"*Studying olive oil* with Nancy Harmon Jenkins has profoundly influenced my cooking. I recommend her book to any food lover, professional or otherwise—Nancy's lessons and recipes will make anyone a better and healthier cook."

—ANITA LO, chef and owner, Annisa

"In *Virgin Territory* Nancy Harmon Jenkins tells us about several of her 'olive oil gurus.' Well, Nancy is now *my* olive oil guru. This is an eloquent book that has the bonus of also being a bit of a memoir as well as a cookbook filled with beloved, mostly Mediterranean recipes. It will help us understand everything we didn't know, or thought we knew but really didn't, or that we might have thought was complicated about olive oil. Nancy tells us just what we need to know in the most understandable, forthright, and personable fashion."

— MARTHA ROSE SHULMAN, author of the *Recipes for Health* blog on nytimes.com and, most recently, *The Simple Art of Vegetarian Cooking*

VIRGIN TERRITORY

VIRGIN TERRITORY

EXPLORING THE WORLD OF OLIVE OIL

Nancy Harmon Jenkins

Photography by Penny De Los Santos

Houghton Mifflin Harcourt
Boston • New York • 2015

Food styling by Simon Andrews
Prop styling by Hilary Robertson

www.hmhco.com

Library of Congress Cataloging-in-Publication Data
Jenkins, Nancy Harmon.
    Virgin territory : exploring the world of olive oil / Nancy Harmon Jenkins ; photography by Penny De Los Santos.
        pages cm
    Includes bibliographical references and index.
    ISBN 978-1-118-20322-4 (hardcover) ; 978-0-544-18866-2 (ebk)
1. Cooking (Olive oil) 2. Cooking, Mediterranean. I. Title.
    TX819.O42J46 2015
    641.6'463—dc23
                        2014004428

Book design by Vertigo Design NYC

Printed in China
C&C 10 9 8 7 6 5 4 3 2 1

For Nadir, Neviyat, and Tsega

CONTENTS

ACKNOWLEDGMENTS

A NOTE OF THANKS

First of all, I want to thank my children, Sara and Nicholas, along with their partners and offspring, for the love and support they have shown throughout this long enterprise; also heartfelt thanks to all the many hands who have joined us over the years as we harvested the olives, made the oil, and then sat around the table in the Teverina farmhouse kitchen to sample, taste and discuss, analyze the past, and make plans for the future.

To Penny De Los Santos for fabulous photography and great companionship on our olive oil adventures; to Justin Schwartz, Stephanie Fletcher, and the team at Houghton Mifflin Harcourt; to Jennifer Griffin, who had faith in the book when I had lost it. To all of you, I pledge my thanks and a bottle of great olive oil next time we harvest!

Thanks are also surely due to the vast number of farmers and producers of excellent olive oil right around the Mediterranean and on to California and Chile who have been generous of their time and expertise, including especially:

IN GREECE: George and Christine Demetriadis of Biolea; Aris Kefalogiannis of Gaea and the Kritsa Cooperative

IN FRANCE: Mort Rosenblum and Jeannette Hermann of Wild Olives/Huile d'Olives in Draguignan; Jean-Benoît and Cathérine Hugues of Castelas, Vallée des Baux

IN SPAIN: Francisco (Paco) Vañó and his sister Rosa Vañó of Castillo de Canena; Francisco Nuñez de Prado of Baena; John Cancilla and Fadrique Alvarez de Toledo of Marques de Valdueza

IN TUNISIA: Abdelmajid Mahjoub of Les Moulins Mahjoub

IN PALESTINE: Nasser Abu Farha of Canaan Fair Trade and the Palestine Fair Trade Organization

IN CROATIA: Katia Gasparini of AgroLaguna, Poreč

IN SICILY: Mary and Tonino Simeti of Bosco Falconeria, Partinico; Gianfranco Becchina and his daughter Gabriella of Olio Verde, Castelvetrano; the family of Nicola Titone at Azienda Titone, Marsala; Lorenzo Piccione of Pianogrillo, Chiaramonte Gulfi

IN PUGLIA: Catherine and Brian Faris of Pascarosa in Martina Franca; Armando Balestrazzi of Il Frantoio in Ostuni

IN UMBRIA: Graziano Decimi of Decimi oils; Feliciano Fancelli of Frantoio Fancelli

IN MOLISE: Marina Colonna of Azienda Colonna, San Martino in Pensilis; Enrico Colavita of Oleificio Colavita, Campobasso

IN LAZIO: Paola di Mauro of Colle Picchione in Marino

IN TUSCANY: the Stucchi-Prinetti family of Badia a Coltibuono; the Bicocchi family of Tenuta Numero Uno; Gemma Pasquali and her father, Paolo, at Villa Campestri; Helen and Keith Richmond of Podere Boggioli

IN THE VENETO: Mirko Sella of San Cassiano

IN CALIFORNIA: Mike Forbes and Bob Singletary of California Olive Ranch, Oroville; the Yocha Dehe Wintun Nation of Seka Hills, Capay Valley

IN CHILE: Jay Rosengarten and Tomas Garcia of Olisur, Colchagua Valley

Other help, both general and specific, was offered by the following friends, scientists, sages, chefs, and experts, and I thank them all, with the assurance that any errors of fact or interpretation in the book are mine and mine alone: the late Mita Antolini, Arnaldo Antolini, Burton and Nancy Anderson, Nancy Ashe, Eryn Balch, Rolando Beramendi, Caroline Beck, Mario Bertuccioli, Bill Briwa, Chris Butler, Maurizio Castelli, Darrell Corti, Maria Isabel Covas, Barbara d'Agapiti, Salvatore Denaro, Lou di Palo, Carrie Donavan, Greg Drescher, Beth Elon, the late Dun Gifford, Dan Flynn, Don Harris, Roberta Klugman, Alessandro Leone and Antonia Tamburrino, Fausto and Mar Luchetti, Luanne O'Laughlin, Claudio Peri, María José San Román, Lisa Sasson, Rossella Speranza, Antonia Trichopoulou, Beatrice Ughi, Paul Vossen, and Ari Weinzweig.

Olives

Sometimes a craving comes for salt, not sweet,
For fruits that you can eat
Only if pickled in a vat of tears—
A rich and dark and indehiscent meat
Clinging tightly to the pit—on spears
Of toothpicks, maybe, drowned beneath a tide
Of vodka and vermouth,
Rocking at the bottom of a wide,
Shallow, long-stemmed glass, and gentrified;
Or rustic, on a plate cracked like a tooth—
A miscellany of the humble hues
Eponymously drab—
Brown greens and purple browns, the blacks
    and blues
That chart the slow chromatics of a bruise—
Washed down with swigs of barrel wine that stab
The palate with pine-sharpness. They recall
The harvest and its toil,
The nets spread under silver trees that foil
The blue glass of the heavens in the fall—
Daylight packed in treasuries of oil,
Paradigmatic summers that decline
Like singular archaic nouns, the troops
Of hours in retreat. These fruits are mine—
Small bitter drupes
Full of the golden past and cured in brine.

A. E. Stallings
The New Criterion, June 2006

INTRODUCTION

I fell in love with olive oil almost by accident, but I fell hard. Forty years ago, I bought an abandoned farm, 25 acres high up in the hills of eastern Tuscany, hard by the border with Umbria. A dozen or so olive trees came with the property, all of them overgrown and neglected, scarcely discernible amid the tangle of blackberries and wild gorse that infested the terraces below the tumbledown stone farmhouse. Over the years, those olive trees began to fascinate me, even as they led me to wonder: Who planted them? When? And why? Twelve olive trees would not provide enough oil for an individual, let alone the fairly sizable family that had last inhabited and farmed Pian d'Arcello some eight or ten years earlier. And those decrepit trees scarcely bore any fruit at all.

Virgin Territory is in part the story of that fascination and of how it led me on an unending and predictably futile search to find the world's greatest olive oil, a search that led to agronomists and nutritionists, to great research institutions, to small family farms in out-of-the-way corners of the Mediterranean and to vast estates where olives marched in regimented rows to the horizon, and finally back to our own farm, where I eventually added 150 young trees to the collection and where we now make our own superb (if I say so myself) green-gold, Tuscan extra-virgin. It has been a continuing process of education as I have studied and questioned, and as I began to grasp how and why things were done the way they were—and just as important, how and why things began to change.

But something else also happened as I pursued my olive oil education. That was the discovery, beginning in the 1960s, of the "Mediterranean diet," or rather the Mediterranean way of eating. *Diet* implies a regimen, a strict adherence to an eating plan with the goal of losing or, more rarely, gaining weight. But the Mediterranean way of eating—with its emphasis on healthful habits based on the consumption of fresh vegetables and fruits, legumes and complex carbohydrates, not much meat, quite a lot of seafood, and above all else the use of extra-virgin olive oil as the principal fat—is less a regime than it is a totally joyful approach to the kitchen and to the table.

As a founder of Oldways Preservation and Exchange Trust, the Boston food-issues think tank that was primarily responsible for educating Americans about the Mediterranean diet, I played a small but gratifying role in the propagation of this great development. Over several decades at Oldways, with my colleagues Greg Drescher and Dun Gifford, we brought together time and again journalists, scientists, nutritionists, educators, and the general public, organized in forums and conferences in the United States and abroad, where we jointly explored what exactly a healthful diet might be and how it might be made more widely available to Americans.

With Oldways and also on my own, I traveled to many parts of the Mediterranean, revisiting places like Spain, France, Cyprus, and Lebanon where I had once lived, and discovering places, like the North African Maghreb, that were entirely new to me. I visited bakers and cheese makers, wineries and markets, all around the Inner Sea. I talked with farmers and chefs and home cooks, with fishermen and market gardeners and commodity grain growers. I stuck my nose into kitchens of all shapes and sizes, and sampled from the cooking pots and the bake ovens. And of course, always and everywhere, I stopped in olive groves, some as ancient as the millenarian trees of Puglia, some as young as the vast new high-density plantations in Andalusia (and in California and Chile, two places that often look Mediterranean even though they are far distant). I visited olive mills, in season and out, to see and taste firsthand what the best producers were doing and how they managed to achieve their quality. And I tasted plenty of rancid, fusty, musty oil at the same time—all to further a deeper understanding. I learned about the different types of olive oil (extra-virgin, virgin, pure, light, flavored), though it took me—and the rest of the world, too, frankly—a long time to understand that high-quality extra-virgin is unique among all types of olive oil for its remarkable health benefits.

Eventually, as the word has spread about olive oil, so too has the cultivation of the olive. In parts of the world with a Mediterranean type of climate, immigrants and colonists planted olive groves, most of them originally no doubt intended for religious uses of the oil. In California, the first olive trees were set out by Spanish mission priests, who needed oil for baptism, unction, and other rituals. Later, Italian immigrants, especially those who came from Liguria, contributed their own varieties and their own techniques. But olives were not a very important crop in California, and table olives were always more important than olives for oil, a situation that has only recently begun to change. In an old issue of *National Geographic* from the early 1940s, I came across a couple of black-and-white photographs of a California olive mill and of ranks of barrels filled, according to the caption, with olive oil and ready for shipment. Another caption praised local olive producers for gearing up to overcome the oil shortfall from the Mediterranean, cut off by war.

Nowadays, olive cultivation has expanded dramatically in Chile, Argentina, Australia, New Zealand, South Africa, and also California; it is spreading even to what would have seemed, just a dozen or more years ago, extremely unlikely parts of the world—China, India, Pakistan—even the U.S. state of Georgia! Why? Because of the health message, because of olive oil's emergence as a must-have item in sophisticated kitchens, because of the market demand that is a result. If most of the world is not yet suffering—and may never suffer—from a glut of high-quality olive oil (we can't seem to get enough of it, in fact), Spanish producers of less-than-top-quality oils are currently suffering the anguish brought on by overproduction. But the rest of the world continues avidly growing, producing, and consuming what many, myself included, believe to be one of nature's most perfect foods.

Olive oil, especially extra-virgin olive oil, is not without its critics, however. Much of the criticism is justified. Prices for extra-virgin are high, especially if consumers can be persuaded that the oil on the shelf, whether in the local supermarket, low-cost chain, or gourmet products store, is genuinely extra-virgin and worth the asking price. And that's where the problem lies. Because, as has been pointed out over and over again, much of what is labeled as extra-virgin in fact is not; sometimes it is not olive oil—or not entirely olive oil—at all. Olive oil is not the only food product, by any means, that is tainted with fraud, but it is the product that at the moment is most questionable in the public mind. Entirely laudable attempts to explain how the fraud occurs have had the unfortunate effect of stigmatizing *all* olive oil, especially

Spaghetti Ajo-Ojo-Peperoncino

This is the simplest pasta recipe in the world, one that Italian cooks always turn to when "there's nothing to eat in the house," or after a long night of partying when a little sustenance is needed to revive the spirits. To make it, you simply boil up the pasta (which could be spaghetti, linguine, or any other long skinny pasta shape) and dress it with about half a cup of olive oil in which you have heated 4 or more chopped cloves of garlic and a small dried hot red chile pepper broken into 3 or 4 pieces—or a quarter teaspoon or so of hot red pepper flakes. Note that the garlic should be softened but not browned and the chile should be simmered but never left to blacken. Some cooks like to melt a couple of chopped salted anchovies in the oil as well, and a sprinkle of minced parsley at the end adds a nice color contrast. But the trick is to keep it fast and keep it simple—and restrict the ingredients to what every good cook has, or ought to have, in the larder: oil, garlic, dried chile peppers, pasta—*e basta!*

all Italian olive oil.[1] Gresham's Law—bad money drives out good—operates here, as with other products: Cheap, badly made, badly handled, or out-and-out duplicitous olive oils, labeled extra-virgin, are driving the truly excellent oils—and there are many of them, from many different parts of the olive oil world—off the market shelves and out of business.

Now more than ever, with all of this oil from likely and unlikely sources circulating in our markets, it seemed to me important for cooks and consumers to understand what exactly extra-virgin olive oil is, to get a good handle on what determines its quality, and to grasp how to tell good oil from bad. So *Virgin Territory* is also a cookbook and a guide, for beginners and experts alike. Each of the 100 or so recipes included herein uses extra-virgin olive oil, sometimes as a cooking medium, sometimes as a key ingredient, sometimes as a condiment or garnish for the plate—and often as all three of these. Above all, whether you're a chef, a cook, or a garden-variety consumer, I hope you'll find in this book a compendium of invaluable information about olive oil in general and extra-virgin olive oil in particular—how to select it, how to use it at the table, and how and why to make it a part of your cooking, your diet, and your life.

Crusty old Tuscan peasant farmers have come a long way in recent decades, but so too have Americans in their appreciation of olive oil. As recently as 1988, a correspondent in *The New Yorker's* "Talk of the Town" section could write about the "extremely low cholesterol level" of an extra-virgin olive oil sold at Macy's. The oil was made, surprisingly, by then–Chrysler head Lee Iacocca on his Tuscan farm, but if it had any kind of cholesterol level at all, it wasn't olive oil, which, because it's entirely plant-based, could never be a source of cholesterol in any case. Such was the state of knowledge a mere quarter of a century ago, even at a magazine famed for the rigor of its fact-checking department.

---

1. Reviewers of a book by journalist Tom Mueller, *Extra-Virginity*, published in 2011, often make claims like the following: "Most of what we eat today on the cheap is actually lampante." That was in *The Observer* in January 2012. Actually, although he is deeply critical of fraudulent practices, nowhere in the book does Mueller make that claim.

That was the same year in which I first published a story about olive oil, an article in *The New York Times* that asked the perennial olive oil questions, still being asked today: "Is it worth the price?" and "What are consumers getting when they buy extra-virgin olive oil?"[2] In the previous year, Americans had imported 51,000 metric tons of olive oil, only about 5 percent of which was extra-virgin. In 2013, we imported more than 290,000 tons, and 65 percent of that was "virgin"—an astonishing increase in that period of time.

Part of the increase was the result of an aggressive marketing campaign by the International Olive Oil Council (now called the International Olive Council or IOC) in the 1980s and 1990s, but part also was certainly traceable to the growing awareness, among scientists, researchers, public health authorities, and consumers at all levels, of the benefits that olive oil provides as part of a healthful diet. At the same time, in the United States our own homegrown olive industry has burgeoned, mostly in California but with a few out-reaches in places as likely as southern Oregon, Texas, and New Mexico and as unlikely as Georgia and Washington State. And uncomfortable, even disquieting questions have been raised constantly about the quality of what is labeled extra-virgin olive oil, especially extra-virgin olive oil imported from the traditional Mediterranean producing regions, Spain and Italy. Mediterranean extra-virgin ought to be the finest kind, but, as almost anyone who has had the misfortune to sample a bottle of standard supermarket extra-virgin knows, too often it is not. Even when it costs a lot.

The demand is greater, much greater, than it was just 10 or 15 years ago, but the knowledge about quality continues to be abysmal, and the knowledge of what quality actually tastes like, what the flavor characteristics are of the best extra-virgin olive oils, remains, for most consumers in the United States and elsewhere, shockingly low. How did we get to a state of affairs where we understand so little about and treat so badly an ingredient that is not only precious but also honored, lauded as the very symbol of Mediterranean food, a substance that is not only beyond any doubts healthful but also delicious, adding immeasurably to the overall pleasure of the food on our plates? How can we begin to understand what makes a *premium* extra-virgin olive oil, and how can we choose it in the marketplace and use it with confidence in our kitchens and on our tables?

I offer this book to try to help answer these questions. Of course it's important to be aware of fraudulent practices in the olive oil industry—just as it is important to be aware of fraud and deception in milk and honey, two other products that are frequent victims of malpractice—and I deal with that misfortune in many places in this book. But it's also important to understand that there is plenty of excellent extra-virgin olive oil available for mindful and attentive chefs, cooks, diners, and food lovers alike. Once you have trained your palate to recognize excellence, you will easily be able to avoid the false, the counterfeit, and the outdated. And by buying only the best, all of us together, we may even come to put the least out of business entirely. Fortunately, training your palate to recognize great, honestly made oil is an easy task—and very agreeable, too. And if you are a chef or a cook, you will quickly come to understand how the myriad flavors of olive oils can be put to use in the kitchen to enhance every dish in which they are used.

---

2. As far as I can tell, this was the first-ever major *New York Times* story about olive oil in the food section's entire history.

INTRODUCTION

VIRGIN TERRITORY

HOW I TUMBLED *(or stumbled)* INTO OLIVE OIL

I DIDN'T WORRY ABOUT THE TREES AT FIRST. In fact, to be perfectly honest, I hardly noticed that there were a dozen or so scraggly olive trees on the terraces below the crumbling stone structure, all that remained of the farmhouse we had just purchased in what seemed, on reflection, to have been an outbreak of lunacy. It was back in the early 1970s and, after years of wandering, I was bent on investing a very small and unexpected bequest, preferably in land, anywhere in the world or at least anywhere in Europe. As it happened, the land we found, a farm called Pian d'Arcello, was in the hills of eastern Tuscany, as far from the Anglican grandeurs of Chiantishire as the rustic hollows of Appalachia are from the Hamptons or Northeast Harbor.

To dignify it with the word *farmhouse* may be going too far. This place had started life as what in Tuscany is called a *casa dei contadini* or a *casa colonica*, a humble dwelling with surrounding fields that was part of a larger—sometimes much larger—domain. But the *contadini*, the sharecroppers who had once lived at Pian d'Arcello, had departed some time ago—three years earlier, said Gianfranco, the *padrone*, who was anxious to sell the property in order to finance a scientific pig operation on his own land higher up the mountain; others said it had been at least a decade since anyone had inhabited the place and worked the land. I could believe the latter more than the former because the house was in such ruinous shape that it was scary even to contemplate camping out under the gaping holes of the roof, much less actually spending time in the place.

There was no running water and no electricity, and the cart track that ambled down the mountainside for a kilometer or so before reaching the house was exactly that—a track for carts but not for cars. Along with dust and spiders, there were scorpions inside the house and vipers outside; wild stinging nettles and brambles overwhelmed what passed for a dooryard, and the terraces with their scattering of olive trees were thoroughly grown up with gorse, broom, heather, more brambles, and a persistent variety of low-growing and scraggly oak that, even when apparently eliminated, still crops up time and again in half a dozen places. The olive trees were strangled, unable to compete with the menace of the *macchia* (the Italian name for this type of Mediterranean scrubland). So it's no wonder I didn't pay attention to them, either then or for some time afterward as, over the next four or five years, the rude stone walls were dismantled and rebuilt, expanding and opening the house in a style that owed more to California than to the rugged hill country of the *montagna cortonese*, the range east of Cortona that separates Tuscany from Umbria. Gradually, however, once the house neared completion, we began to clear the land, step by step, and the olive trees emerged, twisted, gnarled, spindly, looking like relics from the Late Neolithic—when indeed they might have last borne fruit.

The temptation was to chop them down and start over again. But I have a psychological aversion to cutting down anything with a history that has its roots that deep in the ground. Olive trees are notoriously long-lived. Local boosters and tourist guides alike tout the Galilean olive under which Jesus preached the Sermon on the Mount, or, somewhat more remotely, the tree in Lebanon from which Noah's dove plucked the olive branch to take back to the Ark. Apocryphal as these tales are, there do exist all around the Mediterranean some incredibly old specimens of olive trees, at least a thousand years old or even more. One of these is a Sardinian giant that locals have dubbed Ozzastru, an honorific title. According to Jean-Marie Baldassari, a French olive expert who has studied the tree, it may be as much as 3,000 years old—a good deal older than the Sermon on the Mount if not quite as old as Noah. Quite possibly it was planted by Phoenician explorers who settled Sardinia in the eighth century BCE, bringing with them from the shores of Lebanon olive trees and the whole culture of olive oil. This great old survivor has even created its own specific environmental niche, Jean-Marie pointed out to me, like an open-air terrarium if you will, made up of the tree and its fruits as well as the underground root structure, which is fully as complex and monumental as what we see above ground, along with all the insects, fungi, mosses, parasites, and subsidiary plants, as well as the small animals and birds that inhabit its biosphere. Ozzastru, he said, even has its own weather system.

A tree like that you don't chop down casually, although I'm told that landscapers and their nouveau riche clients will happily pay as much as €18,000 (about $23,000) for a handsome thousand-year-old specimen of Spanish olive tree, to be excavated from its birthplace and transplanted to a classy golf course or perhaps the entrance to a posh estate.

The bedraggled trees on our terraces would not have won any beauty contests, nor could even the most profligate rich man have been persuaded to part with money for one of our survivors. But I am loath to uproot anything that has managed to overcome such adversity, to struggle through generations of human activity, or inactivity in this case. So I did the opposite of cutting them down: I planted a few more. And that was just the beginning.

I GREW UP IN THE KIND OF CLASSIC NEW ENGLAND FAMILY where olive oil was kept in the medicine chest and brought out to rub on the baby's scalp for something called cradle cap, a sort of infant dandruff. It never appeared on the table, not even in salad dressings, which mostly came ready-mixed in bottles marked Thousand Island or Blue Cheese and at best were made, according to the ingredients list, with vegetable oil. It could have been any kind of vegetable, but it certainly was not oil from the fruit of the olive. I am quite sure my mother didn't even know you could cook with olive oil, although the few Sicilian families in our small Maine town must have used it, probably having had it shipped to them from relatives in Boston or Philadelphia. (Those barely assimilated Italians also used garlic, and some of them even gathered wild mushrooms—toadstools, my father called them—the certifiably poisonous effects of which they seemed to be immune from. Something about their religion, we were sure, protected them from these evils.)

I left home as soon as I could safely get away and was shortly thereafter awash in a savory sea of garlic and mushrooms, consuming plates of spaghetti in the North End of Boston and chicken cacciatore in what was not yet called the East Village in Manhattan. I traveled to France and Italy as often as I could save the money to get there, and I cultivated young men who were even more traveled, many of whom, oddly enough for that day and age, also knew how to cook and introduced me to a whole world of flavors that stretched from East Coast America across Europe and Russia and down into the Levant and India before culminating in

China and Japan. I learned to make beef stroganoff and caponata and what was billed as authentic Indian curry (beginning with a full pound of butter, clarified), as well as James Beard's awesomely meaty ragù bolognese, and a savory rice pilaf in the Greek tradition. I tasted squid and octopus, eggplant and artichokes, and many other foods that were not to be found on the coast of Maine. But even as my culinary vistas expanded, olive oil still was not a part of any horizon I could see. Yes, we all used it from time to time when the recipe called for it, but we didn't know what we were buying, and to be honest we didn't really care.

I don't recall anything about that oil, but it almost certainly was not very good (which, come to think of it, is probably why I don't remember it). Most of the oil exported from Italy—especially what was sent to the United States in those years when almost all the oil sold in the United States was Italian—was what is called *olio lampante*, meaning oil fit only for lighting lamps, oil that had been refined or rectified using chemicals such as hexane, more familiar from dry-cleaning establishments, to get rid of its nasty odor; it was combined with a small amount of virgin oil to give it a little distinction. Because the technique had evolved in the oil-producing regions along the Italian Riviera, it was called *tipo Riviera* although not all this oil was a product of Liguria by any means. As for the term *extra-virgin*, it had only recently been adopted and was not at all in general use.[1]

In my ignorance, I was not alone. *Gourmet* magazine, that erstwhile bible of upscale American eating, did not describe olive oil in any detail until sometime in the late 1970s, although plain "olive oil," with no qualifiers, had been mentioned as an ingredient in *Gourmet* recipes from the beginning days of the magazine in the 1940s, especially for any recipes from Spain, Italy, or more frequently southern France. Most often a recipe would call for "olive oil or vegetable oil, or a combination." During the war years, of course, a *Gourmet* reader was hard put to come by any olive oil at all, but in 1944, the great food writer Clementine Paddleford, in her regular *Gourmet* column, recommended an importer who offered a "first pressing of hand-picked ripe olives, grown on the French Riviera slopes." The oil was described as "triply clarified," and "packed in France (but before the war of course)." The price was $1.50 a pint, which works out to $3 a liter, more or less—a steep price for oil that, if it had been packed before the war, was at least five years old.

Even when I went to live in Spain, which I did with my young family for several years in the late 1960s, olive oil was not treasured in my kitchen or on my table. A universal ingredient in Spanish cooking, used lavishly throughout the country, it was also almost universally bad, except for rare samples from small producers who made oil strictly for their own use. But quality oil was not available in commerce. We lived in an old-fashioned part of Madrid called the Fuente del Berro (watercress fountain), a small, self-contained barrio of single-family homes surrounded by little gardens. In summertime especially, kitchen windows throughout the neighborhood were flung wide whenever the maids (the chicas) or the housewives set themselves to cook in the heat of the day. And between one and two o'clock each afternoon from those windows arose a disagreeable aroma—rancid, fusty olive oil heating up for the array of fried foods, from delicate little croquetas to robust, deep-fried fillets of hake, for which Spanish cooks pride themselves.

---

1. Fausto Luchetti, former head of International Olive Oil Council, personal communication, 2010.

Olive oil was (and is) a staple in the Spanish diet, but the only olive oil available in Spain in the 1960s, certainly the only oil available for people who lacked access to a family grove, was almost uniformly bad. Why? The reasons are not complex. With the exception of Portugal, Spain was the poorest country in Europe and the most isolated. The tight control of the Franco dictatorship oversaw every aspect of production from food to steel and, I imagine, guitars, castanets, and bullfighter's capes as well. Franco's goal for Spain, in defiance of European boycotts and trade restrictions, was *autosuficiencia*, self-sufficiency. With that in mind, the government had encouraged the expansion of olive groves, especially in the south, and vastly increased oil production. But there was a problem: Oil made to an industrial standard, its price and market regulated by the government, left little incentive to put out a good product. As a result, the market was flooded with shoddy, poorly treated oil.

But everyone cooked with it and seemed happy to do so, especially as there were various techniques for rendering it less offensive. As evidence, I offer advice from a favorite Spanish cookbook (I have the worn and sauce-spattered paperback copy in my library to this day).[2] Published in 1967, it is still a wonderful compendium of traditional Spanish home cooking. The author, an Englishwoman living in Madrid, gave instructions for making a perfect Spanish tortilla, that flat omelet deliciously filled with potatoes and onions that's a staple in every Spanish tapas bar. She also included this tip for purifying the flavor of "poorly refined oil" by a tried-and-true process called *frito y frío* ("fried and cooled"), in which olive oil must be fried for 10 or 15 minutes with an orange or lemon peel, a piece of bread soaked in vinegar, or a piece of potato, and then cooled before using, "to refine the flavor." It was, alas, standard operating procedure throughout Spain.

IT IS HERESY TO SAY SO, BUT I'M NOT CONVINCED that the olive oil available to most people back then, whether in the olive oil regions of the Mediterranean or elsewhere in the world, was all that different from what I found in Spain. The more I struggle to understand olive oil, the more convinced I am that the high-premium oil to which we are happily growing accustomed today is a relatively recent phenomenon except for a few fortunate people who produced their own oil and set aside the finest for the family cellars and kitchens. I had an experience with that kind of oil when I moved from Spain to Lebanon in the early 1970s— my husband at the time was a foreign correspondent whose posting changed every few years—and discovered the miracle substance that is good olive oil. When I did, my conversion was total. Each winter in Beirut, the rich, thick, green oil from ancient groves all across Lebanon's mountains and valleys flowed into city markets. It had an eye-opening, palate-rousing flavor, especially when combined with crushed garlic and fresh lemon juice and poured over a plate of tabbouleh, the beloved staple of the meze table, a salad of bulgur wheat mixed with parsley, mint, onions, and tomatoes.

For all of Lebanon's later problems, Beirut was still at that time a sophisticated urban culture but with deep roots in the countryside; even Beirut professionals, like our friends the Abu Feisals, both distinguished medical doctors with degrees from and residencies in the United States, journeyed back to the family's mountain village in the autumn to share

2. *The Spanish Cookbook*, Barbara Norman, Bantam Books, New York, 1967.

in the harvest and stock up on a year's supply of that fabulous oil. And we happily joined them. This, I am convinced, was olive oil as it was meant to be—full of flavor, with the pungency that comes from a high level of polyphenols, and not only rich in goodness by itself but also able to transmit that goodness to just about everything it was put into, from a simple bean soup to the complexity of stuffed vine leaves or the crackling goodness of deep-fried falafel from a street vendor along Beirut's seaside Corniche.

But Lebanon was a special case, probably because the chain of supply from producer to consumer was so short, and perhaps because Lebanese farmers, unusually in that day and age, were harvesting early and pressing promptly. That was not universally true throughout the Mediterranean. Several decades later, I was on the island of Crete looking into the history of the Mediterranean diet and the Seven Countries Study that had begun there, back in the 1960s, under the aegis of Dr. Ancel Keyes. Visiting an important olive oil producer in the town of Kolymvari, on the western part of the island, I asked him if the fine extra-virgin oil he was exporting might be similar to what had been consumed 30 years earlier. "Oh, no," he assured me, without hesitation, "back then the oil was much higher in acidity."

Acidity, or the amount of free fatty acid, in olive oil is a measure of rancidity and of quality—at the time I had my conversation with the Cretan producer, the measure had to be 1 percent or less in order to qualify as extra-virgin. (In 2003, that was lowered to 0.8 percent.) It was startling, to say the least, to come up against the realization that the oil consumed when the diet studies began in 1962 was not even certifiably extra-virgin, which means it was probably quite similar to the rancid and fusty oil that I had experienced in Spain. And possibly not dissimilar to the oil my neighbors in the Tuscan hill country were producing when we first uncovered the old olive trees on the terraces at Pian d'Arcello. Was that then the true secret of the Mediterranean diet? Rancid olive oil?

Food writers, and I include myself in this company, all too often wax poetically far from reality as we expound on the old ways of the Mediterranean, back when cooking was simpler, flavors were more direct and natural, and there was a perceived connection between what grew in the ground and what graced the table. And clearly everyone was healthier, happier, and longer-lived as a result. Nostalgia like that may be as old as the written word, certainly as old as Hesiod (described, in an apt Wikipedia entry, as a "deteriorationist," as in "things have really deteriorated since I was a lad") or at least as old as Jean-Jacques Rousseau, who celebrated the good, honest, and simple life of eighteenth-century peasants, reveling in a successful grape harvest: "You cannot conceive with what zeal, with what gaiety, it all is done; we sing, we laugh all day, and work has never gone better. All live in the greatest familiarity, everyone equal and no one overlooked. . . . One eats with appetite the peasant soup, a little raw and rude, but good, healthy and filled with fine vegetables!"[3]

Was that peasant soup dressed with a hearty dollop of extra-virgin olive oil? Doubtful in the Swiss village of which Rousseau was writing, but chroniclers before and since have not hesitated to describe an idyllic Mediterranean world living on a diet of fresh, homegrown vegetables, home-cured pork, home-fermented wine, homemade cheese, and of course home-produced olive oil. But was it ever really like that?

---

3. Thanks to Adam Gopnik for pointing to this quotation in *The Table Comes First: Family, France, and the Meaning of Food* (p. 22).

Tortilla Española

Spain's greatest gastronomic achievement owes a lot to olive oil. No, I'm not thinking of the olive oil gels created by fancy chefs like Dani Garcia and Ferran Adrià. Nor am I considering either paella or gazpacho, delicious as those traditional treats may be. In my opinion, the height of Spanish gastronomy is reached with the humble tortilla, featured at every bar and tapas counter throughout the country. Don't, please, think of Mexico when you think about tortilla. *La tortilla española* is an entirely different beast. Rich with potatoes and onions gently sautéed in olive oil, then combined with eggs to make a flat omelet, a tortilla is a humble, cottage sort of recipe, something a peasant farmwife might whip up for her hungry menfolk when they come in from the fields. But it's also the favorite tapa offering throughout Spain, and back in the day it was always served at room temperature. Nowadays, because of the imposition of European sanitary laws, a wedge of tortilla must be served either stone cold or reheated in a microwave, which inevitably detracts from the sumptuous nature of the treat. But if you can make it at home—and it's easy to do—a tortilla makes a great, quick, late-night supper, a terrific after-school snack for hungry children, or a welcome addition to a copious Sunday breakfast or brunch.

Here's how to make a tortilla for 4 people: Peel 2 medium potatoes, and slice them about ¼ inch thick; do the same with a yellow onion, only instead of slicing it, chop it coarsely. Get out your black cast-iron skillet or similar heavy-duty frying pan, and add to it ⅓ cup extra-virgin olive oil, preferably a top Spanish oil such as Castillo de Canena, Marques de Valdueza, or Dauro. Set the pan with the oil over medium heat and add the sliced potatoes. Let the potatoes cook until they are almost tender. Add the chopped onions and stir, then use a spatula to chop the potatoes in the pan. If you further chop some of the onions at the same time, it's no problem.

Why don't you chop the potatoes before you put them in the pan in the first place? I don't know. This is the way they do it in Spain.

When the vegetables are nice and tender, sprinkle a liberal quantity of salt and some black pepper over them, stir them again, and then drain them in a sieve over a bowl to catch the fragrant olive oil.

In another bowl, beat up about half a dozen eggs—if you have really hearty eaters, add a couple more. Then stir in the drained potatoes and onions.

Back in the skillet, add in about ¼ cup of the oil you used for frying. Tilt the skillet to run the oil all over the bottom and sides, then set it over medium heat. As soon as it starts to sizzle, tip in the egg mixture, again tilting the pan to make it even all around. Cook the tortilla over medium to medium-low heat, using a small palette knife to run around the edge of the eggs to loosen them from the pan and lifting the mixture gently from the bottom, letting the uncooked portion seep through. When the tortilla is almost done but still rather liquid in the center, set a plate upside down over the frying pan and, using pot holders, flip the pan over, then slide the tortilla back into the frying pan with its uncooked top side now on the bottom. A minute or two longer will firm up the uncooked part, and the tortilla will be ready to serve.

If the business with the plate and the flipped frying pan sounds kind of scary, turn on the broiler unit just before you start cooking the eggs. Then, when necessary, you can run the frying pan underneath the broiler's heat to firm up the uncooked surface of the eggs.

Well, yes and no. For many people in many parts of the Mediterranean, life was a constant struggle against poverty and hunger. In Italy, especially in the south, a semi-feudal society endured until long after Italian reunification, indeed until after World War II. One has only to read the emigration accounts of millions of Italian small farmers and landless peasants who left in boatloads for North America, Argentina, and Australia. The Jacini Report was commissioned by the Italian government in 1877. Intended to detail the living conditions of agricultural workers, it took eight years to complete and ended up describing almost unimaginable conditions of poverty. In relatively well-off Umbria, in Central Italy, rural families lived on cornmeal flatbread, beans, rice, pork fat, a few vegetables, and potatoes.[4] The lack of meat was everywhere prevalent, but the overall diet was worst in the south, where field workers often subsisted on a ration of bread, salt, and water, with a few drops of doubtless rancid olive oil added to this "soup." Access to adequate food was a major factor driving emigration, which peaked during the decades after the Jacini Report leading up to World War I.

Even in Tuscany, even in Florence, diets were meager for most people. Talking about his childhood after the First World War, one man recounted: "[I]nstead of buying a flask of olive oil . . . people went with a tiny little bottle to buy it. They bought a half a cup of olive oil at a time because they were so poor." He went on to describe the Tuscan custom called *fare il C*—to make a C, a quick swirl of olive oil, on top of the beans or minestrone—a garnish or, in modern food writers' terminology, a drizzle, meant to add more flavor than substance.[5]

But Tuscany and neighboring Umbria may have been among the few places in this world that I had entered so unwittingly where good, carefully made olive oil was more commonly available than elsewhere, a source of great pride to the farmer who produced it, even if it was too expensive a product for urban working families. Until well after World War II, Tuscany and, to a somewhat lesser extent, Umbria were noted for large and for the most part carefully managed estates that operated under the sharecropping system called *mezzadria*. The *fattore*, or bailiff, in charge of the estate made sure that the landlord's family table was well supplied with fine, thoughtfully crafted wines and olive oils, as well as pecorino cheeses, well-aged prosciuttos, and other products of the estate. Naturally even the sharecroppers and small farmers who depended on the system received their share of this bounty, since they were the ones who actually provided it.

So olives and oil had been a mainstay of the Tuscan rural economy for generations, and olive oil was a key ingredient in Tuscan cooking. But never in abundance. I think of Carlo Cioni, chef of his family's restaurant Da Delfina, in Artimino on the outskirts of Florence, who told me how to make a proper Tuscan ribollita, the iconic dish of Tuscan cuisine. He makes it the same way his grandmother, the original Delfina, made it. *Ribollita* means "reboiled," and it is in its essence leftovers—leftover minestrone, leftover bean soup,

---

4. See Carol Helstosky, *Garlic & Oil: Food and Politics in Italy*, pp. 18–19 and 25.

5. Carole M. Counihan, *Around the Tuscan Table: Food, Family, and Gender in Twentieth-Century Florence*, p. 23.

leftover bread—put together in the most frugal manner, which is what makes it quintessentially Tuscan. And, although many Tuscan restaurants nowadays serve ribollita with lashings of olive oil, Carlo says, that goes against tradition. This is a farmhouse dish, and Tuscan farmers, until well into the latter part of the last century, were cash-poor even when their tables were laden with the products of fields, gardens, and forests. Olive oil was a precious commodity, to be sold for coins to stash in the family mattress. Such frugality demanded imagination and skill from cooks like Carlo's Nonna Delfina, who developed an inventive cuisine from the humblest ingredients, even from leftovers. But oil, her grandson says, she added *a punto di cucchiaio*, just the merest edge of a spoonful. *Fare il C!*

Very often it wasn't even olive oil, or not 100 percent. Many of those who didn't make their own simply could not afford anything but a blend. "When I was a child," Fausto Luchetti told me, "in my grandparents' village in Umbria, the little food shop had signs posted on the wall outside that read: *Vendita di olio d'oliva* and *vendita di olio di semi*"—olive oil sold here, seed oil sold here (seed oil being vegetable oil, probably at that time from sunflowers or rapeseed). Dr. Luchetti, who went on to become head of the International Olive Oil Council (now the International Olive Council) is today, in retirement, still one of the few people in the world with a true understanding of the tangled politics of the international olive oil business. "There were two big containers inside the shop," he continued, "one with olive oil, the other with seed oil, and people asked for a little of one and a little of the other, and the mix was made to order right there in the shop!"

But there was another source of fat that competed with olive oil in many farmhouse kitchens and does to some extent to this very day, wherever religious restrictions don't prevent its consumption—the family pig.

Shortly after I moved with my two young children into our not-quite-finished farmhouse in the summer of 1975, I met Mita Antolini, who lived on the neighboring farm along with her husband, her son, her in-laws (mother, father, sister), and her mother. At the time, and for many years after, the Antolinis provided a classic example of Mediterranean subsistence farming. They lived almost exclusively on what they could produce on the few hectares of fields and woodlot that belonged to them—and lived, incidentally, not so very differently from the way their parents and grandparents had lived on the same property. They had no electricity and no running water except for a pipe in the farmyard that brought water from a natural spring on the mountainside above their house. They had no transportation apart from a cantankerous mule, and when the icy *tramontana* wind blew down from the Alps in winter they huddled close around a drafty, smoky central fireplace, their only source of heat.

But they had a number of resources, none of them luxurious but all of them important to their survival. The most important was manpower. With six adults and a teenage boy in the family, there was labor aplenty for harvesting wheat, grapes, and olives, for making 300 jars of *pomarola*, tomato sauce, to see them through the winter, for laying out onions and garlic, legumes and sliced wild mushrooms to dry in the sun. Yet another great asset was a herd of eight or more Large White pigs (that is actually the name of the breed) that Mita, the youngest female in the family, took across our field and down into the forest every afternoon to forage along the streambed at the bottom for acorns, roots, grubs, baby vipers, and other porcine delicacies. As she walked, she often spun wool into yarn on an archaic spindle she carried with her. (Idle hands make work for the devil, I would think as I called out *buona sera*.)

Those pigs represented both the mainstay of the Antolini pantry and a valuable source of cash in the form of prosciutto hams, meticulously crafted and aged right on the farm, that old Agostino, Mita's father-in-law, sold to the butcher in town. Although they had little in the way of cash income, they did need some, not a lot, to buy coffee, salt, black pepper, sugar, and other staples they couldn't produce themselves. More important even than cash, however, was the addition to the family larder of an array of *salumi*—cured sausages, *gota* or guanciale (pork cheeks), *lardo* (cured slabs of pork fat), pancetta and *rigatino*, *sopressata* (head cheese), and perhaps most important of all, *strutto*, the soft, white, rendered fat of the pig—a substance we call in English lard, leading, like so much Italian-to-English terminology, to endless confusion.

Lardo in Italian means the back fat of the pig, brined in salt and fragrant herbs for months until it has become a savory cured delicacy to slice or chop and add to stews and sauces or to eat with a slice of bread for a panino. What we call lard, on the other hand, is what Italians call *strutto* (or in some regions *sugna* or *'zugna*), made when the pigs are slaughtered, usually sometime between mid-December and the Feast of Saint Anthony the Abbot on January 17. Fresh back fat from the slaughtered pig, chopped into pieces, is cooked over a low fire, in order not to burn it, with a little water and a sprig of rosemary or a couple of leaves from the bay tree to add fragrance. Slowly the fat melts, the water boils off, and the bits of pork that don't melt turn brown and crisp in the bubbling fat. These cracklings, called *ciccioli*, are strained off, salted, and put aside, and the fat itself is poured into earthenware containers to cool.

The result? Don't think Crisco! This is a soft, pure, white fat, fragrant with rosemary or bay and a hint of the meatiness of pork, and it is used for just about everything, but especially for baked goods and for frying. *Cenci*, for instance, the simplest sweet imaginable, are "rags" of flour-and-water dough, rolled out, cut into rough strips, and deep-fried in melted *strutto*, then sprinkled with a little precious sugar or honey. *Strutto* went into the bottom of the *pentola* when Mita started her soffritto of onions, carrots, and garlic, the beginning of just about every soup or sauce in her repertoire; and *strutto* went into the Easter *ciaccia*, a raised bread enriched with lard and with those same *ciccioli* cracklings (or sometimes little cubes of pecorino cheese) kneaded into the dough. Some people even spread a thick layer of *strutto* on bruschetta, adding salt and black pepper, for a snack. Dario Cecchini, the most famous butcher in the world (or at least the most famous in Tuscany), mixes *strutto* with more rosemary, a hint of vinegar, some garlic, salt, and pepper, and sells it by the *etto* (100 grams) as "Chianti butter," *burro del Chianti*, "a food as divine as it is simple, genuine and ingenious, which has for centuries kept hunger at bay with next to nothing," he claims.

I've dwelt on *strutto* at what may appear to be unseemly length in a book about olive oil simply because I think part of our nostalgia leads us to imagine a world in which Tuscan *contadini* and similar families all over the Mediterranean lived to the healthy age of 110 because of a diet that was exclusively based on olive oil. Such was not the case. If it wasn't pork fat that provided necessary calories, it was the blended oil of Luchetti's family village. Or rancid, fusty oil. Or oil that had been refined to make it safe for human consumption. As for

text continues on page 14

RIBOLLITA

Ribollita is a Tuscan classic, a cold-weather bean soup with lots of vegetables, thickened with bread and served with the season's new oil on top. It starts with a soffritto of chopped onion, garlic, parsley, and some kind of preserved pork, usually pancetta or unsmoked bacon. For vegetarians, though, I've found you can leave the meat out of ribollita and it doesn't change the good nature of this satisfying fare. Add a little more extra-virgin olive oil to make up for the loss of the pancetta fat and maybe a few more beans to add bulk and you've got it. And although ribollita started as a way of heating up leftovers and making them more palatable, it's even better if you start afresh each time. Just remember to soak the beans overnight or for several hours before you start cooking.

MAKES 8 TO 10 SERVINGS, DEPENDING ON WHAT ELSE IS SERVED

1 large carrot, finely chopped

1 medium yellow onion, finely chopped

1 thick celery rib, finely chopped

1 garlic clove, finely chopped

About ½ cup olive oil, plus more for serving

¼ cup chopped flat-leaf parsley

1½ cups dried cannellini or borlotti beans, soaked overnight and drained

6 cups boiling water, plus more as needed

1 cup canned plum tomatoes, with juices

1 small dried red chile pepper, if desired

1 leek

2 medium yellow potatoes

1 medium or 2 small zucchini

1 bunch cavolo nero (aka Lacinato or Tuscan kale)

1 bunch green chard

COMBINE the carrot, yellow onion, celery, and garlic with ¼ cup of the oil in a large heavy soup kettle. Set the kettle over medium heat and cook, stirring occasionally, until the vegetables are softened a little and giving off a pleasant aroma. Stir in the parsley and the drained beans and add about 6 cups boiling water. Bring to a simmer, then turn the heat down and simmer, covered, for 30 minutes or so. Stir in the canned tomatoes, breaking them up with your hands or with the side of a wooden spoon. Add the dried chile if you wish—if you don't want it to be too hot, discard the seeds before adding. Bring back to a simmer and continue gently cooking, covered, until the beans are tender—the time will vary depending on the age of the beans but should take 45 minutes to 1 hour in all.

WHILE the beans are cooking, prepare the rest of the vegetables, rinsing and slivering the leek, peeling and cubing the potatoes, and dicing the zucchini into small pieces. To prepare the *cavolo nero*, strip away the central rib and discard it. Sliver the leaves. If the chard leaves are very large, you should also strip them away from the central rib, but don't discard the ribs—simply chop them coarsely and sliver the green leaves. The bread can be used as is, but it's actually much better toasted until it's golden on both sides.

WHEN the beans are tender, add the leek and potatoes along with plenty of salt and pepper. Continue simmering until the potatoes are slightly softened, then add the zucchini, cavolo nero, and chard. Add more boiling water from time to time, if necessary.

1 small loaf stale country-style bread, preferably whole wheat, sliced

Sea salt and freshly ground black pepper

1 medium red onion, very thinly sliced

PREHEAT the oven to 400°F.

IN another heavy soup kettle or a deep ovenproof dish, smear 2 tablespoons of the olive oil over the bottom and arrange several slices of bread, overlapping slightly if necessary. When all the vegetables in the soup are tender, spoon about one-third of the soup over the bread slices. Top with more bread and another one-third of the soup. Then top with more bread and the remainder of the soup. Arrange the slices of red onion all over the top and dribble with the remaining 2 tablespoons oil. Transfer the soup to the preheated oven and bake for about 15 minutes, or until the onion slices on the top are starting to sizzle and brown. The bread will have absorbed quite a lot of the liquid in the soup so that you could almost eat it with a fork. But best to use a spoon. Serve immediately while it's still hot and dribble more olive oil, new oil if available, over the top. If you don't eat it all at once, it gets better with time. Just reheat it in the oven until it's hot all the way through and have plenty of new olive oil on hand to garnish it.

butter, that was simply out of the question almost anywhere in the Mediterranean. Even as some scholars have drawn important historical distinctions between the olive oil cultures of the Mediterranean and the butter cultures of northern Europe, I would go further and add pork to the equation. Of course pork was banned in both Jewish and Islamic religions, but throughout the Christian Mediterranean, for decidedly economic reasons, the fat of the pig had almost equal importance with revered olive oil.

TRUTH TO TELL, UP HERE IN THE MOUNTAINS OLIVE OIL was not important in the diet of farm families until fairly recently. At 700 to 800 meters above sea level—that's 2,000 to 2,500 feet—we are (or were) at the upper limits of olive cultivation, although global climate change is revising that. The trees we found at Pian d'Arcello were small for the simple reason that at least once every 30 years or so, a major and prolonged freeze comes along to cut the olive trees almost literally down to size. You can tell by the gnarled and twisted trunks that some of these trees are very old, but the branches that spring from them are often a good deal younger and suppler. In the south of Italy, especially in Calabria, where there is seldom the kind of deep freeze that afflicts us periodically here in the mountainous middle of the peninsula, the olives grow so high they look like elms. Ours are mere shrubs by comparison.

In the winter of 1985, there was a historic freeze: Temperatures plunged well below zero Celsius and stayed there for days, destroying olive trees all over Tuscany and Umbria, even extending westward into parts of Liguria and Provence. Many improvident growers rushed to clear their groves, replanting with vines or even sunflowers, convinced that the end of olive culture was nigh, olives having proven themselves unviable and uneconomical. In a few places, however, ancient wisdom prevailed, and damaged trees were simply cut back to a meter or so above ground and left to themselves to recover. Today, almost three decades later, most of those olive trees have returned to robust health, possibly all the more vigorous for their stressful experience.

Our trees at Pian d'Arcello, however, had been neglected for a very long time, and we continued this neglect even after we came to live in Rome and could spend school vacation time on the farm, as we called it. We never pruned, never fertilized, never planted cover crops such as traditional fava beans. As for harvesting the olives, that task fell to our neighbors, to Mita and her family. I had no idea when the Antolinis did this; I only knew that some time before we arrived for the Christmas school holiday, the olives had been pressed into a cloudy, yellow oil that was presented to me, with great pride, in two tall 1-liter bottles—2 liters of "our" oil.

What a thrill, I can almost hear you say—your own olive oil from your own trees! But back then, even though I still knew very little about olive oil quality and the factors that produced it, I knew that this oil was not good. It was not rancid or fusty, like the Spanish oil that had so offended me in Madrid. But this Tuscan oil had an unmistakably musty, murky, mushroomy flavor, as if it had been made and stored in a dank cellar, unlike any oil I had had before. In fact, the oil tasted as if it had been stored in a moldy terra-cotta jar, which it very well may have been. I am embarrassed to admit that I accepted with apparent grace the annual gift of oil, produced with such effort, and, when my neighbors had left, I turned it down the sink. I tried to use it for cooking, but even in long, slow-cooked dishes, where its rank flavor should have blended and eventually disappeared in a savory mix of meat, wine, onions, garlic, rosemary, and all the other tasty ingredients of a Tuscan stew, some of that mustiness came through. I certainly couldn't bring myself to dress a salad with that oil even though I had by then convinced myself that this was perhaps the way *olio genuino toscano* was supposed to taste.

Genuino is high praise in Tuscany and used to describe any food or, especially, wine that has not been tampered with. It doesn't mean genuine in the English sense, but more something that is unaffected, natural, unaltered. When sugar is added to wine to boost fermentation, a practice that is strictly against regulations but frequently practiced nonetheless, the wine is said to be *sofisticato*, the opposite of *genuino* and undesirable in the extreme.

So this, I thought, was Tuscan *olio genuino*. So much for that!

It took me some years to figure out why oil that should have been the pride of our valley was so bad. I wasn't there at the time our neighbors were harvesting, so I had no idea when the olives were picked, where they were taken for processing, nor even how they got to the *frantoio*, or mill, with no mechanized transport. In fact, in the years before the Antolinis finally were able to buy a car (an exercise that should be the subject of another book), it was difficult even to get the olives to the mill except on mule back. And the distance to the nearest *frantoio* was considerable—20 kilometers on foot, driving the mule over steep mountain roads, was not the least of their chores, by any means.

Our harvest now begins sometime after mid-October, but back then it was much later, and the *frantoi* didn't even open their doors until the middle of November. The olives would have been totally black by then, rich and plump, if sometimes beginning to shrivel, producing an oil that was sweet and bland, without the typical back-of-the-throat kick that's an indication of abundant polyphenols and concomitant flavors. Then, too, without polyphenols, the oil had less staying power, so that even if it was delicious immediately after being pressed, it quickly lost its personality and vigor.

Another characteristic technique practiced by many farmers back then was to dry the olives after the harvest, spreading them out in a thick layer in a clean part of the farmyard or on a terrace off the kitchen, where they were left to cure for anywhere from three to six weeks. Occasionally they were tossed, stirred, and turned over, in a mostly unsuccessful attempt to prevent mold from forming. The wrinkled black olives made a lighter load for the mule than fresh-picked olives would have, and they also made a lighter load at the mill, where the miller was customarily paid according to the weight of the olives he processed rather than the weight of the oil that came out. At the same time, all over Tuscany, indeed all over the Mediterranean, old-fashioned farmers cherished the belief that olives kept like this after harvest actually yielded more oil than freshly picked fruits.

If they didn't produce more oil, however, these sun-dried Tuscan olives did indeed produce worse oil. Like fish in the hold of a vessel, a pile of olives, no matter how often it's stirred, will start to ferment and grow moldy, building up fusty, musty, earthy flavors that derive from anaerobic and ethyl acetate fermentation. And they will never make good oil—there's no way to correct that rank and musty flavor. Such bad habits were by no means unique to my mountain neighbors. Some years ago, I visited a mill in a Tunisian desert oasis

where olives were kept a full year on farmhouse roofs, after which they were ground to a thick, dry paste and pressed to make the most rancid oil I've ever had the misfortune to taste. Plus, everywhere in the Mediterranean, even to this day, olives are packed into plastic sacks or old burlap bags and carted to the mill where they're left to wait, sometimes for days, for their turn at processing, by which time they have inevitably started to ferment.

So the oil that I was guiltily turning down the kitchen drain, bad as it was, may have been of a better quality actually than much that was available. Harvested in mid-November, our olives were at least pressed before Christmas. For others, olives that might have been harvested anytime in December and January might not be pressed before the middle of March. This tells you something about olives and oil in our mountain community. The olives were already quite spoiled by the time they were pressed, and the oil that resulted was perforce rank and fusty—there was simply no way it could be otherwise. This also suggests why olive oil was not all that important in the diet and cooking in farming communities like the one in which we live, and why the fat of choice for most purposes was cured or rendered pork fat. Pigs were a walking pantry for farm families. Olive oil, on the other hand, was troublesome to produce except in small quantities that were set aside for specific purposes, to dress salads and raw vegetables and to use during periods of the year, especially Lent, when pork fat was forbidden.

It's tempting to think of Mediterranean cultures on the whole as existing in a sort of prelapsarian state where everyone had access to fine fresh oil, the kind food writers adorn today with the out-of-date term *first cold pressing*, the kind that produced extraordinarily good cardiovascular statistics in Crete and southern Italy, the kind that formed—and forms—the foundation of the healthy Mediterranean diet. Yet not all regions around the Inner Sea by any means had access to olive oil, and even fewer to high-quality olive oil. Gianfranco Becchina, who makes an excellent Sicilian oil from his own Nocellara del Belice olives (it's called Olio Verde and is sold in the United States), told me that in his youth, his family kept the best oil for their own use and sold off the rest to be blended and bottled by commercial dealers, or *négociants*. This was not unusual. Many large olive farmers producing oil for commerce reserved the best for home use, especially in places like Spain and Tunisia, where olive prices were set by the government and so there was no market incentive to produce excellent oil. But my neighbors barely made enough for their own scant purposes, and every trick that was purported to increase the quantity, even at the expense of quality, was worth pursuing.

I already knew there was better oil to be had from my experience in Lebanon, and I learned in Tuscany that it was possible to go directly to the *frantoio*, the mill where olives were processed, late in November when fresh, new, just-harvested oil was being made, to buy very good Tuscan or Umbrian olive oil in quantity, laying in a year's supply from the best local mills. Clearly there was more and better oil to be found elsewhere than what my mountain neighbors were producing, even if I had yet to figure out why theirs was so bad. But it took another long while before, ever so slowly, it dawned on me that I too could be making oil—well, maybe not a world-class olive oil but certainly something superior to the local offering, something that I wouldn't be ashamed to use to dress a salad or garnish a Tuscan *zuppa di fagioli*, making a C of oil on top.

When I announced my decision to plant 150 young olive trees, everyone, Mita included, looked at me with trepidation. They'll never thrive, Mita said, they'll be eaten by wild boar, they will freeze and die the first winter, and besides, who do you think is going to take care of them?

Truthfully, the reason for planting olives had more to do with a need to keep the land cleared than it did with a secret dream of becoming a producer of classy olive oil. The forest that surrounds our hilltop farm is beautiful, but it's also dense and dangerous, especially late in a dry summer, when foragers, hikers, or fishermen on their way down to the stream might idly toss a burning cigarette into the undergrowth. To keep the land cleared is not just an aesthetic choice—it's also eminently practical, even a matter of security. Yet cutting back encroaching brambles and broom, the first stages in the forest reclaiming its own, was not a high priority on anyone's list, even at prices I was willing to pay to workers. What could make it more valuable? Wine grapes? Too much work. Wheat? Ditto, and also it has to be sown and harvested every year. Tobacco? Out of the question, despite its importance as a cash crop in our community. Olives? Clearly here was the answer.

After initial efforts to clear and reshape the land, forming several existing narrow terraces into two broader plains, after actually planting the 150 infant trees, hardly more than fragile seedlings, and irrigating them carefully for the first couple of years until they had established themselves—after all that, it seemed, there would be precious little to do: pruning in the spring, mowing in the summer, harvesting in the autumn, fertilizing with well-rotted sheep manure every year or so. And for a family that by then included two active gourmands in my grown children, who had long since graduated from peanut butter and jelly sandwiches, the reward would be a plentiful supply of olive oil made to our own high standards, enough for all with some left over for Christmas presents to friends. Leccino was the variety we selected, with the help of Maurizio Castelli, an old friend and an olive oil guru who had been the consultant for far more eminent olive plantations, at Badia a Coltibuono in Chianti for one, and McEvoy Ranch in California for another. Leccino, Maurizio said, was more cold hardy than the familiar Tuscan Frantoio and Moraiolo olives, and here at around 2,000 feet above sea level, we needed something to resist our frosty winters.

And so in 1999 we planted, and Mita was right—at least a little bit right. Wild boar, apparently trying to scratch their backs, knocked some of the little trees to the ground, and the first winter we lost five of our babies to the cold. But the rest did indeed grow and thrive and, after a long wait, began 10 or 12 years later to produce an oil that is more golden colored than green, a characteristic of early ripening Leccino olives, but that still has the pronounced kick, the back-of-the-throat grip, that characterizes the finest Tuscan oil. The trees took root, and for many years I watched them grow, waiting for them to reach fruit-bearing age. In 2006, we finally had a large enough crop to harvest and press into oil. It was just a little oil at first—a mere 15 liters—but the thrill of that first real harvest, and every harvest since, did more than anything else to teach me about olive oil. There is nothing in my copious library of aromas and flavors that can match the first taste of our new oil as it flows from our own crushed olives.

A few years ago, I watched as my then two-year-old grandson stuck his stubby finger into the thick stream of oil flowing into our big 30-liter stainless-steel containers, called *fusti*, from the separator at Frantoio Landi, near Cortona. He licked his finger, smiled, then plunged it right back into the stream. Clearly the oil had passed his inspection. I tried a taste and smiled, too. The freshly pressed oil had a bittersweet, vegetal flavor that I still can't quite describe. Almonds? Walnuts? Artichokes? Crushed grass? Green apples? Tomato leaves, perhaps? A little of all those and something more? When it's oil from your own orchard, pressed from olives you harvested painstakingly over several days while keeping a wary eye on the rain-soaked clouds piling up in the west, then it truly seems like a miraculous substance.

In early November, Leccino olives are already black and shiny and ready to be picked; they droop on the branches like plump jet beads on a Victorian necklace. That first fall of a major harvest for us, in 2008, the weather was balmy but unsettled, and the very first morning, we were rained out. For lunch, we sat down to grilled sausages and *zuppa frantoiana*, a soup of beans and farro that you're supposed to garnish with fresh new oil. The soup was rich and filling, but we had to make do with oil from a friend's harvest.

Tuscany, I believe, is always happiest during the olive harvest. The *vendemmia*, when wine grapes are harvested and pressed, can be fun, it's true, but nowadays so much wine is produced for commerce that some of the joy has gone out of it. But picking olives is different. At this time of year everyone goes out to the olive groves, and even the shops in town close down for the afternoon. A notice pinned to the door reads: *Sto al raccolto, torno dopo tramonto*—"I'm harvesting, be back after sundown." Mills run far into the night and on Saturdays and Sundays too, and there's a celebratory air, like a big party, the main nourishment at which is bruschetta,[6] crisply toasted hunks of crusty bread liberally dipped in new oil. (This, by the way, is the one time of

6. Note that this is pronounced broos-KETT-ah and not, as so many waiters in American restaurants say, broo-SHETT-ah. And in northern Tuscany, they reject the term entirely, calling the treat *fett'unta* ("oily slice") instead.

year when restaurants set out bowls of oil in which you dip your bread to taste the fresh new stuff; otherwise, this custom, widespread in America, is unheard of in Italy.)

The Landi mill where we take our olives is a 30-minute drive from our house. I like this mill because it gives me a choice between two ways to process the crop. The first is the slow, old-fashioned, crush-and-press method; the second is the modern continuous-cycle process that employs state-of-the-art stainless-steel machinery. You simply dump fresh, clean olives into a chamber at one end, press a button, and, within minutes, an hour at most, fill your cans with lush, green oil at the other end. My traditionalist offspring prefer the old-fashioned way, but I like the modern method for its rapid expression of scrupulously clean oil. But I also like the fact that there are still plenty of my neighbors who continue to do it the old-fashioned way. It's slower, they admit, and exposes the olive paste and oil to atmospheric dangers, but the flavors the great grindstones conjure from the olives as they are slowly reduced to a glistening oily paste—those flavors, they say, are beyond compare.

In all, it took us five days, with on-and-off weather that year, to harvest the olives we brought to Landi's mill. Ideally, experts say, to make good olive oil you should press within 24 to 48 hours of harvest, but this, we have learned, is often impossible. You need at least 200 kilos (440 pounds) of olives to make a single pressing, and that takes a lot of hands. And rain, which can cause just-harvested olives to ferment and spoil, can wreak havoc on your plans. So you wait. Then you pick. Then you pray.

And in the end it's worth it. In 2012 we brought home 120 beautiful liters of unfiltered oil, golden green with flashes of deeper color, so highly perfumed that I felt like rubbing it on my arms, dabbing it behind my ears, and drinking it. I got my first real taste of the new oil by lavishly slopping some of it over a slice of bread that had been toasted over an open fire and rubbed with a cut clove of garlic. The *resa*, or yield, was not high, only around 12 percent (meaning that every 100 kilos of olives produces 12 kilos of oil), but the quality was extraordinary. We stored the oil in 30-liter stainless-steel *fusti* in our cool, dark cellar, and every time we extract a liter or so for the kitchen, the fragrance—apples? tomato leaves? almonds? or maybe just the pure fragrance of good, sound olives?—floods the air, and later perfumes every food over which it is ladled.

OLIVES *and* OIL: THE ORIGINS

SOME YEARS, GREEK EASTER FALLS LATE IN APRIL, and the olive trees on the island of Crete often blossom at the same time, as if to celebrate the festival of rebirth, their branches clustered with tiny white blooms so small you might miss them entirely if you didn't know where to look. At that time of year, an elusive magic in the island's light makes it possible, despite the intrusive clamor of modern tourism, to catch a glimpse of what it must have been like in ancient days, when Crete was the dynamic heartland of the Mediterranean, the birthplace of the oldest proto-European civilization. We call the people who lived here then, from roughly the middle of the third millennium to the late second millennium BCE, Minoan. What they actually called themselves is not known. *Minoan* is a modern name, given them by Sir Arthur Evans, the British archeologist who excavated one of their grandest sites, at Knossos just south of the modern city of Irakleion.[1]

---

1. Minoans from the legendary King Minos, ruler of Crete, who kept the fearful Minotaur at the heart of his labyrinth and fed it an annual tribute of Athenian youths and maidens.

Knossos and similar "palaces" on the island represent some of the most complete remains of what would eventually evolve into Mediterranean culture. And here on this island we find some of the earliest references to olives and their oil.

Nothing speaks of the Mediterranean quite like the olive. The tree, the fruit, the oil are all embedded in the history and mythology of the region as much as in the landscape—and in the food. Wherever you go throughout this splendid part of the world you come across olive trees of all shapes and descriptions: It could be an ancient survivor like the Sardinian tree called Ozzastru (see page 3), or a single half-wild tree clinging to a Syrian hillside, its old trunk gnarled and twisted with time, its sparse, dusty foliage shivering in a dry breeze; or it could equally well be a vast Andalusian orchard of pristinely planted modern trees marching to the horizon, row upon row, until the mind grows dizzy with the prospect. The lands that border this inland sea are varied, from deserts to rocky slopes to river deltas and upland plains, but wherever you travel, the olive tree flourishes, having evolved precisely in this Mediterranean climate of hot, dry summers and cool, rainy winters, a climate that is perfect for the health and vigor of these trees.

So it's not surprising if nothing speaks of Mediterranean culture and cuisine quite like olive oil. Since ancient times it has been food, unguent, balm for the sick, and source of light, as well as the victor's prize in the pan-Hellenic athletic events that so impassioned the Greek world. The three great Mediterranean religions all recognize this—it's no accident that olive oil provides the chrism for Christian baptism and anointing the dying; that the miracle celebrated at Hanukkah commemorates the supply of olive oil to light the temple lamps; or that a surah from the Koran praises it: "A sacred tree, the olive," the Prophet says, "which has an oil so clear that it would give light even if no spark were put to it."

It would be difficult to exaggerate the importance of olives and their oil for the countries and cultures that surround the Inner Sea. The tree itself is the fullest expression, the icon, of Mediterranean civilization, and its fruits and the fragrant oil made from them are the foundations of the Mediterranean diet—or, rather, the Mediterranean way of eating. For millennia the olive tree grew only in the Mediterranean basin. In the rest of the world, it was unknown until modern times, with the realization that what climatologists call a Mediterranean climate, a particular and specific type of subtropical environment in which olives flourish, exists in other parts of the world as well. And only very recently, in the past couple of decades, has olive cultivation expanded in California, Australia, South Africa, and elsewhere. Still, today, more than 95 percent of world production of olive oil comes from the countries of the Mediterranean, principally Spain, Italy, and Greece. And all around the Inner Sea, olive trees continue to define the landscape, just as olive oil defines the Mediterranean kitchen, as it has done for incalculable generations.

Olives and olive oil still play an essential role in the economy of the island of Crete. With more than 30 million olive trees, Crete produces a full one-third of Greece's considerable annual yield of extra-virgin oil. It was no less important some 4,000 years ago. Archeologists find evidence of Bronze Age traders from Crete all over the eastern Mediterranean, in mainland Greece, Cyprus, Anatolia, the Levant, Egypt, and elsewhere. Inscriptions, Egyptian wall paintings, and the residue of destroyed cities and tombs (shards of Minoan and Mycenaean pottery, carved and engraved objects, characteristic weapons and tools) all speak to this Cretan presence. And not surprisingly, since trade is a two-way flow, back on Crete itself there are equivalent traces of Greek, Egyptian, Levantine, and other historic and prehistoric cultures.

The ships in these Bronze Age merchant fleets also carried wine and grain, but oil was a major cargo, exchanged for metals (tin, copper, even gold and silver) and other rare and precious materials. Later, as Greeks and Phoenicians began to branch out, to explore and colonize the western Mediterranean, they took with them the shoots of young olive trees for planting in their new homes at Carthage, Marseilles, and other ports of call across the sea, spreading the culture of olives wherever they went. But because these infant trees took a notably long time to bear fruit and because olive oil was a staple in the diet of both Phoenicians and Greeks, they also welcomed regular shipments of oil from their mother cities.

Back on the island of Crete, it seems clear that agriculture flourished even in Minoan times. Regulated by the governing palaces, it provided plenty of what could already be considered a Mediterranean triad—grapes for wine, grain (wheat but also barley) for bread and porridge, and olives for precious oil. An abundant supply meant that in most years surplus commodities, especially easily transportable wine and oil, could be shipped to less fortunate cultures and lands. Knossos was just one among many sites on the island, although it may have been the most important. In the west wing of the Knossos palace, Evans uncovered some 150 intact giant *pithoi*, or storage jars. In all, there may have been more than 400 jars, each of which may have contained as much as 1,000 liters of oil—or wine or grain.

Many more *pithoi* were found at other sites, and not just on Crete. The island of Cyprus also had production centers for commodity exports. At Pyrgos-Mavroraki, in the northwest corner of the island, Italian archeologists discovered the remains of an oil mill from the early second millennium, 4,000 or so years ago, along with storage jars similar to those at Knossos. Each jar, they estimated, might hold as much as 500 kilos (1,100 pounds) of grain or liquid (olive oil or wine)—an impressive capacity, far beyond the needs of the local population, and convincing evidence of the importance of such goods in a redistributive Bronze Age economy.

It's clear that olive oil was a major part of that economy, a commodity in great demand. But for what purpose? For food, for light, for cleansing and perfuming the body—these are the standard answers, but we can't ever be certain and, as usual, scholars differ mightily in their interpretations. Some have even argued that olive oil was not intended for food at all. Instead, they say, oil was used primarily to fill the little terra-cotta and carved-stone lamps that provided a spark of light on dark days and that are found in profusion in archeological sites from the Early Bronze Age practically down to the present day. Oil also filled more grandiose and ornate lanterns and candelabra that lit the homes of gods and goddesses— and presumably of rulers and dignitaries as well. One such, the pride of the Etruscan museum in Cortona, my Tuscan hometown, is still to be seen there, a great bronze *lampadario*, elaborately crafted with mythological figures and a circle of 16 lamps that once flickered in the tenebrous depths of an Etruscan shrine.

Some historians of the ancient world, however, think that olive oil's primary use was as a fragrance. There's plenty of evidence, on Crete and elsewhere, of the economic importance of the perfume industry, which created a high-status, value-added product by infusing the basic substance with a gamut of natural aromas from leaves, blossoms, roots, resins, and berries—roses and lilies, lavender, laurel, orris root, cinnamon, juniper, coriander, mastic resin from the island of Chios, and peppery bergamot (think Earl Grey tea), a musky citrus native to southern Italy. Imagine the heady fragrance of an ancient city—the pungent odors of unwashed bodies, sweat, human sewage, animals and their dung, smoking piles of garbage—and you quickly understand why aromatic oils were a necessity. They conveyed both pleasure and prestige, while the industry that grew up to produce them made the fortunes of many ancient cities. Pyrgos-Mavroraki, the Cyprus site, was destroyed by earthquake some 4,000 years ago. Just recently, in addition to the oil mill, the Italian archeological team uncovered substantial workshops where "perfumes must have been produced on an industrial scale," according to the lead archeologist, Maria Rosa Belgiorno.[2] Not surprisingly, Aphrodite, the sweetly perfumed goddess of love (her skirts were said to waft odors of cinnamon and roses), came from Cyprus, and it was to Cyprus she repaired when, overcome with love for Anchises (father of Aeneas, the Trojan refugee who, myth says, eventually founded Rome), she prepared herself to seduce him: "[T]he Graces bathed her with heavenly oil such as blooms upon the bodies of the eternal gods—oil divinely sweet . . . filled with fragrance."[3] Archeologist Belgiorno concludes that essences like these were probably used daily, even in the most modest homes.[4]

Olive oil was also used for cleansing the body—in classical Greece, athletes rubbed themselves with oil after their strenuous contests, then used a sort of crescent-shaped blade with a dull edge, called a *strigil*, to scrape the oil, dirt, and sweat from their bodies. (Try it sometime—it actually works, especially after a sweat bath or sauna, and will leave your skin feeling clean, soft, and supple.)

But aromatic oils had functions beyond mere personal adornment. Throughout human history, they have also been used, and are used still today, to signify consecration, whether of priests or of royalty, of the living or of the dead. Sweet-smelling Aphrodite, again, anointed dead Hector's body with rose-scented oil to prevent it from defilement, and in Egypt, perfumed oils were used to prepare mummies for the tomb. In modern Christian ritual, babies are still christened with fragrant holy oil, and the same is used to give extreme unction to the dying, while priests receive the chrism of oil when they are ordained. The very title "Christ" comes from the Greek Xristos, meaning the one who is anointed (as does "Messiah," from Hebrew).

Only an olive oil of the highest quality would do to make perfume for Aphrodite—an oil, that is, whose fragrance would complement but not overwhelm the aromatics steeped in it.

---

2. The excavation reports also make a strong argument for the use of olive oil in the furnaces for smelting copper, another valuable Cypriot export.

3. Homeric Hymn to Aphrodite, trans. by H. G. Evelyn-White. http://ebooks.adelaide.edu.au/h/hesiod/white/complete.html#chapter3.5, cited on blogs.getty.edu.

4. Cinyra, Cyprus and the notes of music, of wine and perfumes. http://www.erimiwine.net/erimiwine_g000002.pdf.

Olive Oil in Ritual and Religion

Anthropologists speak of the three pillars of Mediterranean agriculture—wheat, the vine, and the olive, each one of such cultural importance that it has a place in Mediterranean religions as well.

Think of the sacramental bread and wine offered in the Christian mass or the oil used for unction—christening, preparing soul and body for death, anointing of priests and kings. Bread, wine, and oil are part of Jewish Mediterranean culture too—the Friday challah bread, the sweet wine of the Sabbath. And if much of Jewish ritual use goes on in the home rather than in the house of worship, public anointing or ordination is prefigured when the prophet Samuel marks Saul, the future king, for his elevated status: "Then Samuel took a flask of oil and poured it on Saul's head and kissed him, saying, 'Has not the Lord anointed you leader over his inheritance?'" (I Samuel 10:1) And it was of course olive oil that miraculously kept the temple lamp, the menorah, lit for eight days—the miracle that is celebrated each year at Hanukkah.

Potato pancakes, fried in copious amounts of olive oil, are the symbol of Hanukkah for most American Jews, but other fried treats are also offered, including some delicious little jelly-filled doughnuts that are delightfully similar to the zeppole, deep-fried sweet beignets (or *bignés*) that Neapolitans consume by the cartload for the feast of San Giuseppe—Saint Joseph—on March 19. In my town of Cortona, in Tuscany, sweet rice fritters used to be the ritual treat for San Giuseppe, and in other parts of Italy it's fried cream puffs, filled with the cook's choice of crème anglaise or Nutella. Whatever the feast, wherever the culture, oil, it seems, is a necessary symbol of abundance.

Palm Sunday is called *Domenica delle Palme* in Italy, but it's not palm branches that are carried to church. Rather, it's crossed olive branches that are often braided into elaborate designs. Blessed by the priest, the olive branch cross is taken home and kept high under a roof beam to transfer the blessing to the household—unless, that is, there's some threat to the wheat crop, in which case the olive cross is taken down and burned over the wheat fields, the smoke conferring further blessings. And on Holy Saturday, I'm told (though I've never actually seen this), olives themselves are burned and the coals brought into the house as a protection against earthquakes.

There are darker uses of olive oil, too, in traditional Mediterranean cultures. If you're afraid you've been cursed, there's only one solution in southern Italy: Take a bowl of water and set in it olive leaves to float on top in the shape of a cross. Then drop in olive oil. If the drops of oil separate, it's certain there's a *malocchio*, a curse or evil eye, that's been called down upon you. And what do you do then? The most effective recourse is to recite a series of prayers, ending with: "*Gesù, Giuseppe, e Maria, se c'e il malocchio, mandatelo via!*"

And if you think all that is hopelessly old-fashioned, peasant superstition, out of touch with modern life, consider this: In 2012 journalists reported from the Liberian capital, Monrovia, that after the sudden death of a member of the legislature and the unexplained collapse of the speaker, legislators began to carry about with them little bottles of olive oil with which they anointed chairs, desks, and doors to their offices. Oil that had been blessed in church was said to be especially efficacious but, it was noted, legislators were also sucking on limes.

The best oil for the purpose, according to Theoprastus, a fourth-century BCE botanist and close associate of Aristotle, should be pressed from raw, unripe olives. Truly there is nothing new under the sun—even today, olive oil connoisseurs know that the finest olive oil is made from olives that are not fully mature and that are pressed without the application of heat—*cold-pressed* is the term modern food writers use, somewhat inexactly.

What, then, about olive oil as food? It's all too easy to be dismissive of oil's importance in ancient diets until you apply a dash of common sense to the question. Human history in its essence is about guaranteeing the food supply, but archeologists in the past paid little attention to what people ate and how they grew and processed it, ignoring the fundamental nature of diet. In part this was an argument in absentia: Except for animal bones and occasional carbonized seed remains, there's precious little evidence of food left in ancient sites. But modern methods, such as isotope analysis of ancient bones or simple flotation techniques using water to gently process soil from excavations, revealing seeds, roots, microscopic grains of pollen, carbonized remains of food, and other evidence, are helping to bring more information to the fore. Still, beyond the commodities exchanged in international trade and described in long lists of palace stores, we know very little about what people actually ate. It seems impossible, however, that anything as nutritious, as fundamental in the economy, and as easy to produce even by primitive methods as olive oil would not be significant, as much so in the ancient diet as it is in the kitchens and on the tables of modern cooks all across the Mediterranean.

Everything we know about Bronze Age nutrition—and we don't actually know much—leads to the conclusion that most of the people most of the time lived on bread or grain porridge, wine, legumes, and mostly foraged wild greens, with precious little meat except on major feast days when meat offerings were made on altars. Bread, wine, legumes, and vegetables are notably deficient in fat, and fat is essential to human metabolism. Hard as it may be to believe in our own time of fat-free this and low-fat that, we actually must consume fat in order to metabolize certain vitamins and to develop vital membranes in our bodies. Without fat, we are, quite simply, malnourished.

So where did our Bronze Age Mediterranean ancestors get the fat they needed? Not from meat, because they didn't actually have a lot of meat. And not from fish, because fish, apart from inshore species, were difficult to catch and, once caught, hard to preserve for a table more than a few kilometers distant from the sea.[5] It almost goes without saying, then, that a lot of the necessary fat in ancient Mediterranean diets must have come from olives and olive oil. Modern Greeks are world champion olive oil consumers, drizzling an average of 50 kilos of olive oil per person annually over, in, and around their food. In ancient times, archeologist and ethnohistorian Lin Foxhall has estimated, per person consumption for food (lighting and bathing were calculated separately) was somewhat lower—not more than 35 kilos per person.[6]

---

5. Except for tuna, which from early times was caught on its annual migrations; the fish was valued precisely because its flesh could be salted and preserved. For this reason, tuna was sometimes called "the pig of the sea."

6. In *Olive Cultivation in Ancient Greece: Seeking the Ancient Economy*, Oxford University Press, 2007.

Foxhall is speaking of wealthy Athenian households in the classical period. Still, if I'm doing my math right, at the upper estimate that's 860 calories per person per day from olive oil—or at least 30 percent of total daily intake.

If we don't know much about the diet of Bronze Age Greeks, things get a little clearer as we move along in history. By the fourth century BCE, Greek colonists had spread out from the mother country, establishing city states across much of the Mediterranean. Of course they brought their beloved olive trees with them, whether to Sicily or southern Italy or farther afield. One such overseas Greek was Archestratus, a gastronome, an early foodie if you will, who lived a life of *luxe, calme, et volupté* back in the fourth century BCE in the Greek city of Gela, on the southern Sicilian coast. He traveled widely throughout the Greek world and wrote exhaustively about the foods and dishes he discovered—and in which he clearly delighted. His long poem, which was titled possibly *Gastronomia* or perhaps *Hedypatheia*, meaning "The Life of Luxury" (or as James Davidson translates it, "Dinnerology"[7]), has been lost. All that we know of Archestratus's writings are fragments preserved, somewhat like quotations, within a later work called *Deipnosophistai*, or "Philosophers at the Dinner Table." This was written a good 500 years after Archestratus by another Greek, Athenaeus, who lived in the Egyptian Delta town of Naucratis.

Archestratus, food historians like to say, is the first real cookbook writer, or at least the first real Mediterranean cookbook writer.[8] The importance of olive oil in the classical kitchen is unmistakable from the recipes and presentations, abbreviated though they are, that are preserved within the *Deipnosophistai*. Food historians Andrew Dalby and Sally Grainger compiled *The Classical Cookbook* with Dalby's translations and Grainger's adaptations of classical recipes for modern cooks, beginning with those of Archestratus. Lots of these "recipes" or table notes are for fish, a luxury that was prized on the banquet tables of the Athenian upper classes, and most of them call for cooking in olive oil or dressing with olive oil before sending the dish to the table. Modern chefs would do well to pay heed to the simplicity of Archestratus's instructions; far more attention must be paid, he says, to the quality of what Italian cooks still call the *materia prima*, the fundamental ingredients, than to the manner of preparation. Probably best known are his instructions for tuna, but not just any tuna: a large female tuna . . . "whose mother-city is Byzantium." This was to be sliced, roasted, sprinkled with salt, and finally garnished with olive oil. "But if you serve it sprinkled with vinegar," Archestratus councils, "it is ruined."[9]

And maybe Archestratus wasn't actually history's first food writer after all, for we have a very few fragments, also in the *Deipnosophistai*, from an even earlier author, Mithaecus by name, also a Sicilian Greek, whose recipes are even more admirable for their brevity: "Cut off the head of the ribbon fish. Wash it and cut into slices. Pour cheese and oil over it."

7. Davidson, James, *Courtesans and Fishcakes,* New York, 1999.

8. The Li Chi, a Chinese text that included many recipes, was almost contemporary, but of course there was no connection between the Mediterranean and China.

9. Fr. 38 = Athen. Deipn. 7.303e, quoted by Daniel Levine in http://www.uark.edu/campus-resources/dlevine/AIWFLecture.html. See also Dalby & Grainger, *The Classical Cookbook.*

OLIVES AND THEIR OIL CONTINUED TO GROW IN IMPORTANCE THROUGHOUT the classical period. By the time the Romans controlled much of the known world, from Hadrian's Wall to the second cataract of the Nile, from the Caspian Sea to the Atlantic coast of Morocco, trade in olive oil was one of the engines that drove the empire. In the late second century CE, oil was added to the *annona*, the annual grain allotment to which at least one-third of Roman citizens were entitled. The need for grain and oil, for both the *annona urbis* to supply the lower classes, called the *plebs frumentaria*, and the *annona militaris* to furnish the army, created a dangerously self-perpetuating demand that successive Roman governments struggled increasingly to fulfill. More land had to be sought and conquered to produce the grain and oil, larger armies charged with controlling the land had to be supplied, and meanwhile the Roman populace grew ever more voracious and the state ever more burdened. (Soon pork and wine were added to the *annona urbis* on top of oil, grain, and salt.)

In Rome you can still see, even today, the most telling evidence of this insatiable demand and its consequences. Walk down the left bank of the Tiber, along the Lungotevere Aventino, until you come to the Lungotevere Testaccio, which borders Rome's old slaughter-house neighborhood, the site until 1975 of the central abattoir or *mattatoio*; then duck up a side street away from the river, past the remaining *mattatoio* buildings, many of which are now converted into art galleries. You will come to a curious, large, terraced knoll that is unmistakably a relic of some sort. And indeed, this mound, this hill, Monte Testaccio, 35 meters (115 feet or about six stories) high with another 15 meters below the level of the modern street, almost a kilometer in circumference, is composed of the broken shards of what archeologists have estimated to be a cool 53 *million* amphorae.[10] Most of them were made along the banks of the Guadalquivir River in far-off Andalusia, then a Roman colony called Baetica, whence they were shipped to Rome. Archeologists estimate the total represented 6 billion liters of Andalusian olive oil, not all of which came at once, of course. Monte Testaccio probably represents the accumulation of a couple of centuries of olive oil imports, culminating in the late second century. But any way you look at it, it's a powerful amount of oil—and a powerful testimony to the consumption habits of imperial Rome. If Foxhall is correct in her estimation of oil consumption in Greece of 35 kilos annually per person, that would be oil sufficient to furnish 171 million people over the years. Impressive!

Modern Spanish oil producers have complained for years that much of the oil in Italian bottles actually comes from Spain, but the remains at Monte Testaccio suggest that this is a very old story. Whether the oil was good or not is anyone's guess. It risked all manner of mishaps during its long transit from the farm where it was produced to the shores of the Guadalquivir, then by barge down the river to Seville (Hispalis, the Romans called the city) and by sailing ship or rowing galley around through the Gates of Hercules, up past the south coast of Sardinia and into the mouth of the Tiber at Ostia, to end up on the river banks in Rome. Actually, about its quality, I really don't have to guess at all: The oil must have been pretty damaged by the time it reached its destination. Nonetheless, Spanish oil was in great demand, much as it is to this day, in the cheaper end of the market.

---

10. Other estimates run from 25 to 35 million. But most sources agree with the figure of 53 million.

And even in ancient times, dealers in olive oil were sensitive to charges of fraud, especially with oil coming from such a great distance. The shards piled up at Monte Testaccio are concrete evidence of their caution. Most of the amphorae were labeled with inscriptions, *tituli picti* they're called, painted or stamped on the outside, recording the weight of the empty amphora, then the weight of the oil that filled it and its provenance, along with the name of the person who actually weighed it and recorded it. Traceability was a forceful concept even in antiquity.

Meanwhile, oil from other regions was also bought, sold, and distributed in the ancient economy, and not just to Rome, although Rome, with its obligations to feed a voracious population as well as a burgeoning army, was the dominant market for oil, grain, and other staples.

North Africa, from the Nile to the Atlantic, was a vast Roman colony devoted to supplying the imperial mother ship. Leptis Magna, on the Mediterranean coast of modern Libya, is but one example. This opulent city—the ruins of Roman Leptis are among the most impressive in the entire Mediterranean—was one of the largest North African centers for olive oil. Leptis Magna needed oil to supply the annual tribute that Julius Caesar had imposed on its citizens, who had backed the wrong side in his Civil War. An astounding three million pounds (more than a million liters) of oil was shipped to Rome annually in a "tax" that lasted until the reign of Constantine in the fourth century CE. In the Gebel Tarhuna, the high plateau south of Leptis and north of the pre-Sahara, a full-scale oil industry, with thousands of trees and hundreds of mills, plus potteries that turned out amphorae to contain the oil (and possibly, an archeologist of the region suggests, also wine), had developed to supply this demand.[11]

Other parts of North Africa also provided impressive supplies, while Italy itself continued to produce quantities of oil, not all of it premium by any means. Horace, the great Roman satirist of the late first century BCE, described the oil produced by his neighbor Ofellus: "You'd detest the smell of his olive oil," he wrote, "yet even on birthdays or weddings or other occasions, in a clean toga, he drips it on the salad from a two-pint horn with his own hands."[12] Indisputably, most of the oil in antiquity was much worse than even the most ordinary oil that is available today. Milling procedures were primitive, and, despite what almost all the Latin agronomists recommended, little effort was made to produce oil cleanly and rapidly from sound olives at an early stage of maturity, so that it is no wonder the result was rancid, fusty, musty—all the characteristics that are overwhelmingly rejected by the best modern oil producers.

11. Rural Settlement and Economic Activity: Olive Oil and Amphorae Production on the Tarhuna Plateau during the Roman Period. Thesis submitted for the degree of Doctor of Philosophy at the University of Leicester by Mftah A. M. Ahmed (DoA Tripoli, Libya), School of Archaeology and Ancient History, University of Leicester, March 2010. The author points out that this quantity of olive oil could not have sprung up overnight but must have been in development for at least the previous century if not longer, possibly going back to when Leptis Magna was founded by Phoenicians in the eighth or ninth century BCE.

12. Horace, Book II, Satire II: 53-69.

Epityrum: An Ancient Way with Olives

This reads like the original, pre-caper recipe for tapenade (see page 120 for a modern recipe). It was recorded by the great Roman statesman, soldier, and historian Cato the Elder (234–149 BCE), who also wrote an agricultural treatise, *De Agricultura*, that was full of wise, homely advice:

"Make epityrum [translated as 'a dish of preserved olives' or 'olive relish'] of green, black and variegated olives: Remove the stones from green, black or mottled olives. Chop the same, adding oil, vinegar, coriander, cumin, fennel, rue, mint. Mix in an earthenware pot and serve with olive oil covering them." ("On Agriculture," CXIX.)

This will make 2 cups. For this recipe, I like a light, smooth oil, preferably from Greece or Lebanon. If you have access to wild fennel, use the soft green fronds; otherwise, you will have to make do with cultivated fennel, available in supermarket produce sections, but select fennel with plenty of green fronds. Be careful of the quality of olives you choose. They should be fresh tasting and flavorful. Above all, do not use canned black olives, sometimes called California-style.

I have not specified quantities of herbs to use—start with a tablespoon or so of each, then experiment, adding a little more of one or the other as you wish.

Serve epityrum with crusty bread or crackers.

¼ **pound pitted green olives**

¼ **pound pitted black olives**

¼ **cup red wine vinegar**

5 **tablespoons olive oil**

Minced fresh cilantro

Minced fresh mint leaves

Minced green fennel fronds

Small pinch of ground cumin

CHOP the olives together to make a coarse paste. You may do this in a food processor, but be careful not to process to a mush—there should still be a certain heft and texture to the mixture.

TRANSFER to a bowl and stir in the vinegar and 4 tablespoons of the oil. Add cilantro, mint, fennel fronds, and cumin, mix well, and taste. Adjust the seasoning. Spoon the remaining 1 tablespoon oil over the top before serving.

Still, some oils were more highly prized than the ordinary Spanish and North African oils, or even Italian home production, like that of Horace's neighbor. Presumably better oils commanded higher prices from connoisseurs, as they do today. Venafrum oil, from the hill country where modern Molise, Abruzzo, Lazio, and Campania come together, was "of the very highest renown," according to Pliny the Elder. Yet another lauded oil came from Liburnia, an Adriatic territory roughly corresponding to modern Istria in Croatia. Both these regions still produce notable oil. And ancient cooks also had a way, as we learn from Apicius, the Roman gastronome who came along much later, to correct Spanish oil and make it seem like high-quality Liburnian: Take elecampane (*Inula helenium* L., an herb used in the modern production of absinthe), along with Cyprian rush (*Cyperus esculentus*, earth or tiger nuts) and green bay leaves that are not too old, he advised, and crush them together to reduce to a fine powder. Sift this into your Spanish oil, add finely ground roasted salt, and stir industriously for three days or more. Then leave to settle. "Everybody will take this for Liburnian oil," Apicius concludes. (Compare this to the instructions for improving oil in my old Spanish cookbook; see page 6.) Another way to correct oil was by steeping herbs or flowers in it, or if not correct, at least disguise the flavor of bad oil, much as "Persian lime" or "sun-dried tomato" or "genuine essence of white truffles" can almost—but not quite—disguise the flavor of indifferent oils today. The chronicles of olive oil prove yet again that such trickery and deception have a long, if undistinguished, history. Unscrupulous oil producers in Italy and Spain (and elsewhere, I'm sure) still try to persuade a gullible public that the oil in those bottles is truly extra-virgin and truly high quality, even when it's demonstrably not.

On the whole, however, Italians in classical times seem to have been more careful than Greeks about the quality of their olives, more conscientious about harvesting and pressing, and consequently more cognizant of the quality of their oil. Greeks, as shown in a well-known black-figure vase from the sixth century BCE, now in the British Museum, knocked the olives out of the trees with long poles, then picked them up from the ground. And many modern Greeks harvest olives by this method to this very day.

Roman agronomists, and they were many, from Cato to Varro to Columella, advised that olives must be harvested by hand to produce the best oil. "You should pick by hand rather than beat from the tree," Cato instructed, "and in picking by hand it is better to do so with the bare fingers rather than with a tool because the texture of a tool not only injures the berry but barks the branches and leaves them exposed to the frost." Green oil (*viride* in Latin), made in late October from olives that were still green or just starting to ripen and turn color, was the finest, Roman agricultural writers cautioned. Greeks preferred the lush flavors of oil made in December or even into January, when the olives were fully ripe and black. Interestingly, these preferences persist to this day in much of Greece and Italy, with Greeks appreciating sweeter, fruitier oils, while Italians, especially in the north, still look for bitter, pungent flavors from less mature olives.

Columella, one of the greatest of these ancient agronomists and the one who has come down to us with his work most intact, called the olive "first among trees," evidence of the honor and respect with which those ancient Romans valued the olive.

OLIVES IN THEIR NATURAL STATE, FRESHLY PICKED, ARE ALMOST UNBEARABLY bitter and acrid.[13] Anyone who's ever popped an olive, green or black, ripe or not, direct from the tree into her

---

13. This is not universally true. In the Italian region of Puglia, and possibly in other places as well, there is a type of black olive that, when harvested fresh from the tree and immediately cooked in plenty of olive oil, is utterly delicious, sweet, and lush, especially when sopped up with crusts of bread. It's a great feature on farmhouse tables and in many restaurants—Antichi Sapori in the farmland outside Andria is a great place to sample this local delicacy.

mouth will tell you that this is no way to pleasure your taste buds. Indeed, the flavor and texture of a raw, uncured olive is disgusting, pure and simple, so acerbic that it puckers the mouth, with a bitterness that lingers for hours afterward. What causes that are glucosides in the olives, particularly the compound called oleoeuropein; interestingly, they are the same properties that account for the salutary benefits of olive oil. It was a daring innovator who first discovered the delights hidden behind that unappealing taste. And who was that? Who dared go beyond the repugnant flavor of a fresh olive? Who was the first person to realize that the caustic fruits could be cured to something delicious and that, moreover, when pressed, they yielded a savory, sweet, and nutritious oil that had so many uses—balm for the skin, light for lamps, an essential ingredient on the table?

It seems obvious, when you stop to think, that oil must have come first, long before it was understood that olives, properly cured, could be eaten. Olives that drop from the trees in their overripe state leave oily blotches where they fall, as anyone who has ever trod the streets of Berkeley, California, in late October and November will attest, and the oil eventually oozes out. It won't be very good oil, at least not by today's standards, but it will be oil nonetheless, without the bitter harshness of fresh olives, a useful item in the kitchen for

cooking and for adding nourishment to food. I'm guessing that the earliest use of the wild olives that flourished in many parts of the Mediterranean was simply for the oil they exuded, and only later some brave soul discovered that there were ways to extract the nastiness and produce . . . mmm, something indescribably delicious, a salted or brine-cured olive (see page 117 for suggestions for curing raw olives). Once its innate bitterness was tamed or eliminated altogether, the natural sweetness of the fruit came forth.

Wild olives were apparently growing throughout the Mediterranean basin even tens of thousands of years ago. This is the kind of climate an olive tree loves: long, hot, dry summers with clear days and sunny skies, followed by cool, rainy winters when snow falls but rarely and almost never at sea level, and there is seldom penetrating frost except on the mountaintops. Fossilized leaves of wild olive trees have been found on some Aegean islands from 35,000 years ago, possibly long before any humans were around to talk about it, and not only leaves but also the fossilized larvae of the olive fly, still to this day a pest for olive farmers. But it is quite a lot later, perhaps around 4500 BCE, and a little farther to the east, in the northern Jordan valley and on the slopes of Mount Carmel in modern Israel and Palestine, that we begin to find clues to early, very primitive olive processing. Neolithic farmers in these parts made oil with rudimentary methods, simply crushing olives with a stone in a basin (just as they crushed grains), then flooding the crushed olives with water so that the oil would float to the top.

Whether they were wild or domesticated olives the Neolithic farmers crushed is not clear. Wild olives flourished throughout the Mediterranean, but they are hard to distinguish from domesticated ones since cultivated olives, if neglected for a time and left unpruned, will revert to a feral state. Tramping the hillsides around our farm in eastern Tuscany, we often come upon ancient olives: long abandoned and left unpruned, they bristle like a witch's tree with shoots and water spouts and suckers that spring up from the base. On the island of Pantelleria, way out in the middle of the Mediterranean between Sicily and Tunisia, I came across a whole grove of what I was told were wild trees, although I suspect from the regular pattern in which they were growing that they were actually feral olives. Stunted, windswept, and impenetrably thick with growth, they may have been the island's characteristic Biancolilla variety. Each bush had just a few olives and they were almost bluish in color but still hard as little pebbles in late July. This habit of reverting to the wild is why archeologists have a devil of a job figuring out when and where olive trees were first domesticated. Even with modern technology, it is hard to distinguish between the carbonized pits of true wild olives and those of domesticates, or between wild and feral olives. Wild olives are small and difficult to harvest amid the tree's thorny branches, and they are less productive, with an extremely bitter oil compared to cultivated olives. Some people actually treasure wild olives for that very bitterness. Near Kritsá, a village at the eastern end of Crete that is renowned for its production of excellent olive oil, a wild olive tree was pointed out to me, growing on a hillside next to the bleached stones of an ancient gate to the ruins of Bronze Age Kreta Lato. "Does anyone ever harvest that tree?" I asked the young enthusiast who was showing me around. "Oh yes," he said. "Old people do. Old people mix it with oil from the regular trees. They say it adds flavor." Old people often know a lot more than young people do—about olives and olive oil if not necessarily about cell phones and Facebook pages. So these old Cretans mix wild olives into their harvest for the flavor—and they probably get a huge input of health benefits too from wild oil's high content of bitter polyphenols.

Jump ahead several thousand years: The last Minoan olive farmers have long since disappeared from the island of Crete, and now we're in the seventh century BCE at a Palestinian/Philistine site (now in Israel) called Ekron. A leading city in ancient Philistia, one of the five cities of the Philistine pentapolis mentioned in the Bible, Ekron was an amazing producer and exporter of olive oil—at least 500 tons of oil annually, making it the largest oil production center discovered so far in the ancient world. More than a hundred large oil presses have been detailed at the site, although only a few have been excavated. The Israeli

Ministry of Foreign Affairs has a good description[14] of how Ekron's factories (at this scale, that's exactly what they were) produced oil, first crushing the olives with a cylindrical stone that was rolled back and forth in a large rectangular stone basin. On either side of the basin stood presses. The crushed olives were transferred to fiber baskets that were placed in the presses, one basket atop the other, on wooden slats that covered the stone vats in which the oil was received. A heavy wooden beam pressed down on the stack of baskets. One end of the beam was inserted into a niche in the wall, while the other hung free but with heavy stone weights suspended by ropes to add pressure to the stack. The oil produced from the pressing flowed into the vat and from there was transferred to jars, where it was allowed to separate from its watery residues. This is exactly the system, according to Italian archeologists, that had operated at Pyrgos-Mavroraki on Cyprus 1,300 years earlier.

It's also very similar to, although a bit more primitive than, the system that was used in oil mills near Leptis Magna and at Volubilis, modern Walili, at the other end of the Mediterranean, in Morocco, when the Roman colony, or the Berbers who were the Romans' subjects, produced prodigious quantities of olive oil for the markets of the mother country in the early first century CE. By this time, however, there had been a major evolution. From excavation reports and drawings, it appears that in earlier mills, such as Ekron, cylindrical stones were rolled back and forth in rectangular basins to crush the olives to an oily paste. At some point in the history of technology, probably by the third century BCE, this cumbersome structure was replaced by a circular basin with an upright circular stone, like a mill wheel or disk set vertically, rather than horizontally as it would be for grinding grain. The wheel was turned around the basin by means of a long shaft piercing the center of the stone. This is precisely the system that was still in use during the lifetimes of some of my very old acquaintances, Italians, Greeks, Spanish, and others from traditional parts of the olive oil world. On a Tunisian desert oasis, I saw just such a mill in which the motive force came from a blindfolded camel that plodded patiently round and round the basin, grinding the olives to a paste. It was also the system used on an old-fashioned farm in southern Tuscany, which you might think of as one of the most advanced places in Italy, where in the early years of the present century, a small horse still patiently turned the crushing stone and workers spooned the oil from the top of the vats with metal scoops, leaving the murky residue, the *morchia*, behind. (That residue, by the way, is useful. Smeared over the outside rinds of whole rounds of pecorino cheese, it protects and preserves them during the aging process.) The baronessa who owned the mill insisted that this was the only way to get the finest oil. She died only recently at the age of 100, so perhaps she knew what she was talking about.

But the process has always been that simple: crush, press, strain, or separate. It's the way olive oil has been made down through the millennia. The major change that takes place from time to time is the energy source, from humans (often slaves) to animals (mules, horses, camels) to steam to electricity—but the system itself has remained much the same.

---

14. http://www.mfa.gov.il/MFA/History/Early%20History%20-%20Archaeology/Ekron%20-%20A%20Philistine%20City.

Is there any other human technology that has changed so little over four or five millennia? I can't think of one. Today, with our continuous-cycle, two-phase, stainless-steel mills that operate cleanly and rapidly to produce very high quality olive oil, the system is the same: crush, extract, separate, and strain or filter. The hammer mill crushes the olives; the malaxer, or *gramola*, a long box of a kneading machine that is essential to the quality of the oil, helps pull the molecules of oil together; and the separator operates like a centrifuge, spinning out the oil rather than skimming it off the top, but in essence a Bronze Age oil producer, perhaps a little dazed by the scope of the operation, would still be right at home in a modern Tuscan *frantoio*.

Portrait of an Oil Maker: Lorenzo Piccione

The *contrada* of Pianogrillo sits below the imposing heights of Chiaramonte Gulfi, a Baroque city of white buildings, domes, and spires tucked into the southeastern corner of Sicily. Almost the entire *contrada*, or hamlet, is taken up by the farm and olive groves of Lorenzo Piccione, who makes oil from trees planted by his father, his grandfather, his great-grandfather, and other past olive growers going back at least 800 years to a carved and twisted ancient tree in the courtyard of the farmhouse.

"We call that tree a *saraceno*,[1]" he says. "We call all the ancient olives *saraceni*. The Arabs were here for 150 years or more, but they didn't just pack their suitcases and leave. Their influence has stayed. There is something Arab in almost every Sicilian."

Picciones have been making oil here, says Lorenzo, for at least 300 years, and others before them for much longer: "We've found millstones here that date to the third century AD." He jumps up from the vine-shaded outside table where we're having lunch to pull me into the living room. The shelves of a glass-fronted cabinet are filled with bits and pieces of antique ceramics, painted wares, and Roman glass, all found on the property, much of it from classical times or even earlier. In the courtyard outside there are larger pieces, most of them having to do with the milling process—a worn black-lava stone with a hollowed out top, he explains, is where olives were crushed to a paste before the oil was extracted. "Probably by the water method," Lorenzo explains—you immerse the paste in water so that the oil rises to the surface and can be skimmed off. It's a method so old it's recorded in the Bible.

Of course, it's obvious, this was no way to make great oil, since the water, some of which inevitably remained in the oil, would cause fermentation.

("Where there's water, there's life, and where there's life, there's fermentation.") Still, it's impressive to think of people making oil at all, even as primitively as they once did.

Lorenzo has 70 hectares, about 175 acres, planted to olives, almost all of them a prized local variety called *Tonda iblea* (from the Iblean Mountains that surround us on all sides). These olives make a prestigious oil with a much appreciated fresh flavor that experts liken to the fragrance of crushed tomato leaves.

Lorenzo also keeps a hundred or so pigs, a small local heritage breed called *maialino nero*, which simply means "little black pig." These are similar to the famous Iberian pigs from western Spain, although not as large. (British writer Elisabeth Luard claims this breed was brought into Italy and Spain by Celts.) Lorenzo's pigs are slaughtered when they're fully mature, but they only get to about 120 kilos (around 260 pounds) instead of the 250 kilos (550 pounds) of what they call *razze pesante*, or heavy modern breeds—Duroc and Large White principally. His boar is named Silvio, for Berlusconi, but unlike the former prime minister, this Silvio can service four sows in succession. A skittish little herd of piglets rushes up to meet us, then dashes off when Lorenzo lifts an arm to point out where they find water. He turns on a hose pipe and it shoots an arc of water across the dusty pigpen, which stretches beneath the olives. The piglets all scramble to take advantage of the fresh cool water. In another few weeks, these growing critters will be released with the adult pigs to roam the oak forest below the olive groves. Completely free, although in an enclosed area, they develop wonderful flavor as they feed the way pigs love to, on roots and grubs and lizard eggs.

---

1. *Saraceno*, Saracen, is an old term for Arab Muslims, still widely used in Italy, especially in the South.

The pigs are not without a lesson to teach, even though we're here for olives, not pigs. "The breed had almost disappeared," Lorenzo explains. "If you're a peasant farmer, you want a pig that's going to give you the most meat in the shortest time possible, whether you're eating the meat in your family or sending it to market it doesn't matter. It's like the local breed of chickens, Sicilian Buttercup—they only exist now in America. Now we have a standard breed called l'Ovaiola, the Layer. What's important is which one gives you eggs all year round. And that's not Sicilian Buttercup. And what was always important was getting the most oil out of the olives that you possibly could get."

To that end, local farmers traditionally went for quantity over quality, harvesting late in the season when the oil content of the olives was at its peak and then holding the olives to dry for weeks, in the mistaken belief that that practice too would raise the quantity of oil. "You paid the miller by the kilo, so anything that would reduce that weight was a good thing," Lorenzo explains. A late harvest of thoroughly blackened olives gave a lot of bland, almost flat-flavored oil, without the exciting aromas and flavors the cultivar was capable of. If it had any flavor at all, Lorenzo tells me, the oil was avvinato, a technical term for over-fermentation that literally means "winey," a solvent flavor like nail polish remover, that you don't want in your olive oil. Piling all the olives together, those picked or beaten from the tree along with those collected from the ground, leaving them for weeks to boost the yield, crushing for as long as two or three hours, all the while exposing the paste to light, air, and ambient temperatures—that was the way oil was made around Pianogrillo. "Then they stacked it up in mats and pressed them for 30 to 45 minutes to get as much oil out as possible—it was oxidation à gogo," he says, using a term I hadn't heard in years.

Lorenzo's family has always made oil on the property. His father was a surgeon, like his grandfather, with a distinguished practice in Milano, but they always came back to Pianogrillo in the autumn when it was time to harvest olives. Lorenzo had made another life for himself as an industrial designer—his most recent achievement is a sweet little individual oil container, an oliera, made in the shape of a stainless-steel olive, for Alessi—but 15 years ago, when he began to spend more time at Pianogrillo, he also began to understand that good oil, excellent oil, could indeed be made here and that it wasn't difficult to do so.

He was considered a revolutionary when he began harvesting early and pressing immediately. Then when he changed from the old-fashioned crush-and-press system to an Alfa Laval continuous-cycle extraction machine, the locals were sure he had lost it completely. This is the kind of story you hear throughout the olive oil world. Someone comes along—usually someone younger who loves the whole world of olives but has been out in the world enough to know there are better ways of doing things. That person invests a lot of money in doing things right—around $300,000 for the Alfa Laval machinery, I'm told—and all the old-timers raise their eyebrows and pity the poor father who has produced such an imbecile. And then, when they see what comes out and the prices it commands, very soon, everyone else is following suit.

It happened like that at Pianogrillo and other communities nearby. "They would bring me samples of their oil," Lorenzo says, "and they were so proud. I had a hard time but I had to tell them it wasn't any good."

With so much history all around him, it's understandable if he calls on the past as his witness. "*Sicilia Felix*," he says. "I'd love to see us return to the paradise that was here once upon a time." In the past 30 years, he's quick to point out, most of Western society, in Europe and North America, even in Sicily, has grown richer, in goods as well as in ideas, than the world our grandparents knew. "We have begun to value quality over quantity," he says. "It's the *figlio della richezza*, the offspring of richness. The market is beginning to appreciate the quality small producers can provide, and that's a good thing."

TURNING OLIVES *into* OIL

LIKE MOST OLIVE FARMERS IN THE NORTHERN HEMISPHERE, we actually begin to make our oil each year around the time of the spring equinox in March. If that seems early, it's just at that point that one of the most important activities of the entire season takes place—pruning and fertilizing the trees.

We don't prune each and every tree every year, although some producers do, especially those with dense, super-intensive olive orchards, the trees planted in such close hedgerows that they look from a distance like a vineyard. (In fact, this is sometimes referred to as "hedgerow planting.") Unlike a traditional olive orchard, a super-intensive grove is designed for mechanical pruning and harvesting, using equipment similar to that originally developed for mechanical cultivation of vineyards. For this reason, the trees must be pruned every year to keep them tight and compact. Mechanically pruning and harvesting, proponents of super-intensive cultivation say, saves enormously on labor expense, even if the oil produced by these methods isn't prime quality and the environmental costs, in water use and pollution, can be defeating. (For a more detailed discussion of super-high-density planting, see pages 52 to 53.)

But our labor, like that of most producers of premium olive oil, is all by hand—and mostly our own two (or four, or six) hands. Because of that, we prune half our trees one year, and half the following, then wait a few years before starting again. While we're pruning, cutting out excess wood that won't bear fruit, nipping back suckers and shoots that spring from the base of the tree, we're also fertilizing, giving each pruned tree a good dose of an organic fertilizer guaranteed to help the tree recover from its surgery and boost it into healthy production of fruit.

"It's not really a tree, the olive, it's a bush, or it wants to become a bush," Gemma Pasquali, my latest (and youngest-ever) olive guru, tells me: Our job as olive farmers, she says, is to keep them from doing that. With a PhD in agronomics from the University of Florence and post-doc work in plant genetics at the University of Florida, Gemma knows what she's talking about. Her own trees at Villa Campestri in the Mugello, north of Florence, are pruned to keep them shapely, to open the inside of each tree to the light, and to make the eventual fruits easier to harvest. And also, she says, pointing out to me one of her elderly Frantoio trees, they are pruned into the vase shape that is traditional in Tuscany, to keep them from degenerating into bushes as they are wont to do. This particular tree was knocked down by the infamous freeze in 1986 that struck olive groves all over Central Italy and extended as far as Provence. "The base didn't die," Gemma says, "but the trunk did and it's painful. You have to wait many years for it to grow back." There are four sturdy limbs now growing from the base where the trunk was cut back after the freeze. They look like four separate trees, though united at the base, and almost 30 years later they are producing plenty of oil.

The olive tree's vascular system, just like that in humans, transports nutrients, in the tree's case from its roots deep underground up to the foliage and fruits; at the same time, carbohydrates formed from photosynthesis are carried from the leaves back down. When the vascular system is damaged—by frost or disease, or by improper pruning—it leaves a wound that can prevent the system from operating properly. The beauty of olive trees, at least for painters and tourists if not necessarily for olive farmers, is in their gnarled and twisted shapes created by age and the afflictions of time. Venerable old olives often split open, hollowing their trunks or giving the appearance of three or more trees growing inter-twined, yet within the structure is a single tree, its vascular system continuing to operate on the outside of the trunk, its limbs continuing to bear. "The amount of genetic informa-tion in this one tree," says Gemma, "is just amazing." She explains that a tree this ancient is not just a Frantoio cultivar but that it also has absorbed genetic information from the whole population of trees that neighbor it on this high Mediterranean savanna.

Olive trees, icons of the Mediterranean, really want to run wild, and if you don't keep taming them, that's exactly what they will do. I noted earlier that archeologists, looking at carbonized olive pits from ancient digs, find it difficult to differentiate between pits from domesticated olives and those from wild plants, or between wild and feral plants—trees that were once cultivated and have reverted to the wild. The semi-wild trees sprouting on abandoned land around our hill-country farm are telling witnesses to that process. Without the discipline of pruning, their fruit is skimpy, small, and bitter—or nonexistent. It makes me realize that the olive tree is similar to Indian corn (maize) in that it exists in an intimate symbiosis with humankind. Without human intervention, neither corn nor olives would thrive. Both plants depend to a great extent on humans for their continued existence, just as their human cultivators also depend on them. In *The Botany of Desire*, Michael Pollan described this mutual interdependence, this synergy, in terms that suggested that perhaps it's a mistake to speak of humankind domesticating certain plants. Rather, he argued, it may be the case that certain plants have domesticated us instead.

But olive trees, unlike corn, even when they have apparently ceased production completely, can be reborn, as my old journalist colleague Mort Rosenblum has shown on the farm he bought on a steep Provençal hillside some years ago. Mort and his wife, Jeannette, through rigorous pruning, generous fertilizing, and backbreaking labor for a desk-bound journalist, have successfully pruned, hacked, and chain-sawed back into productivity a hundred or more "wild" olive trees that had been abandoned years earlier. Mort, who has a gift for naming, calls his place Wild Olives, which, he notes, if pronounced with a French accent, comes out sounding much like *huile d'olive*. And he's very happy with an annual yield of around 50 liters of opulent, excellent oil.[1]

It's difficult to understand what excellent oil is all about, and why it's so expensive, until you begin to comprehend the method, from start to finish, by which it is made, the step-by-step chain that links each stage to the next and the critical points in that chain that determine success or failure. The process really does begin in March, with pruning and fertilizing, well before the new growth emerges. Well-rotted sheep manure is what old-timers always recommend to spread beneath the olive trees—*la crème de la crème* of manures, Alice Toklas called it, writing years ago about her garden in France. I would prefer sheep manure to our commercial organic fertilizer, but it's hard to find. Until the years after World War II, when rural life throughout Tuscany changed forever, sheep were plentiful up in these hills, part of every farm's endowment. Our village, Teverina, used to host a sizeable sheep fair every August where farmers traded lambs, along with fresh ricotta and pungent pecorino cheeses made from their mothers' milk, but today there are almost no sheep farmers left anywhere around. Getting manure means a trek to a far distant sheep farm and hiring a wagon of some sort to haul it back to Pian d'Arcello. It's a lot easier to dip a gloved hand into a big plastic sack of clean organic fertilizer and swirl it around each tree's roots.

The wild boar also do a great job of cultivating our trees. They obviously adore the olive orchard, because they're out disporting themselves in it almost every night. Fortunately the trees are big enough now and sufficiently sturdy that the boar do no damage when they use the trunks as back-scratching posts. If I wake at three or four in the morning when the moon is full, I can see from my bedroom window their hulking shadows wading through the meadow grasses as they steadily munch on whatever it is that tickles the boarish palate—roots, no doubt, and grubs and, my neighbors say, any sort of lizard, snake, or viper eggs they come across, thus helping to keep the viper population under control. The boars' deposits fertilize the trees, and at the same time their grunting grub work helps to turn over the soil.

---

1. For more of Mort's passionate insights into olives and their culture, see his highly entertaining book *Olives: The Life and Lore of a Noble Fruit*.

Weather-wise, March is often the worst time of the year up where we are, on the high dividing line between Tuscany and Umbria. Pruning trees is fun when days are warm and sunny, even with an occasional spring shower, but much of the time cold rain, lashed by the wind, drives us indoors before nightfall. When it's a harsh winter—and winters are more severe now than when I first came here in the 1970s—the harshness is most piercing in February and March. Last winter the snow came in February, stunning everyone, first with its beauty; it's not often that you get to see this countryside, where every vista seems set to provide the backdrop for a Renaissance Annunciation or Nativity scene, made even more enchanting by a thick blanket of white. ("*Ha visto la neve, signora?*" Margherita in the bottega asks me: "Have you seen the snow?" Well, honestly, Margherita, how could I have missed it—it's a meter deep in the field behind the house!) But once folks had got somewhat accustomed to the beauty, then the worries set in—the isolation (many farmhouses were unreachable for weeks), the cold (temperatures went below zero Celsius and stayed there, also for weeks), and the effects on the olive trees.

By the time spring finally rolled around, they had new worries: We didn't have any rain all winter, just snow, people said, so it's gonna be a dry summer, bad for olives. I could have recited the old Maine farmer's litany about snow, especially late snow, which back in New England is called "poor man's fertilizer," because it melts slowly and carries moisture and nourishment deep into the soil. Much better than the usual driving winter rainstorms of Central Italy, the runoff from which simply carries precious nutrients down into the streams. But I didn't because I knew no one would believe me. Still, by May the olive trees had come back in force and were covered in glorious drifts of tiny, almost insignificant white blossoms that looked like cotton fluff (or snow) on the branches. From our perspective, it seemed like the beginning of a better-than-ever year for olives.

The beauty of growing olives is this: Once the hard work of pruning and fertilizing is over, there's really not much more to do until late summer or early autumn. Old Columella recognized that back in the third century CE: The olive "is held in high esteem because it is maintained by light cultivation and, when it is not covered with fruit, it calls for scarcely any expenditure," he counseled.[2] Less work, less worry, less cost, especially when compared to vines or grains, the other staple crops of the Mediterranean.

Of course, Columella's received wisdom fails to mitigate the conscientious farmer's anxieties as she checks on the swelling buds throughout April and the flowering in May. The grass in the orchard gets cut two or three times through the spring and summer months, and some farmers turn the soil beneath the trees as well. I don't because I'm convinced that this practice simply dries out the earth. Our trees need every drop of moisture they can find.

What about irrigation then? When the trees were young and just getting established, we watered them well, but we stopped once they were on their way to adolescence. Irrigation is a way to reduce the olive tree's rather irritating habit of producing in alternate years—one year abundance, the next year skimpy, and so on. In this, olives are not unlike other fruit trees, especially apples and pears. Commercial producers, who want to ensure a steady

---

2. *De Re Rustica*, Book V, 8.

supply of olives year in and year out, irrigate to give a good-size crop every year, and super-intensive producers must rely on irrigation just to keep trees alive. But there is growing evidence that the quality of the oil suffers. A study developed at the University of Extremadura, funded by Spain's National Research Institute for Agriculture and Food Technology, confirmed that reducing irrigation, while it produces a smaller harvest, actually produces a higher-quality oil with greater concentration of phenolic compounds,[3] confirming what the old-timers say. Irrigating, they all concur, will make a less pungent oil, and pungency is a valued quality, especially here in Tuscany, where our oils are noted for a sharp kick in the back of the throat that leads unwary tasters to cough.

Such pungency is an indication of the presence of the polyphenols that contribute to olive oil's beneficial power in our diets, so it's something we want in olive oil. Polyphenols also give the oil great staying power, meaning that, if the oil is stored correctly, it can keep, undisturbed, even for three or four years. (This is not true of bottled oils on supermarket shelves, which almost invariably are not stored correctly.) New World farmers in South America, Australia, and California, many of them with high-density plantations, are big on irrigation, but, says my neighbor Brian Chatterton, an Australian who grows olives in Umbria, optimum oil production comes about when olives get less water.

---

3. Higgins, Charles, "Less Watering Improves Olive Oil Quality, Study Finds," www.oliveoiltimes.com, April 3, 2012.

Besides, I'm convinced that the olive tree evolved to fit a typical Mediterranean environment with long, dry summers—and if that's the way nature intended olives to be, that's the route I want to follow.

So our olives grow and flourish throughout the warm Tuscan summer. By late June, where once there were flowers, there are miniature olives, hard green babies. In hotter climates—in Sicily and southern Spain, in Tunisia and Palestine, on the island of Crete and the Aegean coast—the olives not only flower earlier, but they also grow much more rapidly. By the solstice, their olives are double or triple the size of ours in Central Italy. But at summer's height, no matter where you are in the olive world, hail is what's most feared. In August, when dark thunderclouds loom on the western horizon, we cross our fingers, cross ourselves, light candles, say prayers, do whatever juju seems called for to keep away a damaging summer ice storm that could leave fruits so battered they're good for nothing when it's time to harvest. Mold, insects, diseases—they all love the rot that comes from battered fruit. One of the worst threats for many farmers is the olive fly, *Bactrocera oleae*, a marvelously evolved insect that has existed for as long as olive trees have and does major damage to the fruits when it invades a grove. Damaged fruit is no way to make good oil, but avaricious farmers, eager to wring every drop of oil, good or bad, from their olives, still bring to the mill sacks full of fetid olives to be converted into oil that can never qualify as extra-virgin. Olive oil, the experts often say, unlike wine, is made in the field and not at the mill. To a large extent they're right. You can manipulate poor-quality wine through fermentation and aging, you can add sugar to boost the alcohol, but you can't do a thing with bad olives except make bad oil.

Up to this point, we've not done much with our olives that Columella would not have recommended. In fact, any of those Roman farmers, and even Greek Hesiod, the oldest agronomist of all, would doubtless look on our inconsiderable labors and approve, despite the fertilizer that comes out of a plastic sack instead of the business end of a sheep. But by autumn, things start to change, and one of the major changes, one that is a critical determinant between excellent oil and indifferent oil, is the time of harvest. It is true that Cato and Columella, among other ancient writers, insisted on the virtues of an early harvest, when the olives were not fully mature, but this smart and sensible practice seems to have been ignored by most growers, then and since, in favor of quantity. Later harvests give more oil; earlier harvests give better oil. For most farmers throughout history and even today, it has not even been a toss-up—quantity wins over quality every time. But those times are changing.

Jean-Marie Baldassari is a Provençal consultant who works with producers in underserved parts of the olive oil world to help boost the quality of their production. Over the years, he has spent many seasons in Palestine, where olives and their oil are both an economic resource and a compelling symbol of Palestinian culture and history. I watched him in action one hot day in mid-October at a mill in Burqin, near Palestine's northern border with Israel. He was instructing a group of a dozen or so youngish men, jointly called the *shabab* or "the boys," who work in and around the mill, which is run by a cooperative called Canaan Fair Trade; most of the *shabab* are also farmers, members of the cooperative who

Portrait of an Oil Maker: Nasser Abu Farha

If you saw Nasser Abu Farha in a suit and tie, strolling along the streets of Madison, Wisconsin, you would take him for the college professor he almost became instead of the Palestinian olive oil producer that he is. But the story of how he came to be head of a prominent Palestinian olive oil cooperative actually begins back at the University of Wisconsin with his doctoral dissertation for the anthropology department at Madison. The dissertation, published as a book in 2009, *The Making of a Human Bomb* (Duke University Press), is a study of violence and its roots in disconnectedness and despair, about how and why young Palestinian men (and occasionally women) become suicide bombers, martyrs for what seems, from the outside at least, to be a hopeless and some would say an invalid cause. Arguing from the evidence, Nasser became convinced that only through positive economic change and the organization and structure that could bring that about, and not necessarily through military or guerilla action, could Palestinians develop the strength and resilience, not to mention the dignity within their own community, that would give them the power to confront the overwhelming threat represented by the State of Israel. A strong and viable Palestinian economy, in short, was one important step toward re-asserting Palestinian rights to their own land, rights that have been subverted by successive Israeli governments as well as by the illegal and insidious network of Israeli colonial settlements that surrounds Palestinian communities on the West Bank.

To achieve his goal, Nasser had to change the way Palestinian farmers made their olive oil. The entity he formed, Canaan Fair Trade, is a cooperative of 1,700 very small farms in the territory around Jenin, the northernmost important town in the West Bank, and incidentally home to an enormous refugee camp that is a constant thorn in the side of the Israelis. Extra-virgin olive oil, certified organic and fair trade, is the company's main focus, produced in a state-of-the-art mill in nearby Burqin. (They also produce other traditional ingredients, many sold in U.S. gourmet products stores, among them sun-dried tomatoes; maftoul, large-grain Palestinian couscous, handmade and dried in the sun; and za'atar, the Middle Eastern blend of herbs and spices, a favorite of American chefs.)

In the process, many traditional ways have had to change. The changes taking place in Palestine are indicative of similar ones throughout the olive oil world, wherever producers try to reach beyond strictly local customers. Increasingly, the international market demands high-quality oils that are certified to be what they say they are on the label—100 percent extra-virgin, produced in a specified place and within a specified time frame, and with a flavor profile that is easy for consumers to appreciate. These are some of the key areas where enormous improvements have taken place just in the past 30 or so years, and they have had a huge impact on the quality of extra-virgin olive oil. In the Middle East in general, these advances have come much later than in Italy, Spain, and Greece, but the entire olive oil world is alert now to the economic value such progress can bring.

Working with French olive oil expert Jean-Marie Baldassari as a consultant (see pages 43 to 47), Nasser has pushed farmers to accept ideas that have often been positively revolutionary for deeply traditional farmers—ideas like early harvest and quick, clean processing at low temperatures. Beyond that, the oil, once processed, is stored in scrupulously clean stainless-steel containers under a flush of nitrogen to protect it from the atmosphere. It all sounds quite simple, but that's without factoring in the unique difficulties Palestinian farmers experience.

Over dinner, which he prepared at his home north of Jenin, Nasser explained to me some of those unique difficulties, especially with regard to water supply: Throughout the West Bank Palestinian territories, it is illegal to drill a well without Israeli military permission, which is seldom, if ever, granted; furthermore, Palestinians are forbidden access to either the Jordan River or the vital aquifer that lies mostly beneath the West Bank, the waters of which are diverted into the Israeli National Water Carrier. Equally problematic is access to historic Palestinian olive plantations, which often requires passage into or through illegal but powerful Israeli settlements that are openly hostile, and very often life-threatening, to Palestinian farmers. The construction of the infamous Wall, a concrete barrier variously 18 to 25 feet high that stretches for miles, has further cut farmers off from their own groves of olives.

Still, the fact that Canaan Fair Trade is able to pay its farmers almost twice as much for their harvest as they earned less than a decade ago, and that they have been able to upgrade their extra-virgin olive oil to international standards and to provide high-quality foods that are in demand in markets from the United States to Germany and Japan, has meant renewed faith in a product that has been a symbol of this region for millennia and a renewed commitment to struggle with a situation that might otherwise seem intolerable.

Nasser Abu Farha is determined that Palestinian farmers will share in those improvements. (Canaan Fair Trade's variety of olive oils and other products are available at canaanusa.com/shop.) In fact, he was one of three entrepreneurs recognized in 2013 at the San Francisco Fancy Food Show with the first annual Specialty Food Association Award for Leadership.

bring their olives here to be processed. "Your olives," Baldassari explained in French, drawing a graph on the whiteboard behind him, "reach organoleptic maturity in the first half of October and then they begin to decline. But the oil matures, it reaches a peak, and the yield is greatest between mid-October and mid-November. The organoleptic maturity precedes by several days the optimum yield—and *that*"—he jabbed a finger at the point on the graph—"that's when you need to harvest."

Collectively, the *shabab* were somewhat incredulous. Growers in Italy and France deliberately harvest for lower yield? "Yes," affirmed Jean-Marie decisively: "You renounce yield, some of it at least, for the sake of quality and flavor in the oil."

This has been a difficult notion for many oil producers, not just Palestinians, to comprehend. For generations, indeed for millennia, the goal has been quantity and not necessarily quality. After all, the oil had to last for two years, given the olive tree's disquieting habit of producing well only in alternate years. To be safe, a farmer had to have enough oil in the family cellar to last until the next good harvest, and moreover enough surplus to sell in order to tuck gold coins under the family mattress. In Central Italy, as the old *nonna* at an Umbrian mill explained to me, the harvest traditionally took place *fra la Madonna e Candelora*, meaning between the Feast of the Immaculate Conception on December 8 (la Madonna) and Candelora on February 2, the purification of the virgin after the birth of Christ (also Groundhog Day).[4] By February, olives in Umbria are going to be thoroughly ripe and black, weeping oil, possibly having suffered more than one freeze, if not actually shriveling on the trees. Nonetheless, that's when people have traditionally harvested, at least in part because that's when the oil content of the fruits appeared to be at its peak.[5] At that stage, it is almost impossible to make good oil.

In Puglia, the heel of Italy's boot, where about 60 percent of all the oil in Italy is produced in any given year (and much of that of indifferent quality), farmers still today attach orange-colored nets beneath their trees and leave them there, suspended from the branches, to catch ripened olives as they fall. The nets stay in place throughout the season. When enough olives have collected to make a big enough load for the mill, the farmer bundles the whole lot up and takes it off to the *frantoio*, replacing the nets under the trees for another session of falling olives. This practice lasts until all the olives have detached themselves from the tree and been "harvested." Problematically, olives start to deteriorate the minute they are separated from the mother tree. (In this, they are not unlike apples and oranges, although the decline with olives is much more rapid than with any other fruit I can think of.) Like fish in the bottom of the boat, olives might well sit in the bottom of the net for a couple of weeks, festering and fermenting and infecting the more recent windfalls so that no good oil can ever come out of it.

---

4. If a candle is lit outside on this day and you cannot see the flame—because the sun is so bright—there will be six more weeks of winter to endure, very close to the myth of the groundhog's shadow.

5. I say "appeared to be" because the oil in fact had reached its peak, as Baldassari pointed out, back in November. After that, as the olives start to dry on the tree, they give up water. So the percentage of oil per weight of the olives goes up—but the actual quantity of oil remains the same.

Back in ancient Greece, methods were no less elementary. In a practice that continues in some regions to this day, Greek farmers harvested by beating the olives out of the trees with long reed sticks or poles, as evidenced by a marvelously vigorous black-figure amphora from the late sixth century BCE in the British Museum. The vase, which was actually found near Viterbo in Etruscan Italy, shows three trees, high in one of which a boy has perched, the better to beat the olives out of the tree. Two men are also knocking the branches with long poles, while another lad harvests the fallen olives from the ground beneath the tree. Though I'm told on good authority that farmers in some parts of Greece continue to do this, it is not recommended since the olives, in order to detach themselves, must be super-mature; and then, of course, even if they are undamaged, they will not produce good oil.

Another widespread tradition, one I've mentioned earlier that is still practiced in many Mediterranean regions, is that of piling the olives up in a corner of the farmyard, or even at the olive mill, in the vain expectation that the yield in oil will be greater if the olives dry for two or three weeks. There is no way to increase the amount of oil in an olive once it has reached its peak. Instead, the amount of water in the olives diminishes as they dry out, so the yield of oil per weight of olives may appear to be greater but in fact it is exactly the same as it would have been had the olives been pressed fresh. Except of course that the quality of the oil suffers enormously from this treatment. The olives start to ferment and rancidify and, again, no good oil will come from them. But since the miller is actually paid by the weight of the olives and not by the quantity of oil, a canny farmer will try to beat down the price by deliberately reducing the weight of his crop.

Despite all these nefarious time- and tradition-honored practices, there have always been some few farmers who harvested earlier, when the fruits were starting to change color, no longer completely green nor yet completely black, but a mixture of some green, some black, and some olives that are streaked with darker rays as the fruits began to mature—a stage called by the pretty Italian term *invaiatura*. The better Tuscan producers were and are especially noted for harvesting olives early to produce green oils with rich and complex aromas and flavors, oils with a pleasingly pungent bite and a degree of bitterness to balance the sweetness of the fruit. Often these early harvest oils were set aside for family use, or for the landlord. Science confirms that this oil is not only better tasting but also better for you, with a higher content of the polyphenols that bring countless health benefits along with appealing flavors. And because of the high content of polyphenols (for a discussion of polyphenols, see pages 83 to 87), the oil has a much longer shelf life—which may have been what motivated those canny old Tuscan farmers in the first place.

"As the olive matures," Baldassari explained to his rapt but still skeptical group of Palestinian farmers, "the aromas change from greenness to nuttiness, and that moment of change is also the point of polyphenolic concentration. Today's market is looking for oils that are very rich in polyphenols—the contest in the oil is between fruitiness and bitterness." Depending on the region and the climate, as well as on the individual variety, that moment could come anytime between the first of October and the middle of November. And still, even in Tuscany with its rather advanced theories about olive culture, there are farmers who won't even enter the olive groves, let alone start harvesting, before St. Martin's Day, San Martino, on November 11.

When we first came to live in Tuscany in the 1970s, no *frantoio*, or olive mill, ever opened before the middle of November. In other parts of the Mediterranean such as Andalusia, it was often as late as mid-December before the harvest began, and it lasted until well into March. Since that time, there has been a determined move toward earlier and earlier harvests, as a direct consequence of market demand for higher-quality oil. A producer in the Cilento, on the Italian coast south of Naples, I was told, even harvests olives during the first week of September to make an oil described as "explosive" with bitterness—and no wonder: At that stage, olive oil is simply medicine, nothing more or less. As Baldassari explained to the Palestinian farmers, striking the balance between peak flavor and peak yield, and between the fruitiness of oil from rich, ripe olives and the pungency and bitterness of that from immature ones, has become a juggling act for conscientious olive oil producers all over the world.

Timing of the harvest, in fact, is one major reason for the immense quantities of indifferent oil coming out of southern Spain. In Andalusia, where a good 40 percent of the entire world's olive oil is made each year, the reach of olive groves is breathtaking, truly awesome; they carpet the rolling land in all directions, as far as the eye can see from a very high hill. But it is simply impossible to harvest all that fruit early and to process it promptly—the capacity of the groves to produce fruit far exceeds the capacity of the mills to make oil. So the harvest in southern Spain continues over months, with fruit growing ever riper on the trees while harvested olives pile up at the mills, waiting their turn to be processed and deteriorating as they wait.

American olive expert Paul Vossen, who works with the University of California's Cooperative Extension Service, calls this "the infamous Picual controversy." Something like 80 percent of the vast olive plantations of Spain are devoted to Picual, a cultivar that, when harvested late, as it most frequently is, makes an oil that, according to this expert, "tastes and smells . . . to trained olive oil tasters" overripe and defective, "with a very distinctive flavor described kindly as 'eucalyptus.'" And because so much of the world's olive oil comes from Spain, and so much Spanish oil comes from defective, overripe Picual olives, the fusty flavor and often rancid smell of that oil are what many consumers confidently assume are the characteristic flavors and smells of properly made olive oil. The result is a little like children who grow up never tasting anything but orange juice made from frozen concentrate. Give them a sip of truly fresh, just-squeezed juice and they turn their little noses up at the taste. So too with olive oil: It's predictable and even understandable that, for millions of consumers for whom the flavor of overripe, fusty Picual is the "true" flavor of olive oil, a well-made oil with its balance of fruity, pungent, and bitter flavors will be not only incomprehensible but downright disagreeable.

In fairness, I should point out that there are a number of Andalusian producers who control their own production from start to finish, harvesting at the right moment and pressing immediately, and consequently turn out excellent oils from Picual olives that stand out in any competition anywhere in the world. Castillo de Canena is one such brand, while Almazaras de la Subbetica, Manuel Montes Marin's Portico de la Villa, Oleum Viride from Zahara de la Sierra in the far west of Andalusia, and Melgarejo from Aceites Campoliva

are others. And there are more. Still, at least 80 percent of Andalusian olive oil is, speaking as kindly as possible, quite ordinary when it's not out-and-out defective. And much of the fault lies in delayed harvesting.

Global climate change has also affected the time of harvest. Unusually harsh winters in many parts of the Mediterranean are only part of the story; Mediterranean summers are drier, hotter, and longer than ever, lasting well into the autumn. It worries Paco Vañó, who makes Castillo de Canena's prize-winning oils, including an excellent monocultivar Picual (thus proving that it is entirely possible to make a first-rate oil from this problematic olive[6]). In order to initiate the enzymatic process called lipogenesis, when oil begins to swell in the olives on the trees, Paco told me, you need autumn rains and lower temperatures—10°C (50°F) for at least a couple of hours every night. In his rustic old Land Rover, we were bouncing across the deeply rutted roads that connect a few of the 3,750 acres of olive trees he maintains. It was late September, and he kept glancing at the outside temperature gauge on the dashboard. By then, pre-dawn temperatures should have been down in the 10°C mark and summer's heat a distant memory. "But look," he continued, pointing at the thermometer, which was hovering around 30°C, "it's still summer weather. Strange times."

6. Castillo de Canena's Picual took a well-deserved gold medal at the 2011 Fancy Food Show in Washington, D.C., the first Spanish oil ever to be so recognized.

Strange times, indeed! Not only hot summer temperatures extending into autumn, but also ongoing drought, only occasionally relieved by torrential rainfall (almost as damaging as drought), have had serious implications for Andalusian agriculture in general and for olives and oil in particular. The region, a broad belt that extends across southern Spain, produces annually between 30 and 40 percent of the world's olive oil. With the rains and cooling temperatures of autumn, Vañó said, the oil should start to increase while the critical content of polyphenols, which determine much of the flavors in the oil, optimizes. In the Picual cultivar, that means a softening of flavor. Harvested too green, Picual olives give an overwhelmingly bitter oil; too ripe and the oil will taste too much of what California's Vossen politely called "eucalyptus." At the moment where greenness and ripeness balance each other, just as Baldassari pointed out to his Palestinian students, a smart farmer can get the maximum yield of oil rich in polyphenols. Just a week or 10 days later, while the oil may have increased in quantity, the quality will be diminished.

Timing the harvest accurately can also affect particular flavors in many oils, as Mirko Sella, a young producer in the hills northeast of Verona, found out. Grignano is an obscure variety grown widely in this very restricted area and until recently was not held in particularly high regard. But Sella, working with agronomists at the University of Padua, discovered that for a particular three-week period in October, Grignano olives produce an oil with a refreshingly citrus or tart apple flavor that is no longer apparent when the olives are left to mature. Now he bottles his October-harvested oil as Grignano Monte Guala, and it is increasingly prized by fastidious collectors.

There are still some philosophical holdouts against early harvesting, however. Those are producers whose goal is a bland and unaggressive oil without the assertive flavors most knowledgeable consumers are looking for. Late November is considered an appropriate time to start the harvest in Liguria, along the Italian Riviera, and in much of the south of France, where olive picking may well go on, a few days at a time, throughout the winter. Traditionalists in regions from Italy's Cinque Terre around through Liguria and into Provence, even down into the Catalan coast of Spain, vaunt the quality of their oil, usually a rich golden color, indicating that it's pressed from fully ripened olives. When it's well made, the oil has a pronounced fruity taste but not much depth of flavor and no challenging complexities. It has no staying power, and the olive cultivars that are grown in these regions, particularly Taggiasca from Liguria and Arbequina from Catalonia, are characteristically low in polyphenols even at their peak. Ligurian gastronomes claim the bland, sweet flavor of their Taggiasca oil is an ideal condiment for the seafood that is such a feature of local cuisine, and they may be right. Still, most connoisseurs today are looking for the complexity and intensity of early harvested oil from cultivars rich in polyphenolic content.

Last year we started picking at the end of October, when the weather was still balmy but autumn skies were lowering, metallic clouds stretching across our high valley in layers heavy with rain. Never harvest olives in the rain, Gemma Pasquali tells me: It's bad for the trees, bad for the olives, and bad for the pickers. Wet olives develop mold and the moldy flavor will contaminate the oil, giving it the negative characteristic that official tasters call "musty"—which is exactly the flavor of the oil that my Tuscan neighbors produced back in the old days. For the same reason, we don't harvest early in the morning, not until the dew has dried on the trees. So we rush to get the olives in after they have dried and before rain begins to fall and wreak havoc with our harvest. The rough wicker baskets that we strap around our waists with a piece of rope or an old belt are shaped like a curving quarter of a globe. I buy them from the old man who makes them himself by hand and brings them to the Thursday market in Camucia, where he sells them for €35 (about $45 at this writing). We pick rapidly, using a two-handed downward motion that a Cortonese farmwife described to me as "milking" the olives, showering the fruits down into our baskets or a broad net tucked under each tree as we proceed through the orchard. There are six of us working together at the beginning of the week, but the crew quickly expands to eight and then ten, the house overflowing, and then we contract back to six again. The pickers include various relatives, friends, neighbors, and assorted hangers-on—in fact, anyone who says, as many people do, "Gee, I'd love to come help you pick olives."

And when the rain comes, we stop and wait. And we cross our fingers and hope.

The second day of picking, the weather clears, and we get down to it with serious intent. But then the clocks are set back to winter time and the sun goes down behind the high ridge of the Cerventosa by 4:30, cutting the day extremely short. Under such constraints, it takes a lot of enthusiastic hands to assemble the 440 pounds of olives we need in order to do a single pressing without combining our olives with someone else's.

Picking by hand is an agonizingly slow process, and there are constant efforts to improve it and speed it up. Some growers harvest mechanically, using battery-operated plastic combs that vibrate along the branches, agitating the olives and knocking them off. There's even a dinosaur-like machine that embraces the whole trunk and shakes it brutally so the olives drop into a giant inverted umbrella beneath. Even if I could afford such a machine, I wouldn't use it—it damages the olives, and damaged olives won't produce good oil. Moreover, the olives have to be very ripe before they'll drop off the tree, even with the violent shaking the machine produces. Some folks like to use plastic combs to rake down the branches, but that rakes off leaves as well, which then have to be removed before the olives can be processed. I have a set of hollowed-out goat horns that I bought in the market in Sfax, one of the centers of Tunisian olive oil production—you put one horn on your index finger, one on your middle finger, and rake down the branches like that. My friend Deborah, who grows olives in the next valley over, used to seek out used opera gloves in Paris flea markets; they made good hand protectors, with the tips of the fingers cut away. But the market in opera gloves seems to have dried up, like so many onetime accoutrements of the good life.

So we pick, family and friends together, going tree by tree, spreading the nets, moving ladders, talking, telling stories, listening, stopping for a quick lunch under the trees and a fortifying swig of *rosso toscano* before we go back to work again. Each day ends at sundown as we amble slowly back to the house and tip our final basket-loads into the airy plastic bins in which the fruit will be carried to the mill.

Super-High-Density: The Future of Extra-Virgin?

In the broad and verdant Colchagua Valley of Chile, some 50 miles south of the country's capital, Santiago, a vast enterprise called Olisur is under way. The brainchild of Chilean entrepreneur Alfonso Swett, Olisur is only a decade old but already produces nearly three million liters of olive oil annually from 3,500 acres of trees, planted tightly together in serried rows, around 700 trees to the acre. (Traditionally, olives are planted anywhere from 100 to 250 per acre, depending on soil conditions and rainfall.) Each little tree is no more than six feet tall, kept at that height by rigorous pruning. They are so closely planted, five feet from the one in front and the one behind, that from a distance the olive grove looks like a very large vineyard—or a series of dense parallel hedgerows.

Alfonso Swett came to olive farming fairly late in life, but that has limited neither his ambition nor his enthusiasm. With at least 3,000 more acres ready to plant in the years immediately ahead, he sees a promising future for southern hemisphere oils in North American markets, especially Olisur's Santiago and O-Live brands. Harvest time in Chile is in May, meaning new, fresh, well-made olive oil can be ready for northern markets at just about the time Mediterranean oils are starting to lose their fresh-harvest punch.

"This is the largest super-intensive farm in the world," Olisur's export manager, Tomas Garcia, told me as he showed me around the plantation. It is truly state-of-the-art technology for olive cultivation. The system, more often called super-high-density planting, or SHD for short, evolved in the past couple of decades, the result of efforts on the part of AgroMillora, a Spanish nursery company that is the main resource for both the expertise and the baby trees. The cultivars provided by AgroMillora are selected and developed specifically for intensive cultivation, whether modern clones of antique varieties such as Arbequina and Koroneiki, with long histories in Catalonia and Greece respectively, or newer hybrids such as Sikitita (called Chiquitita in the United States), a cross between Arbequina and Spain's mightiest cultivar, Picual. About 80 percent of the trees at Olisur are the Catalan cultivar Arbequina.

Super-high-density planting is inarguably the most important development to take place in olive agriculture since—well, one could argue that it is the only development of consequence in olive cultivation since the great Latin agronomists instructed farmers back in the days of the Roman Empire. So what are its advantages? First of all, terrific savings in the two costliest parts of producing olive oil: pruning the trees, which conventional growers do every year or two, and annual harvesting. Given the nature of a traditional olive grove, like those I see all around me in Tuscany, both of these activities are highly labor-intensive and are one of the main reasons why fine olive oil is so expensive. Each year in early spring, pruners go through the groves, tree by tree, carefully trimming no-longer-productive limbs and opening the trees up to bring light and air to the center and make the eventual harvest easier. Then in the autumn, to make the best oil, fruits must be removed by hand, almost one by one. (True, some mechanical aids have been developed, but even using battery-operated combs that pull fruits from the tree is essentially handwork.) In high-density groves, on the other hand, both operations are done by machine, using over-the-row harvesters and pruners developed for the wine industry and adapted to olive trees. It all happens much more quickly and at much lower cost.

Further, since these SHD plantations are perforce brand-new, most growers have sited their milling operations practically in the middle of the grove, cutting down the amount of time between harvest and processing. At California Olive Ranch (COR), another giant operation in the northern Central Valley, Bob Singletary, in charge of milling operations, cheerfully boasts that his olives go from tree to mill in just two hours. Singletary, who was an independent olive processor for 30 years, has happily gone over to running COR's mill, which he operates with just one other person. Together, these two men handle 55 tons of olives an hour to produce 80,000 gallons of oil every 24 hours during the season. And the mill runs, Bob tells me, 24-7 from early October to early December. Which is one reason why COR's gamut of oils sell on average at about half the price of oils of similarly high quality from more traditional operations.

Super-high-density planting has been adopted with enthusiasm by growers in the New World, but especially in California and South America, as well as in many parts of Spain. But if this revolutionary system—and the adjective is, I think, justified—means more good oil at a better price than conventional, traditional olive agriculture, are there drawbacks? Yes, of course there are. One is cost—although the cost of maintaining an SHD orchard is lower in terms of pruning and harvesting, the initial investment is very large and moreover requires heavy inputs of irrigation water and often nutrients to spur growth in the infant trees, both of which are costly. Beyond that, many traditional growers are appalled at the idea that the trees themselves become exhausted and must be replaced after 15 years. But COR's plantation in Oroville is 14 or 15 years old already and continues to produce well, or so I was told when I visited. Still, when so many olive trees around the Mediterranean are revered for their centenarian and even millenarian status, it's painful to think of olives being treated like just another commodity crop.

And the oil? Taste a COR Miller's Blend or Olisur's Santiago against the very finest Tuscan, Sicilian, Greek, or Spanish oil, and you will doubtless find that the complexity of Mediterranean oils puts them in a category by themselves. "It's good honest oil," one California expert told me, "but it isn't going to make anyone write poetry." For everyday use, and for the majority of people who would rather not be challenged by super-intensive flavors, these SHD oils provide a welcome solution. Economical, honestly made, high in quality, they stand in relation to an oil like, for instance, Pianogrillo from Sicily's Monte Iblei region or Fritz Blauel's Greek Organic from the Mani peninsula as a well-made California Cabernet Sauvignon stands in relation to a Bordeaux Premier Cru. The latter is not for everyday drinking, but when you taste it, you unquestionably realize what is missing from your everyday wine.

I think of a Robert Frost poem I've always loved, "After Apple Picking":

For I have had too much
Of olive-picking: I am overtired
Of the great harvest I myself desired.
There were ten thousand thousand fruit to touch,
Cherish in hand, lift down, and not let fall.
    (Apologies to the poet.)

In the end, it took us four days to complete the harvest.

WHAT ACTUALLY DETERMINES THE QUALITY OF AN EXTRA-VIRGIN OLIVE OIL? The care and cleanliness with which olives are grown, harvested, and pressed is one big part of the equation. The variety of olives used and their stage of maturity when picked is another. How carefully the oil is stored is also very important. But these are specifics. The two most critical factors in producing high-quality olive oil, the two issues that enter into the picture throughout and most affect the outcome, from the first olive picked to the last drop of oil out of the *frantoio*, are more generalized:

Time.

And temperature.

Time means speed—speed of harvest, speed in getting olives to the mill, speed in milling the oil. "Olive oil is like music," Tunisian producer Majid Mahjoub told me a few years ago. His family company, Moulins Mahjoub, makes an apple green and fragrant oil from their own groves of Chetoui olives in the Mejerda Valley, west of Tunis. Majid is a philosopher at heart who spends a lot of time thinking—and then linking his thoughts in unlikely ways. So what does he mean, like music? "Music is an expression of time," Majid explained. "It's a way of controlling time. And you can't make quality oil without controlling time—time of harvest, when olives are turning from green to black; time between picking and pressing; time the oil sits in storage before it's used. All this means the difference between great oil and, um, not so great."

The temperature factor is equally important. We hear a lot about the virtues of "cold pressed extra-virgin olive oil," but in fact *all* extra-virgin olive oil is or should be expressed at temperatures below 27°C (about 80°F)—otherwise it cannot be called extra-virgin. And the oil will be much better if the entire process takes place at temperatures far below that mark. (Recently, I was introduced to a new marketing term, "ice-pressed" oil—I hope the producer was not planning actually to freeze the olives; that would seriously damage them and make any oil obtained highly questionable.) Maintaining temperatures at or below 27°C might seem easy enough, but in fact temperature is often the most difficult factor to control. In the Palestinian olive groves I visited recently, for instance, the daytime temperature in October was well above 30°C (90°F), so the harvested olives were consistently, inevitably, and unavoidably exposed to undesirable temperatures.[7] And the same holds true in many other parts of the Mediterranean. With all the care in the world, rushing to the

———————————

7. Why not harvest at night? Few Palestinians would be foolish enough to venture forth at night. The risk of being shot by Israeli army patrols or assaulted by West Bank settlers is too great.

mill with tenderly handled, scrupulously clean olives, the oil still inevitably suffers when temperatures soar.

Another function of time: To make good olive oil, the olives must be pressed as quickly as possible, ideally, experts say, within 24 to 48 hours of harvest. Commercial producers are constantly pushing the envelope, trying to reduce the gap. Many of the big producers I've visited in California and Chile claim the olives go into the crushing machines less than an hour or so after they have been picked. Throughout the Mediterranean, fine producers like Priego de Cordoba in Spain or Titone, near Marsala in the west of Sicily, make sure each day's harvest is processed that evening before the next day's harvest begins. For small operations like our own, this is not as easy as it sounds. Like most olive mills, the mill we use on the Arezzo road just north of Cortona, Frantoio Landi, requires at least two *quintales* (200 kilos, or 440 pounds) of olives to make a single pressing. Any less and our olives must be mixed with someone else's, and there's no guarantee that those other olives will be any good. So if we arrive at the mill with less than the stipulated quantity, we risk contaminating our beautiful, clean, fresh olives with those from some much less fastidious farmer.

I would love to say that we proudly get our olives to the mill within 12 or 24 hours of picking them, but the truth is quite a bit broader. Usually it takes us four days—and that's four days of brilliant autumn weather, golden from sunrise to sunset—to accumulate 440 pounds of olives, even with ten pairs of hands at work. Days are short, weather threatens, and even the most good-hearted helper is, after all, simply that—a helper and not a paid employee that the manager can fire if he or she slacks off.

Most of the loyal clients of Mr. Landi's mill are like us, small individual producers making oil for their own uses and perhaps a little to sell on the side. Despite the reputation of Lucca as home to some of the industry's major global firms, like Bertolli and Filippo Berio, the true backbone of Tuscan oil is the output of much smaller enterprises, including some very well-known and prestigious brands that market internationally and are often also home to

Tuscany's finest wines. They might be a good deal larger than our mini farm, but still, to Californian and Spanish advocates of super-technological, super-high-density olive oil assembly, the individualist, small-scale, family-size production in Central Italy looks hopelessly old-fashioned and backward. Even at renowned estates like Badia a Coltibuono, Castello Volpaia, Frescobaldi, and Capezzana, this small scale is maintained—and these and similar family units produce some of the very finest and most prestigious olive oils on the market.

I favor the Landi mill especially because it offers a choice between the old-fashioned crush-and-press sort of operation and modern, continuous-cycle, stainless-steel machinery. Until just a few years ago, almost all the mills in Tuscany and Umbria that catered to small producers were the old style. Traditionalists continued to hold sway throughout Italy much longer than elsewhere in the olive oil world. It was still crush-and-press even back in the 1990s, when, wherever else I traveled in the Mediterranean—in Spain, in Tunisia, in Greece—what I found were mills that proudly vaunted clean, modern, continuous-cycle machinery, much of which, ironically, was actually made in Italy even if it wasn't much used there. Two firms in particular were evident, Rapanelli from Florence and Pieralisi from Jesi on the Adriatic, and they continue to this day to be in the vanguard, covering the world market for oil-processing machinery, although Alfa-Laval, a Swedish concern, also has made great inroads. Gruppo Pieralisi, a family firm in business since 1888, leads with 60 percent of the market. The smallest continuous-cycle machine made by Pieralisi today costs a bit less than €30,000—or a bit more than $50,000—which is a quick answer to the frequently asked question: "How come you don't have your own olive press at home?"

One other system for extracting oil should be mentioned. Once heralded as a solution for producing the very highest quality of oil, this system, called *sinolea*, has not acquired the following that was once predicted, although it is still talked about. It is the gentlest possible method of extraction, made by inserting thin steel blades into the olive paste. The blades drip oil, but *drip* is truly the word for it—drop by drop the oil slowly accumulates in a process that is almost meditative in its agonizing pace.

Old-fashioned mills are precious relics if only because they are directly descended from the ancient Roman *trapetum*. Two or three giant stone wheels, standing on their edges, turn steadily around a central axle on a wide basin, at the same time that each wheel turns on its own axis. The olives, previously rinsed of orchard dust and with the leaves blown away, are dumped into the big basin and the wheels turn, slowly crushing the olives, pits and all, to an oily mash the dark color of mud. (The aromas, however, that arise from the mash are seductive and not mud-like at all—in fact, it's sort of like the appetizing fragrance of a good tapenade.) When the olive mash or paste has reached the right consistency at the Landi mill, it is piped into the malaxer, or kneading machine, a long metal box, open at the top, that contains a slowly turning double screw. This is a critical element in the production cycle, Mr. Landi explains. Crushing the olives in the mill has emulsified the oil and vegetable water inside each fruit, so the malaxer's job is to separate these two and over the course of 30 to 40 minutes to tease the minuscule droplets of oil into larger drops that will be more easily and efficiently separated in the press. Once that point has been reached, the paste is spread directly onto broad circular mats, made of plastic woven to imitate the esparto grass that was once used. The plastic mats are stacked as they are filled, one on top of the other, to make a tower or *castello*. Every six mats or so, a steel plate is inserted to maintain the stability of the tower, which is then towed on a cart to a hydraulic press. There the stack of paste-covered mats is gently but firmly squeezed for at least 40 minutes or as long as an hour while the vegetation liquid gushes out and down over the mats and the oil oozes slowly forth, drop by precious drop.

Years ago, I visited an olive mill in a Tunisian desert oasis that operated on very much the same principal as Mr. Landi's old-fashioned mill. In fact, the oasis setup would have been familiar to the long-ago residents of Volubilis in Morocco, where you can still see the ancient Roman olive-processing machinery that has been in place there since the last Roman soldier-farmer left at the end of the third century. At the Tunisian oasis, I was told by officials from the International Olive Oil Council (IOOC) who had arranged the visit, the villagers, olive farmers all, still spread their olives on the flat roofs of their houses and keep them for a full year before pressing. Even though it wasn't the right season, the mill had been set into operation for the benefit of me and a couple of other visiting journalists. It was tucked into a low-ceilinged cave, and the grindstone—there was only one in this case—that crushed the olives was powered by a blindfolded camel plodding slowly in an unending circle round and round as the mangy beast turned the crushing wheel. Presumably the camel added certain flavors to the volatile paste. In any case, when later at lunch I was presented with a little dish of the oil and reached for it, the swift arm of an IOOC official grabbed my hand and pulled me back. "No," he muttered, "don't touch that. It could be dangerous."

Even if operated by a conscientious producer like my Mr. Landi, there are other disadvantages to this system. First of all, it's slow, and because it's slow, olives tend to pile up at the mill. Even if your olives are perfect and clean, picked at exactly the right stage of maturity, and you've struggled to get them to the mill within hours of harvest, you may still have to wait your turn, sometimes as much as a day or even more. Then throughout the time the olives are being crushed, the paste is exposed to air and consequently oxidizing. And even more exposure takes place during the hour or so that the mats are stacked up in the hydraulic press. All told, the olives are subjected to much greater risks from oxidation. If, moreover, your olives are next in line for processing after a farmer who is a good deal less scrupulous than you, and if the mats and the grindstones alike have not been meticulously cleaned after use (a requirement that is seldom honored in the bustle of an olive mill at the height of the season), you risk contaminating your oil with thoroughly undesirable aromas and flavors from the batch produced by the negligent farmer who proceeded you.

In the early 1990s, before I even thought about planting trees and making oil, I often helped friends with their harvest. Olives got picked over the course of weeks rather than days, so they might arrive at the mill already ten days old, tightly crammed into burlap sacks. And there they would sit, waiting their turn, throughout the slow process of producing oil. The great stone wheels turned slowly, steadily, night and day without cease throughout the period of the harvest, but the process was so slow that big burlap sacks crammed with olives backed up, stacked willy-nilly at the entrance to the mill. Everything was orderly but nothing was very clean—there simply was no time for cleanliness in the frantic rush to get the olives crushed. You left your olives in sacks heaped up in a corner and then there might come a telephone call, perhaps at 10 PM, perhaps saying, be here at two o'clock, meaning 2 AM, because that was the time when your olives would be crushed and woe betide anyone who missed out. It was not only bad form but also bad practice to miss your own processing—who knew what the miller, that wily stock trickster from folklore, might be up to without a canny farmer watching him weigh the take. And then—once the olives were crushed to a paste and spread on mats (none too clean, themselves, after a day or two of continuous pressing) and the mats stacked high, the *castello* was moved into the press, where it would be left for an hour or so as the vegetable water gushed down over the tower and the olive oil leaked out slowly, drop by drop. Often hot water was poured over the tower to encourage the oil to issue forth, which of course raised the temperature of the paste.

Now, even in Tuscany and Umbria, those old-style mills have almost disappeared, replaced by the modern, continuous-cycle machinery that I have come to prefer. Only in a few places, like our Mr. Landi, or Feliciano Fancelli's delightful old mill in Capodacqua up above Foligno in Umbria, can visitors still see the time-honored process, now considerably cleaned up from what I witnessed years ago. Mr. Landi offers a choice between old-fashioned and modern, but Mr. Fancelli is noteworthy because he is steadfast in his belief that the old-fashioned way is the only way to produce high-quality olive oil. In fact, he opens very early, in mid-October each year, to accommodate Italian singer-songwriter Francesco de Gregori, who insists that the olives from his nearby estate be pressed in the traditional manner and pressed first, before anyone else has access to the mill.

The malaxer or kneading machine is one of the keys to high-quality oil.

It's great to watch this old way of doing things at Fancelli's mill, to think about the generations that have preceded us and done the same as in centuries past, following the rhythms, anxiously awaiting the moment when the oil is finally extracted, weighed, calculated—and then the first taste of the new oil, almost hot with the complex and unsubdued flavors of the olives. In the old mills, there was always, tucked away in a corner of the room, a hearth with a low fire burning and a group of old guys sitting around, toasting bruschetta—that rarest of treats, thick slices of rough, country-style bread, toasted on a grid set over the embers, then rubbed with a cut clove of garlic and lavished with the new oil and a sprinkling of salt—a surefire way to convert skeptics to the incredible taste of fresh oil. In a singular bow to modern times, the Fancellis have moved the hearth to a separate room in order not to contaminate the oil with wood ash or the fragrance of a smoky fire. But it's still an unstinting hand that pours the bright green new oil.

All the time I'm watching this old-fashioned process in utter fascination, however, I'm also thinking about the olives, the olive paste, the crushed mass churning in the open air of the malaxer, and the amount of time it has all been exposed to air, to light, to the warmth of the mill and the friction of the turning stones. Light, heat, atmosphere—these are the enemies of high-quality olive oil. And even though the oil from Fancelli's mill is extremely high quality, it requires constant vigilance to make it so. After six weeks of producing oil, he needs a long winter vacation.

So my own preference, in this if in nothing else that has to do with food, is to go with the modern process. I like to compare the continuous-cycle process to a bread machine (although believe me, I would *never* make bread with a machine!): You dump the ingredients in at one end, press a button, and in a matter of minutes, an hour maximum, what issues forth is something utterly delicious.

Clean, cool, and fast, continuous-cycle milling is almost single-handedly responsible for the fact that more good extra-virgin olive oil is available at prices that most people can afford than there has ever been throughout history. Our olives are weighed and rinsed and defoliated within minutes of our arrival at the mill. Then they disappear into the stainless-steel innards of the machine. Here's what happens inside: The olives are crushed, pits and all, by hammers or steel knives, to the same dun-green paste as in the traditional crusher. Then, as with the traditional process, the paste goes into the malaxer (called the *grammola* or *grammalotrice* in Italian, *batidora* in Spanish, kneader in English), a long double screw that interweaves within the mass and slowly turns the paste for a period of 30 to 40 minutes. This piece of the process is critical to the success of the continuous-cycle machine. The purpose is to pull the molecules of oil together and make the extraction more efficient. But the effect is also to control the bitterness in the final product. More kneading of the paste, I was told by Fadrique Alvarez de Toledo, means a less bitter oil. Fadrique and his father, the Marques de Valdueza, make an elegant Spanish oil called, appropriately, Marques de Valdueza, in the western Spanish region of Extremadura, where the family estates are located. This is how he explained it: "The longer you have the mash in the mixer (*batidora*), the more velvety the oil; that is, less bitterness, less pungency. Our olives are early picked to get complexity, but we mix longer (but stop before excessive emulsions form, from which the oil cannot be easily extracted) to soften the taste." So once again, time enters the picture and the producer chooses between extracting more oil with a sweeter flavor profile or less oil but with the pronounced bitterness and pungency many (but by no means all) prefer.

Oil is made in the field, I have heard over and over again; the job of the processor is not to ruin it. Terroir—that wonderful French vineyard concept that wraps up soil structure, climate, weather conditions, and the *je ne sais quoi* that adds mystery to flavor—terroir is key. Yet in modern oil production, it's clear that the kneading action of the malaxer plays a critical role. The late Marco Mugelli, a world-renowned Tuscan expert on olive oil production, criticized many California oils for being milled to too fine a paste and left too long in the malaxer. My guess is that the producers in question were trying to make Tuscan-style oil, without understanding the role of both cultivar and terroir in producing that complexity of flavors.

Once the malaxing is done, the paste moves on again to the final stages, the separation of good, fresh oil from the gunk (*morchia*) and the vegetable water that inevitably accompanies the process, no matter how it is done. And that's it: The process is done, the circle is complete, and we set our stainless casks, called *fusti*, under the spout and watch the unctuous green-gold roll into the tin and head for home to celebrate the new oil.

And here's what we feast on:

TUSCAN BEAN *and* FARRO SOUP *for the* OLIVE HARVEST

This is the hearty soup we serve for lunch during the olive harvest. If fresh oil isn't available, use an oil with good, strong flavors, one from Tuscany or Umbria that will stand up to the robust dish; a Picual from Andalusia or a Coratina from Puglia would also be a good choice.

1½ cups dried beans, preferably speckled cranberry beans or borlotti, soaked for several hours or overnight

1 medium carrot, chopped

2 small yellow onions, 1 chopped

1 or 2 bay leaves

1½ cups farro

4 garlic cloves

½ cup olive oil

Sea salt and freshly ground black pepper

8 to 10 thin slices dense, grainy Italian country-style bread, preferably at least a day old

4 to 6 tablespoons olio nuovo (fresh new olive oil), if available, for serving

2 tablespoons finely minced flat-leaf parsley, or more

DRAIN the beans, and discard the soaking water. Place the beans in a large saucepan with carrot, chopped onions, and bay leaf (or leaves). Cover with fresh water, bring to a boil, lower the heat, and simmer, covered, until the beans are very soft, 40 minutes to 2 hours, depending on the age of the beans. Keep a kettle of water simmering, and add more water to the beans as they absorb the liquid. They should always be just covered with water but never swimming in it.

THE farro should not need soaking, but it should be rinsed briefly in a colander to get rid of any dust. In a medium saucepan, cover the rinsed and drained farro with boiling water to a depth of 1 inch. Bring to a simmer and cook, covered, for 20 to 30 minutes, until the farro is tender.

WHEN the beans are very soft, set aside about ½ cup whole beans. Discard the bay leaves and puree the remainder of the beans, with all their liquid and the vegetables that were cooked with them, in a food processor or put through a food mill. Drain the farro and add to the pureed beans. Stir in the reserved whole beans.

CHOP the remaining onion with 3 of the garlic cloves until finely minced. Over medium heat, sauté the onion and garlic in ¼ cup of the oil until soft. Add to the pureed beans and mix well. Taste and add salt and plenty of pepper.

LIGHTLY toast the bread slices. Halve the remaining garlic clove, and rub the slices well with the garlic on both sides. When ready to serve, set a toast slice in the bottom of each soup plate and dribble a liberal dose of fresh new oil over each slice. Spoon hot soup over the bread and add another dollop of oil to the top of each serving, without stirring it in. Sprinkle with the parsley and serve immediately, passing more fresh new oil to pour over the top.

WHAT *is* EXTRA-VIRGIN *anyway and* WHY SHOULD YOU *(or I)* CARE?

MAURIZIO CASTELLI IS PART OF A SMALL CLUB THAT I CALL MY OLIVE OIL GURUS, a club so exclusive its members probably don't even know they belong. More than that, Maurizio is widely acknowledged as one of Italy's leading experts on the cultivation of olives and the production of high-class oil. He is the talent behind some important New World endeavors too—not the super-high-density, get-it-out-and-sell-it-fast operations but more thoughtful, slow, traditional estates like the award-winning McEvoy Ranch in Marin County, California. So I listen carefully when Maurizio speaks. And right now he is speaking half-jokingly but with an edge of seriousness of the American woman who asked him about the olive trees that are spread in silvery profusion down a terraced Tuscan hillside: Were they extra-virgin olive trees, she wanted to know, or just the regular kind?

No, Maurizio explained with great patience, there is no such thing as an extra-virgin olive tree, nor are there extra-virgin olives. But extra-virgin olive oil is very real and there is more of it than ever before, in part because of improved production methods, as I noted in the previous chapter, and in part because of market demand. (Not all of that is truly extra-virgin and some of it is not olive oil, or not entirely olive oil, but I will get to that later.)

Producers are scrambling to fill that demand as more and more consumers around the world clamor for olive oil, even in unlikely places such as China and India. Olive oil imports in China soared in the past decade, from an insignificant 605 tons in 2002 to more than 108,000 tons in 2011. And who would believe that "health-conscious, upwardly mobile Indian consumers," in the words of a recent business publication, would make olive oil "the cooking medium of choice"? Is India not the land of ghee?[1]

So what is this extra-virgin olive oil and why should I—or you—care?

Let's start with the definition of "virgin olive oil." Back in the eighteenth century, and for a long time thereafter, virgin olive oil, which was always considered the finest kind, referred to an oil that had not been pressed at all. The olives were crushed, using the big stone wheels, and then the oil that naturally floated to the top of the paste was carefully skimmed off—and that was virgin. Apart from crushing, the olives and their paste experienced no stress and certainly were not subject to crude treatments such as having boiling water poured over the paste to extract more oil, a common practice back then. Alfredo Mancianti's "Affiorato" oil, made on the shores of Lake Trasimeno in Umbria, and "Flor del Aceite," made by Nuñez de Prado in Baena, Andalusia, are both examples of this free-run kind of oil. But it is rare, and priced accordingly.

The International Olive Council (IOC)[2] is an industry group chartered by the United Nations in 1959 to promote consumption of olive oil of all kinds. IOC members include almost all the major olive oil–producing countries—as countries, not as companies—from Albania to Turkey (notably absent are the United States and Australia, two countries that show every intention of becoming important producers). The IOC defines the various categories of olive oil in a way that has become, for its member states, the legal classification. Virgin olive oil's definition is straightforward: It is "obtained from the fruit of the olive tree (*Olea europea* L.), *solely by mechanical or other physical means* [my italics], under conditions, particularly thermal conditions, that do not lead to alterations in the oil." Furthermore, olives and oil must not undergo any treatment other than washing, decanting, centrifuging, and filtering.

What this means in practical terms is that olives, and only olives,[3] are crushed, pressed, and extracted mechanically, using either traditional milling (crush-and-press) or modern continuous-cycle techniques, but no chemical solvents or other nonmechanical methods

---

1. We're not talking extra-virgin here. V. N. Dalmia, whose company is the largest importer, says olive pomace oil is most suited for Indian cuisine because of its neutral taste and high smoke point. The smoke point business is a myth, though widely promulgated. As for pomace oil, most olive oil traditionalists consider it inedible. "But we are here for a very long innings," one Indian industry executive told a reporter.

2. Formerly the International Olive Oil Council (IOOC) and still sometimes referred to by that designation.

3. The current U.S. fad for flavored olive oils most often involves crushing lemons or oranges or garlic or possibly coffee beans (no, I made that up!) along with the olives. How the oil thus obtained can still be called "virgin" or "extra-virgin," according to the IOC definition, is, frankly, beyond my comprehension.

(such as steam deodorizing), and without the application of heat above 27°C (80.6°F) at any point in the process. So think of virgin olive oil as simply the juice of olives, decanted or centrifuged after processing to separate the oil from the vegetable water in the fruit, and possibly but not necessarily filtered at the end. The definition also excludes from the virgin category any olive oil that has been mixed with even a bare minimum of other kinds of oil. It goes without saying that, for the oil to be good quality, the olives themselves should be fresh, sound, and healthy, and they should be processed at an appropriate stage of ripeness, as described in the previous chapter.

So much for virgin olive oil. And I defy you to find a bottle of it on a shop shelf anywhere in America[4]—or in Italy, for that matter. It's what my Australian colleague Brian Chatterton, who produces excellent extra-virgin oil in Umbria, has aptly called "ghost oil," much talked about but almost never seen. "Use extra-virgin for drizzling," chirps the usual food blog, "and virgin oil for cooking." Ask that food blogger where she gets her virgin oil and she will be stumped. Because it simply does not exist commercially.

What does exist, and is widely available on shop shelves all over North America, is *extra*-virgin olive oil, and here we move up a notch, or two or three. Extra-virgin olive oil is extracted by those same mechanical methods that define just plain virgin, but it has several characteristics that move it into a more exalted position. Most important, in laboratory tests the oil must have a free acidity, expressed as oleic acid, of not more than 0.8 percent— no more than 0.8 grams of free oleic acid per 100 grams of oil. Chem 101 alert: Free acidity is caused by the breakdown of triglycerides in the oil due to hydrolysis or lipolysis. I don't understand what that means but I know it is a measure of degradation in the oil and it has nothing to do with an acid flavor. I have to repeat that: Oils that are unacceptably high in free oleic acid do not necessarily taste acidic or sour. In fact, you will probably not be able to detect by taste or smell alone a high acid content.

But the most important thing for you to know is that producers of premium olive oil would slit their wrists and sell their oil to the nearest biodiesel plant if it tested out anywhere close to the 0.8 percent free oleic acid that the IOC permits. The producers I know and have encountered over the years count on a free acid measurement no higher than 0.2 percent, and 0.1 percent is optimum.

There are other laboratory measures of quality required by the IOC, including testing for peroxide levels, which indicate the amount of oxidation to which the oil has been subjected. The IOC definition of extra-virgin oil permits a peroxide level of 20 mep (whatever that means) but, again, conscientious producers of premium oils want peroxide levels down around 5 or 6 mep, no more, which is to say, a quarter or less of what the IOC allows.

The overall IOC parameters for extra-virgin, in other words, are generous, much more so than conscientious producers of high-quality oils would accept in their own oils. And the

---

4. Recently, Jean-Benoit and Cathérine Hugues have started to export Fruité Noir oil, which they produce in Provence. It is indeed marketed as "virgin" rather than "extra-virgin" because of the peculiar characteristic of fustiness, a major defect for extra-virgin oils. See page 72 for more information.

hurdles for extra-virgin qualification are set much too low. In brief, just because an oil qualifies as extra-virgin doesn't necessarily mean that it's any good.

Beyond laboratory testing, however, to be categorized as extra-virgin, the oil must also pass a taste test. This is a completely blind tasting by a panel of at least eight trained professional tasters. Just as with wine, just as with tea, just as with chocolate, these tasters have undergone rigorous training, supervised by the IOC, to evaluate olive oil for "perfect organoleptic characteristics"—meaning the oil must have perfect flavor and aroma, with no discernible defects whatsoever. Professional tasters will tell you this is easy, but believe me it is not. For nonprofessionals, even for people like me who've been around a lot of olive oil over the years, defects can slip past—and just a little vinegary or musty note in the oil will be sufficient to knock it out of the extra-virgin category. Beyond that, perfection is such a delicate, even fragile, concept that I often think it is best considered an attribute of divinity rather than of mere olive oil. But there are those, and there have been those down through the ages, who have associated olive oil directly with divinity in any case, so perhaps I am splitting hairs.

Professional tasting, it cannot be denied, is a serious business. A great deal of money can ride on whether or not an oil merits extra-virginity. The scientific laboratory criteria (free acidity, peroxide content, and so forth) are specific and measurable, but tasting itself is a relative business at best, so conclusions are never reached based on one person's opinion alone, but rather on a consensus. And tasting, in the end, is what counts. An oil might pass the lab tests with three stars for excellence and still fail the taste test with mustiness or fustiness, or muddy or vinegary flavors, any or all of which will disqualify it. And a single dissent on the tasting panel can be enough to kick an otherwise deserving oil out of the extra-virgin category.

Tasters sit in a room together, but each person is in an enclosed cubicle with no opportunity for communication among them. The samples are doled out anonymously, each oil in a blue tasting glass—blue to disguise completely the color of the oil—that can be easily cupped in the palm of the hand. The cupping is important because warming the oil to body temperature helps to release volatile aromas and flavors. So the taster sits, swirling oil in the glass in the palm of one hand with the palm of the other hand securing a flat glass lid, until the oil has reached body heat, whereupon the taster opens the lid a little and takes a deep sniff, or two or three, to inhale all the ephemeral fragrances. Then back goes the lid for another swirl, another lift of the lid, and the taster sips from the glass, not more than a teaspoon or so of oil, holds it on the tongue, presses it out to the sides of the mouth, then inhales sharply, stretching the mouth to draw in air through the sides, slurping the oil. Finally, carefully considering, the taster swallows, and then notes all applicable impressions.

Like riding a bicycle, this sounds much more complicated than it actually is.

But what is the purpose of the ritual—for ritual it most certainly is? First off, the aromas: They hardly need explanation, but it is primarily fruitiness, or lack of it, that is detected through the initial smelling. Then, once the oil is in the mouth, it is sensed by all those tiny papillae on the surface of the tongue—bitterness is especially apparent on the

An Olive Oil Tasting

Once you start to get a little comfortable with olive oils and their multitude of flavors, you may want to organize an olive oil tasting with friends and colleagues as a way of spreading the word. You can do this with as few as three oils or as many as five or six. More than that, however, and palate fatigue will start to set in and you'll find it hard to distinguish among them.

The fresher the oils are, the more their flavors will be distinctive and interesting. This is not always possible, since in North America we usually don't receive new harvest oils from the Mediterranean until February or March at the earliest—although some California producers are making an effort to get first-of-the-harvest oils to markets in the rest of the country. But do try to have all the oils you're tasting from the same harvest year; it simply is unfair to the producers to taste a two-year-old oil against a couple of fresher ones. You could restrict the oils to all Spanish or all Greek or even all Tuscan, or you could have a range of oils from the Mediterranean, California, and even New Zealand or Chile. But keep in mind that southern hemisphere oils are harvested on a different schedule, the harvest taking place usually in late April or May and the new oils reaching northern markets around July.

It's also a good idea to include among the selection one oil that you know to be defective, just to give people a sense of what's at stake. That oil unfortunately will be easy to find—just pick out the cheapest extra-virgin on the shelves of your local supermarket and it's bound to be fusty and/or rancid, if not both.

Have a series of tasting cups, one for each oil for each person. So if you have five oils and four people tasting, you'll need 20 tasting cups or glasses. These could be special tasting glasses like those used at Villa Campestri, a Tuscan olive oil estate. Or they could be stemmed wineglasses. (The International Olive Council insists on blue glasses to disguise the color of the oils; others, myself included, believe that color should be assessed as part of the aesthetic value of an oil.)

If necessary, have available a "lid" for each glass, even as simple as a piece of paper or a small paper plate. (You could just cover the glass with the palm of your hand, but if you've used any soap or hand cream, it may transmit flavors to the oil.) If you want to do a blind tasting, cover the bottles and number them, keeping a list of what oils the numbers refer to. Put just a couple of tablespoons of each oil in the appropriate glasses.

Taste each oil in turn. Cup your palm around the bowl of the glass, keeping the lid, whatever it's made of, on the glass so the oil doesn't spill out, and swirl it gently to warm the glass until you detect only a slight difference from your body temperature. Remove the lid and sniff deeply, turning the glass, so you get all the complex aromas, and think about what you smell—fresh grass, artichokes, wild herbs (chamomile perhaps, or rosemary), the fragrance of citrus or of fresh almonds. Then replace the lid, give the glass another swirl, and take a small sip; just a teaspoon of oil is sufficient. Hold it in the front of your mouth at first and think about it, then push the oil out to the sides of your mouth and think again. Now stretch your lips into a smile and suck in air, pushing the oil to the back of your mouth. Swallow (don't worry if you cough—it's hard at first to get accustomed to the feeling of the oil going down). At that point, you'll experience what sensory scientists call a retronasal sensation, as the fragrance and flavor of the oil pass through the back of your throat where smell and taste come together. With a fine oil, you should sense a balance of fruitiness (either green fruit or mature fruit) with bitterness and pungency, plus the individual flavors of each different oil.

In between tasting, clear your palate with fizzy water or slices of tart green apple. We do not taste using pieces of bread to dip into the oil, as is sometimes done, since the flavor of the bread, if it's any good, will interfere with the flavor of the oil—and if it's not any good, there's not much point in tasting it.

Don't worry about identifying aromas and flavors too precisely. There really is no right or wrong answer in a tasting—it's a matter of comparing and talking about what you sense and savor, and understanding that there is a vast world of aromas and flavors to be appreciated in the finest oils.

sides of the tongue, and then in the back, as the oil is swallowed, the sensation of pungency is paramount. Actually, as you probably know, our human perception of taste, as such, is limited to sweetness, sourness, saltiness, and bitterness, the four tastes that the tongue distinguishes. (Many people now agree on a fifth sensation, called by the Japanese term *umami*, but that "meaty" taste doesn't seem to apply to olive oil.) So the complexity of flavors in olive oil is not really tasted so much as it is smelled or experienced by what professional tasters call a retronasal gustatory sensation or retronasal olfaction—a mouthful of words to describe the way almost every "taste," from orange juice to fine wine to cheap beer, is actually most fully experienced by swallowing and passing the substance through the retronasal area (the "internal nares") in the back of the throat so that aroma and flavor become combined.

What is in that complexity of flavors in extra-virgin olive oil? Taste and aroma depend on so many factors, starting with the cultivar or variety of the olive itself and its maturity at harvest, then the climate and soil structure where the tree grows, the weather throughout the growing season, and the precise moment when the harvest occurs. To a great extent it also depends on how the olives are treated after harvest, how quickly they are milled and under what conditions, and how the oil is handled once it has been made.

Just as with grapes, different cultivars have very different flavors—and the flavors differ too depending on the degree of ripeness of the fruit, the time and manner of the processing, and indeed the way the oil has been handled in the pipeline from producer to consumer. Some olives taste of almonds, others of green apples; some have ripe tropical fruit flavors like mangoes or melons; some taste of freshly cut grass or artichokes. There's a cultivar called Grignano, for instance, that grows in a small area of northern Italy, east of Lake Garda in the province of Verona; picked and processed at a certain moment in October, Grignano olives have a decided citrus flavor and aroma that comes from the olives themselves and not from any lemons or other citrus added during the processing.[5] Harvested three weeks later, Grignano oil, while still being very good, will lack that distinction. Another example is Arbequina, a typical olive from Catalonia, where the oil produced has a distinctive and delicious flavor, when fresh, of almonds; but Arbequina produced from olives grown in other parts of the globe—for instance, in California or Chile, where it is a favorite cultivar for super-high-density planting—is simply a bland oil that needs blending with other, different cultivars to create an oil of character.

No matter what the variety, however, all oils should have easily discernible flavors of the olive fruit itself, whether the fruit is ripe, green, or on the way to maturity, with no off-flavors, nothing metallic or musty; and this fruity flavor should be most apparent when the oil is fresh and new. Bitterness and pungency, contrary to what you might have thought, are not defects, but positive attributes, indicating the strong presence of valuable polyphenols. These qualities will diminish as the oil ages, and some connoisseurs prefer softer oils that are past their peak of freshness for this very reason. By June, even the most pungent Koroneiki oil from Greece or Coratina from Italy, made the previous autumn, will have

---

5. Mirko Sella produces an excellent example of this oil in his Monte Guala monocultivar Grignano, not easy to find but worth looking for.

calmed and become detectably sweeter. The hot flavors just post-harvest, so exciting to taste, will be replaced by a roundness on the palate; one can almost speak of the tranquility of oils in that stage.

Beyond fruitiness, bitterness, and pungency, professional tasters recognize many different flavors, most of which are positive traits in extra-virgin oils. An oil can taste of ripe fruitiness or, on the contrary, of green, immature fruitiness. Sweeter oils, often made from riper olives, may have flavors of apple, or ripe tomato, or of nuts such as almonds or hazelnuts; green sensations in oils are described as flavors of artichoke or green tomato, sweet green pepper, or even herbal flavors of freshly cut grass. Intense flavors may depend more on the age of the oil, with fresher oils obviously having much greater intensity and a robust concentration of flavor, while older oils can be smooth and mellow, almost buttery. But that contrast, too, can depend on variety. Flavor in olive oil is an ever-changing, ever-intriguing subject. The best way to experience it and begin to understand it is through tasting a gamut of four to six oils, made from different cultivars and from different regions. If you've never done this, you may be astonished by the differences that are easy to distinguish even if you can't quite describe them yet. And you don't need "official" blue tasting glasses—a simple wineglass with a bowl small enough to cup in the hand will do very nicely.

Of course, and I regret to say it, some oils unfortunately are also redolent of all those musty, muddy, fusty, rancid flavors we have met with frequently in this book. And some oils, indeed, taste of nothing at all, meaning they are so old and flat by the time they reach your palate that all the aromatic properties you might once have enjoyed have completely vanished.

Now, diverging briefly from extra-virgin, there are other classes of olive oil defined by the International Olive Council, but you will not see them as such on the shelves of your local supermarket. Virgin oil is one, but, as noted, it hardly exists except in the minds of the IOC classifiers. The lowest quality of all is called *lampante*, and it is a seriously defective oil, as its Italian name indicates, an oil that is only good for lighting lamps. Even though it is "virgin," meaning produced mechanically, it is not intended for human consumption.

What you will see at the supermarket, however, is another highly visible category of oil. This is simply called "olive oil," or sometimes, but more rarely these days, "pure olive oil," suggesting, quite incorrectly, that it is somehow purer and better than extra-virgin. This is oil that, for whatever reason, failed to make the extra-virgin grade, either because the olives were defective in the beginning or because of a fault in the milling, a time delay being the most common problem. This substandard oil is then rectified or refined to remove all its nasty flavors and aromas, and the result is a tasteless, odorless, colorless oil to which a small amount of extra-virgin is then added in order to give it some character. In effect, the polyphenols are removed from the oil, leaving a product that is still rich in monounsaturated fatty acids, which are good for you, but deprived of the polyphenols and antioxidants, which are even better for you. It's perfectly fine to use in a pinch, and some cooks prefer this to extra-virgin olive oil, especially for deep-fat frying. I don't. I take my cue from generations of Mediterranean cooks at all levels, from the humblest homestead to the most exalted restaurant kitchen, and *only* cook with extra-virgin olive oil.

In the United States, you may also come across an olive oil marketed as pomace oil or *olio di pomace*; while other grades of olive oil can be used in an economic pinch, pomace oil

is, in my view, to be avoided at all costs. It is extracted from the waste of the oil mill by the use of chemical solvents and undergoes further refinement to remove the solvents, at which point it is said to be fit for human consumption—but I do not trust it. And with good oil available, why bother? Still, 5 percent of the 300,000 tons of olive oil imported into the United States in the 2011–2012 season consisted of pomace oil, most of it destined for food service or for packaging (for example, canned sauces, tinned fish products, mayonnaise made with olive oil, and the like).

There is actually far more high-quality extra-virgin olive oil offered today than at any time in the past. In that same season of 2011–2012, nearly two-thirds of U.S. imports consisted of what the IOC calls "virgin grade," which is almost exclusively extra-virgin. This is a huge change from the past. Until recently, no import statistics distinguishing between extra-virgin and just plain or pure olive oil were available, but it was clear to people in the trade that extra-virgin represented a very small portion of the overall quantity of imported oil even as late as the 1990s.[6]

Partly the increase in availability of extra-virgin olive oil is the result of modern technology that makes it possible to harvest and process oil much more rapidly, and partly it's because of consumer demand. As more and more health-giving properties of extra-virgin oil have been confirmed, consumption has increased dramatically. At the same time, olive oil has become a signature, the mark of an up-to-date kitchen; restaurant chefs, more and more, turn to it to show off their prowess. Alas, far too many restaurant chefs, at all levels

6. Personal communications and conversations with the late Arlene Wanderman, the IOOC's chief U.S. spokesperson for many years until her death in 1996.

of the profession, don't really understand high-quality olive oil, how to select it and how to use it in their kitchens. Thus we have the unhappy phenomenon of defective extra-virgin olive oil, rancid or fusty or simply old and flat, displayed in a tasting dish, possibly disguised with a dollop of what purports to be "balsamic" vinegar or a sprinkling of dried culinary herbs, proudly presented to restaurant patrons along with bread for dipping in it.

What it takes to make high-quality extra-virgin olive oil, as we saw in the previous chapter, is this: Sound, healthy olives from well-maintained orchards, harvested by hand or by the gentlest of machines, at a point of maturity that precedes, but not by too much, full ripeness, crushed and milled in a scrupulously clean environment within 24 hours of picking, and stored in stainless-steel containers in a cool, dark space. This is not rocket science. It is exactly what my family does on our Tuscan olive oil farmlet (apart from the rapid processing, which is impossible for us to achieve), like thousands of other growers and producers, large and small alike. It's a fully transparent process followed right around the olive oil world, from the Mediterranean to the newest areas of cultivation in California, Australia, South Africa, and even China. Not only that, but it's a process that, apart from improved technology, is essentially unchanged down through the ages—it comes with a millennial guarantee of history and of tradition behind it.

What, then, goes wrong? Because, although as I've said there is far more high-quality olive oil available today, there is also a vast ocean of bad and even fraudulent oil. I define bad oil as honestly made extra-virgin oil that has been severely mishandled en route to the consumer or kept until it is over the hill. Fraudulent oil is oil that has been deliberately made to defraud consumers, either by mixing refined oil with extra-virgin or by marketing other oils as extra-virgin when they've never come near an olive. Hazelnut oil is a prime candidate for this treatment, but even soy oil can be doctored with additives to make it taste just enough like olive oil to convince naive consumers.

And not just in the United States. We Americans have been told over and over in recent years that we are uniquely targeted by European scam artists, principally but not entirely Italian (hence, an unspoken assertion, most likely run by the mob), who are intent on dumping bad oil on our innocent and ingenuous salads. The assertion is not without an element of truth, but the fact is that bad oil is a round-the-world phenomenon. It is just as easy to find very bad oil on the shelves of Italian, Spanish, Turkish, French, you-name-it supermarkets as it is to find it in North American markets. Olive oil producer Gemma Pasquali leads remarkably informed and informative olive oil tastings at Villa Campestri, her family hotel in northern Tuscany's Mugello valley. She always begins with a defective oil as a baseline for mediocrity, and she has no trouble at all finding an example or two at her local supermarket. No, the major difference between there (Italy) and here (North America) is that it is much easier there than here to have access to high-quality oil. But the bad stuff? The indifferent stuff? It's everywhere in the world, including in far too many high-end restaurants.

The two most common defects in olive oil are rancidity and fustiness, and they are almost ubiquitous in what I call, for brevity's sake, supermarket oils. That they are also prevalent in oils sold in many fine, upscale gourmet stores and exclusive restaurants also goes without saying. The simple reason is that most of us, including shopkeepers and chefs, are profoundly ignorant of what high-quality oil tastes like, what it *ought* to taste like. When

Gemma Pasquali opens her tasting sessions with a rancid oil, you can look around the table and see heads nodding in familiar acknowledgment: "Mmhmm, this is olive oil, this is what we expect." And then she moves on—offering perhaps an oil from the Monte Iblei in the southeastern corner of Sicily, followed by a prized Andalusian Picual from the south of Spain or a Greek oil from Kalamata or a fresh, lemony oil from Verona in northern Italy or a high-grade California oil from Marin County, and then ending with the oil produced from her family's trees just outside the door. And as she progresses through the tastings, moving from the green tomato flavors of the Sicilian oil to the spiciness of the Picual and the richness of the Kalamata to the prodigious complex of flavors in the Tuscan oil, expressions change from murmurs of recognition to astonished explosions. "Wow!" you hear from one corner of the tasting table and then from another: "Wow! Amazing!"

"I had no idea olive oil could have such a range of flavors," the editor of an important American food publication said after one such tasting, blinking as she emerged into the sunlight from the cool depths of the stone-walled tasting room in the villa's old wine cantina. "I've always loved olive oil but I had no idea it could be so *good*." She was eloquent in her simplicity, and she echoed the thoughts of most people who experience the flavors of truly fresh, well-made oils for the first time.

The fact is that our palates have learned over the years to expect and to accept rancidity and fustiness (the two defects often go hand in hand) in olive oil, so much so that we often see these two characteristics not as faults but as positive attributes. "Very buttery," said the owner of a retail shop near my home in Maine, proudly offering me a taste of a new French oil he had just received. But buttery in his view was unquestionably fusty in mine.

What does "fusty" taste like? A little like the taste of certain table olives, whether green or black, that are purposely meant to undergo some fermentation during processing. But what is desirable in table olives is not necessarily so in oil. Fustiness comes about when olives are kept too long piled up, at the mill or the farmhouse, before pressing. The interior of the pile begins to undergo a kind of anaerobic fermentation that produces the characteristic flavor. (To me, "fusty" tastes like, if you can imagine it, a bale of hay that's been left on the barn floor all winter. The damp, slightly rotten fragrance of that hay is for me the fragrance of fustiness.)

Fustiness can also be deliberately induced in olive oil. Jean-Benoît Hugues makes an intentionally fusty oil at his domain near Les Baux de Provence, where the gnarled and ancient olives were famously painted by van Gogh. "We started because our neighbors asked for it," he explained. "And then we decided to put it on the market." He looked a little wistful when he said: "I sometimes think you don't get the true taste of a Provençal aioli except with fusty oil." Jean-Benoît and his wife, Cathérine, make an excellent extra-virgin oil, called Castelas, which is exported to the United States; their fusty oil, also sold in North America under the brand name Fruité Noir, is one of the very few oils marketed as "virgin," not "extra-virgin," because of this resolute flaw, which absolutely knocks it out of the extra-virgin category.

As for rancidity, although it can happen when already rancid olives are pressed for oil, it's a defect that most often occurs post-production because of improper storage and handling of the oil. The term refers to the decomposition of fats and oils, especially unsaturated fats and oils, when they are exposed to light, heat, and atmosphere. You don't need a trained nose to recognize it. Most cooks have had the experience of rancid walnuts or whole wheat flour, two foods that spoil as easily as olive oil, and for the same reasons. In fact, it's the oils themselves, naturally present in walnuts and whole wheat flour, that rancidify or oxidize. Extra-virgin olive oil, because of the antioxidants that we taste as bitterness, astringency, and pungency, is naturally protected against oxidation, but eventually, unless it's carefully stored, even olive oils that are very high in antioxidants (such as Picual from Spain, Koroneiki from Greece, or Coratina from southern Italy) will turn rancid.[7]

One year as an experiment, I poured some of our bright and lively fresh-from-the-mill oil into a glass mason jar and left it standing on a sunny window ledge in the kitchen. Within a week. it was transformed from healthy green to a pallid yellow color, and after another week, all its vigorous flavors and aromas were gone, replaced by a decided taste of turpentine, the result of chemical transformations in the oil. Despite antioxidant polyphenols, olive oil is extremely fragile. Yet again, a lot depends on the cultivar and the amount and structure of the polyphenols therein. Our oil is made from Leccino olives, not notably high in antioxidants. Had I been able to make a single-cultivar oil from the few Frantoio trees in our orchard, it would most likely have stood up better to my harsh treatment. But not forever.

The uncomfortable fact is that most rancid and fusty oils are not seen as defective by the public. On the contrary, in a great many tastings over the years it's the slightly rancid, decidedly fusty oils that too often win top billing. Even at tastings conducted by "gourmet" journalists and their publications, self-styled food experts to a man or a woman, the prize most often goes to oils that any truly educated taster recognizes as seriously defective. Both *Cook's Illustrated* and *Bon Appétit* are guilty of promoting oils that are quite obviously—to an expert, that is—deficient.

Such persistent consumer ignorance creates big problems for producers. In California a survey by the Olive Center, the University of California at Davis's research program, showed that most Californians surveyed actually preferred the taste of fusty, slightly rancid oil. No surprises there, but the experts were confounded when a similar survey in Spain, conducted by experts at the University of Jaén, right in the heart of the heart of Spain's olive oil country, indicated that less than one-third of regular consumers of olive oil knew what the grade "olive oil" means (that is, a mixture of virgin olive oil and refined olive oil). A mere 3 percent of those surveyed got the definition right, and only 10 percent of respondents knew what a single-variety olive oil was. This comes despite recent labeling reforms that encourage producers to label bottles with much more information, including both origins and olive cultivars used. The authors of the UC Davis study suggested that consumer preferences for defective oils probably are due to the great amount of defective "extra-virgin" olive oil available on the market. But almost three-quarters of the consumers interviewed disliked the oils that were identified as high-quality by expert tasters.[8]

7. Smart producers nowadays keep their oil stored under a flush of inert nitrogen gas, which protects the oil from the effects of the environment; some even bottle the oil with a plug of nitrogen on top, beneath the lid.

8. The California study appeared in the journal *Food Quality and Preference* in March 2011. The study of 110 Northern California olive oil consumers was conducted by UC Davis sensory scientists Claudia Delgado and Jean-Xavier Guinard.

Well, Why Don't They Do Something About It?

"They" being, in this case, the United States government, in the form of the Federal Food and Drug Administration and/or the Department of Agriculture, both charged with overseeing various aspects of our food supply and protecting consumers from fraud, misrepresentation, and contamination. The plea comes from U.S. consumers: Why don't they do something about the amount of bad, out-of-date, downright fraudulent olive oil there is in the U.S. marketplace?

The short answer is that "they" don't have the time, personnel, or money to spend chasing olive oil fraud. Fake extra-virgin just doesn't stack up against the threat of E. coli, listeria, and salmonella, nor does it rate very highly when compared to problems with the meat supply or with adulterated vaccines that can and do actually kill people. (Come to think of it, the federal government doesn't spend a lot of time chasing bad or fraudulent wine, either, except to make sure taxes are paid on it.)

In 2013, according to the North Atlantic Olive Oil Association, the U.S. imported 290,614 metric tons of olive oil, 65 percent of which was extra-virgin. Consumption has increased steadily since the 1990s to the point that the United States is now in third place after Italy and Spain—and ahead of Greece.[1] It used to be said that the increase was owing to the fact that those who already consume olive oil were upping their intake, but it's now become clear that olive oil use is spreading beyond a fairly elite and educated consumer group to engage more of the population at large. Has the U.S. market reached its saturation point? Probably not. Or at least not yet, although the actual rate of increase may have reached a plateau. Meanwhile, California (and lesser producers in Texas, Arizona, southern Oregon, and Georgia) is seeking a bigger share of the market. California alone, with 30,000 acres in production, plans to add 5,000 more acres every year until at least 2020. Someone is going to have to consume all that oil. At the University of California at Davis, Dan Flynn, director of the Olive Center, which promotes California's youthful olive oil industry, told me their goal is to see California's share of the national market climb to 10 percent within the next decade. So it's not surprising that the California Olive Oil Council (COOC) has been a fierce proponent for more federal regulation to weed out suspect foreign olive oil.

Early in 2010, the USDA finally adopted new standards for olive oils; to be called extra-virgin, an oil must conform to the International Olive Council's

---

1. This is total consumption—in per capita consumption, the United States is at the very bottom of the list, way behind Mediterranean countries, especially Greece, the undisputed world champion at 18 kilos (39.6 pounds) per person annually.

definition, which, as we have seen, is not notably rigorous. That is, the oil must be mechanically pressed, free of defects, and with an acidity of no more than 0.8 percent. But this is merely a recommendation, without any force of law. Nonetheless, any bottler who complies and submits an oil for testing can put a seal indicating such on the label. The first outfit to do that was Pompeiian, hardly a brand that leaps to mind when one thinks of high-quality olive oil.

The California council, with more than 400 members among growers, producers, and retailers, is justifiably proud of the way it has introduced certification procedures for California oil. But in their zeal to control *all* olive oil, they may well create a nightmare of regulation that will drive out of the U.S. market altogether producers of excellent olive oil from other parts of the world (and they are many, and growing). In the 2012 farm bill, a complex piece of legislation that governs U.S. farm policy over a period of five years, olive oil has been added to the list of commodities under import controls. (The current farm bill expired on December 31, 2012; it was not clear as of this 2013 writing when the new farm bill would be approved.)

Along with that, American producers have also proposed a federal marketing order that, if adopted, would create quality standards for olive oil produced in this country, including olive oil grades that are a good deal more stringent than those established by the International Olive Council. When the farm bill with its olive oil addition is passed, these quality standards would also apply to imported olive oils. Marketing orders, which exist for many food products, oranges and tomatoes most prominent among them, are enforced by the U.S. Department of Agriculture. The proposed regulations would include new labeling requirements, including best-by dates and the origin and grade of the oil. In addition, oils would have to be tested for adulteration, and the extra-virgin grade would have to meet a limit of 0.5 percent of free fatty acids (the IOC's current limit is 0.8 percent, but, as we have seen, producers of premium oil aim for something closer to 0.2 percent or less).

All of this could be seen as a legitimate response to a UC Davis report that found, as reported on the Olive Center website, out of 52 samples of 14 top-selling imported olive oil brands, 73 percent were so defective that they failed the IOC's own sensory standards. Certainly, there is a crying need for accurately measurable and enforceable standards throughout the industry. But there are a number of problems with the report and more with the way it has been interpreted by the media, much of which has confidently adopted the stance that 73 percent of *all* imported olive oil is seriously defective, suspect, and "not really extra-virgin at all."[2]

If the proposed legislation sounds on the surface like a benign and much needed program to protect American consumers, I'm enough of a cynic to see in it a very calculated attempt to grab the market for California—at the expense of some of the finest producers in the world and, in the end, at the expense of the American consumer.

---

2. The conclusion of the UC Davis report was that 73 percent of the tested oils were defective. Since only 52 samples of 14 brands were tested, that is hardly representative of *all* imported olive oils. Moreover, the decks were stacked by the organizers since they selected industrial, commodity imported oils and compared them with what were for the most part high-end California oils. Moreover, the report was paid for by the California Olive Oil Council and a few prominent California brands, including California Olive Ranch. This is hardly an argument for objectivity.

Paul Vossen, who oversees the olive oil sector for the University of California's Extension Service, says marketers are simply giving consumers what they want and are used to. U.S. supermarkets are full of rancid and fusty oil, Vossen says. "Most restaurants serve rancid olive oil to their guests mixed with a bit of vinegar, and they love it." Unfortunately, giving people what they want in this case is bad for their health. But Vossen, who is deeply involved in the promotion of California olive oil, is optimistic about the future. "Consumers will eventually learn what fresh, defect-free olive oil tastes like," he says, "and they'll prefer it to the rancid, fermented oil on the market now."

And what's the harm in the end? If most people like the flavors of rancidity and fustiness, and prefer what they call buttery fruit flavors, why not accept that and make it part of the parameters for olive oil excellence? I honestly don't know how to answer that except to say that, just as we have learned to refuse corked wines and stale coffee, so we must learn to refuse rancid, fusty olive oil. Moreover, as Vossen indicated, it is indeed bad for you. Oxidation in our food is something we want to avoid. Nuts, grains, and oils with the distinctive taste of oxidation are not exactly poisonous, but if consumed steadily over the years they will do you no good and can in fact do a great deal of harm. (I'll explain this a bit more in the next chapter.)

At the farm end, it's easy to avoid these problems by focusing on good sound olives, harvesting early, and rushing olives to the mill. At the mill end, it's also easier now than it has ever been in the past to process rapidly at low temperatures. But there is one critical place in the chain where everything falls apart—and unfortunately, most producers of fine oil have no way to intervene. By that I mean what I call the pipeline from the producer to the consumer.

In an ideal world, the distribution chain that connects these two, producer and consumer, would be as short as possible. That's why, as I noted earlier, it's easier to find really good oil in Italy or Spain or California, or wherever oil is produced, than it is in the rest of the world. For the rest of us, the ideal is seldom realized. The oil goes from producer to shipper to the dock and the container ship. Then across the Atlantic (or increasingly the Pacific, from Australia, New Zealand, and Chile) to another dock and another shipper, to the importer's warehouse, and then out to subsidiary distributors and then finally, possibly months later, to the shelf of a gourmet food store in your neighborhood. The delays and the exposure, even inadvertently, to light and unacceptably high temperatures all work their nefarious magic on the oil in the bottle. And there are other perils along the way: A colleague has described a wooden container of olive oil that arrived with a customs seal on it declaring that the container had been deliberately exposed to very high temperatures in order to kill any organisms the wood itself might harbor. An excellent way to protect the U.S. environment from invasion by suspect bugs, but a terrible way to protect olive oil. Furthermore, once the oil actually arrives in that gourmet food store, an ignorant shopkeeper will all too often display, with great pride, his or her new arrivals—on a shelf under bright lights, if not actually in a sunny window. (A wise shopkeeper, though there are few of them around, would display one bottle only, and keep the rest in a dark, cool closet in the back of the shop.)

There have been several attempts to correct this situation. One of the most innovative is the so-called OliveToLive system developed by Tuscan oil maker Paolo Pasquali (father of

Gemma, mentioned previously, and co-owner of Villa Campestri). In his system, which is intended for use in commercial enterprises, such as shops or restaurants, the oil, from the time it leaves the producer, is protected under nitrogen and maintained at low temperatures, then dispensed directly to the consumer. The distribution chain is as short as possible, practically from producer to consumer through only one intermediary. But it's complex and involves an ungainly machine. It's clearly not for everyone, and certainly not for the home kitchen. And Pasquali himself has been timid about marketing it.

The system originally depended for its supply of olive oils on evaluations by an organization called Tre E (three E's—for excellence, ethics, and economics), which was founded at the prestigious Accademia dei Georgofili agricultural institute in Florence under the aegis of Claudio Peri, a chemical scientist with a passion for olive oil. Since a very high percentage of extra-virgin oils have what Peri calls, with exquisite politeness, "prominent sensorial defects," he proposed to take olive oil "beyond extra-virgin," to create a new culture of olive oil that would stress excellence above all and would monitor every aspect of oil from production through storage and distribution, eventually to uses of excellent olive oil in the kitchen and at the table. A distinguished panel of sensory scientists and other experts would select these premium oils and monitor them through production, then Pasquali's OliveToLive would be the chief marketing arm.

In the event, the organization proved as unwieldy to operate as Pasquali's machine, and it required an investment of time and money with very little by way of payback. On the whole, Spanish producers of mass-market oils—and the bulk of mass-market oils originate in Spain—have resisted the idea of superpremium oil; instead, their goal is to expand the market for Spain's enormous overproduction of olive oil—and that does not mean high-quality extra-virgin. "All too often we think that producing an excellent oil will result in good business," Dr. Peri noted reluctantly, "but this is absolutely false."

The best solution to the problem of fraudulent oil, surely, is education—of consumers, importers, shopkeepers, chefs, restaurateurs, and every other link in the long distribution chain. And that education must begin with consumers who, once they understand what good, fresh olive oil tastes like, will refuse the rancid, fusty stuff on offer, just as they refuse rotten apples or sprouted potatoes, or meat or fish with a suspect odor, or corked wine or stale coffee. And just as you, the consumer, would return rotten apples or corked wine, so should you return rancid olive oil to the place where you bought it and demand a refund or a replacement.

DESPITE THE ACCUSATIONS THAT MUST HAVE SEEMED IN THE PUBLIC eye to be an all-out campaign to tar Italian olive oil, it was Italian oils that once again took the gold at the Los Angeles International Extra Virgin Olive Oil Competition in March 2013. The oils are judged in three categories—delicate, medium, and robust. Out of hundreds of entries from as far afield as Japan, Turkey, Croatia, Slovenia, Portugal, and the United States, it was an Abruzzese oil made from Gentile di Chieti, Intosso, and Leccino olives that won in the delicate category; an oil from the far northern region around Lake Garda in the medium category; and a Tuscan oil, a blend of several cultivars from the hills south of Florence, in the robust category.

Portrait of an Oil Maker: Katja Gasparini

Katja Gasparini had the translucent glow of a young woman who has just learned she's expecting and is thrilled at the prospect when I visited her in July 2011. Only two months pregnant and beaming with joyful pride, she was already planning her most immediate future. "The baby isn't due till January," she said, "so I'll be fine for the harvest. Even if I'm . . ." And she curved both arms around an imaginary big belly. "And then, by next year's harvest, the baby will be old enough so I'll bring him to work with me."

The harvest she was planning is olives, lots of them, some 700 tons that will be turned into more than 130 tons of splendid Istrian olive oil, some of the finest oil in the Mediterranean. Oil from Istria was already praised, if in a rather backhanded way, when the Roman poet Martial suggested in the first century BCE that it was better than oil from Venafrum, a town in modern Molise that was and still is famed for its oil. A century later, Roman aristocrats had established large estates in Istria for the purpose of supplying vast quantities of olive oil to the imperial army in the Danube region. Istrian oil ought to be as well known today as it was in Roman times, and if AgroLaguna, the company that employs Katja Gasparini as its operations manager, has anything to say about it, it will be.

Istria is that large, heart-shaped peninsula that drops down from the European continent into the northeast corner of the Adriatic. As a distinctive region of Croatia, it has been contested between countries, religions, and cultures throughout the twentieth century and long before. For now, however, the scene is peaceful, with a landscape that looks like a cross between Italy and Greece, which it is in a way. Unmortared walls of white limestone define ancient vineyards and olive terraces, while wheat fields, burnished gold under the hot July sun, roll down to the sea. Villages, identified by the steeple of the local church, either hide away in the clefts of valleys or display themselves prominently, walled medieval fortresses perched confidently on the very hilltops. It's no wonder that Istria, almost surrounded as it is by the blue-green waters of the upper Adriatic, and despite strong ties to Central Europe, has always identified itself with Mediterranean culture, and of course with the Mediterranean trinity of wheat, vines, and olives.

AgroLaguna, the largest olive oil producer in Croatia—and also, incidentally, one of the most important wineries—began back in the 1950s as a worker's cooperative; it was recently acquired by Agrokor, a holding company that is a Balkan powerhouse with interests in supermarkets, bottled water, ice cream, and dozens of other enterprises, including the cut flowers market. But it was the high quality of Ol Istria olive oil, produced by AgroLaguna and sold at Zingerman's Deli in Ann Arbor, Michigan, that had brought me here. I hadn't actually tasted it—not yet—but it came highly recommended, and I looked forward to our promised tasting.

"We make four different oils," Katja explained to me as she set out the blue tasting glasses. "Three monocultivars—Ascolano, Picholine, and our native Istarska Bjelica or Istrian White. And then a blend that might include any of the others but usually tends to have more Ascolano." The olives, marketed under the Ol Istria brand, are all produced on AgroLaguna's 220 hectares (about 500 acres) of groves, more than half of which grow in the blood-red soil of Istria's western coastal plain. And they are all milled here, just outside the resort town of Poreč. In super-modern, super-clean, continuous-cycle machinery with stainless-steel surfaces that gleamed in the dim light of the *uliara*, or olive mill. The machinery was familiar—Pieralisi, an Italian company that is in the forefront of modern oil production.

"We have two lines," Katja pointed out, "one of which produces two tons and the other one a ton an hour. So we're able to start making oil within an hour from harvest." This, of course, is one of the most important guarantees of quality in olive oil production: the speed with which freshly harvested olives can be turned into oil before the olives begin their inevitable breakdown. Once the olives are crushed, the paste goes into a *grammola* or malaxer, which gently kneads the paste for up to 40 minutes at a controlled temperature—around 25° or 26°C, Katja said—in order to pull the molecules of oil together and make the final extraction cleaner and more efficient. And then it's a question of centrifuging the mix to separate the oil from the murky liquid that makes up the greatest part of any batch of milled olives.

"What about filtering?" I asked, remembering that there are strong arguments made for both filtered and unfiltered oil. Unfiltered oil, its proponents say, is tastier, but filtered oil, according to the other side, is more stable and has a longer life. "I'm thinking about it," Katja answered. "It's a decision I'll make in the future." She plans, she said, to set aside two identical batches of oil, one to be filtered, the other not, and then to make the comparison six months or more afterward to see what develops. This is not just a question of personal perception, however, for Ol Istria maintains a state-of-the-art laboratory right at the mill and oils are constantly tested, throughout the production cycle, to prevent any defects.

In AgroLaguna's spacious tasting room next to the *uliara*, we tasted the 2011 harvest—the three monocultivars and the company's blend, the production of which Katja also oversees. In Istria's hot climate, olives ripen early. The 2011 harvest began at the end of September and went on into early November, so in July the oils we tasted were already up to eight months old. They had been stored in large stainless-steel tanks at a constant temperature of 18°C (just under 65°F), but still the flavors and aromas would not be as vibrant as when they were young. The oil made from the Ascolano olive (which is used more for table olives than for oil production in its native Marche region of Italy) was deliciously fruity with a ripe tomato flavor and just a slight tomato-y bitterness; the Istarska Bjelica, also sometimes called Bianchera (recalling that Italian is almost as prevalent in Istria as Slavic or Croatian) had a decidedly grassy nose and a nice pepperiness but was not bitter except in the aftertaste; and the Picholine had a very bitter nose but not so in the flavors, which were redolent of fresh almonds.

Some of the oldest olive trees in the Mediterranean grow in Istria. One in particular, on the island of Brijuni off the west coast, is said to be at least 1,500 years old. So these Istrians have some experience in the art of olive oil. And yet, even here, it is only because of changes that have taken place in the very recent past that the future for olive cultivation looks bright. Cleaner, quicker methods, more attuned to the needs of the oil itself in order to maintain its fresh taste and aroma, are the keystones of modern olive production, and Katja Gasparini represents that change. In a world that has been dominated by tradition—we do it this way because our grandfathers did it this way—it's refreshing to see a young woman take charge and say, we do it this way because this way is proven best.

THE SCIENCE

ONCE WE START TO SAMPLE A VARIETY OF EXTRA-VIRGIN olive oils from different parts of the world, tasting them in sequence, we begin to comprehend the enormous range of flavors to be distinguished among them. These flavors are the products of volatile compounds that are released when the fruit cells are broken, either when the fruit is damaged or when it is deliberately crushed in the milling process to extract the oil. The nature of these compounds depends on many factors, but especially on the cultivar itself, as well as on the place where it was grown and the climate in which it was produced: An austere Cornicabra oil from high in the Toledo mountains south of Madrid has very different flavors, a different sensory style, from what's in a rich Nabulsi oil from the rocky terrain of Palestine at the other end of the Mediterranean, and both are quite distinctive when measured against, say, a spicy Koroneiki oil from the volcanic soils of the island of Crete. But despite the differences, it's the volatile compounds in all these oils that help to produce the flavors. Those same compounds will also determine whether an oil is good or bad. Sink your nose into a glass of fresh, green, premium olive oil straight from the mill and you should smell lovely aromas of freshly cut grass, of green or ripe fruit, and possibly other fragrances, such as almonds or tomatoes or artichokes or green tomato leaves or citrus or crushed thyme—all aromas that are produced by volatile compounds in the oil.

Now leave that glass of oil out next to the stove in your kitchen for a week or so, and then sink your nose into it again. The aromas will be very different, possibly quite subdued, and the color will have changed from a bright or gentle green, perhaps with golden highlights, to a hue we might describe politely as the color of pee. All this is caused by the dispersal of those earlier compounds—it's not for nothing that they're called volatile—and the emergence of others that come about through oxidation. If you're lucky, the oil will smell of nothing at all, or of old straw or hay; if you're unlucky, it may actually have begun to stink of rancidity, the main clue to oxidation. What does rancidity smell like? Open a bin of whole wheat flour that has been kept closed for several months, or a bag of walnuts or peanuts forgotten in the back of the pantry shelf—that's the smell of rancidity. Like the flour and the nuts, the olive oil, too, should be discarded. Not only is rancidity not good for you, but taken in quantity over time, it can also be downright dangerous.

And what makes one oil taste so very different from another is directly related to the positive effects olive oil has on human health and metabolism.

Years ago, when I first started to get more than casually interested in olive oil, this was not so well understood. In 1993, Oldways Preservation and Exchange Trust, a nonprofit I helped establish and with which I worked closely at the time, joined with the Harvard School of Public Health to organize the first Mediterranean Diet Conference in Cambridge, Massachusetts. Back then, we thought, along with just about everyone else who'd looked into it, that the role of olive oil in sustaining the remarkably good health of people who followed a traditional Mediterranean diet was the result of two facts: 1) olive oil was the principal fat in the diet, sometimes accounting for as much as 40 percent or more of daily calories; and 2) olive oil is primarily made up of oleic acid, a monounsaturated fat. Nutritional scientists were largely in agreement that monounsaturated fats (or MUFAs, as they're sometimes called in the literature) work in human metabolism to regulate serum cholesterol, reducing dangerous low-density lipoproteins (LDLs), called "bad" cholesterol, and maintaining or even boosting high-density lipoproteins (HDLs), the so-called "good" cholesterol.[1] Olive oil contains anywhere from 55 percent to 83 percent monounsaturated oleic acid, depending on the cultivar, the maturity of the fruit at harvest, and the terroir of the orchard or field, that is, the nature of the soil, the altitude, the climate (cool climates produce oils with more oleic acid), and the weather throughout the growing season.

---

1. This is not the place for a discussion of primate metabolism. Suffice to say that a lipoprotein is made up of a fat, a lipid (that's the cholesterol), combined with a protein. A low-density lipoprotein has more cholesterol than protein, and that isn't good. A high-density lipoprotein has more protein than cholesterol, and that is what we're looking for when we look at healthy cholesterol levels. For a much more comprehensive discussion, see the Harvard School of Public Health's website: http://www.hsph.harvard.edu/nutritionsource/what-should-you-eat/fats-full-story.

Another reason for the importance of MUFAs is their stability against oxidation—unlike the polyunsaturated fatty acids (PUFAs, naturally) that are in vegetable oils (corn, soy, sunflower, canola, and so on), MUFAs combat the production of free radicals that are linked to carcinogenesis.

What this means in effect is that all olive oil, both extra-virgin and the regular stuff (just plain olive oil, that which has been refined or rectified as described on page 90), is regarded favorably as a good source of the kind of healthy fats that help fend off cardiovascular disease. Those who heard him will never forget Dr. Walter Willett, the esteemed chair of the Department of Nutrition at the Harvard School of Public Health, when he said with regard to the U.S. Department of Agriculture's food pyramid, "As far as I'm concerned, you can just take the whole pyramid and pour olive oil over it." That was a profoundly revolutionary statement about a food that is primarily a fat, at a time when the good-nutrition mantra chanted by every academic dietician and nutritionist was: low fat, low fat, low fat.

But as it turned out, MUFAs are only part of the story, an important part, it's true, but there is much, much more going on with extra-virgin olive oil than even authorities like Dr. Willett imagined back then. Note that I wrote *extra-virgin*. Although plain olive oil—which is, just like extra-virgin, a monounsaturated fat or MUFA—is good for us, the very process of refining it, stripping the oil of compounds that produce flavors and colors, also strips it of some major health benefits. The two go hand in hand—the aromas, flavors, and colors that give extra-virgin olive oil such a unique place in the kitchen and on the table are testimony to the presence of the vital compounds that make the oil indispensable in a healthy diet. So olive oil is good for us, but extra-virgin olive oil is better. And the better the oil, the more complex its flavor, the deeper its color, the better it is for our health. In a way, this is analogous to consuming whole grains naturally rich in vitamins, minerals, active compounds, and fiber versus consuming highly processed grains stripped of these vital nutrients.

Almost every week, it seems, nutritional scientists find new evidence of the beneficial impact of extra-virgin olive oil. Cardiovascular disease, diabetes (especially type 2, so-called adult onset diabetes), many types of cancer, including breast and prostate cancers, even Alzheimer's disease are among the catastrophic illnesses for which extra-virgin olive oil is believed to have therapeutic or preventative (or sometimes both) effects. And new conditions get added to this list just about every month or so as scientists and nutritionists continue their research. At this point it's believed that extra-virgin olive oil, especially at its freshest, seems to have a profound anti-inflammatory outcome because of an element in its composition that accounts for the catch in the back of the throat that's typical of fine fresh oils.

The positive effects of extra-virgin olive oil come about largely because of the presence of powerful antioxidants that are naturally present in the oil, especially as polyphenols with suggestive names like oleuropein, oleocanthal, hydroxytyrosol, tyrosol, and many others, some of which have yet to be identified. The presence of these extremely valuable antioxidants is indicated by those same volatile compounds that you smell and taste in fine extra-virgin olive oil. That is, while "there is no direct relationship between the amount of antioxidants and the aromas perceptible in an oil," says Mario Bertuccioli, professor at the

University of Florence and one of Europe's leading figures in sensory science, "we can say that the aromatic freshness of an oil is a good indication of a quantity of antioxidants." It would be difficult to overemphasize the importance these antioxidants play in a healthy diet.

No doubt the most impressive polyphenol in olive oil is hydroxytyrosol (which, interestingly, is also present in white wine), sometimes called a "superstar" because of its ability to absorb free radicals and protect cells against oxidative stress.[2] If you look up hydroxytyrosol online, you will find a number of sites that guarantee equivalent effects from hydroxytyrosol supplements. Be skeptical: That's not a great idea. Despite the fact that it has been heralded as the most potent antioxidant found in nature, no one so far has been able to tease out the synergistic effects of any of these elements that make olive oil so good for us. Might it be that the magic bullet, the potion that will restore health and ensure a long life, is not hydroxytyrosol alone but hydroxytyrosol and fat, or hydroxytyrosol and cooked vegetables, or hydroxytyrosol and garlic, or hydroxytyrosol and all of the above, including other antioxidants present in olive oil?

The prize for the polyphenol with the best back story surely goes to oleocanthal, which was "discovered" back in 1999 when Gary Beauchamp, a biologist and director of the prestigious Monell Chemical Senses Center in Philadelphia, was given a taste of oil fresh from the mill while visiting friends in Sicily during the olive harvest. The burn or sting he experienced in the back of his throat would be familiar to anyone who has ever tasted very fresh oil, an overwhelmingly pungent sensation that often leads to a coughing attack—and also leads some wags to refer to olive oils as one-cough, two-cough, or three-cough oils. The Monell scientist, however, recognized that back-of-the-throat pungency as a characteristic of ibuprofen, a non-steroid anti-inflammatory drug (NSAID) widely available in over-the-counter remedies for aches and pains, especially those associated with inflammation—arthritis, rheumatoid arthritis, menstrual pain, and injuries. (Advil is probably the best known brand-name NSAID to American consumers.) Dr. Beauchamp's crew at Monell spent three years studying the effects of olive oil, concluding, not surprisingly, that the more coughs the oil produced, the more of the valuable polyphenol oleocanthal it contained.[3] Anti-inflammatory drugs like ibuprofen are also associated with lowering the risk of certain cancers, heart disease, stroke, and dementia, and oleocanthal, it appears, has a similar

---

2. A brief explanation: Oxidative stress results from the normal process of living. We need oxygen in order to survive but, as with many essential elements, too much of it can be a bad thing. The oxygen in the air we breathe helps convert food into energy. But this basic metabolic process, without which life cannot continue, also creates by-products called free radicals, which can destabilize the organism entirely. Free radicals thus come about through the very process of living, breathing, and aging, although they are also created by pollution in the air, water, and food we eat, and in toxic substances such as tobacco smoke. All these effects combined are what we call oxidative stress. And antioxidants help defend us against its effects.

3. Their results were published in the weekly journal *Nature*: 437 (September 1, 2005), Beauchamp, Gary K., et al., "Phytochemistry: Ibuprofen-Like Activity in Extra-Virgin Olive Oil."

effect.[4] Although structurally unrelated, both oleocanthal and ibuprofen are potent anti-inflammatory compounds, and both produce the same effects, inhibiting enzymatic reactions in the body that promote inflammation.

At about 10 percent of the total phenolic compounds, ibuprofen-like oleocanthal is one of many positive elements in extra-virgin olive oil, which, it appears, might just be nature's most perfect food after mother's milk, providing beneficial fats and good antioxidant vitamins and polyphenols to protect us, and in fact providing just about everything we need in life except for protein. (But if you want protein, take a plate of beans cooked slowly with garlic, a slice of onion, and a few leafy greens, and pour a healthy dollop of olive oil over, as generations of Mediterranean cooks have done down through the ages, and you have something close to a perfect meal. And one that's good for you, too, as modern generations of scientists are proving almost every day.)

But there's more. Alessandro Leone, an agronomist from the University of Foggia, in Puglia, explains it: "Pungency in the back of the throat," he tells me, "is not negative. On the contrary, it is absolutely positive because it's a symbol of the enormous quantity of polyphenols that the oil contains." And beyond their implications for human health, Dr. Leone tells me, polyphenols carry another benefit: "They're also indications of an oil with a long life, one that will maintain its organoleptic qualities for a very long time." Of course, the oil must be protected from exposure to light, heat, and the atmosphere, but even so, an oil rich in polyphenols, with, let's say, around 400 ppm (parts per million), like one from the massive ancient Ogliarola and Coratina trees that Leone's family maintains in a magnificent grove below the whitewashed town of Ostuni in Puglia, will endure with most of its structure intact far longer than a sweeter Taggiasca oil from Liguria, for instance, or a Biancolilla from Sicily. Oils from olives such as Biancolilla, Taggiasca, and other varieties that are naturally low in polyphenols, as low as 80 ppm, are often delicious when fresh, but within six months or so, even if carefully maintained, they will lose their flavor impact, their polyphenolic structure, and their positive effect on health.

Green, bitter, pungent: That's the word on extra-virgin olive oil from Maria Isabel Covas, head of the Cardiovascular Risk and Nutrition Research Group associated with the Ospedal del Mar in Barcelona and a renowned Spanish researcher into the effects of olive oil on health risks and oxidative stress. "Use any oil you like," Dr. Covas says with her typically unstoppable enthusiasm, "as long as it's green and bitter."

---

4. For a more scientific discussion of this than I can possibly provide, see: Monti, Maria Chiara, Luigi Margarucci, Alessandra Tosco, Raffaele Riccio, and Agostino Casapullo, "New Insights on the Interaction Mechanism between Tau Protein and Oleocanthal, an Extra-Virgin Olive-Oil Bioactive Component," published in Journal of the Royal Society of Chemistry and cited as DOI: 10.1039/ c1fo10064e (www.rsc.org/foodfunction); received April 29, 2011, accepted June 14, 2011. This study, by a group of research scientists at the Università degli Studi di Salerno, concluded: "The reduced risk of neurodegenerative pathologies as AD [Alzheimers disease] in Mediterranean area has been associated with high consumption of extra virgin olive oil, which also exerts beneficent effects on cancer and cardiovascular diseases. These healthy properties have been attributed mainly to minor phenolic compounds found in extra virgin olive oil, which also bear antioxidant, anti-inflammatory and anti-thrombic activities."

Look up *bitterness* in a thesaurus and you will not be surprised to find that the primary synonyms for the word are all negative: acrimony, anger, having a sharp, strong, unpleasant taste. Look up *pungent* and it's almost as bad: strong smelling, caustic, overpowering. Why then should we be seeking bitterness and pungency in olive oil?

Dr. Covas described for me an important study that she conducted along with colleagues in four Spanish cities—Barcelona, Valencia, Navarre, and Seville. It is to date one of the few large controlled studies, using human subjects, of the effects of olive oils with different phenolic structures on cholesterol levels.[5] The greater the polyphenolic content of the oil, the study found, the greater the increase in HDL cholesterol ("good" cholesterol) in blood samples taken after eating. And it's precisely the bitter flavors and pungent impact in fine extra-virgin olive oil, Dr. Covas assured me, that indicate the presence of polyphenols in the oil—polyphenols that are strongly protective against chronic illnesses related to oxidative stress. Other researchers have suggested that olive oil has a positive effect on many other debilitating conditions and problems—osteoporosis, for example, and depression, and even, quite tentatively, on the outcomes of infertility treatments.[6]

---

5. http://www.fasebj.org/content/24/7/2546.abstract.

6. I have no medical training and am not in a position to give professional medical advice. But for those willing to seek it, there is plenty of information available to link monounsaturated fats that are high in phenolic compounds with positive health outcomes. The one fat that fits that definition is extra-virgin olive oil.

How does it all work? Atherosclerosis, cardiovascular disease, many types of cancer, metabolic syndrome, diabetes, and quite likely neurodegenerative conditions such as Alzheimer's are triggered by an inflammatory reaction that is derived from oxidative stress. And polyphenols in olive oil, in turn, trigger a genetic response that combats inflammation. These antioxidant components—called "minor components" because in fact they form a very small but critical part of the overall composition of olive oil—seem to repress the genes that lead to inflammation. Genetic expression is simply the latest in ongoing research by very distinguished scientific institutions throughout the world to identify where, what, and how olive oil can produce such positive effects.

Genetic expression was featured in a project carried out at the University of Cordoba's Maimonides Institute for Biomedical Investigation, led by Dr. Francisco Pérez-Jiménez, chief of internal medicine at the Reina Sofia Hospital in that city. The study, which involved 20 subjects, all with metabolic syndrome, concluded that olive oil with a high phenolic content influenced the regulation of almost 100 genes, among them those linked to obesity, high blood fat levels, diabetes, and heart disease. Admittedly, this was a very small sampling—only 20 subjects—and admittedly it was carried out at an institution located in the very heart of Spanish olive oil production. Still, Dr. Pérez-Jiménez is highly regarded by his peers as an impeccable scientist and his conclusions, while positive, are cautiously so. "Several of the repressed genes are known to be involved in pro-inflammatory processes," he said in a press statement, "suggesting that the diet can switch the activity of immune system cells to a less deleterious inflammatory profile, as seen in metabolic syndrome."

Polyphenols are not the only hard-working guardians of good health in extra-virgin olive oil. There are also hundreds, possibly thousands, of other active compounds, "and we don't know what most of them are," explains Antonia Trichopoulou, head of the World Health Organization Collaborating Center for Nutrition at the medical school of the University of Athens (Greece) and a longtime advocate for the traditional Mediterranean diet. Some of these other factors, she pointed out to me, include tocopherols (think vitamin E), carotenoids (think beta carotene and lutein), and squalene (with strong tumor-inhibiting properties), all powerful antioxidants that work in our bodies to fend off (*scavenge* is the word scientists use) free radicals caused by pollution, tobacco smoke, the exigencies of daily life, and the normal process of aging, as well as those caused by the excess of omega-6 fatty acids that's so typical of modern diets.[7]

We know, too, that all of these compounds react with each other to produce distinctive aromas and flavors. But Dr. Trichopoulou stresses, "It's not about a set of individual components, or even individual foods. It's really about how all these factors interact with each other. Maybe olive oil facilitates the absorption or even the metabolism of other food elements. Maybe wine does that too. But we should not try to medicalize the Mediterranean

---

7. Omega-6 fatty acids are not bad for us. They are essential, meaning our bodies cannot manufacture them. The problem is an imbalance: We get plenty of omega-6 through our heavily meat-laden diets and through vegetable oils, including olive oil, but not enough omega-3, found mostly in fish.

diet." In short, we shouldn't try to reduce olive oil, as some have tried to do, to a series of extractable components that can then be put into a pill to swallow on a regular basis.

So important are polyphenols to sustaining good health that Dr. Covas in Barcelona believes they should be listed on bottle labels, just like the free oleic acid content and the harvest and bottling date. But there's a problem with that. As we saw at the beginning of this chapter, between olive oil fresh from the press and possibly year-old olive oil left to sit on the counter of a heated kitchen next to the stove for a week, the polyphenolic content can change drastically. A polyphenol-rich olive oil may be full of a delicious complex of flavors, bright in color and seductive in aroma, when it leaves its producer's care, but there is absolutely no guarantee that all those positive characteristics will be sustained and maintained over the long journey from the producer to the consumer. In the very ordinary course of events, a shipment of oil may well be exposed to excessive heat, if not necessarily to light. You only have to imagine a container of oil sitting on a sunny dock in New York City for a day or two in August waiting to be picked up by an importer to understand that the perishable product will be assaulted and rendered deeply defective by the experience.

Beyond that, however, there is a further problem in the very long chain from producer to consumer. That is that wholesalers and retailers alike don't understand the product and don't know how to treat it. Or perhaps they do know and simply find it easier to be sloppy in their administration. And I'm not just talking about North American retailers. All over the world, it seems, olive oil is treated as if it were a product like seed oil or corn oil or canola, or any one of a dozen different highly refined (and thus highly stable) products, instead of as the precious and somewhat delicate product that it is.

Too much fat in the diet has been cited as a primary cause behind so many modern diseases that it is quite amazing to find a single dietary fat that can provide major health benefits. But olive oil's anti-inflammatory, antioxidant effects are more and more established as important partners in a healthful diet. It is increasingly recognized that heart disease, for instance, is not so much caused by a buildup of fat as it is by an inflammatory response in the arteries that leads to atherosclerosis (narrowing of the arteries). That inflammatory response can be triggered by environmental factors—diet, tobacco smoke, air pollution, water pollution, pesticides—and by the very process of human existence as we grow, mature, and age. And extra-virgin olive oil combats it.

Olive oil alone, in no matter what quantity, no matter how high in antioxidants, will have a hard time defending a body against a steady diet of Big Macs, fried potatoes, Coca-Cola, and so forth. But a diet that stresses fresh vegetables, beans and other legumes, seafood rather than red meat, and a very low to nil consumption of fast food and highly processed food—that diet, whether Mediterranean, Asian, or somewhere in between, coupled with plenty of olive oil, plenty of physical activity, and another element we might call the luck of the genes—can be effective in promoting a long and healthy life.

Olive oil is the common thread that runs through it.

IN *the* KITCHEN, ON *the* TABLE: CHOOSING *and* USING *the* BEST

IN THE SUMMER OF 2012, AN AMERICAN drugstore-supermarket chain in my Maine neighborhood was advertising Filippo Berio olive oil—plain, light, or extra-virgin, take your pick—in half-liter (16.9-ounce) containers for just $2.99. That's a little like offering condensed cream of mushroom soup at 10 cents a can. Anyone who falls for it probably deserves the bad soup or bad olive oil in his or her market basket. And it will be bad, believe me. I expect the Berio oil on offer, apart from any other qualities, was seriously out of date, although it was impossible to tell from the information provided on the containers.

It is a situation that is all too typical—out-of-date olive oil (that was not great oil in the first place), offered at fire-sale prices to shoppers who don't actually have any idea what they are getting.

Often the most difficult fact for consumers to understand is that the finest kind of extra-virgin olive oil is never cheap. Even when you make it yourself. Burton Anderson, an American journalist best known for his writing about Italian wines and winemaking, has lived in Italy for many decades. He also produces his own Tuscan olive oil when he's not deep in some cantina sampling the latest vintage of Barolo or Brunello. Anderson once went through his accounts and estimated that his own oil, harvested and produced by himself and his wife with a little help from their friends, cost him far more than he could buy it for on the open market anywhere near his home in the hills north of Arezzo. And still he continues to produce it, for the pleasure involved in making his own oil and for the comfort in knowing that it has been made precisely to his own high standards. If he tried to sell it, he said, few would buy. The cost would be prohibitive, simply because the time and effort that go into producing it, in his words, "exceed rational limits."

There are several reasons why fine oil is costly: A good harvest of sound, healthy olives relies on considerable hand labor, since the olives are harvested almost one by one. Beyond that, it takes a keen and sensitive eye to oversee all stages of the production cycle. The finest kind of oil, as described in Chapters 3 and 4, is almost invariably made from olives handpicked before they are fully mature and rushed to the olive mill within hours of harvesting. The mill must be scrupulously clean and the mill operators must know what they are doing, including accurately judging temperatures and the length of time for the various parts of the operation in order to get the best flavor profile for the oil. And then there's the question of post-production handling: Oil must be filtered or racked periodically to remove any natural sediment that collects; it must be stored in a dark, cool place, preferably under a flush of inert nitrogen gas to protect it from atmospheric contamination; and it must remain there until it's time to bottle it and send it out to market. It must be shipped expeditiously, not allowed to linger in the hot sun of a shipping dock in the middle of summer, and then, once it has reached its destination, it must continue to be handled in a correct manner, something no producer can possibly guarantee, especially not small producers who have no way of controlling distant markets once the oil has left their careful hands.

So olive oil is not a cheap commodity. And the fact that there is money to be made from what we might term an essential luxury has led to a range of unscrupulous and illegal practices that make cheap oil, like what I saw in that Maine drugstore-supermarket, even more suspect. Often it's simply a question of old oil, for olive oil, unlike wine—and this cannot be said often enough—does not get better with age. In fact, the opposite. So a producer, importer, or distributor, left with a large stock of two-year-old oil unsold, may well try to get rid of it by lowering the price. There's nothing wrong with that practice so long as it's honestly conducted. If you can be sure of the date when the oil was actually produced, and not just when it was bottled, you might find a bargain cooking oil on your hands. (Like most Tuscan peasants, in our farmhouse kitchen we count on last year's oil, even oil that's two years old, for almost all our cooking.) All too often, however, if you didn't actually make it yourself, there is no way to tell from the label when the oil in question was made, since the expiration date required by law is 18 months from *bottling* rather than from harvest.

Beyond slapdash handling, however, there is also a good deal of out-and-out fraud practiced on an unsuspecting public. There are many ways to deceive. Certifiably extra-virgin oil may be blended and "stretched" with large amounts of cheaper refined or rectified oil; that is, with oil that failed to meet the extra-virgin standard and has been corrected chemically or physically to make an inert oil with no flavor or aroma. Again, like old oil, this isn't necessarily bad if you know what you're buying. But it is completely fraudulent to label it extra-virgin and price it accordingly.

More often, olive oil may be adulterated with chemically refined vegetable or nut oils. Turkish hazelnut oil was a big favorite for some time, and also palm oil and corn/maize oil. Marketing this as olive oil, extra-virgin or not, is, again, fraudulent and illegal, and authorities in countries such as Greece, Spain, and Italy, where high-quality olive oil is produced, are increasingly on the alert to protect their national reputations.[1] (This has not always been the case, as detailed in my colleague Tom Mueller's exhaustive book, *Extra-Virginity*.) In late 2011, a pair of Spanish businessmen were sentenced to two years in prison for adulterating olive oil with up to 80 percent sunflower oil. Earlier, several Italian processors were convicted of completely faking extra-virgin olive oil by coloring sunflower and soy oils with chlorophyll and beta-carotene to give them the seductive look of green-gold extra-virgin. And those are just the ones who have been caught.

But cases like these, convictions, fines, even jail sentences, don't actually have much impact on the world of illegal olive oil production. Fraud continues to be practiced, primarily because penalties are light and often impossible to enforce, and the profits to be made by such practices can be stunning.

Possibly even more alarming than faking oil is the practice of altering low-quality olive oil through a process called deodorizing to mask it as extra-virgin. Defective oil, oil made from damaged, overripe, or fermented olives, develops chemical signs called alkyl esters, which remain in the oil even when its nasty flavors and aromas have been removed by steam deodorizing. A test for alkyl esters, recently adopted by the European Union, thus should indicate whether or not the oil was defective to start with and distinguish deodorized oil from true extra-virgin. But it is not clear that the test is accurate, and in any case producers of high-quality oils say the level allowed by EU regulations, 75 milligrams of alkyl esters per kilo of oil, is much too high. Or rather, Italians feel 75 milligrams is way too high; Spanish producers would like to see the permitted level at 100 milligrams. Hence the compromise at 75. But a quality oil, produced from sound olives pressed immediately after harvest, should have a level of not more than 10 or 15 mg of alkyl esters per kilo, much, much lower than the level allowed by EU regulations. A defective oil, deodorized to make its defects no longer apparent, is not only fraudulent but is moreover cheating consumers of the full nutritional benefits of extra-virgin olive oil.

Don't imagine that Americans are the sole victims here. In Italy's Marche region a few years ago, the regional environmental agency conducted a test of alkyl esters in extra-virgins produced locally and of supposedly extra-virgin oils produced elsewhere but purchased in local supermarkets. The conclusion? Up to 150 milligrams per kilo of alkyl esters in the supermarket oils, while oils from local olive mills were in the range of 15 milligrams per

---

1. Spanish authorities have been particularly vigilant since the 1981 so-called "toxic oil scandal," in which 1,000 people are said to have died as a result of poisoning. Despite popular misconceptions, however, the event did *not* involve olive oil and may in fact not have been caused by oil at all but rather by pesticide residues on Spanish-grown tomatoes. See Bob Wiffenden's excellent analysis in *The Guardian* of some years ago: http://www.guardian.co.uk/education/2001/aug/25/research .highereducation.

kilo. Italians too, like the Spanish and doubtless like Greek and French consumers as well, are being cheated of full value when they buy a supermarket "extra-virgin" oil blended from products from all over the olive oil–producing world. That blend typically will include any number of deodorized and otherwise rectified oils.

Add to all this the quantity of mass-produced oils that manage to qualify as extra-virgin, in the sense that they fall within the very loose parameters of free oleic acid (0.8 percent) and peroxide levels (20)—or might have done so at one time before exceeding a normal lifespan—but do not taste all that different from Wesson or Mazola or Crisco, the three barely differentiated brands that dominate the U.S. market for vegetable oils. True, if you were to put an unmarked tasting glass of, say, Carapelli or Bertolli up against a tasting glass of Crisco canola oil, you would likely be able to identify which glass has the olive oil. But the industrial olive oil won't taste like much of anything at all beyond a hint of olives and a decided fustiness if not out-and-out rancidity. Such industrial oils are most often created by judiciously blending bulk oils from all over the Mediterranean in order to arrive at a uniform flavor, texture, and aroma that does not differentiate one bottle from another or one year from another. The goal, in other words, is to produce a standard product that the consumer can rely on—like McDonald's hamburgers, it will always and everywhere taste exactly the same, just like Wesson, Mazola, and Crisco.

The perceptibly fusty taste (a taste that's familiar as the flavor of poorly processed green or black table olives) in almost all of these oils is a defect, say the experts, but it is deliberate. Fustiness comes about when olives have been fermented in a willy-nilly manner, and it is present in these industrial oils because manufacturers believe, correctly, that fustiness is a flavor the American public finds desirable in olive oil. (And not just the American public—there are untold numbers of fusty industrial olive oils on the shelves of supermarkets throughout Spain, France, and Italy, indeed throughout the world.) Yes, it may legally qualify as extra-virgin, but it has nothing to add to your kitchen or your table.

U.S. consumers spend more than $700 million annually on extra-virgin olive oil, the good, the bad, and the ugly, almost all of it imported. It's the third largest specialty food product in the United States, after coffee and chocolate. The United States is the major market for European Union olive oils, which is to say most of the olive oil in the world. Since the publication of Mueller's book in 2011 and its resultant publicity, however, U.S. consumers have grown ever more leery of the product, and especially—unfairly in my view—of Italian olive oil. The fact is that Italy produces some of the very finest extra-virgin olive oils in the world. That the country is also responsible for much of the fraud is equally undeniable, although Spain shares a good part of the blame.

There's an old joke retold old too often in the olive oil world: Where is the best oil from? Answer: Spain. And where is the worst oil from? Answer: Spain. And it could be said equally of Italy or Greece, which are, along with Spain, the top suppliers of olive oil for the U.S. market.

To be fair, much of the fraud practiced by European olive oil farmers and producers has little to do with the quality of consumer products and more to do with false claims for subsidies collected from the European Union's Common Agricultural Policy, or CAP. Spain alone, which makes a little less than half of the world's entire production of olive oil (and exports a little more than half[2]), receives subsidies from Brussels to the tune of a cool 40 percent of the value of its own olive oil market. This has, predictably, encouraged Spanish farmers to plant more and more olives, many in the intensive system of cultivation that was actually developed in Spain in the 1990s. Over-planting, in turn, has led quite predictably to massive over-production and a glut of Spanish olive oil. But this is not premium extra-virgin in fancy containers costing upward of $40 a liter. Think instead of the bottles stacked on your local supermarket shelves, bottles that often bear what looks like an Italian name or an Italian image on the label. Many are produced by a single Spanish multinational and filled with cheap, undated oil from the huge plantations of Andalusia. Carapelli, Bertolli, and Sasso all started out life as reputable Italian firms, but as their market grew larger and larger, they looked ever farther afield to source cheap oil. Soon they became acquired by Unilever, the massive Dutch multinational, which then sold the lot of them off to SOS, a Spanish not-quite-so massive multinational, which promptly changed its name to Deoleo, and has now joined with the Hojiblanca Group, a huge association of 90 producer cooperatives in Andalusia, to form the world's largest olive oil company. Gresham's Law, a historic economic dictum that goes back to very ancient times, states, in brief, that bad money drives out good. This new association, it seems certain, will dominate the market, pushing cheaply made Spanish bulk oil—and in the end, bad oil will drive out good.

This is olive oil as a commodity: produced in quantity, priced cheaply, supported by government subsidies, and intended for a growing global market to compete with canola and other vegetable oils. This is olive oil as kitchen grease, pure and simple. It should be no surprise that subsidies produce gluts, which in turn create lower prices and the need for more supports, in a continuing downward cycle that debases the identity of one of the most superb products that nature and humankind have joined together to produce. It is Gresham's Law in its purest operation.

EARLIER, I TALKED ABOUT THE DIFFERENT CATEGORIES OF OLIVE OIL, but let me sum up once again what we can find in stores in America (and in Italy and Spain and probably elsewhere too, for that matter):

> EXTRA-VIRGIN OLIVE OIL: Purported to be the highest quality of oil, produced mechanically, without chemical inputs, to standards established by the International Olive Council (see page 64) and evaluated for its excellence with both laboratory testing and by a panel of IOC-certified tasters.

> OLIVE OIL (SOMETIMES STILL PRESENTED TO AN UNWITTING PUBLIC AS "PURE" OLIVE OIL): Like extra-virgin, produced by mechanical means but because it has failed to make the extra-virgin grade, has been corrected, rectified, or refined—all

---

2. That is to say, in a normal year Spain exports 54 percent *by volume* and 46 percent *by value* of the world's olive oil. 2012–2013, however, was not a normal year, as long-term drought, blamed on global climate change, led to a predicted 37 percent shortfall in Spanish production.

three terms are used—to create a flavorless, odorless oil to which a small amount of extra-virgin oil may be added to give it some taste and aroma. I have to point out another widespread myth about olive oil, that this category is produced from a "second pressing." Even some of the most reputable sources (such as, alarmingly, the BBC Web site) have repeated this untruth. It cannot be said often enough: With modern extra-virgin olive oil production, there is no second pressing.

LIGHT OLIVE OIL: Rectified or refined oil, like the previous category, that is deliberately created with very little aroma or flavor but otherwise similar to the olive oil grade—olive oil, in brief, for people who really don't like olive oil.

POMACE OIL (AKA OLIVE-POMACE OIL): Cheap oil produced by extracting the small amount of oil remaining in the dregs (the pomace—pulp, skins, and pits) of olive processing, using solvents, most commonly hexane; the oil must be further rectified to remove the solvent and make it acceptable for human consumption. While technically considered edible, pomace oil is banned in some countries. In the United States, it is used, legally, in many low-end food service operations such as pizzerias. As Curtis Cord, editor of the excellent website Olive Oil Times, put it: "Pizza makers . . . simply don't know the difference and neither do their customers."

In this book, as I've stated frequently, I deal only with extra-virgin olive oil since I believe it is the only olive oil that counts, the only oil that is interesting to use, and, frankly, the only oil that is interesting to write about. All else is like kitchen grease made in such quantities solely to compete with cheap vegetable oils that do nothing for your health or your diet. But clearly extra-virgin comes in many stripes and colors too. Given the confusion of labels, most of them misleading when not downright fraudulent, what is a poor cook to do? How can buyers know when the oil they are purchasing is genuine, unadulterated, 100 percent extra-virgin? And even more important, how can they know, if it says it's extra-virgin, that it's actually any good?

What, in short, is the best extra-virgin olive oil? It's a question I am often asked by worried consumers. My old pal Mort Rosenblum, an astute journalist and author of *Olives: The Life and Lore of a Noble Fruit*, asked that same question of Juan Vicente Gomez Moya. To which the very genial Gomez Moya, then director (now retired) of the Spanish oil export organization ASOLIVA, replied: "What's the best cheese? What's the best wine?"—pointing out what is not always obvious, the absurdity of the question. If you stop to think for a minute or two, it becomes clear that the value of an olive oil, like the value of a cheese or of a wine, depends entirely on the uses to which it will be put. That and the personal taste of the buyer.

But there are some rules of thumb to follow when faced with the bewildering array of olive oils on offer.

First of all, *don't be seduced by cheap prices* and loss leaders. I can assure you that the oil on offer unquestionably will not be very good. Unfortunately, the converse is unreliable: Just because a bottle comes at a fancy cost is no guarantee that the oil contained therein will live up to its price tag. Some of the most expensive—indeed, I dare say, the two *most* expensive—oils on the market are not worth the prices being asked.

Second, *stay away from oil in clear glass bottles*. Light is one of the greatest enemies of fine olive oil, and there is no excuse for a conscientious producer bottling his or her oil in clear glass. (The excuse offered is that "the customer likes it that way"—but consumer perceptions are changing, as well they should.) Oil should be packaged in dark glass, UV-resistant glass, or, best of all, in opaque tins.

Third, and as a corollary, *don't buy any oil, even in a tin, that has been displayed in a sunny shop window* or on a high shelf under hot, bright shop lights. Even the tin will not protect the oil from eventual contamination in such situations. You could mention to the shopkeeper that it's a disgrace to display a fine oil in such a manner—but, in my experience, the shopkeeper probably won't welcome your advice and won't act on it.

Fourth, *read the labels*: As of mid-2012, European legislation requires olive oil producers to state on the label both the origin of the olives and the place where they were processed; if and when oils from various origins have been blended together by the producer, that too must be clearly stated. I expect that olive oil producers from other parts of the world will follow suit if they have not done so already. Place of origin is no guarantee of quality, but at least if the label suggests the oil was made in Italy by Old World crofters and the print states that it actually comes from many sources around the Mediterranean, you will know better than to pay an elevated price for the stuff.

Sometimes information on the label is in excruciatingly tiny type but eventually, even if you have to use a magnifying glass, you may find a line that says: "Produced in Bari, Italy, from olives grown in Greece, Morocco, and Tunisia." Or something similar. More conscientious producers may give you more information, such as the variety of cultivars used, the date of the harvest, and the date of bottling. Only the date of bottling, or the use-by date, which is 18 months from bottling, is at this writing required by law. Harvest date is the most relevant information of all, but only the very top producers include it on the label. Olive oil, both top-quality and industrial, is customarily kept in silos and only bottled right before it is sent to market. Thus an oil can be and often is bottled two, and sometimes even three, years after harvest. The expiration date, curiously, doesn't go into effect until the oil is bottled. So an oil that was made in October 2011, say, might be bottled in July 2013 and carry a "use-by" date of January 2015—at which point it will be almost four years old. All perfectly legal, if demonstrably unscrupulous—as an Australian producer told me, "Two-year-old olive oil should feed the biodiesel industry." (I don't agree with his observation, but I get his point.)

All things being equal, an ideal label might read something like this: "Made from Koroneiki olives grown on our Astikas estate in the PDO [Protected Denomination of Origin] Kolymvari Chania, on the island of Crete. Stone-ground and milled on the estate. Harvested in November 2012 and bottled in April 2013. Certified organic." This is an actual label from Biolea, a lovely oil produced by George and Christine Dimitriadis on their family farm in the mountains of western Crete.

But isn't it enough that the label says "extra-virgin"? Is that not a guarantee of quality? Well, no, unfortunately. Some of the most indifferent oils on the market fall within the parameters of extra-virgin, which, after all, is a pretty loose definition. I noted earlier that 0.8 percent free oleic acid and a peroxide level of 20, the limitations set by the International Olive Council, are not in fact very stringent. Indeed, producers of fine oils that I know all over the Mediterranean would fall on their swords rather than send out an oil with those qualifications. In brief, producers of the finest oils are looking for quality markers below 0.2 percent maximum free oleic acid and around 5 or 6 for the peroxide content.

What about "first cold pressing"? The terminology is still used by many producers, both artisanal and industrial, on their labels, and it is beloved of food writers, who wax into almost orgasmic descriptions of the aromas and flavors of "first cold pressing." But, honestly, the term has little meaning and even less value as a descriptor. All extra-virgin olive oils, in order to qualify for that grade, must come from the first extraction of the olives— and there is no other separation of oil from the fruit, unless it is the chemical treatment of the dregs that produces pomace oil, as noted previously. To be called extra-virgin, oil must be from the original, and the only, pressing of the olives. Furthermore, even to talk about "pressing" gives a misleading idea, since almost all extra-virgin oil in commerce these days is made by centrifugal extraction rather than by crushing the olives and pressing the paste. Even the few producers who still crush olives with granite stones usually extract oil from the paste by centrifugal flow rather than by pressing. Perhaps labels would be more

accurate if they read "original extraction," but unfortunately the words don't have the same crème-de-la-crème tone as "first cold pressing."[3]

Another quality marker that you will find on labels is "protected denomination of origin" (DOP in Italy, DO in Spain, PDO in Greece, AOC in France), a designation that is granted by EU authorities in Brussels but regulated by a particular country's Ministry of Agriculture, working with local producers to set standards. If you're familiar with the French wine term *appellation controlée*, you know that this means the product (wine, oil, cheese, or other artisanal food) is produced within a specified geographic area and certain well-defined limits. In the case of olive oil, the limits almost always include the varieties of olive that can be used and possibly the harvest dates permitted, but there will also be quality controls that go beyond what has been set up by the International Olive Council, the idea being to create a flavor profile that is particular and distinctive to a region. Tasting panels determine whether or not an oil will receive the coveted seal indicating a protected denomination of origin, and this panel test must take place each time a product is finished. In other words,

---

3. It is sometimes stated that "extra-virgin olive oil" comes from the first pressing, while plain "olive oil" comes from a second pressing. As noted on page 93, this is simply not true.

just because your olive oil received the seal last year is no guarantee that its quality will be sufficient to receive the seal this year.

So, yes, a seal of controlled denomination of origin, or its less stringent counterpart, PGI (or IGP), protected geographic indication, can point you in the direction of a well-made oil. (For Denomination of Origin, all phases of production must take place within a specified geographic area; for Geographic Indication, not all phases must take place there—so you could presumably have olives grown in another region and processed in Tuscany, for instance, hardly a stout recommendation.) But keep in mind that all these designations are assigned *at the time the oil is produced*. What happens to that oil between the moment of production and the moment your hand reaches for it on a grocery shelf is unfortunately unknowable, and all sorts of dire things could be hiding behind that label.

So the final bit of advice for purchasing good, reliable, well-made olive oil is this: Taste. And taste. And taste. As often as you can. Not every store, by any means, will permit tasting or even think that it's a remarkably efficient sales pitch. Some years ago, when I was in the business of selling olive oil, among other food products, I could not convince my partners that opening a bottle of a prized oil and offering a sample to customers would in any way increase sales. All they could see was the price of the opened bottle, and to their minds, it was a waste. But shops run by smart retailers, such as Market Hall Foods in Oakland, California, Zingerman's in Ann Arbor, Michigan, Di Palo's in New York City, and others in other parts of the country, have learned over the years that the best way to seduce customers into buying fine oils is to first give them a taste. And encourage them to taste some more.

Another fine opportunity to taste is offered at the Culinary Institute of America at Greystone in the Napa Valley, where the unique OliveToLive system, developed at Villa Campestri in Italy, allows visitors to the school's Wine Spectator Restaurant and Flavor Bar a chance to sample a selection of oils from Italy, Spain, and California, all in a state as close to immediate post-harvest freshness as is humanly possible. And if you find one or two that you especially like, you can have a bottle filled fresh from the OliveToLive machine to take home. If the system can demonstrate success, which is still uncertain at this writing, perhaps others will invest in similar methods of guaranteeing high quality and fresh flavors.

As well, there are more and more small shops dedicated to olive oil opening across the United States. In my experience, most of these are in some way offshoots of an outfit in Berkeley, California, called Veronica Foods, which provides the expertise and the oils for such places. In my experience, too, most of the olive oils come from the southern hemisphere, and while the quality is generally good, it is seldom exceptional. These are good places to get introduced to olive oil but not to experience excellence. There is, moreover, an unfortunate concentration on flavored oils (and flavored vinegars) with odd ingredients. You will never be able to understand the true taste of high-quality oil when it has been flavored with an extract of, say, Persian lime or chipotle peppers or something called "Tuscan herbs."

In rare parts of the United States where olive oil is actually produced—and that means, to all intents and purposes, in California, although production is spreading in Texas and southern Oregon, among other less likely regions—you should be able to taste on the spot, just as you can at a winery. While this will give you a sense only of one producer's oils, it will give you a very strong understanding of what fresh, well-made oil should taste like, especially if you can arrange this during the autumn harvest. (In California, that means late November.) Of course, best of all, for those who can afford it, is a trip to any part of the olive oil world at the time of harvest and processing, from late September until almost Christmas, depending on where in the world you are.[4] Traveling the back roads from mill to mill and from farm to farm, tasting as much as possible on the spot and in local restaurants, which almost always vaunt local production, will give you a terrific sense of the gamut of olive oil and what it can do.

And that explosive first taste of an oil fresh from the press is nothing short of a miracle. Would to god more people could experience it—the world of cheap industrial oils would quickly be wiped off the shelves.

Once you start tasting olive oil, really tasting it, you will become aware of the astonishing fact that extra-virgin olive oils come in an enormous gamut of flavors. This is what sensory scientists call a sensory profile, and they spend a great deal of time trying to figure out the profiles of various oils and how to describe them. One such description, widely used, consists of a spider graph—it looks like nothing so much as a rather lopsided spider web— that will show whether an oil is particularly bitter or spicy or has a pronounced flavor of, say, green tomatoes or citrus. Sometimes smart producers will put one of these spider graphs on a label as a way to help consumers understand before tasting what they can expect. I have to admit that I have never found these to be very helpful and in fact most of the time can't figure them out. And relating such a spider web profile to what I find in the bottle when I taste the oil is often impossible.

Another way of describing oils, which I find much more helpful, is verbally, in terms of what they actually taste like. Most oils can be classified under three broad generalizations (and do keep in mind that we are talking about fine extra-virgins, not about light or pure olive oils):

lightly fruity oils with a softness and delicacy to the flavor, and very mild hints of bitterness and pungency or piquancy;

more flavorful oils, with medium fruitiness and a rounded mouthfeel, well balanced among fruitiness, pungency, and bitterness, with a clean, fresh aroma;

intensely fruity oils, strongly flavored, with very perceptible bitterness and pungency, still well balanced but with what wine connoisseurs would call very forward flavors.

Beyond these generalizations, there is a broad range of aromas and flavors in individual oils. A lightly fruity Arbequina from Catalonia is often distinguished by fresh almond flavors, while a similarly lightly fruity Taggiasca oil from Liguria will recall ripe apples or even bananas. One slender volume in my ever-increasing library of books about olive oil has

---

4. In the southern hemisphere (New Zealand, Australia, South America, South Africa), that would be in April and May.

14 pages devoted to the different cultivars and different DOP and PGI blends in Italy alone. And it only discusses a mere 38 of the more than 400 cultivars that are known to exist in the country, not all of which are in even minor production.[5]

A person could clearly become quite obsessive about the whole question of pairing specific oils with specific foods or preparations, and I think we will see more and more chefs turning to this previously ignored field in the future, as more of them become aware of the fact that high-quality extra-virgin olive oils can be almost as varied in flavor profiles as fine wines and deserve a similar attention from conscientious cooks.

As far as home cooks and consumers are concerned, playing around with the many different flavors available in olive oils can be a lot of fun. Certainly any good kitchen should have at least two oils, one for all-purpose cooking and one for critical garnishes. But it's also good to keep in mind that for untold generations, cooks and chefs alike in Mediterranean countries have had one oil and one oil only—whatever was produced locally. This year's oil was used for garnishing, last year's for cooking, and that was that. So don't get too wound up in the task of making sure you have exactly the right oil for your tomato salad and that it's unlike the one you use for frying eggs. If you want to use the same oil for both, by all means do so. You are the final judge, and it's your own palate that will decide.

OKAY, SO NOW YOU HAVE TASTED, SAMPLED, STUDIED, SELECTED, AND paid for your olive oil and brought it home. What happens next?

You might be tempted, if it's an especially handsome bottle or tin, to display it proudly next to your stove, where all your guests and friends can see how astute you are in your olive oil selection.

Don't do that!

Keep your olive oil stored in a cool, dark cupboard. The heat and lights of the kitchen are damaging to olive oil. In Tuscany, we keep our oil stored in a dark and unheated cantina (like an above-ground cellar) in stainless steel containers called *fusti*. In Maine, I'm lucky to have an unheated pantry where the oil is kept in tins in dark cupboards. On the counter space, in both kitchens, is enough oil for a couple of days' use, no more, kept in closed containers. Yes, of course it's boring to have to replenish the supply every two or three days, but better that than fine olive oil slowly deteriorating from the heat and light of a normal kitchen. Another tiresome but necessary task: Before replenishing that kitchen container, make sure it has been thoroughly drained, rinsed, and dried. The practice of simply topping up an olive oil cruet is the source of much of the rancid oil in restaurants: If the oil in the bottom of the container has already gone bad, fresh good oil added to it will quickly go bad also, contaminated by the bad oil left in the container.

One question I'm often asked: What about refrigerating olive oil? Isn't that a good way to keep it? I can think of situations where you might consider refrigerating olive oil, but

---

5. Capano, Giuseppe, & Luigi Caricato, *Olio: crudo e cotto*. Caricato is also the editor of the website Teatro Naturale, which frequently discusses, in Italian and unfortunately poorly translated English, issues relating to olives and olive oil.

they are not many. The biggest problem with the practice is the condensation it creates inside the container. The condensation drips into the oil and the water in the oil creates problems. In the presence of moisture, fermentation takes place and mold develops. However, in a very hypothetical situation—let's say you live in Phoenix, Arizona, you are going to be away for much of the summer, you can't leave an air-conditioner turned on, temperatures can get well up over 90°F and stay there for days at a time—in that case, yes, I would probably refrigerate olive oil if I had no cool basement in which to leave it. But that's an extreme state of affairs.

As for freezing olive oil, Graziano Decimi, a passionate producer who makes extraordinary olive oils all by himself on the banks of the Tiber River in Umbria, explained to me what happens when you freeze the precious substance: "It's fine as soon as you take it out of the freezer," he said. "But you have to use it right away because it will deteriorate rapidly." In brief, if you wanted to preserve the fresh taste of just-made olive oil for a salad in, say, May, freeze a small quantity in November, just enough to dress that salad. Any more than what you need will not be worth the effort, as it will go bad very quickly.

And now that you have your oil properly stored and a small container (or two or three if you have, like me, multiple oils) in the kitchen, it's time to start cooking.

How do you cook with extra-virgin olive oil?

Fearlessly!

Generously!

Use it, as home cooks and restaurant chefs do throughout the Mediterranean, for everything: sautéing, frying, stir-frying, poaching, baking, roasting, braising, as well as for garnishing both raw and cooked dishes, salads and bean soups, and eggs and tomato sauces, and with meat and fish and vegetables, and in desserts. In the next section you'll find a selection of recipes that all require extra-virgin olive oil to be all that they can be. But I would like for the moment to assume that you are a complete novice with extra-virgin olive oil and to introduce you to a few simple things that may convince you—if you still need convincing—of the virtues of this miracle ingredient. Then, once you are convinced, you may wish to go on and try a whole variety of different olive oils with different flavors, sometimes very subtly varied, at other times quite dramatically diverse.

Keep this in mind: Olive oil can exalt particular flavors in a dish but it can also suppress undesirable flavors (too much bitterness, for instance), as well as pull flavors together to meld them into a more integrated whole. Bill Briwa, a senior chef-instructor at the Culinary Institute of America's Greystone campus in St. Helena, California, is a man with a true gift for assessing flavor profiles and an inexhaustible curiosity about the uses to which olive oil can be put in the professional kitchen. Chef Briwa offers an example of a Picual olive oil from Spain (he uses Castillo de Canena's award-winning Picual) that, when added to a tomato sauce, gives new emphasis to the balance of sweetness and acidity in the sauce. Conversely, a Tuscan oil, with its natural bitterness (and here he uses Villa Campestri's Olio di Cosimo), actually loses that bitterness when poured in a little stream over slices of a fine beefsteak grilled rare.

So let's try a few experiments.

First of all, let's make a very simple salad dressing, since that seems to be the most natural, most common use of extra-virgin olive oil on the American table. Take out your favorite salad bowl. Use the flat blade of a knife to crush a clove of garlic on a chopping board. Coarsely chop about half of that clove (save the other half for the next little experiment) and put it in the bottom of the salad bowl along with a half teaspoon or so of fine sea salt. Now use the bowl of a soupspoon to crush the garlic into the salt, working it together until it makes a smooth paste. Stir in three spoonfuls of your favorite olive oil and another spoonful of freshly squeezed lemon juice or a mild or aged wine vinegar, whichever you prefer. (The size of the spoon you use doesn't matter—the important thing is the ratio of three to one, oil to acid.) Stir together, then pile rinsed and dried salad greens on top. Add whatever you wish by way of cucumbers or spring onions, radishes or tomatoes, and toss the salad ingredients in the dressing just before you bring the bowl to the table.

If you liked that (and I can't imagine you didn't), try it again, this time with a different olive oil, perhaps a spicier oil or a sweeter one, and compare the results. You can also play around with the mixture, adding fresh green herbs, such as basil, flat-leaf parsley, chives, chervil, tarragon, or mint; lovage is a favorite at our house. A French cook would probably stir in a small amount of fine Dijon mustard with the vinegar. A Greek cook might add a pinch of dried oregano. A Lebanese might stir in lemony-flavored sumac at the end.

I would be the first to admit that making this little mix is not quite as easy, nor quite as cheap, as opening a bottle of Wish-Bone dressing. If you use top-of-the-line Badia a Coltibuono olive oil, for instance, you will spend about $4 to dress a salad for six to eight people. (I don't calculate the rest of the ingredients, which cost pennies.) A cheaper but still very good Sicilian oil might cost $2.50 for the same quantity. But while that Wish-Bone costs as little as 14 cents an ounce, the advantages of a fine olive oil, in flavor, in nutritional value, and in satisfaction are enormous. Just check the ingredients list: Unlike commercial dressings, the one we've just made together is crafted almost exclusively from fine extra-virgin olive oil, while the commercial variety is made up of water (the number one ingredient in most commercial dressings), soybean oil (number two), and sugar (usually number three). I rest my case.

Let's try another experiment: Take a 28-ounce tin of best-quality whole canned plum tomatoes. Chop the rest of that garlic clove (or get out a fresh one) and add it to a small saucepan along with a couple tablespoons of olive oil. Set the pan over medium-low heat, and when the garlic bits have softened but not browned, add the whole tomatoes, crushing them in your hands as you add them to the pan. Leave the juices behind in the tin, in case you need to use them to thin out the sauce later. Let the sauce cook until it is very thick and the tomatoes are falling apart. Take the pan off the heat and, as soon as it has cooled a bit, use a stick blender (an immersion blender) to puree the tomatoes. If they seem very thick, add a little of the juice in the tin, but be sure to blend it in thoroughly. Now, off the heat but with the puree still hot, blend in about a third of a cup of extra-virgin olive oil, adding a couple of tablespoons at a time. Taste and add salt. Sometimes a bit of sugar is necessary to boost the flavor of canned tomatoes. You could also add a pinch of crushed dried chile pepper if you wish, or several grinds of black pepper from a mill. This will make a sauce that is unctuous, rich, and delicious, perfect for plain pasta and as good as ketchup (no, better!) to spoon over hamburgers or sliced meat loaf or grilled chicken.

One final experiment, easier than all the others:

STEP 1: Put a nice big russet potato into a 375°F oven and bake it until it is tender throughout—40 to 50 minutes should do it, depending on the size of the spud.

STEP 2: Put it on a plate and crack it open. Immediately douse it with a liberal help-ing of your finest extra-virgin—none of those food-writerly drizzles here, add a proper glug or two of oil. Plus a sprinkle of flaky sea salt and a couple of turns of the pepper mill.

STEP 3: Eat.

I can guarantee this will woo you away from butter and sour cream forever. One caveat, however: Nothing but the best extra-virgin will do. Any hint of rancidity or fustiness will only be emphasized by the heat of the potato.

And now, let's move on to cooking with olive oil:

What has caused more confusion than almost anything else having to do with extra-virgin olive oil is the question of the smoke point, the point at which an oil—any oil—when heated starts to smoke and break down into glycerol and free fatty acids. Not only does a smoking oil or fat give food an unpleasant taste, but there is also a good deal of evidence that consuming such fats on a regular basis is a very unhealthy practice.

Over and over again I have been told, by earnest, well-meaning chefs and accom-plished cooks alike, that "you can't cook with extra-virgin olive oil." This is a dictum taught in some of our finest cooking schools and repeated authoritatively in food magazines and newspaper food columns as well as on television food programs. The chorus sings almost with one voice: Regular olive oil for cooking and extra-virgin for garnishing only.[6]

Why?

Because the smoke point of extra-virgin is too low.

In fact, the chorus is wrong. It cannot be stated often enough or loudly enough: *The smoke point of extra-virgin olive oil is not low.* And the polyphenols in extra-virgin olive oil, which barely exist, if at all, in other oils, are a further protection against the breakdown of the oil under heat.

According to the International Olive Council (IOC), extra-virgin olive oil has a smoke point of 210°C (400°F). Other, less prejudiced experts say the smoke point is between 380° and 410°F, depending on the free acid level and the number of impurities (filtered oil is bet-ter for frying than unfiltered). Is that temperature low? I don't think so. *The Joy of Cooking*, that American household bible, recommends deep-fat frying at between 350° and 365°F. That is, if you want fried food that is cooked all the way through with a golden, crisp, greaseless coating, whether it's fish and chips, Southern fried chicken, apple fritters, or

---

6. Sometimes virgin olive oil is recommended for cooking, but as we've seen, virgin olive oil is a category that practically does not exist in commerce.

Maine fried clams. The whole purpose of deep-frying food, whether it's floured or not, breaded or not, in a batter or not, is to create a crisp, caramelized outer shell that seals the food quickly and protects the juiciness of the interior. Think of that Southern fried chicken and the pleasure of biting through the buttermilk-flour coating to reach the tasty, warm, and succulent bits of flesh inside—at a higher temperature than 355° or 360°F, you risk burning the outside coating while the inside may still be unpleasantly raw. Alternatively, if you fry at lower temperatures, the coating will absorb a great deal of fat, it will be soggy, and it will never develop that satisfyingly rich, golden, crunchy crust.

So where does this myth about the low smoke point of olive oil originate? It's not at all clear, but it has become ubiquitous. A corollary myth has it that somehow when you fry with olive oil it becomes a trans fat. This is physically and chemically impossible in a home or restaurant kitchen.

Most of the time, in any case, unless you're the proprietor of Freddie's Fabulous Fries, you will not be deep-fat frying, so there is no excuse for not using extra-virgin olive oil. But if you are the chef de cuisine at Freddie's, one thing to keep in mind is that olive oil for frying should not be used more than twice or maximum three times, since any oil (not just olive oil) degrades with each successive heating. All cooking oils, including extra-virgin olive oil, if used over and over again at high temperatures, as for deep-fat frying, will eventually oxidize and turn rancid.

California food writer (and expert olive oil taster) Fran Gage, whose book *The New American Olive Oil* gives the skinny on California producers, even deep-fries perfect french fries using California extra-virgin—and there's no reason to think other extra-virgins might not work just as well. Gage soaks the potatoes before peeling and slicing them, and soaks them again once they've been prepared. Then she heats the oil to precisely 380°F and away she goes. Even a little higher than that temperature, she says, will work, and the oil will definitely not smoke.

I do not suggest that you use an expensive, high-quality extra-virgin olive oil for deep-fat frying, any more than I would suggest that you use a Premier Cru Mouton Rothschild in your coq au vin. Not only would it be ridiculously expensive, but the extreme heat of frying (or of boiling) would end up destroying all the flavor complexities of both oil and wine. But a less expensive extra-virgin can be a fine choice for the occasional exercise in deep-fat frying—there are any number of Greek and Spanish oils that are reasonably priced, especially if bought in 3- or 5-liter tins, and these are excellent for the task. And extra-virgin olive oil, heated to the correct temperature before the food is added, is notably lighter and easier to digest than food fried in other fats.

All the other methods of cooking apart from deep-fat frying are also excellent ways to use extra-virgin olive oil. In this, as in so many kitchen techniques, I follow the lead of expert cooks all over the Mediterranean. Sautéing meat or fish, frying an egg for breakfast or a late-night supper, poaching a center cut of salmon, tossing steamed greens, or starting off a soup or stew or pasta sauce with that Mediterranean standby, chopped onion-garlic-carrot-celery-parsley—all call for extra-virgin olive oil, and the oil used almost always adds immeasurably to the flavor potential of the dish in question.

The late Marcella Hazan, dean of Italian cooking in America, rose to the olive oil challenge when she took to task science journalist Harold McGee, who wrote about science and food for *The New York Times*. McGee claimed that using extra-virgin olive oil for cooking is a waste of money, since the oil, once heated and held for a period of time, loses all its flavors. Nonsense, said Marcella; what matters is not how the oil tastes when you're done with it but how the good flavors of a fine oil are transferred to whatever is cooked in it, whether simple vegetables, braised chicken or fish, an aromatic pasta sauce, or even a humble fried egg. "What a good olive oil transfers to the food that is cooked in it," Hazan went on to say, "is something that *only* a good olive oil can bestow: aroma and depth of flavor." Just fry an egg in extra-virgin and you'll agree.

María José San Román is the chef-owner of a string of eating establishments in the southeastern Spanish city of Alicante—a delightful port town with a broad, palm-shaded esplanade running along the seafront. One of her restaurants has a Michelin star and another was hailed in the gastronomic press as the best tapas bar in Spain. When I first met her, María José was the Spanish saffron queen. She had made herself an advocate for locally grown saffron and was earnestly developing recipes for that brilliant spice. Since then, however, she has discovered olive oil. No, that's wrong: María José, like all Spanish cooks, has always used olive oil. But, like most Spanish cooks, previously she used it with considerable indifference. It was for her, as we've said so often, kitchen grease, pure and simple.

"There's an intensive use of olive oil all over Spain," she said to me when I visited her in Alicante. But the quality, she admitted, was not something she had ever paid much attention to, and at that time she was using seed or vegetable oil for frying. And then she was introduced to some of the top producers of southern Spanish oil, in particular to Rosa Vañó, marketing director of the Vañó family firm, Castillo de Canena, and María José's life, or that is to say her kitchen, changed. "Why are my calamari, my rice, my tomatoes so much better?" she asked me rhetorically, as we sat at the bar of her Taberna del Gourmet on the Alicante esplanade and munched on fried potatoes with a bowl of garlicky aioli for dipping. "I only started using olive oil to this extent two years ago," she said, "but it has made such a difference. We have two fryers with 25 liters of olive oil each and we change them every two days. Yes, I spend more. But I can charge more too because the quality is so much greater. We live on olive oil—it's my new religion."

Of course, I think back to my introduction to olive oil in Spain way back in the 1960s, when the oil was uniformly rancid and the odor of frying oil from the cooking pots of my neighborhood in Madrid was overpowering every day at lunchtime. What a long way Spain has come since then, supplying much of the world with some of the finest olive oils in existence. It has been a great leap forward . . . but there is still a long, long way to go. I dream of a day when most forward-thinking consumers will understand exactly what superior extra-virgin olive oil is, how it's made, what it tastes and smells like, and how it can be used in the kitchen and at the table. I dream of restaurants that understand the precious nature of this ingredient and how it must be treated and presented, with respect and even, perhaps, with love. And I dream of healthy children growing up with sound, wholesome diets based on Mediterranean principles of fresh food enhanced with the most nutritious, most delicious, and most interesting condiment, extra-virgin olive oil.

INTRODUCTION *to the* RECIPES

Most of the recipes in this collection come from Mediterranean kitchens, where cooks and chefs have been using olives and olive oil for thousands of years, developing an impressive body of culinary wisdom as they have experimented, studied, tasted, learned from each other and from previous generations and then passed that learning on—exchanging information, adding new ingredients (the tomato above all), and refining and improving basic ideas. At the same time, I've also included a few recipes from other parts of the world, even from India, a cuisine that is only now discovering olive oil for its healthful properties and adapting recipes to use oil instead of traditional ghee, which, as a butterfat, is high in saturated fat. I've also added a few fundamental American recipes like chile-stuffed steak, buttermilk biscuits, and Southern fried chicken, all of which have been adapted to olive oil—just to prove that you don't have to have a Mediterranean grandmother to cook with olive oil.

In truth, olive oil can be used in almost any recipe that calls for fat, whether butter, lard, coconut oil, or some more esoteric substance. In most cases, it's simply a straightforward exchange, a tablespoon of olive oil for a tablespoon of butter or whatever. Only in baking must the cook be attuned to the fact that olive oil is a liquid, whereas both butter and lard are solids. So a simple exchange doesn't always work and some adjustment is required. But I'll explain all that in the section on cakes, where it's most important.

Be advised that the olive oil used herein is always and only extra-virgin. This is the only oil allowed in my kitchens, whether in Tuscany, Maine, or New York. Sometimes I do use a little butter—I find it helpful for that business of "greasing and flouring" a cake pan, when olive oil doesn't really stick to the sides of the pan. But regular olive oil, light olive oil, or—perish the thought—pomace oil has no place in any kitchen that is dedicated to creating healthful, delicious food. Only extra-virgin will do.

A Note About Ingredients

OLIVE OIL: I cannot stress it strongly enough: The only olive oil used in my kitchen is extra-virgin olive oil. I don't call for extra-virgin as such in the recipes that follow because I want cooks and readers to understand that it is a given and that there's no reason to use regular olive oil or light olive oil. Extra-virgin is the key to excellence for everything—cooking, garnishing, topping the breakfast toast or the baked potato for supper, dribbling atop the soup at lunch, whatever. Except on rare occasions, I don't use fine estate-bottled oils for cooking—that would be a waste of the exquisite flavors that tend to dissipate with heat. Instead I buy from trustworthy distributors

3- or 5-liter tins of excellent-quality extra-virgin that has nonetheless been economically produced to give good value for money. You'll find some of these listed in the Appendix (page 326).

OLIVES: The selection of olives in American supermarkets has improved enormously in recent years, and we now have available brine-cured green olives, salt-cured black ones (often mistakenly referred to as "oil-cured"), purple tart-sweet Kalamatas, tiny green Picholines, big fat Gordals or Sevillanos and even fatter Bella di Cerignola. Beyond supermarkets, specialty food stores stock an even greater variety, and you might find small Amfissa olives from Greece or black salt-cured Nyons and tiny wrinkled Niçoises from France; seek these out and taste them—you may discover as many different uses as there are olives.

One type of olive to be avoided is the canned black olive, often called, somewhat unfairly, "California style." These are artificially ripened green olives, cured in a lye solution to turn them black, canned and then heat-treated to prevent contamination. Any flavor is, to put it gently, absent.

SWEET AND HOT (CHILE) PEPPERS: I use a wide variety of different kinds of peppers, starting with sweet peppers, meaning mild fresh peppers with plenty of flavor but no discernible heat. The most familiar are bell peppers, available throughout the year in every supermarket produce section, but there are also seasonally available, in supermarkets and farmer's markets alike, peppers such as banana, cubanelle, pimento, ox horn or bull's horn, and others, all of them "sweet" in the sense that they're not at all hot. If a recipe calls for sweet peppers, any one of these may be used unless a specific kind is mentioned.

For fresh hot chile peppers, I tend to use whatever my market offers me, usually serranos or jalapeños—but not fiercely hot ones such as habaneros or Scotch bonnets.

For dried chiles, there is a remarkable selection from all over the world, although not every one of these is available everywhere. My first choice for dried ground red chile pepper is almost always *piment d'Espelette*, from the Basque region of southern France—a ground chile that, while spicy, fragrant, and flavorful, is lightly pungent but not at all fiery. After that come various ground chiles from Spain: *pimentón de Murcia*, or its smoky cousin *pimentón de la Vera*, both of which come in hot, medium, and sweet (*dulce*) varieties; then the flaked or crushed red chile pepper, so-called Aleppo (little enough actually coming from Aleppo these days, unfortunately) or Turkish red pepper, from the Middle East. Occasionally, whole dried red chiles are called for, and when that's the case, I look for the milder flavors of New Mexico (Anaheim), pasilla, or ancho chiles.

TOMATOES: The very best tomatoes, of course, are those that come fully ripened in the sun fresh from your own or a neighbor's garden. But tomatoes are also one of the vegetables (fruits) that take well to canning, and good cooks are never afraid to use canned tomatoes. Just be sure you get the very best quality you can find. This does not always mean imported. San Marzano tomatoes from the countryside around Naples in Italy are probably the finest in the world, but they are expensive, and Muir Glen tomatoes, organically grown in California, run a close second. When a small amount of very intense tomato flavor is required, I use tomato paste, also sometimes called tomato concentrate. Sicilian *estratto di pomodoro* (extract of tomatoes) is a dense paste made by crushing fully ripe tomatoes and drying the paste in the hot Sicilian sun; if you can find it, it's the best of all and seems to give a sunny Sicilian flavor to whatever it's added to.

CHEESE: The finest imported parmigiano reggiano is, in my humble opinion, the greatest cheese in the world. But it is expensive and, if you wish, where parmigiano reggiano is called for, you may substitute a similar type of Italian cheese called Grana Padano.

RICOTTA: True ricotta is made by reheating the whey after cheese is made. The word comes from the Italian and means "re-cooked." There is a regrettable fad, especially in restaurants, for "homemade" ricotta—basically, whole milk to which a small amount of lemon juice or vinegar is added to curdle it. This is a far cry from the real thing.

One good source for real ricotta: Paula Lambert's Mozzarella Company (www.mozzco.com). They are located in Dallas but will ship all over the country.

HERBS AND SPICES: Parsley, sage, rosemary, thyme—all such green herbs, including basil and tarragon, are far, far better fresh than dried. The singular exception is oregano, which has a far more pungent flavor when dried. If you can find it, Greek or Sicilian oregano has the finest flavor.

Two rather unusual dried herbs are used in the recipes: Wild fennel pollen, made from the mustard yellow flowers of wild fennel that grows in abundance all over Italy; and za'atar, a combination of wild thyme, sesame seeds, and tart sumac that is a favorite seasoning in Lebanon and Palestine. Both are available from specialty stores and mail-order outlets.

Spices used here are commonly available—cinnamon, cloves, caraway, cumin, and so forth. But they are all much more flavorful if they are ground to order, so to speak. Keep a small coffee grinder especially for grinding spices (and wipe it out after each use so as not to contaminate the next spice with a previous one). And take a tip from the Indian kitchen and, before grinding, roast spices in a dry skillet just until the aromas start to arise, then transfer to the coffee mill for grinding. The flavors are astounding.

PANCETTA, BACON, PROSCIUTTO, GUANCIALE, JAMÓN SERRANO, AND JAMÓN DE PATA NEGRA OR JAMÓN IBÉRICO: These are all slightly different types of cured pork, made mostly in Italy and Spain, and used both as hors d'oeuvres or tapas and, when chopped with onions, garlic, parsley, and other aromatics, to flavor many dishes. The last is a very expensive ham from Spain, but pancetta, guanciale, and *jamón serrano* should not break anyone's budget for the small amount used as the basis for soups, stews, and pasta sauces.

BREAD AND BREAD CRUMBS: I refer often to "a rustic country loaf," by which I mean a bread that is full of flavor and texture, usually made at least in part with whole wheat flour, and with a thick crust that comes from or mimics baking in a wood-fired oven. I keep the ends of such a loaf and when I have an accumulation, I whizz them in the food processor to make bread crumbs. The crumbs can be frozen for long storage, or they can be toasted in a low oven to dry them thoroughly, after which they don't need refrigeration.

SMALL DISHES:
ANTIPASTI,
MEZE, TAPAS,
and SNACKS

I T MIGHT BE AN ARRAY OF ANTIPASTI IN A SICILIAN SEASIDE TRATTORIA (fine slivers of cured bottarga served with lemon juice and a dribble of Nocellara del Belice oil) or a selection of tapas at a crowded standup bar in Barcelona or San Sebastian (tiny baby squid called *chipirones*, fried to a crisp in Catalonia's sweet Arbequina oil); it might be a rich assortment of meze in a restaurant on Beirut's Corniche (plump falafel with their cumin fragrance, deep-fried in oil from the Janoub, the hills of southern Lebanon) or something similar near the Galata Bridge in Istanbul (*midia dolmasi*, mussels stuffed with savory rice and onions sautéed in oil from Turkey's Aegean coast). But wherever you go in the Mediterranean, you'll find menus so abundant with these little dishes that it's hard even to know where to begin. Whole cookbooks could be written, indeed have been written, about the small dishes of the Mediterranean, and I encourage you to consult other writers for ideas.

Above all, in your antipasti or meze selection, don't by any means be limited to what I've included here. Many other dishes in this book could serve in the same role. On the other hand, some of these small dishes could easily become main courses or sides if served with a few other things to flesh out a meal. The zucchini fritters on page 127, for instance, are terrific with any kind of lamb dish, while the roasted red peppers on page 125 are a delicious accompaniment to braised pork or grilled pork sausages. And the Provençal tarte au chèvre (page 133) makes a fine lunch or light supper dish when served with a fresh green leafy salad.

·

BRUSCHETTA, FETT'UNTA, *and* PA AMB TOMAQUET

Toasted bread lavished with olive oil—you can't get more basic than that. Bruschetta (or *fett'unta* in some parts of Tuscany) is the universal treat in Italian olive mills as the new oil comes from the press. There's often a fireplace in a corner of the mill with a couple of old guys patiently toasting slices of bread over the embers. Once done, each slice is rubbed gently with a cut clove of garlic (and in Tuscany and Umbria, where unsalted bread is the rule, sprinkled with a bit of sea salt) and then generously lavished with fresh new oil. And that's as good as it gets.

In Catalonia, the treatment has evolved into a universal breakfast, served all over the region all year round, but especially gratifying in the café bars inside Barcelona's Boqueria market. *Pa amb tomaquet* is Catalan for "bread with tomato," and in this case, after the garlic but before the oil, a half of a very ripe tomato is rubbed over and over into the toasted bread until all the juice and flesh have been absorbed and nothing but the tomato skin remains to be discarded. Then the olive oil goes on top and the treat is consumed, along with a big cup, a bowl really, of milky coffee.

For years my breakfast has regularly consisted of a slice of toasted bread with a spoonful of fresh olive oil poured over the top. To friends who look askance I say: Don't knock it till you've tried it. And I've gained lots of converts that way. But it must be really good bread, nicely browned in the toaster—or better yet over a wood fire when it's possible—and of course, it goes without saying, it must be the finest, freshest olive oil you can find. A little crunchy Maldon salt on top makes a perfect breakfast.

PANE CUNZATA *(Garnished Bread)* *from a* SICILIAN FRANTOIO

During the harvest in Sicily, you're apt to get a more elaborate treat at the *frantoio*, or olive mill. There it's called *pane cunzata*, meaning garnished bread. On the island they favor a sesame-coated bread made from locally grown and milled semolina, preferably in the form of small buns or loaves, one to a person, hot and fresh from the oven so the bread fully absorbs all the added flavors. But failing that authentic touch, a soft baguette will do, as will a crusty ciabatta.

If you're familiar with the fabled New Orleans sandwich called a muffaletta, filled with olives, sliced meats, and cheese, you'll recognize *pane cunzata* as its direct ancestor, no doubt brought by Sicilians who flocked to the Crescent City in the nineteenth century.

Note that marinated white anchovy fillets, widely available at deli counters, could be substituted for the salted anchovies.

MAKES 6 SERVINGS

6 freshly baked small breads, 1 per serving, preferably sesame-coated semolina breads

¾ cup fine olive oil, preferably fresh Sicilian oil (olio nuovo or olio novello)

2 tablespoons dried oregano

Sea salt and freshly ground black pepper

6 small ripe tomatoes, very thinly sliced

4 ounces pecorino toscano or caciocavallo cheese, very thinly sliced

6 salted anchovies, rinsed, boned, filleted, and chopped, or 12 to 15 anchovy fillets

½ cup coarsely chopped pitted black olives

½ cup coarsely chopped pitted green olives

THE bread should be fresh and hot. If you haven't made it yourself, set the loaves in a hot (375°F) oven for 15 minutes or so, to warm all the way through and crisp the outside crust. Remove the breads from the oven and slice each one in half.

OR, if you're using regular bread, slice it about ½ inch thick and toast it brown on both sides.

DOUSE each half or each slice while still hot with an abundance of oil and sprinkle heavily with the oregano, salt, and pepper. Then on one half of each bread, arrange slices of tomato and cheese, as well as the anchovy bits and the olives. Top with the other half and press together firmly.

SET aside for 15 minutes or so to let the bread absorb the flavors before serving.

Note: The simplest *pane cunzata* is made just with olive oil, oregano, salt, and lots of black pepper, but more elaborate combinations are also possible, such as adding pickled vegetables and/or salami or other cured pork sausage to the above ingredients. Keep in mind, however, that whatever you add should be thinly sliced—and that the point of the sandwich is to appreciate the flavors of fresh new oil.

SICILIAN FRIED ALMONDS

Gianfranco Becchina makes Olio Verde at his picturesque estate in Castelvet-rano, southern Sicily, where the Nocellara del Belice olives—so called because the round, green fruits look just like unripe walnuts (*noce* in Italian)—stand in disciplined rows, interspersed with lemon trees that may account for some of the citrusy flavors in Olio Verde.

Sicily also produces outstanding almonds, so the combination with great olive oil is a natural. But be careful: These are addictive.

One other caution: Do, please, use a frying thermometer to be sure the oil is the right temperature. It always seems to take much longer to get up to 360°F than I anticipate. For more advice, see the section on cooking with olive oil, pages 100–105, and the instructions for frying on page 126.

If you have a source of freshly blanched almonds, so much the better, but you may have to blanch the almonds yourself. To do so, bring a large pot of water to a rolling boil, add the almonds, and let them return to a boil for about 30 seconds, then drain into a colander and run cold water over them. The skins should slip right off. Spread the blanched almonds on paper towels and pat them dry; otherwise, they will make the hot oil splatter, risking burns. If any of the skins don't slip off easily, return them to the boiling water for another 5 to 10 seconds.

MAKES 2 TO 3 CUPS ALMONDS

1 to 2 cups olive oil

1 pound freshly blanched almonds (see headnote)

Sea salt

YOU may fry the almonds in batches, in which case you may only need 1 cup of the oil. Heat it to frying temperature (about 360°F) in a deep, heavy saucepan suitable for deep-fat frying. Next to the stove, have a rack or a colander covered with paper towels on which to drain the almonds. When the oil is hot, add half (or all, depending on the size of your saucepan) the almonds and cook, stirring gently with a wooden spoon, until the almonds are evenly toasted and golden. This will take 4 to 6 minutes. Just as soon as they are golden, use a slotted spoon to scoop them out and set them to drain on the paper towels. Don't let them get too dark: The almonds actually will continue to cook a little after they've been removed from the oil.

continued

WHEN all the almonds are done, toss them in a bowl with sea salt. Set aside for an hour or so to cool, then serve. The almonds keep well in a cookie tin. Leftover oil may be strained through a fine-mesh sieve and used once or twice more for frying, after which it should be discarded.

Notes: American cooks may want to use a less expensive oil than Becchina's Olio Verde, but it should still be extra-virgin olive oil of high quality with a softly rounded, not too fruity flavor.

Roasting the almonds in the oven is another possibility. The nuts don't roast as evenly, but the process uses much less oil. To roast, heat the oven to 350°F. Combine the almonds in a bowl with ⅓ to ½ cup oil and toss to make sure they're all well covered, then spread them in a single layer on a baking sheet and transfer to the hot oven. Roast for about 5 minutes, then remove, stir the nuts, and return to the oven for another 5 to 10 minutes, until they are golden.

A nice touch: While the almonds are still hot, that is, right out of the frying pan or the oven, toss them with some sea salt, a little ground red chile pepper (*piment d'Espelette* is great), and a dried herb. Indians use ground ajwain seeds mixed with cardamom and cumin, while Middle Easterners might use a finely ground aromatic mix called za'atar, made up of wild thyme, sumac, and sesame; in Mexico, Provence, and southern Italy, dried oregano could be sprinkled on. Whatever you use, however, be cautious—the herbs, like the olive oil, should accent but not dominate the rich flavor of the almonds.

Curing Olives, Sicilian Style

October 4, the feast day of St. Francis of Assisi, is the day to start pickling or curing olives, or so says Salvatore Denaro, a Sicilian chef who has lived and worked in Umbria for years. "After that date," Chef Salva says, "the olives start to make oil"—and then they're no good for pickling. He calls olives the food of Ulysses, reminding me of what Lawrence Durrell, the great Mediterranean memoirist, said about their flavor: "Older than meat, older than wine, a taste as old as cold water." Salvatore cures his olives with the umbrella-like seed cases of wild fennel, pushing green olives, or ones that are streaked with darker color, down into the brine and then pressing the wild fennel on top. Covered but not sealed, the olives cure for several months, after which they are deliciously redolent of the wild fennel's pungent, anise-like flavor. Then he takes them out of the brine and transfers them to a jar with plenty of chopped celery leaves, dried red chile peppers, and lots of fresh oil to bathe them.

OLIVES

Curing Your Own

If you are lucky enough to have access to freshly harvested olives, whether green, partially ripe, or fully ripe and black, there are a number of easy traditional ways to cure them.

FOR FULLY RIPENED BLACK OLIVES:

This is best done in a basket set over one of those old basins or mixing bowls that you have tucked away in the back of a kitchen cupboard—one you don't mind staining with the liquid that drains from the olives.

Layer the olives with large-grain sea salt; first a layer of salt, then a layer of olives, another layer of salt, and so on until the olives are all used up. The topmost layer should be salt. Set aside for several weeks but do not refrigerate. Gradually, the olives will yield their juice (but not their oil) and absorb the salt. Stir the olives occasionally; you may have to add a little more salt from time to time. In the end, the olives will be quite shriveled and both meaty and salty in flavor. Shake the salt off completely, then coat the olives very lightly with a small quantity of olive oil—they should not be sitting in oil. These are often sold as oil-cured olives. Of course they're not cured in olive oil at all, but in salt.

They will keep for several months and just get better with time.

FOR GREEN OR RIPENING—JUST TURNING COLOR—OLIVES:

In the Mediterranean, adept home cooks crack each olive with a stone. I find it easier to make a little cut along one side of each olive, discarding any bruised or otherwise defective olives. Rinse the olives to rid them of any dust, then pack them in a large mason jar or similar lidded container.

Add seasonings to the jar: Dried wild fennel blossoms are used in Tuscany and Umbria, but they may not be easy to find. You could add a spoonful of fennel seeds or celery seeds (or both) to the jar; a small dried hot chile pepper; a spoonful of pickling spices; some cracked black peppercorns; or fresh dill or fennel tops, rinsed and dried.

Make a strong brine: For every 2 quarts (8 cups) water, add 1 cup white vinegar and ¾ cup pickling salt, meaning uniodized salt—not ordinary table salt. When the salt has dissolved in the mixture, give it a stir and pour it over the olives in the jar. Close the jar tightly and set aside in a dark cupboard or pantry for at least 3 weeks, turning the jar over every couple of days to redistribute the seasonings.

These will keep in their jar for 3 or 4 months, or even longer. If they form a little white scum on the top, simply lift it off and discard it.

MARINATING CURED OLIVES

The olives sold from bins in the deli department of most supermarkets often seem all to taste alike. You can boost the flavors and personalize the selection by marinating them for several days or even weeks. For a pound of plain cured black olives, I use a basic mixture made up of ½ cup cool water, ¼ cup red wine vinegar, and ½ cup olive oil. Taste the olives and if they are salty, add just ½ teaspoon salt to the mix. If they're not salty, you can add as much as a full teaspoon. Put all these ingredients in a glass jar and add aromatics as you wish. Here are some suggestions, but please don't put all these in the jar at once. One or two or perhaps three will suffice, among them crushed red chile pepper (*piment d'Espelette* is especially nice if you can find it), crumbled bay leaf, dried oregano, dried orange peel, slivered fresh orange or lemon peel, very finely minced garlic, smoked paprika (Spanish *pimentón de la Vera*), crushed cardamom, or coriander. Experiment with various spices and spice mixtures—but be cautious. Always remember the less-is-more admonition of the great food writer Elizabeth David: "Just because a teaspoon of something is good doesn't mean that two teaspoons will be twice as good."

Shake the jar vigorously, then pour the contents over the olives. You should have enough liquid to just immerse the olives. Cover the container and set aside in a cool place to marinate for several days before using.

For a pound of plain green olives, I use the following, slightly different mixture:

1 teaspoon coriander seeds

½ teaspoon cardamom seeds

½ teaspoon cumin seeds

1 teaspoon or more good-quality ground or crushed red chile pepper, such as piment d'Espelette or Aleppo pepper

3 tablespoons olive oil

1 tablespoon freshly squeezed orange juice

1 tablespoon freshly squeezed lemon juice

4 garlic cloves, crushed

Very thinly sliced orange wedges, peel and all

COMBINE the coriander, cardamom, and cumin in a small skillet over medium heat and toast the seeds until the fragrance starts to rise; be careful not to let the seeds burn. Transfer the toasted seeds to a clean coffee mill or spice grinder and add the chile pepper. Grind briefly—to a coarse texture, not a fine powder. Combine the spices in a bowl with the oil and citrus juices.

MINCE the garlic and coarsely chop the orange wedges and add to the bowl. Add the olives, stirring to mix well and coat the olives with the spicy mixture.

COVER the bowl with plastic wrap and set aside to marinate at room temperature for at least 6 hours before serving. The olives may also be stored in a jar, refrigerated, for 2 to 3 weeks, but they should always be brought to room temperature before serving.

Olive Oil with Popcorn

This is not a recipe but one of those tricks that at first glance astonishes and then quickly wins over the skeptic. Simply air-pop the popcorn and while it's still very hot, toss it with a tablespoon or two of olive oil, along with sea salt, just as you would with butter. For an added fillip, use the back of a spoon to crush a clove of garlic to a pulp with salt, then dissolve that in olive oil in a small skillet over low heat. Just warm the garlicky oil, but don't let the garlic actually cook. A pinch of ground red chile pepper is a nice addition, or a very small pinch of curry powder—just enough to make people say: Hmm, what's that interesting flavor, but not actually to recognize it.

TAPENADES

Tapenades, or olive pâtés, are typically served as part of an appetizer or antipasto with toasted grainy bread or crackers, but they also have a number of other kitchen uses. The word *tapenade* actually has little to do with olives. In fact, it refers to capers, which are called *tapéno* in Provençal, and capers are critical to the success of the pâte. If you're using salted capers, which most cooks prefer, be sure to allow 10 or 15 minutes to soak them in very warm water to rid them of excess salt. Drain them well and pat dry with paper towels.

Other uses of tapenades: Spread green or black tapenade on top of chicken breasts before roasting them in the oven, or smear over lamb chops immediately after grilling. Stir a dollop of tapenade into a warm bean or potato salad, with slivers of red onion and crumbled hard-boiled egg, and let the tapenade melt into the dish before serving. Or mix it with a fresh, young goat cheese to make a different take on the usual dip or spread. A tapenade is also great on pasta, with a little more oil added to make it more of a sauce.

Both of these tapenades can be made in advance and kept in the refrigerator with a thin film of oil on top until ready to serve. Bring them to room temperature before serving and stir the oil film down into the tapenade before setting it out. Spread the tapenade on crisp crackers or toasts, top with a caper, and serve.

CLASSIC PROVENÇAL BLACK OLIVE TAPENADE

Many different black olives will work with this but *not* the so-called California style, most of which come in a can. These are not really black olives at all but rather green olives that have been blackened by a chemical process that leaves them quite flavorless. If you use Kalamata olives, which are very juicy, pit, chop, and drain them well before adding to the tapenade to avoid having too much liquid in the mix.

MAKES 1½ TO 2 CUPS

1 pound pitted black olives, coarsely chopped

¼ cup salted capers, soaked, drained, dried, and chopped

1 garlic clove, coarsely chopped

½ (6-ounce) can yellowfin or albacore tuna, drained

1 to 2 tablespoons brandy

½ cup olive oil

Juice of ½ lemon

COMBINE the olives, capers, garlic, tuna, 1 tablespoon of the brandy, and the oil in a food processor and buzz briefly, pulsing, just until all the ingredients are well combined. Tapenade should not be a smooth paste but should have a coarse texture. Stir in the lemon juice. Taste and add more brandy or a few more drops of lemon juice, if you wish.

Pinzimonio

Too simple to be dignified with the term recipe, this is made up of a selection of crisp, seasonal raw vegetables, appropriately trimmed and cut into slices or strips, and served with the very finest, freshest extra-virgin olive oil you can afford, plus flaky sea salt and fragrant black pepper, served in a mill for grinding. Each person at the table should have a little bowl or plate in which to combine oil with salt and pepper, and then dip vegetables in the combination. For vegetables, include at least three or four of the following: cucumbers, carrots, radishes, red or green sweet peppers, fennel, celery, thin wedges of red radicchio or green cabbage, artichokes sliced vertically if they are young and tender without a choky center, spring onions or scallions, slender spears of raw asparagus, or crisp raw green beans in season. A plate of fine prosciutto and thin slices of bread are a nice accompaniment, but anything else would be gilding the lily. Don't forget paper napkins, however, for sopping up spills.

GREEN OLIVE TAPENADE

Use plain, brine-cured green olives for this. The combination of anchovies, capers, and olives can result in a very salty mixture. The almonds help to balance the saltiness, but be sure to rinse the capers very well. Taste the olives and if they are also very salty, soak them for half an hour or so in warm water, then drain thoroughly before using.

2 plump garlic cloves, crushed and finely chopped

Grated zest and juice of ½ orange or 1 whole lemon, preferably organic

6 to 8 anchovy fillets, coarsely chopped (optional)

2 heaping tablespoons capers, preferably salted capers, soaked, rinsed, and dried

4 or 5 sprigs fresh thyme, leaves only, chopped (½ teaspoon)

1 cup coarsely chopped pitted green olives

¼ cup finely chopped raw almonds

¼ to ⅓ cup olive oil

Pinch of crushed or ground red chile pepper or freshly ground black pepper (optional)

COMBINE the garlic, orange zest and juice, anchovies if using, capers, and thyme in a food processor and pulse briefly to blend. Add the chopped olives and the almonds and pulse again to make a rough paste. With the processor on, slowly pour the oil into the mix. It can be as rough or as smooth as you wish. You may not need all the oil—there's sometimes a lot of oil in the olives themselves. Taste when it's the right consistency and add a little chile if you wish, or some black pepper. You may also wish to add a little more orange juice or some lemon juice if the mix is very salty.

Note: Greek cooks often add a teaspoon or more of ouzo to give a green olive tapenade just a hint of aniseed flavor.

ROASTED RED PEPPERS *with* ANCHOVIES *and* TOMATOES

My take on the pepper-and-anchovy antipasto that is so deservedly popular with Italian cooks is a little different from the usual, and very easy to throw together. Serve it as an antipasto, or a *contorno* to go with grilled meat or fish, or chop the finished peppers with all the other ingredients and use it to top a dish of pasta. I use big late summer peppers, mostly red but throwing in a few yellow ones for a colorful touch. I figure on half a pepper per serving—so two peppers will serve four, but use your judgment: Smaller peppers from the farmer's market might come out two to each serving.

MAKES 4 SERVINGS

2 big sweet red peppers (or 1 red and 1 yellow) or 4 medium peppers

Olive oil

2 garlic cloves, thinly sliced

5 or 6 cherry or grape tomatoes, cut in half

4 anchovy fillets, each one cut in 3 or 4 bits

2 tablespoons salted capers, rinsed

About ¼ cup fresh goat cheese (chèvre)

6 pitted black olives, coarsely chopped (optional)

Freshly ground black pepper

Chopped fresh basil leaves for garnish

PREHEAT the oven to 375°F.

CUT the peppers in half the long way and remove the seeds and inner white membranes, but leave some of the stem to keep each half intact. Lightly oil a baking dish in which all the halves will fit comfortably in one layer and set the peppers in the dish, skin side down. Now add to the inside of each half: a few thin slices of garlic; 2 or 3 cherry or grape tomato halves, cut side down; 3 or 4 bits of anchovy fillet; and a half dozen or so capers. Add a dab of the goat cheese and some of the chopped olives, if using, but don't get too carried away. Remember, simpler is always better in the kitchen. Now top each pepper half with 1 or 2 teaspoons olive oil and several grinds of black pepper. No salt, because the anchovies and capers will take care of that.

SLIDE the dish into the oven and let the peppers roast for 40 to 50 minutes, until they are tender all the way through and the edges are brown. Remove and serve immediately; or set aside and serve later at room temperature. They make a great addition to a meze or buffet table, although they're hard to eat standing up. For an extra touch, sprinkle some chopped fresh basil over each half just before serving.

FRYING WITH OLIVE OIL

Don't be afraid to fry with extra-virgin olive oil. There is no better, healthier medium for deep-fat frying. Popular mythology holds that extra-virgin oil has a low smoke or flash point and is thus unsuited for deep-fat frying, but that is quite simply not true. The smoke point of extra-virgin olive oil is up around 400°F, well above recommended frying temperatures. Moreover, because of its high content of polyphenols, extra-virgin olive oil is more stable and resists high heat better than most vegetable oils. If you fry at the correct temperature (350° to 360°F), the food will absorb a minimum of fat. In fact, there is more fat in a stew made with a half a cup of oil than in a plate of properly cooked fritters.

GREEK ZUCCHINI FRITTERS
Kolokythokeftedes

A favorite in every Greek taverna from the borough of Queens to the island of Ikaria and back again, these tasty fritters are excellent with a glass of chilled white wine. Even as a toddler, my grandson loved them—they're a great way to get more vegetables onto a toddler's plate.

MAKES 16 TO 20 FRITTERS

1 pound zucchini, grated on the large holes of a grater

Sea salt

½ cup minced flat-leaf parsley

½ cup freshly grated aged pecorino or parmigiano reggiano cheese

½ cup dried bread crumbs

1 medium yellow onion, grated or minced

1 large egg, beaten

Freshly ground black pepper

Pinch of cayenne pepper

Olive oil, for frying

MIX the zucchini in a strainer with a couple of pinches of salt; set a weighted plate on top and let the zucchini drain for 30 minutes, then transfer to a clean kitchen towel and squeeze out the liquid. Mix the zucchini, parsley, cheese, bread crumbs, onion, and egg in a bowl. Season with pepper and a little pinch of cayenne. Shape small handfuls of the mixture into fat patties about ¾ inch thick.

HAVE ready a wire rack covered with paper towels to drain the fritters.

ADD the oil to a deep-sided pot to a depth of 2 inches and heat over medium-high heat until a deep-fry thermometer reaches 350°F, or when a small cube of bread browns in about a minute. Working in batches, fry the patties until browned and crisp, 5 to 6 minutes. Transfer the browned fritters to the rack to drain.

SERVE immediately, while still hot.

FALAFEL *(Bean or Chickpea Fritters)*—THE REAL THING, *with* TAHINI

This is the way I learned to make falafel when I lived in the Middle East many years ago, and I've been making them that way ever since. I won't claim perfection because that would be tempting the gods, but this is darned close to it and so much better than those cold, pasty things you get in far too many delis. It's worth spending the time and effort to make real falafel at least two or three times a year.

The tahini sauce can be made a day or more in advance and kept, covered, in the refrigerator until ready to make the falafel. By the way, tahini also goes very well with fried or grilled fish.

You can find dried peeled fava beans in many Italian and Middle Eastern specialty grocers, but if peeled beans aren't available, buy whole dried beans with the peel or skin still attached. Soak them for several hours or overnight, after which you can pull off the tough skins and discard them.

For a bigger flavor impact, grind whole spices (cumin, coriander, and chile) in a coffee grinder or a mortar.

MAKES ABOUT 24 FALAFEL BALLS (8 TO 10 SERVINGS)

For the tahini sauce:

½ teaspoon thoroughly crushed and minced garlic

1 cup tahini

Freshly squeezed juice of 1 lemon

Sea salt

For the falafel:

1 cup dried peeled fava beans, soaked for several hours or overnight

½ cup dried chickpeas, soaked for several hours or overnight

1 small yellow onion, finely minced

TO MAKE THE TAHINI SAUCE: Combine the garlic and tahini in a bowl. Add water, 1 teaspoon at a time, stirring well, until the sauce is the consistency of heavy cream. An odd thing about tahini: The more water you add, the thicker the cream will be. If it seems too watery, just stir in a little more water! When it's the right dipping consistency, add the lemon juice and salt to taste.

TO MAKE THE FALAFEL: Drain the soaked beans and chickpeas and combine them, uncooked, in the bowl of a food processor. Pulse briefly, just enough to break up the beans, which should be soft enough to crumble easily.

ADD the onion, parsley, cilantro, garlic, baking powder, salt, pepper, cumin, coriander, and chile and pulse, scraping down the sides of the bowl. When you have a coarse paste, continue pulsing while adding a few tablespoons of cool water through the feed tube.

½ cup finely minced flat-leaf parsley

¼ cup finely minced fresh cilantro

1 garlic clove, crushed

1 teaspoon baking powder

1 teaspoon or more sea salt

½ teaspoon or more freshly ground black pepper

1 teaspoon ground cumin

1 teaspoon ground coriander

Pinch of ground red chile pepper (optional)

Olive oil, for frying

NOW stop the processor and extract a little bit of the falafel mix. The texture should be gritty but it should hold together in a little ball when gently squeezed. If necessary, add a little more water. When the mixture seems just right, transfer it to a bowl and set it aside to rest for 15 minutes or so. (You can make the batter ahead of time, but cover the bowl with plastic wrap. In hot weather, it should be refrigerated.)

WHEN you're ready to cook, heat about 2 inches of oil in the bottom of a deep frying pan until a deep-fry thermometer reaches 360°F. (A small cube of bread, dropped in the hot oil, will brown in about a minute.) Have ready a wire rack covered with paper towels.

SCOOP out rounded patties of the falafel mix, 2 or 3 tablespoons each, and shape gently into round balls or patties about 2 inches in diameter. Drop the balls into the hot oil. Fry in batches until crisp and brown, turning once to brown on all sides. Remove with a slotted spoon and set on the rack to drain.

SERVE immediately, with the tahini sauce.

SHRIMP FRITTERS *from the* SOUTH *of* SPAIN

Called *tortillitas*, or "little tortillas," in the region of southwestern Spain where they are a very popular bar snack or tapa, these are made with tiny shrimp harvested from the mouth of the Guadalquivir River. I make them in winter with little Maine shrimp. If you can't find them, try to get wild-caught shrimp and simply chop them coarsely once they're peeled.

Note that the *pimentón* or Spanish paprika used here is not the smoky kind called *pimentón de la Vera*, but plain *pimentón* made from sun-dried but not smoked red peppers. It can be sweet, medium, or hot—*dulce*, *agridulce*, or *picante*—so take your pick.

MAKES 32 TAPAS-SIZE FRITTERS

1 cup olive oil

2 large eggs

Pinch of sea salt

1 cup unbleached all-purpose flour

1 pound small shrimp, peeled and coarsely chopped

1 medium yellow onion, chopped or coarsely grated

¼ cup chopped fresh cilantro

2 tablespoons chopped flat-leaf parsley

Pinch of Spanish paprika (pimentón), sweet or hot

HAVE your *mise en place* ready—that is, have all the ingredients prepared, set out, and ready to go. Add the oil to a deep skillet or wok and set it over medium heat to warm up while you mix the fritters.

WHISK the eggs with the salt in a bowl, then whisk in 1 cup water. Now whisk in the flour, a little at a time, to make a creamy batter. (You might need to add a bit more water—much depends on ambient humidity.) Once the batter is adjusted to the consistency of heavy cream, fold in all the remaining ingredients and mix well. The shrimp pieces should be spread evenly throughout.

HAVE ready a wire rack covered with paper towels to drain the fritters.

WHEN the oil is hot enough to fry—when a deep-fry thermometer reaches about 360°F or when a small cube of bread browns in about a minute—drop in a big spoonful (about 2 tablespoons) of shrimp batter and test it by frying, turning once, until it's golden all over. Taste the fritter and adjust the seasoning in the batter, if necessary. Then fry the rest of the fritters. Smaller ones can be served with drinks; larger ones can make a first course, two per serving on a tangle of interesting salad

continued

131

greens. If cooking larger ones, don't try to do them as balls or they won't cook all the way through; instead, flatten them slightly with a spatula so they look like a rounded shrimp burger. As they finish cooking, transfer to the wire rack.

SERVE them immediately—they're best hot from the frying pan.

Notes: In a pinch, I once used lobster meat in these fritters. Chopped quite fine (by hand, not in the food processor) and used in place of the shrimp, it was delicious!

New England codfish balls make another great fish fritter. Use equal parts cooked fish (halibut, haddock, or cod) and mashed potatoes and season with salt and pepper, minced onion and garlic, and fresh flat-leaf parsley, dill, or basil. Flour the balls lightly before dropping into the hot fat. As with the shrimp fritters, you could do them in small balls for cocktails or in larger patties for a first course. In New England, we often serve these with our Saturday night baked beans.

Eggplant Fries

These are the eggplant sticks traditionally served with salmorejo in Cordoba, Spain (see page 144), but they are very good on their own too, or with a tomato sauce (see page 293) for dipping. In Italy they might be served as part of a *frittura mista*—a mixed fry that would include other vegetables and fish, and perhaps some bits of organ meats.

Simply bring a cup or more of olive oil up to frying temperature (when a deep-fry thermometer reaches 360°F or when a cube of bread will brown in about a minute). While the oil is heating, cut the eggplants into sticks or batons, about ¾ inch by 2¼ inches by ¼ inch, dry them thoroughly, then dip them in all-purpose flour seasoned with salt and pepper. Once the oil is sufficiently hot, drop the eggplant sticks into it and let cook quickly until golden on all sides. Transfer to a rack covered with paper towels and serve immediately.

TARTE AU CHÈVRE
Fresh Cheese and Tomato Tart

These tarts were made for a teatime treat by the wife of a cheese maker near the village of Ampus in the olive oil country of Provence, using fresh white cheese from her husband's own herd of goats.

If the recipe looks complicated, analyze it: The tart shells, the tomato sauce, and the cheese cream can all be done well in advance and then combined quickly and easily when you're ready to bake.

If you don't have time for the yeast dough, a package of frozen puff pastry is a fine substitute. Cut it into circles to fit the bottom and sides of two 9-inch tart pans, preferably the kind with a fluted edge and a removable bottom.

In late summer, when the finest tomatoes are available, use fresh, dead-ripe, red tomatoes, first peeling and juicing them—but keep the juice in case you need to add it to the sauce. Out of season, make the sauce with the finest canned tomatoes.

MAKES TWO 9-INCH TARTS (8 SERVINGS)

For the dough:

1 teaspoon instant yeast

2 cups unbleached all-purpose flour

1 cup very warm water

½ cup cornmeal

2 tablespoons extra-virgin olive oil, plus more for the bowl

Sea salt

For the tomato sauce:

6 to 8 small shallots, finely minced (about ½ cup)

5 garlic cloves, finely minced (about 2 tablespoons)

¼ cup olive oil

continued

TO MAKE THE DOUGH: Combine the yeast and 1 cup of the flour with the warm water in a bowl, stirring to mix well. Cover with plastic wrap and set aside in a warm place for about 1 hour or until the sponge rises slightly and bubbles. Now stir in the remaining 1 cup flour and the cornmeal along with the oil and salt to taste. Mix, first using a wooden spoon and then your hands. When the ingredients are combined but still raggedy, turn them out onto a lightly floured board and knead with your hands for a few minutes, until the dough is softer and more elastic. Rinse out the bowl and then grease it lightly with a few drops of oil. Return the dough to the bowl, cover again with plastic wrap, and set aside in a warm place to rise for 1 hour.

TO MAKE THE TOMATO SAUCE: Over medium-low heat in a saucepan, gently sweat the shallots and garlic in the oil until the vegetables are soft, about 10 minutes. Do not let them brown. Add the tomatoes, rosemary, thyme, and bay leaf. Stir in the sugar and salt. Raise the heat slightly and continue cooking the sauce, adding a little of the reserved tomato juices if necessary to keep the tomatoes from burning. Break up the tomatoes with the edge of a spoon as they cook down. After about 20 minutes, you should have a thick, coarse-textured sauce. Remove from the heat and stir in the orange zest.

continued

About 1¾ pounds fresh, ripe, red tomatoes, peeled, seeded, chopped, and drained, juices set aside for later; or 1 (28-ounce) can whole tomatoes, drained and chopped, juices reserved

1 small branch fresh rosemary, leaves only, chopped

3 or 4 sprigs fresh thyme, leaves only, chopped

1 bay leaf

1 teaspoon sugar

½ teaspoon sea salt

Grated or julienned zest of 1 orange

For the cheese cream:

12 ounces creamy, fresh, young goat cheese

4 large eggs

½ cup finely minced flat-leaf parsley

¼ cup finely minced shallot

½ cup skim milk

⅓ cup olive oil

To finish the tart:

½ cup pitted black olives, preferably wrinkled, dried olives

¼ cup freshly grated parmigiano reggiano cheese

Freshly ground black pepper

TO MAKE THE CHEESE CREAM: In a bowl, combine all the ingredients, first mashing the goat cheese with an ordinary table fork, then stirring in the eggs. Use a wire whisk to beat all the ingredients together to make a thick cream.

PREHEAT the oven to 400°F.

PUNCH down the risen dough and divide into two equal portions. Roll each one out into a disk about ⅛ inch thick to fit a 9-inch tart pan, preferably the kind with a fluted edge and a removable bottom. Set the disks into the pans, pressing the bottom edge in well and fluting the top edge. Prick the bottom with a fork. Bake the shells for about 10 minutes or until they are golden and firm. Remove from the oven and set aside to cool.

REDUCE the oven temperature to 375°F.

TO FINISH THE TART: Spoon half the tomato sauce over the bottom of each tart shell. Top the tomato sauce with the cheese cream. Dot the cream with the black olives and sprinkle each top with 2 tablespoons grated cheese and black pepper. Bake for about 20 minutes or until the tarts are firm. Remove from the oven and let cool slightly before serving.

SAGANAKI
(Grilled Halloumi or Kasseri Cheese)

This very simple Greek meze gets its name from the frying pan, the *saganí*, in which it is cooked. It's dead easy but does require a certain kind of halloumi or kasseri or a similar cheese that is slightly rubbery in texture and not at all crumbly nor so soft that it oozes. No salt is called for because the halloumi is quite salty. If using another kind of cheese, taste it for salt and add if you think necessary.

MAKES ABOUT 18 MEZE-SIZE SAGANAKI

1 pound halloumi, kasseri, or similar cheese

½ cup unbleached all-purpose flour

1 tablespoon dried Greek oregano

1 teaspoon freshly ground black pepper

½ cup olive oil

Lemon wedges, for serving

CUT the cheese slices into batons, ½-inch-thick rectangles 1 inch wide by 2 to 3 inches long.

COMBINE the flour, oregano, and pepper and toss with a fork to mix well.

ADD the olive oil to a large frying pan and set over medium heat. Have ready a wire rack covered with paper towels. Once the oil is hot, dip the cheese batons into the flour, patting them so the flour adheres all around, then drop them straight into the frying pan. Let the cheese batons brown and crisp on both sides—the flour should form a crisp coating around the melting cheese and keep it from escaping.

TRANSFER the browned saganaki to the rack to drain.

SERVE with lemon wedges to squeeze over.

SOUPS

COLD SOUPS

COLD SOUPS OR HOT SOUPS, BEAN SOUPS OR FISH SOUPS, SOUPS TO START A MEAL OR SOUPS TO MAKE A WHOLE MEAL IN themselves; Whatever your pleasure, a dollop of olive oil as a finishing touch can make the difference between everyday and extra-special. In using olive oil to garnish, think about the aromas and flavors you want to emphasize—if you serve a sweet soup that is focused on a single, direct taste, such as a pureed carrot soup, for instance, you don't want a super-assertive olive oil; on the other hand, if you're serving a complex fish stew with many different flavors from garlic to fish to perhaps fennel or even coconut, a robust oil like a Koroneiki from the island of Crete can be just what's called for.

COLD SOUPS

Anytime you make a cold soup—or a cold preparation of any type, for that matter—olive oil is ideal because it retains its texture and flavor at room temperature or even chilled. (Even if olive oil firms up when refrigerated, it takes a while for it to do that, and when it's thoroughly amalgamated into the flavors of a soup, it doesn't present a problem—unlike butter, which will become greasy, lumpy, and unpleasant in a chilled soup.)

Gazpacho and Salmorejo

These two cold soups are close cousins and beloved of cooks in Andalusia, the hot southern region of Spain. "We have a jug of gazpacho in the refrigerator all summer long," one young Sevillana told me. "We just help ourselves to it whenever we need a pick-me-up."

The difference between the two soups is slight. Salmorejo, claimed by the ancient city of Cordoba as its heritage, is thicker than gazpacho because more bread is added, and it's often served accompanied by deep-fried eggplant sticks (see page 132). The hot, crispy, salty eggplant dipped into the cold, sweet, soft puree of the soup is a delight. Another difference: Gazpacho is most often served in deep bowls or even in cups to sip from, while salmorejo is more likely to be served in a proper flat soup plate.

For making a very fine puree, a blender works better than a food processor, but an immersion blender also does a good job.

GAZPACHO

1 (2-inch-thick) slice stale rustic crusty bread

3½ pounds ripe red tomatoes, peeled and coarsely chopped (about 6 cups)

1 red or green sweet pepper, chopped

1 medium cucumber, peeled, seeded, and chopped

½ small red onion, chopped

2 or 3 garlic cloves, chopped

1 cup olive oil, preferably Spanish Picual, plus more for garnish

2 tablespoons aged sherry vinegar, or more to taste

1 teaspoon ground cumin

Pinch of ground red chile pepper, hot or mild, preferably Spanish pimentón de Murcia

Sea salt

Sugar, if needed

Garnishes: finely diced cucumber, green sweet pepper, spring onions or scallions, finely minced fresh flat-leaf parsley or mint

TEAR the stale bread into small chunks and set in a bowl. Add about ½ cup of cold water. When the bread is soaked thoroughly, gently squeeze out the excess water and set the bread aside.

IN a blender, combine the tomatoes, sweet pepper, cucumber, onion, and garlic. Pulse or whiz briefly to puree—it may be easier to do this in small batches. With the blender lid ajar, continue to process the vegetables while you pour in the oil and then the vinegar.

STILL blending, add the softened bread, the cumin, and chile pepper and process until the ingredients are thoroughly blended.

TASTE and adjust the seasoning, adding salt or even a small bit of sugar to bring out the sweetness of the tomatoes. A little more vinegar may be to your taste as well. If the puree seems too thick, add ice-cold water until you get to the consistency you want. Some people like gazpacho thick enough to eat with a spoon, while others prefer it thin enough to sip from a cup.

IN any case, the important thing is to chill it thoroughly before serving. It should be a light, smooth soup, quite creamy in consistency. Taste again after chilling: It may need more salt or sugar at that point.

GAZPACHO is often garnished with chopped raw vegetables or minced green herbs, like those mentioned here. Or each of these garnishes is set out in little bowls on the table, along with diced toasted croutons. A dribble of olive oil over the top of the soup when served is de rigueur, and one Spanish friend always serves gazpacho in a cup with a stick of celery, just like a bloody Mary.

TOMATO-CUCUMBER SOUP *with* AVOCADO CREAM

A refreshing treat on a hot summer day, this is very pretty if you swirl the green avocado cream into the pale red soup. Pack the tomato soup in a Thermos to take on an August picnic and bring the avocado cream in a container to add on-site.

For the soup:

¼ cup olive oil

1 cup finely chopped yellow onion

2 pounds ripe red tomatoes, peeled and cubed (4 cups)

4 long thin cucumbers, peeled, seeded, and cubed (4 cups)

4 cups chicken or vegetable broth

Sea salt and freshly ground black pepper

For the avocado cream:

1 large ripe Hass avocado

½ cup heavy cream

2 tablespoons olive oil

1 teaspoon freshly squeezed lemon juice

Sea salt

2 tablespoons chopped fresh chives, for garnish

TO MAKE THE SOUP: Combine the oil and chopped onion in a heavy saucepan over medium-low heat. Cook, stirring frequently, until the onions are very soft, but do not let them brown. Add the tomatoes and continue cooking and stirring. The tomatoes will melt and almost dissolve into the onions. Add the cucumbers. Stir in the broth, add salt and pepper to taste, and bring to a simmer.

COVER the pan and let the soup simmer for 25 to 30 minutes. When the soup is done, remove and process in a blender or food processor. You should have a very smooth mixture, but if it is a little grainy, pass it through a sieve to strain out the bits. Chill the soup until ready to serve.

TO MAKE THE AVOCADO CREAM: Combine in a blender or food processor the avocado, cream, oil, and lemon juice and process until you have a green cream. Add a little more oil and/or lemon juice if the cream is too thick. Taste and add a little salt if necessary. Spoon the chilled soup into bowls or mugs and swirl the avocado cream on top, then sprinkle with the chives. Serve immediately.

SALMOREJO

This soup is a variation on traditional gazpacho, thickened with more bread—but still liquid enough to eat with a spoon—and traditionally garnished with sliced hard-boiled egg and strips of serrano ham. The bread used should be a rustic loaf, preferably whole grain; remove the crusts and simply tear the bread apart into pieces.

MAKES 8 SERVINGS

2 cups packed torn stale bread, crusts removed

2 garlic cloves, coarsely chopped

Sea salt

1 teaspoon freshly ground black pepper

1 teaspoon ground cumin

Pinch of dried saffron threads

½ cup olive oil, preferably Spanish Picual, plus more for garnish

1 tablespoon aged sherry vinegar, or more to taste

3½ pounds ripe red tomatoes, peeled and coarsely chopped (about 6 cups)

½ cup finely minced onion

Garnishes: 1 peeled red sweet pepper, cut into thin slivers; 3 hard-boiled eggs, coarsely chopped; 4 slices serrano ham, cut into thin strips

Eggplant Fries (page 132), for serving

ADD 2 cups water to a bowl along with the bread. Let the bread soak for 20 to 30 minutes, then drain and gently squeeze out the excess liquid from the bread. You will have a couple of handfuls of big, damp, loose pieces of bread.

POUND the garlic in a mortar with a pinch of salt, then add the black pepper, cumin, and saffron, and work into a paste. Slowly add ¼ cup of the olive oil and the vinegar.

IN a blender, puree the tomatoes and onion until smooth, then add the spicy oil and vinegar mix from the mortar and whiz once more to blend well. With the machine running, gradually blend in the bread and the remaining ¼ cup olive oil. If the soup is too thick, add ice-cold water, a little at a time, until it reaches the right consistency, but keep in mind that it should be much thicker than gazpacho. Taste and adjust the seasoning, adding more salt or vinegar.

WHEN all the ingredients have been incorporated and the seasoning is correct, transfer the soup to a large bowl. Chill thoroughly before serving.

SERVE the soup garnished with pepper strips, chopped eggs, and/or ham strips, as well as a thread of olive oil. Deep-fried eggplant sticks are a traditional accompaniment.

CLASSIC TOMATO SOUP

This is the soup I turn to on chilly days when the world looks bleak and gray and I feel a cold coming on. It's a burst of sunshine in the middle of winter, although there's nothing to stop you from making it with fresh, red, ripe tomatoes at the height of summer too. Use any of the suggested garnishes, along with the ritual dribble of olive oil—if I have it on hand, I like that to be a well-made Spanish Picual.

You can vary the seasoning of this soup in many interesting ways. Add ginger and cumin to give it more of an Asian flavor, for instance, or cilantro and lime juice to lend a hint of Latin America.

MAKES 4 TO 6 SERVINGS

2 medium yellow onions or 2 fat leeks, coarsely chopped

2 garlic cloves, crushed

¼ cup olive oil, plus more for garnish

2 (28-ounce) cans whole plum tomatoes, preferably organic

1 teaspoon sugar, or more to taste

½ teaspoon dried crumbled thyme

½ bay leaf

Sea salt and freshly ground black pepper

Optional garnishes: ¼ cup slivered fresh basil leaves; 1 tablespoon ground cumin; grated lemon or orange zest; pinch of ground or crushed red chile pepper (piment d'Espelette or Aleppo pepper); a handful of diced stale bread, gently toasted in garlic-flavored olive oil

MIX the onions and garlic with the oil in a heavy saucepan over medium-low heat. Cook gently, stirring, sweating the onions until they are soft and golden but not brown. Toss in the tomatoes, breaking them in your hands as you do so. Reserve their juices to add later if necessary. Add the sugar, thyme, and bay leaf, season with salt and pepper, stir to mix well, and bring to a boil. Cook, uncovered, until the tomatoes are disintegrating into a sauce-like consistency, 15 to 20 minutes. Puree the soup using a food processor or blender—an immersion blender is fine for this. If the soup is too thick, return it to the heat and add some or all of the juices from the tomatoes. Taste and adjust the seasoning, adding plenty of black pepper.

SERVE with a dollop of olive oil and one or more of the suggested garnishes.

Note: For a variation, my friend John Lyons, an accomplished cook and gardener who frequently posts recipes on his Facebook page, adds fennel to the tomato soup, a flavor pairing so right that when you taste it you think: Hey, how come I didn't think of that? To the basic soup, he adds, along with the tomatoes, 2 fennel bulbs, trimmed and sliced to make 2 cups, along with a spoonful of chopped celery or lovage leaves and either bruised fennel seeds or, even better, wild fennel pollen, available from Zingerman's, Market Hall Foods, and other online purveyors (see page 326).

PUREED VEGETABLE SOUP:
Chunky, Creamy, or Silken, your choice (a basic recipe with variations)

This is a basic recipe that can be varied almost infinitely, depending on what is in season. Don't feel bound by any of these ingredients. You could also combine two or three vegetables to make a more interesting soup. You start with what Italian cooks call a soffritto, a chopped vegetable combination that sets the flavor of the soup. It almost always includes a member of the *Allium* genus (onions, leeks, shallots, scallions), sometimes several in combination. To this is added garlic, carrot, chopped parsley, and often chopped celery as well. These are gently sautéed or sweated in olive oil, then the principal vegetable is added, also to sweat in oil, before adding water or stock, along with the seasoning. A potato, peeled and diced, can add heft to the soup, but not all soups will require it, especially if your aim is a light, delicate soup for a summer lunch. Blending in heavy cream, sour cream, mascarpone, or yogurt is a nice touch at the end, but if yogurt is added, do not let the soup come back to a boil lest it separate.

Be discreet with the seasoning. You can always add more, but you can seldom take away or correct the situation if you've gone too far overboard. If in your enthusiasm you've dumped a ¼ cup of curry powder into a cauliflower soup (when a slight touch of curry would make an intriguing difference), you'll have to pretend that you're serving an Indian dish—either that or start all over again with more cauliflower.

And do use olive oil to garnish the soup as you serve it. If you've used basil, for instance, in the soup itself, mixing a little minced basil into the olive oil garnish is a nice way to boost the flavor.

MAKES 4 TO 6 SERVINGS

For the soffritto:

3 tablespoons olive oil

1 medium onion, or 1 leek, or 2 scallions, or a combination, coarsely chopped to make about ⅓ cup

1 garlic clove, coarsely chopped

1 medium carrot, coarsely chopped

¼ cup coarsely chopped fresh flat-leaf parsley

For the main vegetable:

1 large head cauliflower, broken into florets; 2 pounds fresh peas, shelled; 1 pound carrots, chopped; 1 pound peeled and cubed butternut or other firm squash;

1 pound beets, peeled and cubed; 1 pound onions, coarsely chopped; 2 pounds fresh tomatoes or 1 (28-ounce) can whole tomatoes with their juices; 1½ pounds celeriac (celery root), trimmed; or 1 to 2 pounds other fresh vegetable, trimmed as needed; or a combination

Sea salt and freshly ground black pepper

For the seasoning, any one or two (but no more) of the following:

1½ teaspoons curry powder; ½ teaspoon crushed red chile pepper; 2 bay leaves; any of the following, minced or slivered: 1 tablespoon fresh thyme, 2 tablespoons fresh flat-leaf parsley, 1 tablespoon fresh lovage, 1 tablespoon fresh dill, 2 tablespoons fresh basil

1 medium potato, peeled and cubed (optional)

5 to 6 cups chicken or vegetable stock, or plain water, or mixed stock and water

1 tablespoon freshly squeezed lemon or orange juice, plus ½ teaspoon grated zest; or a few drops of white wine vinegar (optional)

¼ cup heavy cream, sour cream, mascarpone, or yogurt (optional)

Olive oil, or minced fresh herbs (use any of the herbs you used for seasoning) mixed with ¼ cup or more olive oil, for garnish

TO MAKE THE SOFFRITTO: In a medium soup pot, combine the oil with the onion, garlic, carrot, and parsley over medium-low heat. Cook, stirring occasionally, until the vegetables are soft.

ADD the main vegetable (or two or three—cauliflower plus carrots, or peas and onions, for example), along with salt and pepper. Stir to mix it well, and let the vegetables cook with the soffritto to absorb some of the flavors, 5 to 6 minutes.

ADD the seasoning—one or two of the recommendations, but by no means all of them.

IF you want a thicker soup, stir in the potato cubes.

ADD the stock, stir to mix it all together, and bring to a gentle simmer. Cover the pan and cook gently for 20 to 25 minutes, until all the vegetables are fork-tender. Taste the soup when done and adjust the seasoning, adding more salt or pepper. A touch of lemon or orange juice and zest or a few drops of white wine vinegar can also help to boost flavors.

REMOVE the pan from the heat. For a chunky soup, put the contents through the coarse disk of a vegetable mill; for a creamy texture, puree in batches in a food processor or blender, or use an immersion blender right in the soup pot; for a silken texture, like the kind of soup you're often served in fancy French restaurants, put the puree through a chinois, pounding to extract all the flavors. Add the cream, if you wish, and return to the heat. If you add yogurt, do not let the soup return to a boil.

SPOON the hot soup into a tureen or individual soup plates and garnish with a thread of oil, or with fresh herbs mixed into olive oil. Serve immediately.

Note: Because these soups are made with olive oil instead of butter, they can also be chilled without fear that the fat will congeal. For a hot summer day, a chilled beet soup, mixed with fresh dill and yogurt, for instance, is a wonderful treat.

ROASTED SQUASH SOUP *with* CUMIN

Another simple and delicious pureed soup, but in this case the flavors are boosted by roasting the squash or pumpkin and onions in the oven before transforming them into a soup. For the squash, I like to use a *rouge vif d'Étampes* (actually, I believe, classified as a pumpkin), which I find in farmer's markets, but you could also try any one of the hard winter squashes, from butternut to Hubbard, or a pumpkin—as long as it's not a pie pumpkin bred for sweetness. A little sweetness is fine, but too much turns this into a dessert soup, which is not what we are looking for.

¼ cup olive oil, plus more for garnish

1 to 2 pounds peeled squash (see suggestions above), cut into chunks

1 large yellow onion, diced

1 small garlic clove, crushed

Sea salt and freshly ground black pepper

1 teaspoon curry powder (more or less, to taste)

1 teaspoon ground cumin

Pinch of ground or crushed red chile pepper (optional)

¼ cup dry white wine

2 cups chicken or vegetable stock

Honey (optional)

1 cup light cream

PREHEAT the oven to 400°F.

IN a bowl, combine the oil with the squash, onion, and garlic. Add a good sprinkle of salt and several turns of pepper and toss to mix well. Spread the vegetables out in a single layer on a baking sheet that has slightly raised sides (so the oil doesn't drip off) and transfer to the hot oven. Roast for about 45 minutes or until the squash pieces are very tender.

WHEN the squash is tender, transfer all the vegetables to a soup pot or saucepan, including the oil and any browned bits from the baking sheet. Set over medium heat and stir in the curry powder, cumin, and chile pepper, if using, along with the wine. Let the wine bubble up and evaporate slightly, enough to get rid of some of the alcohol, then add the stock.

BRING to a simmer and taste, adding salt and pepper if necessary. If you think it needs a boost of sweetness, stir in a tablespoon or two of honey. Simmer the soup very gently, covered, until the squash pieces are falling apart in the stock, 15 to 20 minutes, then remove from the heat and let cool slightly before pureeing—an immersion blender is ideal, or transfer the soup to a blender or food processor.

ADD the cream and bring the soup back to a simmer before serving.

WHEN you serve the hot soup, garnish each serving with a dribble of fine olive oil.

Note: Croutons made from bread cubes browned in a little olive oil are also a nice garnish.

SAVORY BEAN SOUP *with* SPICY GREENS

For a bright garnish at the end, add some strips of sweet red pepper, either sliced from peppers you've roasted yourself (see note, page 198) or from a jar of high-quality roasted red peppers.

MAKES 6 TO 8 SERVINGS

1½ cups dried cannellini or borlotti beans, soaked overnight

6 cups chicken or vegetable stock

6 ripe plum tomatoes, or 6 canned whole tomatoes, coarsely chopped

1 or 2 bay leaves

1 celery rib, including the leaves, diced

1 medium yellow onion, diced

1 cup dry white wine

Salt and freshly ground black pepper

Pinch of ground or crushed red chile pepper (optional)

1½ to 2 pounds greens, such as mustard greens, chard, or kale (if necessary, remove and discard tough center ribs), chopped into bite-size pieces

¼ cup olive oil, plus more for garnish

2 medium fennel bulbs, diced

2 garlic cloves, minced

2 tablespoons chopped mixed fresh herbs, such as rosemary, thyme, and flat-leaf parsley

Roasted red pepper strips, for garnish (optional)

DRAIN the soaked beans and place in a pan with 2 quarts fresh water. Bring slowly to a simmer, then cover and cook gently until the beans are tender but not falling apart, 40 to 45 minutes. Check the beans from time to time and add boiling water if necessary to keep them always covered with water to a depth of at least ½ inch.

MEANWHILE, combine the stock with the tomatoes, bay leaves, celery, onion, and wine. Add salt and pepper to taste, along with a pinch of chile pepper if you wish. Bring to a simmer, cover, and cook gently for about 40 minutes. Strain the stock, pressing the solids in the colander to extract the flavor. Discard the remaining solids and return the stock to the pan over medium-low heat. Taste the stock and adjust the seasoning if necessary. Bring back to a simmer.

ADD the greens to the simmering stock, cooking the greens just until they are wilted—5 to 10 minutes, or more, depending on how coarse the greens are. (Delicate mustard greens will cook quickly, while kale may take as long as 10 to 15 minutes.)

ADD 2 tablespoons of the oil to a sauté pan over medium heat. Stir in the fennel and cook, stirring, until it just starts to brown. Add the garlic and mixed herbs, along with the remaining 2 tablespoons oil and ½ cup of the bean cooking liquid, and cook gently until the garlic is soft. Scrape the contents of the sauté pan into the stock with the greens, then use a slotted spoon to extract the beans from their cooking liquid and add them to the soup. If the soup is very thick, add more of the bean cooking liquid.

TASTE the soup again and adjust the seasoning.

SERVE with an extra dollop of olive oil on top of each serving. Garnish each, if you wish, with a strip of roasted red pepper.

Note: If you have more bean cooking liquid than you need, don't discard it. Freeze it, if necessary, until you're ready to use it as a great flavor boost for other soups and minestrones.

PISTOU

This classic basil-fragrant spring soup from the South of France is one of the two most famous Provençal soups. Think of it as bouillabaisse for vegetables and you'll understand that the two soups are very much alike. Everything fresh and seasonal from great local markets, such as the magnificent Cours Saleya in Nice, is added to this, and then the whole delicious freshness is exalted when a big dollop of basil-rich, garlic-rich, oil-rich sauce is stirred in, with more being served at the table.

To be super-authentic, use a fine Provençal oil, such as Castelas, a controlled appellation (AOC) from the Vallée des Baux. Or try it with a Taggiasca from neighboring Liguria or a Catalan Arbequina oil.

Don't feel restricted by the vegetables listed here. If fresh peas, fava beans, or other greens are available, by all means dice or sliver or chop or shuck, and add them in too. Omit the carrots and tomatoes and you will have a very pretty green and white soup that simply sings of spring.

MAKES 6 MAIN-COURSE SERVINGS

For the "pesto":

4 garlic cloves, chopped

2 cups packed fresh basil leaves

Pinch of sea salt

3 tablespoons freshly grated parmigiano reggiano cheese, plus more for serving

⅓ cup olive oil, preferably Provençal or Ligurian

For the soup:

½ cup dried cannellini or borlotti beans, soaked overnight

1 or 2 bay leaves

6 cups chicken stock, vegetable broth, or plain water

¼ cup finely minced pancetta (optional)

2 garlic cloves, minced

TO MAKE THE "PESTO": (Note that this is a little different from the Genovese pesto that is made on the other side of the nonexistent border between Provence and Liguria.) Pound in a mortar the garlic, basil leaves, and a pinch of salt. When the mixture is a paste, stir in the grated cheese and the oil. Or combine all the ingredients in a food processor and pulse until well blended. Set aside until the soup is done.

TO MAKE THE SOUP: Drain the soaked beans and add them to a saucepan with the bay leaves and 2 cups of the stock. Cover and simmer over medium-low heat until the beans are tender but not falling apart, 40 minutes to 1 hour. When done, set aside in their liquid. (If fresh cranberry or other shucking beans are available, use them instead of dried beans—they will require only 15 to 20 minutes of cooking.)

IN the bottom of a heavy stockpot, combine the pancetta, garlic, parsley, and onion with the oil. (If you are not using pancetta, you may wish to add another tablespoon or two of oil to the mixture.) Set over medium-low heat and cook gently, stirring, until the vegetables are tender, but do not let them brown.

continued

SOUPS

151

¼ cup chopped flat-leaf parsley

¼ cup chopped white or yellow onion

¼ cup olive oil, preferably Provençal or Ligurian

2 leeks, diced

2 medium carrots, diced

2 small zucchini, diced

1 large russet potato, peeled and diced

½ pound fresh green beans, sliced about 1 inch long

½ pound ripe tomatoes, peeled and chopped, or 6 canned whole tomatoes, drained and chopped

Sea salt and freshly ground black pepper

1 cup pasta, either small shapes or vermicelli broken into 1-inch lengths; or ½ cup long-grain rice

¼ small green or savoy cabbage, slivered

3 or 4 large leaves chard (red or green), slivered

ONCE the vegetables in the kettle are soft, add the leeks, carrots, zucchini, potato, green beans, and tomatoes. Stir in the remaining 4 cups stock and bring to a simmer. Cook gently, covered, for about 20 minutes, or until the carrots and potatoes are tender. Stir in the beans with their cooking liquid, and add salt and plenty of freshly ground black pepper. Let the soup simmer for another 5 minutes, then stir in the pasta or rice and continue cooking just until the pasta is al dente or the rice is tender. Add the slivered cabbage and chard, mix well, and remove from the heat. The greens will cook in the residual heat of the soup.

STIR in a big spoonful of the basil sauce right before serving, tasting once more and adjusting the seasoning. Serve more of the sauce and more grated cheese at the table.

Note: Leave out the pancetta, adding another spoonful or so of oil to take its place, and use vegetable stock or water to make this vegetarian. Omitting the cheese as well will turn it into a delicious vegan dish.

LENTIL *and* BULGUR SOUP *with* CHILE-MINT GARNISH

A traditional soup from Turkey, this adds the delightful touch of aromatic oil, flavored with dried mint and red chile pepper, for a garnish.

5 tablespoons olive oil

1 heaping teaspoon ground cumin

Big pinch of Turkish or Aleppo crushed red chile pepper

2 garlic cloves, finely chopped

1 medium onion, chopped

1 tablespoon tomato paste

3 medium tomatoes, peeled and chopped

4 cups chicken broth

1 cup dried split red lentils (also called masoor dal), rinsed and drained

4 cups boiling water

1 tablespoon sumac (optional)

½ cup coarse bulgur

Sea salt and freshly ground black pepper

1 tablespoon dried mint leaves, crumbled

½ teaspoon crushed Aleppo pepper, or to taste

IN a large saucepan over medium heat, combine 2 tablespoons of the oil with the cumin, chile pepper, garlic, and onion and cook, stirring, until the vegetables are soft, but do not let them brown.

RAISE the heat to high and stir in the tomato paste. Continue to cook for just a few minutes, until the red color of the paste darkens. Stir in the tomatoes and cook until the juice the tomatoes give off starts to reduce, then add the broth and the lentils. Decrease the heat to low and simmer, covered, for about 15 minutes, until the lentils start to soften.

HAVE the boiling water ready, and when the lentils start to soften, add the boiling water together with the sumac, if using, and the bulgur. Once the soup is simmering again, cover once more and continue cooking until the grains of bulgur are soft, another 15 to 20 minutes.

WHEN the soup is thick and the lentils and bulgur are tender, taste and add salt and pepper. You may also, if you wish, use an immersion blender at this point to partially blend the lentils and bulgur, but don't try for a smooth puree—the soup is better, and looks nicer, with some texture from the grains and legumes.

PREPARE the mint and chile garnish: Combine the dried mint and Aleppo pepper in a small skillet with the remaining 3 tablespoons oil. Warm just to a brief sizzle and remove from the heat. The oil should be very aromatic.

TRANSFER the soup to a serving dish or individual bowls and garnish the top with a driblet of the flavored oil.

CHICKPEA SOUP

In one version or another, you can find this chickpea soup all over the Mediterranean. Here I combine memories of similar soups in Italy and Spain. If you want a more Provençal touch, add more garlic and use fresh basil in place of the rosemary; if you want a North African style of soup, add a little crushed chile pepper (or a spoonful of harissa) to the mix, along with a teaspoon or so of ground cumin. This is not exactly a quick soup, since it can take as long as 3 hours to cook. But the advantage is that the cook doesn't spend much time at all, unless you enjoy watching a simmering pan. And it can be prepared ahead and saved until the next day. Like most beany soups, it may be even better the day after it's made. But don't garnish the soup until you're ready to serve it.

MAKES 4 SERVINGS

¼ to ⅓ cup olive oil

¼ pound pancetta, prosciutto, or guanciale, diced

2 celery ribs, including the leaves, chopped

1 medium yellow onion, chopped

1 carrot, chopped

1 tablespoon coarsely chopped garlic

1 cup dried chickpeas, soaked for several hours or overnight

½ cup white wine

8 cherry tomatoes, cut in half

2 sprigs fresh rosemary

1 bay leaf

1 cup slivered chard, beet greens, spinach, or other greens

Sea salt and freshly ground black pepper

4 slices country style bread, about ½ inch thick

COMBINE 2 tablespoons of the oil and the diced pancetta in a soup pot over medium heat. Cook, stirring, until the fat starts to soften and melt. It's okay if it starts to brown along the edges, but don't let it turn crisp. Add the celery, onion, carrot, and garlic. Stir the vegetables in the hot fat until the onion turns translucent and the celery and carrot start to soften, 10 to 15 minutes.

DRAIN the chickpeas and add to the pot, along with the wine. Raise the heat briefly to cook off some of the alcohol in the wine, then add water to cover by about 1 inch. Stir in the tomatoes, rosemary, and bay leaf, and bring to a simmer. Turn the heat to low so that the liquid is barely simmering and cover the pot. Cook thoroughly, checking occasionally to make sure there's enough liquid left in the pot. If you must add a little more water from time to time, make sure it is boiling so as not to cool the soup down. When the chickpeas are very tender—when you can pinch them slightly and they squish between your fingers—remove the pot from the heat. (This can take as long as 3 hours, depending on the age of the chickpeas.)

USE a slotted spoon to remove and set aside about 1½ cups of chickpeas. Remove and discard the bay leaf and any twigs of rosemary. Puree the rest with an immersion blender or put it through the coarse disk of a vegetable mill. If you must use a food processor, just pulse it

2 hard-boiled eggs, chopped
(optional)

Freshly grated parmigiano
reggiano or aged pecorino toscano
cheese (optional)

Chopped fresh rosemary leaves,
for garnish

several times to blend. The soup should *not* have a very fine texture. This is a rustic soup and you should be able to see bits of carrot, rosemary, and celery along with the beans.

ADD the reserved whole chickpeas to the soup and return to the stovetop over low heat. As soon as the soup begins to simmer, add the slivered greens and continue cooking just until the greens are tender, about 10 minutes. Taste and add salt and a little pepper.

WHEN the soup is done, toast the bread slices and dribble a little oil on each slice. Alternatively, dribble a little oil over the slices and bake in the oven at 325°F until they are golden. Put a slice in the bottom of each serving bowl.

LADLE the soup into the serving bowls. Top each serving with a sprinkle of hard-boiled eggs and some grated cheese, if you wish. Add more pepper and chopped rosemary, dribble more oil over the top, and serve immediately.

Note for vegetarians: You can leave out the pancetta, but I'd add a couple more tablespoons of olive oil to compensate for the loss of richness. Or, if you don't mind eating fish, substitute 2 or 3 anchovy fillets, chopped, and melt them into the oil before adding the onion.

BREAD, MUFFINS, BISCUITS, CRACKERS, FOCACCIA, *and* PIZZA

BREAD, FOR THE MOST PART, IS SIMPLY MADE OF FLOUR AND WATER, maybe some salt, and leavening, which could be yeast, a sourdough left over from a previous baking, or a chemical leavener such as baking powder. Olive oil, while a common topping, seldom enters into the bread itself except when the baker is making pizza or its near cousin focaccia. So these recipes are very simple and reflect my opinion that olive oil makes a magnificent substitute for any other kind of fat (butter, margarine, vegetable oil) that you might use in baking.

A Note About Flour

In the following recipes, I recommend using unbleached all-purpose flour, often mixed with a measure of whole wheat flour. I use the white (all-purpose) and whole wheat flours offered by the King Arthur Flour Company in Vermont (see their website, www.kingarthurflour.com). Experienced bakers know that for breads, quick breads, and crackers, you can play around with the ratio of all-purpose flour to whole wheat flour, and even make breads that are 100 percent whole wheat flour. (This is not true of cakes and fancy pastry, however.)

Semolina, sometimes called semolina flour, is a little different because it comes from hard durum wheat. While regular flour, whether white all-purpose or whole wheat, is made from bread wheat (*Triticum aestivum*), durum wheat (*T. durum* or *T. turgidum subsp. durum*) makes a grittier flour that is considered ideal for pasta making. Semolina is also used for bread making in many parts of the Mediterranean, but especially in southern Italy and North Africa. Semolina can be as gritty as fine cornmeal grits, or it can be ground finer to make semolina flour or durum flour. My preference is for plain semolina, that is, not the finer-textured durum flour, but I should note that King Arthur's semolina comes with the subtitle "semolina flour." Just don't confuse that with the very soft durum flour.

GLUTEN-FREE OLIVE OIL– BLUEBERRY MUFFINS

I'm no big advocate of gluten-free, but these muffins are so deliciously nutty and light in texture that I could eat them every morning for breakfast. Don't feel restricted to blueberries—other types of berries will work as well, or add some chopped dates or dried figs, or a combination of, for instance, dried cranberries and walnuts.

Almond flour, often sold as ground almonds, is available from many health food and whole foods stores.

MAKES 6 TO 8 MUFFINS

2 tablespoons olive oil, plus more for the pan

2 cups almond flour (very finely ground blanched almonds)

¼ cup sugar

1 teaspoon baking soda

½ teaspoon salt

½ teaspoon ground cinnamon

2 large eggs

1 teaspoon vanilla extract

2 tablespoons plain yogurt

1 cup blueberries

PREHEAT the oven to 425°F. Use a paper towel to wipe 6 to 8 cups of a standard muffin pan with olive oil—or use those little corrugated paper muffin liners.

COMBINE the almond flour, sugar, baking soda, salt, and cinnamon in a large bowl and toss with a fork to mix well.

IN a smaller bowl, mix together the eggs, the 2 tablespoons oil, vanilla, and yogurt, then stir this mixture into the dry ingredients. Don't worry if there are some lumps in the dough—it makes better muffins than a completely smooth dough. Fold in the blueberries with a rubber spatula.

SPOON the dough into the muffin pan, filling each cup to just below the brim.

TRANSFER to the oven and bake for 5 minutes, then turn the oven down to 350°F and bake for an additional 15 to 20 minutes, until the muffins are lightly golden and thoroughly dry on top.

TRANSFER to a rack and let cool slightly, then turn out into a serving basket.

SLOW-RISE OLIVE OIL BREAD *with* BLACK OLIVES

A bread like this was renowned on Cyprus when I lived on the north coast of the island in the 1970s. Along with another bread, equally famous, that was covered with sesame seeds and redolent of fennel, it was a specialty of Turkish bakeries in Kyrenia. The fragrance of those breads, coming hot from an oven in a backstreet bakery, lives with me to this day. But while the bread itself is old-fashioned, the method owes a lot to Jim Lahey, New York City's premier baker, and the no-knead technique he developed at his Sullivan Street Bakery.

Salt-cured black olives are sometimes mistakenly referred to as oil-cured; they are actually cured in salt (see page 117), which accounts for their wrinkled, dehydrated look, and then coated with a little oil to give them a nice gloss. I use Greek oil from the island of Crete for this.

I've given recommended quantities of flour to be used in the dough, but, as bakers know, flour requirements can vary depending on ambient humidity on any given day in your kitchen.

MAKES TWO 2-POUND LOAVES

For the starter:

1 teaspoon instant yeast

1 cup room-temperature water

1 cup unbleached all-purpose flour

For the dough:

3 cups whole wheat flour

3½ cups unbleached all-purpose flour, plus more as needed for dusting

Sea salt

3 tablespoons olive oil

2 cups warm water

¾ cup coarsely chopped pitted salt-cured black olives

TO MAKE THE STARTER: Combine the yeast, 1 cup room temperature water, and flour in a bowl and stir with a wooden spoon until it is combined. Don't worry if it's lumpy. Cover with plastic wrap and set aside for 12 to 18 hours.

TO MAKE THE DOUGH: The next day, in a large bowl combine the starter with 2 cups of the whole-wheat flour and 3 cups of the all-purpose flour. Add salt to taste, keeping in mind that the olives may contribute quite a lot of salt when they are added. Mix together with a wooden spoon. Add 2 tablespoons of the oil to the warm water, whisking to combine well, and immediately pour it into the bowl with the flours. Mix again, using a wooden spoon. (You may use your hands if you wish, but it will be a very sloppy, wet mixture.)

ADD the remaining 1 tablespoon oil to another large bowl and rub it all around the insides. Turn the dough into that bowl, scatter a little more flour, either whole wheat or all-purpose, over the top, cover with plastic wrap, and set aside, again, for 12 hours or more.

SPREAD 1 cup of the remaining flour, whole-wheat and all-purpose mixed together, on a bread board or wooden countertop. Turn the risen dough out onto the heavily floured board and gently stretch it out into a rough rectangle. Scatter the olives over the surface, then fold half of the dough over on top of the other half. Give the dough a quarter turn and repeat the folding. Do this five or six times, until the dough has picked up quite a bit of the flour from the board and the olives are well distributed throughout.

NOW use some of the remaining flour to dust your hands and the board, and shape the dough into one or two round loaves (boules). (Note that, unless you have two ovens, if you make two loaves they must be baked one at a time, in which case you should set the second loaf aside, lightly covered, in a cool place until ready to let it go through its final rise, timing it to be ready to go in the oven when the first loaf is done.)

SET the loaf that is to be baked on a heavily floured kitchen towel. (You may use either whole wheat or all-purpose flour for this.) Cover with a dampened cloth and let rise for another 2 hours. During the last half hour, turn the oven on to very hot (425° to 450°F) and set a heavy covered pot (an enameled cast-iron Dutch oven is perfect for this) in the oven. Let the pot and the oven heat fully for half an hour. Then remove and, working quickly and carefully, lift off the lid and turn the dough from the kitchen towel directly into the pot. Shake it to settle it, clap the lid on, and return the pot to the oven.

BAKE for about 40 minutes. Then uncover the pot and let the bread continue baking for another 10 to 15 minutes, or until the top crust is a rich golden brown.

REMOVE the pot from the oven and turn the bread out onto a wire rack to cool.

OLIVE OIL–BAKING POWDER BISCUITS *with* FRESH HERBS *and* PARMIGIANO

Quick and easy, these biscuits are great to serve with any kind of saucy stew, since they do a fine job of sopping up the juices. I like them with the bean and pork chili on page 194. If you wish, you could use a combination of all-purpose and whole wheat flour. And you could use grated cheddar in place of the parmigiano.

MAKES 8 TO 10 BISCUITS

1 cup unbleached all-purpose flour, plus a little for the board

1 cup whole wheat flour

1 tablespoon baking powder

1 teaspoon salt

2 tablespoons minced fresh green herbs—flat-leaf parsley, rosemary, thyme, chives, or your choice

1 cup freshly grated parmigiano reggiano or other cheese

⅔ cup milk, or a little more if needed

⅓ cup olive oil

PREHEAT the oven to 450°F.

HAVE ready a baking sheet lined with parchment paper. Combine the flour, baking powder, and salt and toss with a fork until well mixed. Add the minced herbs and grated cheese and toss again. Pour in the milk and oil and stir with the fork until just moistened. Don't worry if the dough is a little lumpy. Knead very lightly (biscuits should be handled delicately), just to combine the ingredients. If the dough seems a little dry, add another tablespoon of milk and knead it in.

GENTLY pat or roll the dough out on a very lightly floured bread board. The layer of dough should not be more than ½ inch thick. Use a 2½-inch biscuit cutter to cut out rounds and set them onto the prepared baking tray. Transfer to the oven and bake for 15 minutes, then lower the heat to 350°F and bake for an additional 5 or 10 minutes, until the biscuits are golden on top.

SERVE hot from the oven, or keep warm in a low oven until ready to serve.

THREE-ONION FOCACCIA *or* PIZZA AL TAGLIO

Gabriele Bonci is Italy's star *pizzaiolo*, with a national television show and an amazing following of fans, many of whom flock to his classes at Pizzarium, his Rome studio-outlet-bakery. Neapolitan *pizzaioli* have sworn to me that they never add olive oil to the dough, so I was especially struck by Bonci's use of a couple of tablespoons of extra-virgin in his—it adds to the suppleness of the mixture.

This makes an excellent all-purpose dough for pizzas and focaccias. I think of focaccia as a more home-style version of pizza, although like most things Italian, that requires a little stretching of the truth. But one difference between the two surely is that focaccia is almost always baked in a rectangular pan, while pizza is a circle of dough cast directly onto the oven floor or a pizza stone. And the toppings for focaccia tend to be simpler than those for pizza. A favorite is simply olive oil, salt, and rosemary—bathing the top of the dough with several glugs of olive oil and sprinkling on coarse sea salt and coarsely chopped rosemary leaves. But that kind of focaccia is almost always called *pizza bianca*. So go figure!

In Rome, a big square-pan focaccia like this one is called *pizza al taglio*, because you buy it by the piece (actually by weight) and it's cut (*tagliato*) with a knife. So call it pizza or call it focaccia, and call it delicious anyway!

If you wish, for variety, try substituting a cup of barley flour, whole wheat flour, or semolina for a cup of the all-purpose flour in the recipe.

Note that I use semolina for kneading on the bread board. To my taste, this makes a sturdier and more interesting dough, but if you don't have semolina handy, by all means use all-purpose flour instead.

MAKES TWO 9 BY 13-INCH FOCACCIAS

For the dough:

3½ cups unbleached all-purpose flour

½ teaspoon instant yeast

About 2 cups very warm water

3 tablespoons olive oil, plus more for the bowl

TO MAKE THE DOUGH: In a bowl, combine the flour and yeast and toss with a fork. Add the water, about ½ cup at a time, and mix with the fork. (You may not need all the water; you are aiming for a dough that is quite sloppy and sticky, not like the usual bread dough.) Continue mixing until all the lumps are gone, then mix in the oil and salt. Cover the bowl with plastic wrap and set it aside for about 15 minutes.

1 tablespoon sea salt

1 cup plus 2 to 3 tablespoons semolina, for the board, if available (see headnote)

For the topping:

4 to 6 tablespoons olive oil, plus a little more for the pan

1 pound red onions, halved and sliced

¾ pound yellow onions, halved and sliced

Sea salt and lots of freshly ground black pepper

½ pound trimmed leeks

1 tablespoon sugar

2 tablespoons balsamic or aged sherry vinegar

1 teaspoon crushed red chile pepper, or to taste

½ cup slivered Gruyère cheese

½ cup freshly grated parmigiano reggiano cheese

SPREAD the 1 cup semolina thickly over a bread board or other work surface and transfer the dough to the board. Knead it very gently by folding the dough over on itself, like an envelope, then giving it a quarter turn and folding again, continuing like this until most of the semolina on the board is absorbed into the dough, which should be quite springy and elastic and no longer as sticky as it was when you started.

SET the dough aside, in its bowl, covered with plastic wrap, to rest for 15 minutes, and then repeat the previous process, this time using just a couple of tablespoons of semolina on the board. You can do the whole thing a third time too. (This is the only "kneading" the dough will get. It's reminiscent of baker Jim Lahey's no-knead bread technique, which went viral when it was described in *The New York Times* several years ago.)

RINSE out the bowl and rub it lightly with olive oil. Transfer the dough to the bowl, cover it with plastic wrap, and move it to the refrigerator to rise and develop flavor for at least 24 hours. This is the key to the procedure, because it's where the dough starts to work for you and to develop complex flavor as it continues to ferment.

WHEN ready to continue with the dough, take it out of the refrigerator. Remove the dough from the cold bowl and set it on a bread board. Knead it three or four times, in order to help it warm (you probably will not need any additional flour on the board at this point), then cover with a lightly dampened cloth and let it come to room temperature.

TO MAKE THE TOPPING: While the dough is warming, in a large saucepan, combine 3 tablespoons of the oil with the red and yellow onions, stirring to mix well. Set over low heat and cook very slowly, stirring from time to time and adding a little more oil when necessary, until the onions have reduced to a soft and rather creamy mass. This will take 20 to 30 minutes. As the onions cook down, add at least 1 tablespoon salt and lots of black pepper.

CUT the leeks in half lengthwise, rinse, and slice very thinly. When the onions are thoroughly reduced, stir the leeks, sugar, and vinegar into the mass. Add the chile pepper. Now raise the heat to medium, and cook for an additional 15 minutes. The onions will start to brown slightly as you do this.

SET the oven on the highest temperature that it will allow—450° to 500°F. Cut the dough in half.

continued

AGAIN, have a well-floured (with semolina) work surface ready. Drop half the dough onto the surface and, with your fingers, gently spread it out.

OIL the surface of a sheet pan on which you will bake the focaccia. (I use two 9 by 13-inch sheet pans; the topping described is sufficient for both pans.) Transfer the dough to the pan and continue to stretch it until it fills the pan. Use your fingers, or the handle of a wooden spoon, to dimple it all over with shallow indentations, then spoon half the onion topping all over the top of the dough, smoothing it right out to the edges. Cover the top of the onions with half of the slivers of Gruyère, then with half of the grated Parmigiano. Continue with the second piece of dough on a second sheet pan.

TRANSFER the pans to the preheated oven and bake for 15 to 20 minutes, until the crusts are brown, the tops are slightly crisp and starting to brown, and the cheese has melted.

REMOVE from the oven, cut into squares, and serve immediately.

Note: Other focaccia toppings: Take a dozen or so cherry or grape tomatoes and cut them in half; thinly slice a couple of garlic cloves. Press them all over the top of the focaccia, so they sink slightly into the dough. Then top with olive oil, salt, and, if you wish, about a tablespoon of Greek or Sicilian dried oregano, crumbled between your fingers. Or top the focaccia with the flaked contents, well drained, of a 6-ounce can of oil-packed tuna and about ½ cup of coarsely chopped flat-leaf parsley leaves. Again, add salt and olive oil and several turns of black pepper from the grinder.

And another note: You could, of course, turn this into a more classic Neapolitan round pizza, simply by dividing the dough into four to six balls and stretching each one gently, gently, into a disk.

Top with your favorite tomato sauce, a few slices of real mozzarella (not that rubbery square stuff in the supermarket cheese case), a driblet or two of olive oil, and a sprinkle of grated parmigiano reggiano. Pop into a very hot oven (500°F if you can do it) until done, then immediately throw some fresh basil leaves over the top and serve.

MIDDLE EASTERN PIZZA
Sfiha

Fairouz Shomali, a brilliant cook who also teaches high school history in the Palestinian town of Beit Sahour, near Bethlehem, showed me how to make these delicious pizzas called *sfiha*. She prepares the topping the day before and lets it sit in the refrigerator overnight to develop flavor. Some cooks add ground allspice to the topping before baking and sprinkle pine nuts over the top when the *sfiha* come out of the oven. If you serve these for a light lunch, count on 2 *sfiha* per person—though some hearty eaters can easily down 4 or 5.

MAKES 25 TO 30 INDIVIDUAL *SFIHA*

For the topping:

1 large ripe but firm tomato (about 1 pound)

1 medium onion

2 green or red sweet peppers

1 whole fresh green or red chile pepper, such as jalapeño or serrano

3 garlic cloves

1 pound lean ground meat, all beef, all lamb, or a mixture of the two

½ cup tahini

2 to 3 tablespoons tomato paste

1 teaspoon Aleppo pepper (red pepper flakes)

1 tablespoon sea salt

Freshly ground black pepper

For the dough:

3 cups unbleached all-purpose flour

1 cup semolina

1 teaspoon instant yeast

⅔ cup olive oil

1¼ cups warm water

1 tablespoon sea salt, or as desired

TO MAKE THE TOPPING: Peel, slice, and chunk the tomato, onion, sweet peppers, chile pepper, and garlic and add them to the bowl of a blender or food processor. Process, adding a little cool water if necessary to help with the blending, until the vegetables are very finely minced. You should have about 4 cups of minced vegetables.

COMBINE the vegetable mixture in a bowl with the ground meat. Add the tahini and tomato paste—more or less as you see fit to give a nice ruddy color to the mix—along with the Aleppo pepper, salt, and a good spoonful or more of black pepper. Using your hands, knead well to mix. Cover the bowl and set in the refrigerator overnight or for at least 8 hours. The next day, turn the meat mixture into a colander in the sink to drain out all excess liquid.

TO MAKE THE DOUGH: While the meat is draining, combine the all-purpose flour, semolina, and yeast in a large bowl and then stir in the oil, along with the water. Add the salt and knead thoroughly, just as if it were bread (which of course it is).

WHEN the dough is soft and silky, cover the bowl and set it aside in a warm environment (room temperature should be fine) to rise until doubled.

PUNCH the dough down and shape it, tearing away small lumps to make perfectly smooth balls—larger than golf balls, smaller than tennis balls. You should have between 25 and 30 balls. Set the balls on a tray

continued

or wooden board and cover with a lightly dampened towel. Let rise for about 30 minutes.

PREHEAT the oven to 425°F.

ROLL each ball into a thin circle 4 to 5 inches in diameter. Set the circles on baking sheets lined with parchment paper. (You will have to bake in batches.) Smear a generous portion (about 2 tablespoons) of the meat mixture over the top of each circle, extending it out almost to the very edge and smoothing it with the back of a spoon. Prick the *sfiha* all over with a fork to prevent them from blistering while baking.

TRANSFER the baking sheets to the oven and bake for 20 to 30 minutes, until the topping is thoroughly cooked and the edges of the dough circles are crisp and golden. Watch carefully toward the end to make sure the little pies don't get too brown.

REMOVE and serve immediately. You could also let them cool and serve at room temperature. They're best hot from the oven but can be kept for several days and warmed up when ready to eat.

OLIVE OIL CRACKERS

This recipe comes from a friend, Dawn Woodward, who has a wonderful bakery called Evelyn's Crackers in Toronto. With her partner, Ed Rek, Dawn makes whole-grain crackers, cookies, granola, and other goodies (www.evelynscrackers.com). When I asked Dawn if she had a recipe for olive oil crackers, she immediately sent me this.

Note that you'll find this easier if you have a hand-crank pasta machine for rolling out the dough.

MAKES 32 TO 40 CRACKERS

1¾ cups semolina

½ cup unbleached all-purpose flour, plus a little more for the board

¼ cup stone-ground cornmeal

1½ teaspoons sea salt, plus more to sprinkle on top

1½ teaspoons fennel seeds

¼ cup very finely chopped green olives

2 tablespoons olive oil, plus more for brushing the crackers

MIX the semolina, all-purpose flour, cornmeal, and salt together. Crush the fennel seeds lightly in a mortar and toss into the flours, along with the olives. Mix together the olive oil and ⅔ cup water and beat briefly with a fork, then stir into the dry ingredients. Start to knead in the bowl, then transfer to a very lightly floured board and continue kneading to form a stretchy, well-developed dough, about 10 minutes. Let the dough rest, covered, for at least 30 minutes.

PREHEAT the oven to 375°F.

ROLL out half the dough, keeping the other half covered, into a disk that is as thin as you can make it—a little thicker than an ordinary mailing envelope—about ¹⁄₁₆ inch. (If you have a hand-crank pasta machine, cut the dough into smaller pieces and roll each piece until it is ¹⁄₁₆ inch thick.) As you finish each piece, cut it in strips or lozenges and set on a baking sheet (or bake the crackers as long thin rectangles and then break them once they are baked).

BRUSH the tops lightly with olive oil, then sprinkle with sea salt (Maldon salt will give a nice crunch to these), keeping in mind that the olives may lend a good deal of salt to the crackers. Transfer to the oven and bake for 12 to 15 minutes—but be very attentive. Because they're so thin, they can burn quickly. Once the crackers are dry and golden but speckled with darker spots, remove from the pan and set on a rack to cool.

STORE in a dry tin or cracker box. They'll keep well for a long time—if you can resist them.

BREAD, MUFFINS, BISCUITS, CRACKERS, FOCACCIA, AND PIZZA

TARALLI AL PEPERONCINO E ORIGANO

Down in Puglia, on the heel of Italy's boot, *taralli* are a necessity to serve with a glass of wine late in the afternoon or before dinner. They look sort of like pretzels, and indeed they're made like pretzels (or like bagels), first boiling them before baking them. But the flavor is decidedly different, and the olive oil in the dough gives *taralli* a crunch and crumbly, crispy texture that pretzels simply lack. Serve these with chilled white wine. Or train your children to expect them for a healthy after-school snack.

MAKES 50 TO 60 *TARALLI*

2¾ cups unbleached all-purpose flour, plus a little more for dusting the bowl and the board

2 teaspoons sea salt, plus more for the boiling water

½ teaspoon sugar

1½ teaspoons dried crumbled Greek or Sicilian oregano

¾ teaspoon crushed red chile pepper

½ cup dry white wine

½ cup fruity olive oil, preferably from Puglia

IN the bowl of a food processor, combine the flour, salt, sugar, oregano, and chile pepper, and pulse briefly to mix. With the motor running, pour in the wine and oil and mix to a wet dough. Transfer the dough to a well-floured bowl or other container, dust the top of the dough with more flour, and refrigerate, covered, for 2 hours or overnight.

TURN the dough out onto a well-floured board and knead lightly. Working with half the dough at a time, keeping the rest chilled, cut the dough into walnut-size pieces and roll each piece into a snake about ¼ inch in diameter. Shape the snake into a sort-of pretzel shape, a ring with the two ends crossed at the bottom.

DUST a kitchen towel with flour and set the shaped *taralli* on the towel. Have ready a lightly oiled baking sheet.

PREHEAT the oven to 350°F.

BRING 5 to 6 quarts of well-salted water to a rolling boil. Drop in the *taralli*, a few at a time, and boil until they float to the top. (Italian cooks say, "Until they are *gallegianti*," which suggests the bubbling, dancing nature of the *taralli* as they finish cooking.) Use a slotted spoon to extract the *taralli* and set them on the oiled baking sheet. When the sheet is full, transfer to the oven and bake for 35 to 40 minutes, or until the *taralli* are burnished gold. Remove from the oven, transfer to a rack to cool, and then store in a sealed tin—they will keep for weeks, months even.

Note: There are several other favorite ways to flavor *taralli* instead of chile pepper. Fennel seed is popular and so is plain black pepper—in either case, use about 1 tablespoon of the seeds or peppercorns and crush them lightly in a mortar.

173

PASTA, RICE, *and* LEGUMES

P

ASTA, RICE, AND BEANS, ALONG WITH BREAD, are the foundation of the Mediterranean diet, present on most Mediterranean tables on a daily basis, sometimes even twice a day. But don't think of them as just stodgy filler-uppers: with the right combination of fresh vegetables, of green herbs and aromatic spices, of long-cooked ragùs or meat or fish stews, they can easily become the centerpiece of a healthy meal. And of course extra-virgin olive oil is key, lending flavor, color, and texture to the whole presentation.

SPAGHETTI AGLIO-OLIO-PEPERONCINO *Spaghetti with Garlic, Oil, and Hot Red Peppers*

This is the kind of quick, simple dish Italians often throw together after an all-night party or when spirits are flagging and an infusion of food is called for. Other types of long thin pasta, like vermicelli, linguine, or taglierini, may be substituted. If anchovies are omitted, adjust the salt in the sauce.

MAKES 6 SERVINGS

4 to 6 plump garlic cloves, chopped

½ cup olive oil, preferably a fruity oil from Molise or Sicily

Sea salt

1 pound spaghetti

3 or 4 anchovy fillets, coarsely chopped (optional)

1 small dried hot red chile pepper, crumbled, or ½ teaspoon crushed hot red chile pepper, or more to taste

½ cup minced flat-leaf parsley

BRING 5 to 6 quarts water to a rolling boil in a pasta pot.

IN a pan large enough to hold all the drained pasta, cook the garlic in the oil very gently over medium-low heat just until the garlic softens and starts to turn golden. Don't let the garlic brown.

ADD at least 2 tablespoons salt to the pot of vigorously boiling water, then tip in the spaghetti and give it a stir.

IF you're using anchovies, add them to the oil and garlic. Cook briefly, mashing the pieces into the oil with a fork. Stir in the chile pepper and half the parsley, and carefully add a ladleful of the pasta cooking water. Let it simmer and reduce slightly while the pasta finishes cooking.

START testing the pasta after it has cooked for 4 minutes. When it is still a little chewy in the center, drain it and add to the pan with the sauce. Turn the heat up slightly and cook, mixing the pasta and sauce together for a couple of minutes, until the pasta is done to taste. Turn the pasta into a preheated serving bowl, sprinkle with the remaining parsley, and serve immediately.

TRENETTE, FAGIOLINI, E PATATE AL PESTO *Long Thin Pasta, Green Beans, and Potatoes with Pesto*

The most elegant pasta dish that Italian cooks have ever invented is astonishingly simple to make, especially if you make your pesto with a food processor instead of a mortar and pestle.

MAKES 4 SERVINGS AS A MAIN COURSE, 6 AS A *PRIMO*

2 cups packed tender young basil leaves

¼ cup pine nuts

Sea salt

2 plump garlic cloves, crushed with the flat blade of a knife

½ cup olive oil, or more to taste, preferably a Taggiasca from Liguria

½ cup freshly grated parmigiano reggiano cheese, or more to taste

½ pound small yellow-fleshed potatoes, peeled and sliced about ¼ inch thick

¼ pound tender young green beans, cut into 1-inch lengths

1 pound trenette or other long thin pasta

TEAR the basil leaves into smaller pieces and combine with the pine nuts, 1 teaspoon salt (or to taste), and the crushed garlic in the bowl of a food processor. Pulse until the mixture is coarse and grainy. With the motor running, add the oil in a slow, steady stream. Add the cheese and pulse just enough to mix well. If the sauce seems too dry, pulse in a little more oil. Taste and add more cheese or salt, if you wish. Set the pesto aside.

BRING 6 quarts water to a rolling boil in a large saucepan or pasta pot. Add at least 2 tablespoons salt and the potato slices. Cook for about 5 minutes, or until the potatoes have started to soften but are not cooked through. Add the green beans, and continue boiling for another 5 minutes.

ADD the pasta and stir. Start testing the pasta after 5 minutes. When it is al dente, the potatoes and beans should be tender. Drain in a colander and turn the pasta and vegetables immediately into a preheated bowl. Set aside a couple of tablespoons of pesto to garnish the top. Add the rest to the pasta and mix thoroughly. Serve immediately, garnished with the reserved pesto.

ANNA TASCA LANZA'S PESTO *from* LE CASE VECCHIE

North Americans sometimes think pesto can only be made with basil and pine nuts, so I thought it would be useful to include this example from a little book called *Herbs and Wild Greens from the Sicilian Countryside*, which my dear late friend Anna put together in 1999 and published herself at Case Vecchie, her delightful home on her family's Regaleali wine estate in central Sicily. Since Anna's passing, her daughter Fabrizia Lanza now lives at Case Vecchie and continues to run a cooking school that honors her mother's spirited defense of Sicilian traditions.

This makes a sauce for a pound of spaghetti or linguine, enough for 4 abundant main-course servings or 6 servings as an Italian-style *primo* or first course.

MAKES 4 SERVINGS AS A MAIN COURSE, 6 AS A *PRIMO*

1 cup flat-leaf parsley leaves and tender stems

1 cup basil leaves

1 cup mint leaves

Leaves from 1 sprig sage, chopped (about 1 teaspoon)

Leaves from 1 small sprig rosemary (about 1 teaspoon)

Leaves from 1 sprig thyme (about ¼ teaspoon)

1 fresh hot red chile pepper, seeded

2 garlic cloves

1 cup olive oil

1 teaspoon sugar

½ cup ground or finely chopped blanched almonds

¼ cup freshly grated pecorino or parmigiano reggiano cheese

Sea salt

1 pound spaghetti or linguine

4 ripe medium tomatoes, peeled and diced

COMBINE the parsley, basil, mint, sage, rosemary, thyme, chile pepper, garlic, and oil in the bowl of a food processor. Pulse in spurts until well combined, then add the sugar, almonds, and cheese. Process very briefly, just to mix well—the almonds should not be overprocessed. Taste, and add salt if necessary (there may be enough salt from the cheese).

BRING 5 to 6 quarts water to a rolling boil. Add salt, and when it comes back to a boil, cook the pasta in the boiling water. When the pasta is almost done, extract a ladleful of pasta water and add to the pesto to thin it slightly. Drain the pasta and mix it with half the pesto, then turn it into a warmed serving bowl or platter. Spoon the rest of the pesto over the top and garnish with the diced tomatoes. Serve immediately.

SUMMERTIME PASTA *with a* RAW TOMATO *and* OLIVE OIL SAUCE
Pasta alla Checca

This is not pasta salad; rather, the sauce is cool—actually at room temperature—but the pasta *must* be hot. It's a good quick dish because, even if the sauce requires some preparation (but not very much!), once it's done it simply sits in its bowl, which it can do for hours, until the pasta is ready to serve. This was a family favorite from when I lived in Rome, to be consumed preferably in the heat of summer on a shady terrace as swallows hurled themselves through the blue skies, church bells mingled with children's voices, and the fragrance of good things rose from the neighborhood bakery.

MAKES 4 TO 6 SERVINGS

2 pounds very ripe tomatoes, peeled, seeded, and chopped

4 garlic cloves, chopped or very thinly sliced

Sea salt

½ teaspoon crushed red chile pepper (optional)

⅓ cup plus 2 tablespoons chopped fresh basil

½ cup olive oil

1 pound spaghetti or similar long thin pasta

COMBINE the tomatoes, garlic, a teaspoon or so of salt, the chile pepper, if using, ⅓ cup of the basil, and the oil in a large bowl. Cover and set aside at room temperature to marinate for several hours. If you must refrigerate the sauce at any point, be sure to give it plenty of time to come back to room temperature before serving it.

WHEN ready to serve, bring 5 to 6 quarts water to a rolling boil in a pasta pot. Add salt, and when it comes back to a boil, simply add the pasta, cook, drain, turn into a heated serving bowl, and immediately toss with the sauce. Garnish with the remaining 2 tablespoons basil and serve immediately.

ARROZ CALDOSO CON ALMEJAS
Soupy Spanish Rice with Clams

Along the Catalan coast of Spain, this rice is made with small, sweet Mediterranean clams, which finish cooking right in their shells in the middle of the rice. In North America, I make it with cherrystones or little Manila clams, cooking them separately and shucking them in order to get rid of any sand or grit. Note that I've called for Spanish *pimentón*. This is not *pimentón de la Vera*, which is smoked, but an unsmoked and very fragrant ground red pepper.

Don't think of this as a Spanish clam risotto—it should be somewhat soupy rather than risotto-like.

MAKES 6 SERVINGS

Pinch of saffron threads

1½ pounds cherrystone or Manila clams in their shells

1 cup dry white wine, or more as needed

½ cup extra-virgin olive oil

1 large onion, chopped

1 pound tomatoes, peeled and chopped

3 garlic cloves, crushed with the flat blade of a knife

1 sweet red pepper, diced

1 sweet green pepper, diced

3 sprigs fresh thyme, or ½ teaspoon dried thyme, crumbled

½ teaspoon mild Spanish paprika (pimentón)

¾ cup short-grain rice (Valencia or Arborio)

2 cups boiling water

Sea salt

¼ cup minced flat-leaf parsley

ADD the saffron threads to ½ cup warm water and set aside to steep for at least 1 hour.

COMBINE the clams and wine in a saucepan—there should be about 1 inch of wine in the bottom of the pan. Set over medium heat and cook the clams in the simmering wine just long enough to open the shells. As the shells open, remove them from the liquid and set aside. When done, strain the liquid thoroughly (use a paper coffee filter if you have one, or a double or triple layer of cheesecloth in a colander) to get rid of any trace of grit. If the clams themselves are very clean, leave them whole and add them later, in their shells, to the rice. It makes a nicer presentation, but the clams must be scrupulously free of sand; otherwise, shuck the clams, discarding the shells, but keep them warm in the strained liquid.

HEAT the oil in a large Dutch oven or heavy saucepan. Add the onion, tomatoes, garlic, and peppers, and cook over medium heat until the tomatoes have dissolved in their own juices and the peppers are starting to soften. Add the saffron with its soaking water, then stir in the thyme and paprika.

ADD the clam cooking liquid to the pan and continue cooking for 5 minutes. Stir in the rice and the boiling water. Add a good pinch of salt and let simmer for about 15 minutes; the rice should soften but still be quite firm. Stir in the clams and continue cooking another 5 minutes. Once the rice is tender, remove from the heat and stir in the parsley. Cover and let the rice sit for 5 minutes before serving.

RISOTTO ALLE ERBE
Green Herb Risotto

Many risotto recipes call for butter, but I find it makes a heavy and indigestible dish. In this recipe, I use a light-flavored oil (not a so-called "light" oil but one that has a softer flavor) in order not to compete with the fresh herbs. A lot depends on what the main ingredient is, however, and for the more assertive wild mushroom risotto that follows on page 188, I use a more medium-bodied oil.

Genuine ricotta is made by reheating the whey from cheese making. A type of curdled milk, made with lemon juice or vinegar, is often mistakenly called ricotta. Be sure you get the real thing for this delicious risotto. If the ricotta is very damp, with a lot of whey still clinging to the curds, drain it briefly in a fine-mesh sieve to get rid of excess liquid.

Have the stock simmering on the back of the stove so it will be ready to add to the risotto. Another tip: The spinach, like the ricotta, must be very well drained to make a creamy, not watery, puree.

MAKES 6 SERVINGS

½ cup cooked, well drained spinach

1 cup whole-milk ricotta cheese, drained

6 cups chicken stock, or more if needed

½ cup finely chopped basil leaves

½ cup finely chopped flat-leaf parsley

¼ cup finely chopped rosemary leaves

¼ cup finely chopped sage leaves

1 medium white or yellow onion, finely chopped

¼ cup olive oil, plus a little more for garnish

COMBINE the spinach and ricotta in a blender or food processor and blend to a smooth, light green cream. Set aside.

BRING the stock to just below a boil in a saucepan and maintain this level of heat.

USE a fork to toss the basil, parsley, rosemary, and sage together to mix well.

IN a large heavy saucepan over medium-low heat, sweat the onion and half the herbs (¾ cup) in the oil, cooking gently, stirring, until the onion is thoroughly softened. Mix in the rice and add salt and pepper. Stir slowly and, when the rice starts to turn opaque, tip in the wine, raising the heat slightly.

LET the wine bubble and simmer. At this point, be sure the stock is very hot, just below boiling. As soon as the wine has been absorbed by the rice, start to add the stock, ¼ to ½ cup at a time, stirring it in and waiting for each addition to be absorbed before adding more. Do not let the rice dry out at any point—it should always have a slightly

2 cups short-grain rice (carnaroli, vialone nano, or arborio)

Sea salt and freshly ground black pepper

½ cup dry white wine

½ cup freshly grated parmigiano reggiano cheese

soupy texture. You may not need all the stock to finish the risotto, but you should keep adding it until the rice is done. The grains will still be separate and slightly resistant to the bite but bathed in a thick, herby sauce.

AT this point, remove the pan from the heat and quickly stir in the remaining ¾ cup herbs and the ricotta-spinach mixture. Finally, stir in the grated parmigiano. Cover and let rest for 10 minutes, then serve immediately, garnishing each serving with a thin thread of olive oil.

Note: Make this vegetarian simply by substituting vegetable broth for the chicken stock.

MUSHROOM RISOTTO

Once you've made risotto a couple of times, you will realize what a quick and easy dish it is, despite its reputation for being difficult and time-consuming. For me, it's one of the best ways I know to put an elegant dish on the table, especially when unexpected guests arrive. There is always rice in the pantry and there is always something else that can be added, even if it's just onions or a can of good-quality San Marzano tomatoes, that will make a flavorful dish to set before a prince of the realm.

Any one of a number of different vegetables—spinach, artichokes, squash, tomatoes in season, green peas, asparagus—could be used in this risotto, but the basic procedure is the same.

MAKES 6 SERVINGS

6 cups chicken or vegetable stock

1 medium yellow onion, halved and very thinly sliced

⅓ cup olive oil

2 cups short-grain rice (carnaroli, vialone nano, or arborio)

¾ cup dry white wine

2 to 3 cups chopped or slivered mushrooms, wild or cultivated

Sea salt

½ cup well-drained ricotta cheese

2 to 3 tablespoons finely minced flat-leaf parsley

¾ cup freshly grated parmigiano reggiano cheese

Freshly ground black pepper

HEAT the stock to a bare simmer and keep simmering very gently while you prepare the risotto.

IN a heavy saucepan large enough to hold all the rice when cooked, gently sauté the onion in the oil over medium-low heat until thoroughly softened but not browned, about 15 minutes. Add the rice and stir well with a wooden spoon to coat with the oil. (The wooden spoon will be gentler with the rice as it starts to soften.) Cook for about 5 minutes, or until the rice has taken on a translucent look. Raise the heat slightly and add the wine. Cook, stirring gently, just a couple of strokes, until the wine has evaporated or been absorbed by the rice.

ADD the mushrooms (or whatever other vegetable you choose), and stir into the rice. Add a ladle or two of simmering stock, along with a small pinch of salt, and stir. (Keep in mind the saltiness of your stock and also the fact that the cheese added at the end will contribute to the salt in the dish.) When the rice has absorbed the liquid, continue adding the stock, ¼ to ½ cup at a time, stirring briefly as you add. There should always be liquid visible in the pan. Do not add all the liquid at once; this will produce boiled rice instead of risotto. The rice will be done when it is al dente, with a bit of a bite in the center. Each grain should be well coated with the sauce of vegetables and stock, which should be dense and rather syrupy looking. When it is done, the risotto should be thick enough to eat with a fork and not at all soupy. (You may not need to use all the stock.) Total cooking time will vary from 20 to 30 minutes, depending on the degree of doneness that you're looking for.

WHILE the rice is cooking, beat the ricotta and minced parsley together to make a light, pale green cream.

WHEN the rice is cooked, remove the pan from the heat and immediately stir in the ricotta-parsley mixture along with ¼ cup of the grated parmigiano. Add a few grinds of pepper, cover the pan, and let it sit for 5 minutes to settle the flavors. Taste before serving, and add more salt if you wish. Serve immediately, passing the rest of the grated cheese at the table.

MAQLOUBEH
Upside-Down Rice with Eggplant

In Arabic, *maqloubeh* means "upside-down," an exact description of what happens with this dish, which is cooked in a deep pot that is then inverted over a serving platter so that the rice, which is on the top in the pot, becomes the base of the dish on the platter and all the delicious meat juices and vegetables are a sumptuous crown for the rice. *Maqloubeh* comes in many variations throughout the Middle East but always includes rice, at least one vegetable, and some kind of meat (often lamb, though chicken is almost as frequent). This Palestinian version is from Fairouz Shoumali, an engaging cook and schoolteacher, who makes it for family celebrations in Beit Sahour, just south of Jerusalem.

The melted butter may seem an odd variant in an oil-based cuisine like that of Palestine. I suspect that the original probably used *samneh*, a type of clarified butter that was cultured to preserve it, which was once more widely used throughout the Middle East.

MAKES 6 TO 8 SERVINGS

Sea salt

1 to 1½ pounds eggplant, peeled and sliced ¼ to ½ inch thick

1½ pounds tender lamb, diced

3 tablespoons mixed ground spices (see Note for suggestions)

1 small head cauliflower (1 to 1¼ pounds)

1 medium onion, chopped

2 garlic cloves, chopped

About ¾ cup olive oil

2 cups basmati rice

1 large tomato, very thinly sliced

2 tablespoons butter, melted

1 cup pine nuts

Plain yogurt, for serving

SPRINKLE salt over the eggplant slices and set them in a colander to drain in the sink for about 30 minutes (you may weight the eggplant slices with a plate and a large can, such as a can of tomatoes).

IN a saucepan, cover the meat with about 5 cups water and bring to a simmer. Skim off any froth that rises. When the froth has stopped rising, stir in the mixed spices, cover the pan, and simmer gently for 40 minutes to 1 hour, until the meat is tender.

MEANWHILE, separate the cauliflower into small florets. Combine the onion and garlic and mince together.

PREHEAT the oven to 350°F.

RINSE the eggplant slices and dry thoroughly with paper towels. Brush a sheet pan with a little of the oil, then add the eggplant slices in a single layer and brush with a little more oil. Toast the eggplant in the preheated oven, turning the slices once, until golden on both sides but not necessarily cooked through. Set aside when done.

BRUSH the sheet pan with more oil and set the cauliflower florets on it, brushing each floret with a little more oil, then transfer the pan to the preheated oven. Roast the cauliflower until the pieces are golden. When done, set the cauliflower pieces aside.

RINSE the rice in a colander, running hot water over it, then set aside to drain and absorb any residual water.

IN a sauté pan deep enough to hold all the meat, mix the onion and garlic with 2 tablespoons of the oil. Set over medium-low heat and gently sauté the vegetables until golden but not brown.

MEANWHILE, drain the meat pieces, reserving the liquid and keeping it warm. Add the meat pieces to the onion mixture and continue cooking until the meat starts to look a little toasted and browned—just a few minutes should be enough. Stir in the cauliflower.

NOW it's time to assemble the dish: Smear another 1 tablespoon oil over the bottom of a deep pan with a lid, then lay the tomato slices all over the bottom. Make a layer of eggplant slices, then a layer of the meat and cauliflower combination, then another layer of eggplant and another layer of meat.

STIR the melted butter into the rice and spread it over the top of the pan. Bring the reserved liquid to a simmer and pour over the rice. Bring the pan to a simmer, then turn down to the lowest possible simmer, cover the pan, and cook for about 45 minutes, or until the rice is tender. The broth should not come to a rolling boil or it will toss the ingredients about and mix them up so that they lose their elegant structure of layers.

WHEN the rice is done, remove the pan from the heat. Remove the lid from the pan and set a wide platter over the top. Now, carefully, and using oven mitts, invert the pan so that the rice comes out on the bottom, covered with the layers of meat, cauliflower, and eggplant. Ideally, the *maqloubeh* will be a perfect round mound of savory rice with the richness of its accompaniments as a sauce.

MAQLOUBEH is not usually served immediately but rather set aside to let the rice settle until the dish is at room temperature or somewhat warmer. While it is cooling, toast the pine nuts in a pan with 1 tablespoon oil—watch them carefully because once they start to turn golden they can quickly burn. Spoon them over the top of the *maqloubeh* and serve, accompanied by yogurt.

Note: The spice mixture for this dish should include (all ground to a powder) equal parts cumin, cardamom, black pepper, cinnamon, and allspice, plus just a pinch of curry powder (a modern addition to the Palestinian kitchen).

MIDDLE EASTERN PILAF: SPICED RICE *with* TOASTED ALMONDS

Nasser Abufarha is the head of a Palestinian olive oil cooperative, Canaan Fair Trade, in the northern part of Palestine, but he put himself through graduate school at the University of Wisconsin by running his own restaurant, so he clearly knows where he is in the kitchen. One night when I was visiting, he made this sumptuous rice for dinner to go with a whole leg of young lamb that he had rubbed with an abundance of olive oil, salt, and lots and lots of freshly ground black pepper. "I could add rosemary," he said, "but it would cover up the good flavor of the lamb."

The spices were a traditional mixture that he buys in the market in Jenin and has ground on the spot, but similar mixes are available everywhere in the Middle East. I've made a suggestion of a few spices, but you could add cumin and coriander seeds too. Buy them whole and grind them in a spice grinder or a coffee mill for the most pungent fragrance. You might start with equal proportions of the suggested spices, then vary the mixture to your own taste, adding in cumin or coriander, or perhaps a little of the sour tangy spice called sumac, if you wish.

MAKES 6 SERVINGS

2 heaping tablespoons combined ground spices (cinnamon, cloves, black pepper, allspice; see headnote)

1 cup olive oil, preferably Palestinian or Lebanese

2 cups basmati or other long-grain rice, rinsed and tossed to dry

1 tablespoon sea salt

¾ cup minced flat-leaf parsley

¾ cup blanched almonds

BRING 2 quarts water to a rolling boil. When the water boils, stir in the fragrant spices and let simmer while you toast the rice.

HEAT ½ cup of the oil over medium-high heat in a heavy saucepan large enough to hold all the rice when cooked—such as a 2-quart pan. Let the oil get very hot, then add the rice to the saucepan and toast, tossing and stirring. This will keep the rice from sticking to the pan as it cooks. Toast until the rice has turned translucent, then pour in the boiling spiced water all at once. Add the salt and, as soon as it returns to a boil, turn the heat down, cover the pan, and continue cooking until the rice is done, about 20 minutes. Remove the rice from the heat, stir in the parsley, cover the pan once more, and set it aside for at least 5 to 10 minutes to settle.

MEANWHILE, heat the remaining ½ cup oil in a deep skillet over medium heat. When it is very hot—a deep-fry thermometer should reach about 350°F—add the blanched almonds. Cook, stirring constantly, until the almonds are a rich golden color. As the almonds start to change color, be very careful not to let them burn. When they are done, remove from the oil with a slotted spoon and add to the finished rice, stirring the almonds into the rice at the last minute before serving.

CHICKPEAS *and* GREENS

This is a variation on an old-fashioned Tuscan recipe from the Arno Valley; you could make it equally well with other types of dried beans, such as cannellini or borlotti, too. It should be served as a very thick soup.

You could use other greens than those mentioned. Spinach would be good, but as it needs a minimum amount of cooking, add it at the very end of the cooking time. If you wish, use spicy greens, such as broccoli rabe (rapini) or bitter chicories, although to my taste they cover up the sweetness of the chickpeas.

1½ cups dried chickpeas, soaked overnight

4 garlic cloves, crushed with the flat blade of a knife

1 bunch green chard, Tuscan kale (lacinato kale), or other greens

1 medium red onion, halved and thinly sliced

¼ cup olive oil, plus more for garnish

2 anchovy fillets, chopped

2 tablespoons tomato paste or concentrate

Sea salt and freshly ground black pepper

Toasted slices of country-style bread, for serving

Freshly grated pecorino toscano or parmigiano reggiano cheese, for serving

DRAIN the soaked chickpeas and put them in a pot with fresh water to cover to a depth of 1 inch. Bring to a simmer, and add the crushed garlic. Simmer the chickpeas, covered, until they are quite tender. This may take as long as 1 hour or more—it all depends on the age of the chickpeas.

WHILE the chickpeas are cooking, prepare the greens, slivering them into ribbons. Chard needs simply to be slivered, but if the central ribs are very large, you may prefer to remove them and chop them coarsely separately. They will take longer to cook than the leafy greens. Tuscan kale must have the central ribs removed and discarded, as they are too tough to eat. (An easy way to do this: Assuming you are right-handed, grasp the rib in your left hand and tug at the leafy part at the widest part of the rib to loosen it, then strip right down the rib to pull away the leaf from the rib in one neat stroke.)

COMBINE the onion slices with the oil in a skillet over medium-low heat. Cook the onions until they are soft, then stir in the chopped anchovies. Use a fork to press the anchovy bits into the oil, making a sort of anchovy paste. Dissolve the tomato concentrate in ½ cup very hot water and add to the skillet, along with salt and pepper to taste. Bring to a simmer, and then turn the mixture into the pot of chickpeas. Let cook for another 15 minutes, by which time the chickpeas should be well-done. Stir in the greens and let cook for another 15 to 20 minutes, until the greens are tender. (If using spinach, keep in mind that it will be tender in just about 5 minutes.)

WHEN you're ready to serve, put a slice of toasted bread (a *crostino*) in the bottom of each soup plate and dribble with olive oil. Ladle hot soup over each *crostino* and sprinkle with a little grated cheese and another dribble of oil. Pass more cheese at the table.

PASTA, RICE, AND LEGUMES

CHILI *with* PORK, BEANS, *and* GREENS

With pork, beans, greens, and peppers, both sweet and hot, in abundance, this hearty Southwestern-style stew takes the edge off cold winter nights. Crispy corn tortillas are good with it: Cut fresh tortillas into quarters and fry in olive oil until crisp and golden, then break them up in the stew when you serve it. Cornmeal polenta, a recipe for which follows, also makes a fine base for the stew.

MAKES 8 SERVINGS

1¼ cups pinto beans, soaked overnight

1 pound pork shoulder or stewing pork, cut into ½-inch cubes

½ cup olive oil

3 garlic cloves, chopped

2 medium red onions, chopped

2 green sweet peppers, chopped

2 fresh poblano chile peppers, seeded and chopped

2 fresh jalapeño chile peppers, seeded and chopped

2 cups chopped tomatillos (about 5 large tomatillos)

2 cups water, light chicken stock, or vegetable stock

¼ cup mild paprika

2 tablespoons ground cumin

1 tablespoon, more or less, ground or crushed red chile pepper (not too hot)

1 bunch kale or other winter greens (broccoli rabe, collards)

Sea salt and freshly ground black pepper

1 bunch cilantro, chopped

Yogurt, for garnish (optional)

DRAIN the beans and place them in a saucepan with water to cover by a depth of 1 inch. Bring to a simmer over medium-low heat and cook, covered, for about 25 minutes, or until the bean skins crack when you blow on them lightly. They will not be done—they have more cooking to do. Add boiling water from time to time, if necessary, to keep the beans covered.

WHILE the beans are cooking, combine the pork and oil in a heavy saucepan large enough to hold all the ingredients and set over medium heat. Brown the pork cubes on all sides, then add the garlic, onions, sweet peppers, poblanos, jalapeños, and tomatillos. Stir and continue cooking for about 15 minutes.

BRING the water to a boil. Add the beans, with their liquid, to the pork and then add enough of the boiling water to cover all the ingredients to a depth of 1 inch or so. Bring the liquid to a simmer and taste. Stir in the paprika, cumin, and ground chile pepper. Lower the heat to just simmering, cover the pan, and cook the pork and beans together for 45 minutes to 1 hour, until the beans are very tender.

MEANWHILE, strip the kale from its tough center stems. Discard the stems and sliver the green leaves.

WHEN the beans are tender, stir in salt and pepper to taste and the slivered greens. Let the greens cook until done, 15 to 20 minutes, then stir in the chopped cilantro.

SERVE, if you wish, with crispy corn tortillas or polenta, as suggested in the headnote. Pass a bowl of yogurt to garnish the stew, if you like.

POLENTA

Sea salt

1½ cups coarsely ground cornmeal

BRING 6 cups water to a rolling boil, stir in 1 tablespoon salt, and lower the heat to just simmering. Stirring with a wooden spoon, slowly pour in the cornmeal, stirring continuously while you pour. Cook, continuing to stir slowly, for about 20 minutes, reaching with the spoon all over the bottom of the pan. This is tedious but necessary in order to prevent lumps from forming in what is essentially cornmeal porridge. Protect your stirring arm with an oven mitt. The boiling polenta can act like Mount Vesuvius, sending up volcanic splatters of lava-hot polenta.

CONTINUE cooking for up to 10 minutes longer, or until the polenta is very thick and gives off a pleasant corny aroma. When it has reached the right consistency, stop stirring but leave the pan sitting on the lowest possible heat for another 2 minutes, just to tighten it. Then turn it out onto a heated platter or, for a more traditional presentation, onto a wooden board, and serve with whatever stew, sauce, or meat you've chosen to accompany it.

VEGETABLES
and SALADS

I've INCLUDED HERE MANY SUGGESTIONS FOR SPECIFIC VEGETA-BLES and what I think are good and easy ways to prepare them, but there are also some very general techniques to think about when using olive oil in the kitchen. If you're like me, you frequent farmer's markets and the best produce stands, where you fuss over the gorgeous array and end up taking home far more vegetables than you can ever use in a week's time. Not to worry, however; there are many ways to handle them.

I do want to offer one bit of preliminary advice, one of those little kitchen *trucs* my mother taught me, but it took me years of throwing out limp, over-the-hill vegetables before I realized that she was actually right for a change. This is my kitchen maxim:

Take care of the vegetables as soon as you get them home and the rest will take care of itself.

What this means in practice: Do all the prep work necessary. Rinse the greens and dry them. Scrub the carrots and potatoes (but don't peel them). Get rid of any fading bits and pieces—wilting yellow leaves, bruised or moldy scraps, excess greenery, and so forth. Then tuck away the potatoes and onions (never together) and the garlic in a cool, dark place, and refrigerate the rest of your provender—except for eggplants and tomatoes, which should be used in a day or two to take full advantage of their summery flavors. Neither takes well to the refrigerator's chill.

We all know we should be eating more vegetables, and I'm not sure why we find it so hard to do that—except that it's easier to throw a steak on the grill and bake a potato than it is to do the slightly more busy prep work that vegetables require. But if you take my mother's advice, you'll be halfway there already. That, and the judicious application of delicious olive oil, will make vegetable cooking a breeze and a delight.

We should all take a lesson from the Greeks as far as vegetable cooking is concerned. Greek cooking authority Diane Kochilas confirms that olive oil is an absolute necessity when Greeks cook vegetables—and they cook a powerful amount too. Greeks, she claims, eat on average a pound of vegetables a day. Vegetables often cooked in oil, yes, but also always with a final addition of oil at the end to finish the dish. This is olive oil as it was meant to be—both cooking fat and flavoring agent. "Let the vegetable juices cook down," she advises, "until there's nothing left but the oil, caramelizing and reducing the juices to something very flavorful."

Following are several general techniques that are applicable to a variety of produce and that sometimes generate even better results when you can combine two or three or even four vegetables—no more than that, though, lest the flavors get a little muddied and confused.

Many vegetables, for instance, take well to **oven-roasting**. Think of a selection of summer vegetables—eggplant, tomatoes, peppers both sweet and hot, and onions—cut into rather large pieces, tossed with a generous glug or two of olive oil, a good sprinkle of sea salt, several turns of the pepper mill, and maybe some aromatics, especially garlic and perhaps dried oregano or fennel pollen. The whole tray is then slid into a preheated 375°F oven and roasted until the more slow-cooking eggplant pieces are roasted through and tender and the onions and peppers are starting to crisp nicely and brown on the edges. Pile the vegetables on a handsome pottery tray and serve it as a deconstructed ratatouille or caponata.

In wintertime, a similar technique works with certain of the cabbage family—Brussels sprouts, split in half, are terrific roasted in the oven, but other cabbage-y vegetables, even a firm head of green cabbage cut into wedges, will also do nicely as long as they are well rubbed with oil to keep them from burning. For color contrast, add some good chunks of squash or carrots as well as some quarters of red onion; don't forget the garlic, and again, be generous with the olive oil. Seasoning? Thyme, rosemary, and bay leaves all come to mind. For extra crunch, add a handful of walnut halves or broken pecans scattered through-out. A few potatoes, peeled and chunked, are also good with this. Beets, too—although you may wish to roast peeled beets separately so that they don't color all the other vegetables with their virulent pink, then combine them just as you're serving.

Another great technique is what I call **steaming-and-sautéing**, from the kitchens of Italy and Greece, both champion consumers of vegetables. Markets year-round in these countries are full of a gamut of greens, from wild dandelions and amaranth greens in the early spring through spinach and chard and on into the sturdy, often bitter greens of autumn and winter (broccoli rabe, kale, collards). In North America, the mixture sold as "braising greens," which usually includes kale and broccoli rabe (aka rapini), is also a great choice.

Rinse the greens, discard any thick, inedible stems, chop the leaves coarsely, then steam until tender in a small amount of water, enough to keep them from catching on the bottom of the pan. Keep the initial steaming to a minimum, just long enough to tenderize the greens. Drain the greens thoroughly, even squeezing out handfuls of liquid (which could go in the stockpot if you're so inclined), and chop them again.

When it's time to serve, the greens are tossed in a sauté pan with plenty of olive oil in which some chopped garlic has been stewed, perhaps with a sprinkling of ground or crushed red chile pepper, and a spritz of fresh lemon juice added at the very end. And that's all it takes. The beauty of this: A cook can steam enough for a week of meals and keep the drained greens in the fridge until dinnertime. Then it's just a quick sauté and they're ready for the table. In old-fashioned trattorie in Italy you can order a *mista di verdura cotta*, a mix of cooked greens, as a starter: It will consist of three or four different greens, cooked sepa-rately and arranged on a plate, with more fresh olive oil and lemon juice to dress each one.

Greens prepared like this also make a great sauce for pasta—especially short chunky pasta shapes like orecchiette, the ear-shaped pasta from Puglia that is traditionally cooked and served with broccoli rabe or another of the spicy winter greens Mediterranean cooks love.

Stir-fried vegetables are not something you'll find very often in Mediterranean kitch-ens, but there's every reason in the world to include them in an olive oil–based cuisine, especially as the technique is also a quick, easy way to get a tasty meal on the table. It doesn't have to be Chinese to be stir-fried, although a Chinese wok is the perfect vessel for this ancient technique. The most important trick? The vegetables must all be cut roughly the same size beforehand. Then keep the vegetables refrigerated until ready to use. This ensures that they'll all cook at the same rate and be done at the same time. Keep in mind, though, that dense root vegetables like carrots and turnips, no matter how they're cut, are going to take longer than tender onions and peppers, which really have only to yield up their liquid in order to be done. With stir-frying, you won't need much oil—just a couple of tablespoons to start off with (you can add more if necessary as the vegetables cook).

One secret to success in stir-frying is to keep your batches small. Don't try to do too much at once. If you're cooking a large amount, do the vegetables in batches and combine them all at the end. Another secret is to keep it simple. Don't add every leftover that's in your refrigerator—think about the combination and what goes well with what. (Maybe that leftover mashed squash isn't such a great idea, after all?) Onion, garlic, ginger, peppers (sweet and hot), and one or two other vegetables (broccoli? carrots? fresh or dried mushrooms? leeks? eggplant?) should be plenty. A couple spoonfuls of broth or just plain boiling water will help the cooking along; a handful of freshly chopped green herbs thrown in at the very end of cooking, just as you turn off the heat, is a great idea, and another tablespoon or so of good olive oil on top makes a fine garnish.

Stir-fried vegetables make a great topping for pasta or rice; or serve them along with a plate of beans, again topped with olive oil, for a robust vegetarian supper. Or add slivers of chicken breast or fresh wild-caught shrimp as you start to cook. Remove them when they're done and set aside while you do the vegetables, then add them back at the end.

A final technique I want to mention is a little old-fashioned, but I'd like to see it revived, as it's a nice way to keep vegetables on hand for several days or even weeks. This is the old French method called *à la grecque*, although I'm not sure the Greeks ever had much to do with it. The classic recipe calls for a broth made up of equal quantities of olive oil, dry white wine, and water (say, a half a cup of each to start with), with about half that amount (a quarter of a cup) white wine vinegar, combined with a few cloves of garlic and some dried aromatics (coriander seeds are always part of the recipe, plus bay leaves, black peppercorns, maybe a small red chile pepper, fennel or dill seeds, even star anise or Szechwan peppercorns). Bring this to a simmer and then add your vegetables—carrots cut into batons, baby onions or larger ones quartered, scallions, small mushrooms whole or quartered, cauliflower broken into florets, quartered artichoke hearts, small fennel bulbs cut in half, even peeled whole cloves of garlic. Simmer the vegetables in the broth—do it in batches, one vegetable at a time—until they are just barely tender, still with a little crispness, then transfer them to a bowl and boil down the broth to a syrup. Cover the vegetables with the syrup and chill, then bring them to room temperature to serve as an hors d'oeuvre, or warm them up a bit more to serve as a side dish. You could also combine a number of vegetables *à la grecque* to make a composed salad. In essence, what you've made is a very light pickle. Because of the acid, the vegetables will keep for a week or even ten days in the refrigerator with no problems.

Artichokes

Where I live in Italy I have a choice, depending on the season, of up to half a dozen different varieties of artichoke. This has spoiled me thoroughly. Italians are masters of artichoke cookery—frying them, pickling them, stewing them, eating them raw. When young and tender, they're excellent in a pinzimonio (see page 122), or quartered, battered, and fried to make a traditional Tuscan accompaniment to fried rabbit.

They do require some work, however, and the first thing you'll need once you've got the artichokes in hand is a bowl of acidulated water, water with half a lemon squeezed right into it, to keep the artichokes from blackening once they've been cut. Use the other half of the lemon to rub the cut surfaces as you prepare them; then when they're done, toss each one into the bowl of acidulated water. Remove the tough outer bracts (leaves) by bending them back and breaking them off or cutting them with a sharp paring knife. Keep doing this until you reach the pale, tender insides. Then cut the top one-third off. If the artichokes are large and well developed, you can usually push the inner leaves aside and scrape out the prickly inside thistles (the choke) using a serrated grapefruit spoon. Otherwise, cut each artichoke in quarters and cut away the thistles.

Asparagus

Like artichokes, asparagus, when it's young and fresh, is often eaten raw; in Italy, it frequently forms part of a pinzimonio (see page 122). An asparagus omelet (call it a frittata or a tortilla, if you wish) and asparagus risotto (substitute asparagus in the recipe on page 188) are among the great delights of springtime.

Beets

Beets are great whether steamed or roasted, on their own or in combination with other vegetables. A salad of beets and other root vegetables, roasted together and then tossed with a simple vinaigrette, is a great accompaniment to a wintertime roasted chicken or pork loin. Another popular salad combination I see on the menus of restaurants that vaunt local, seasonal cuisine is beets with dabs of blue cheese and very coarsely chopped walnuts, bathed in an olive oil vinaigrette, an excellent combination. Or try beets *à la grecque* (see page 200)—again, combining them with other root vegetables, or simply with onions and garlic.

OVEN-BRAISED ARTICHOKES *with* POTATOES *and* ONIONS

Artichokes in North America—at least in the part of North America where I live—are usually so hideously expensive that I can't imagine buying them except for very special occasions. For the price of a single artichoke at Whole Foods, I can buy a dozen at any Italian street market, and they are almost always much fresher and tastier too. So I look for recipes that let these crown jewels of the vegetable kingdom be extended, and potatoes and onions are excellent for that purpose. If you can't find small artichokes, use just four of the giant ones from California.

MAKES 6 TO 8 SERVINGS

8 small yellow-fleshed potatoes (yellow Finns are fine)

8 small, very firm artichokes

1 lemon, for preparing the artichokes, plus ⅓ cup freshly squeezed lemon juice, plus lemon wedges, for serving

1 medium yellow onion, halved and thinly sliced

2 garlic cloves, thinly sliced

Sea salt and freshly ground black pepper

2 tablespoons finely minced fresh herbs (chives, thyme, flat-leaf parsley)

2 bay leaves

⅓ cup plus 2 tablespoons olive oil

PEEL the potatoes and slice into approximately ¼ inch slices. Toss the potatoes into a bowl of water as you finish to keep them from darkening.

PREPARE the artichokes as described on page 201, rubbing the cut surfaces with half a lemon and using the other half to acidulate a bowl of water. Cut the artichokes into quarters (or smaller if they are very large) and remove their center chokes if necessary. Toss in the bowl of acidulated water as you finish each one.

PREHEAT the oven to 375°F.

DRAIN the potatoes and artichokes and combine in a bowl with the onion slices and the garlic. Add salt and pepper, the minced herbs of your choosing, the bay leaves, broken in half, and ⅓ cup of the oil. Toss to mix everything well and coat the vegetables with olive oil. Spread the mixture in a gratin dish (one that is safe to use on the stovetop) in which they will just fit without a great deal of overlap.

SET the gratin dish over medium heat and, when the oil starts to sizzle, add the lemon juice and boiling water to come about halfway up the sides of the dish. Trickle the remaining 2 tablespoons oil over the top. Cover the dish securely with aluminum foil and carefully transfer to the oven. Roast for about 30 minutes, then remove the foil and spoon some of the juices over the vegetables. Raise the heat to 400°F and return the gratin dish to the oven, uncovered. Cook until most of the liquid has boiled away and the vegetables are sizzling in the oil, about 15 minutes longer.

SERVE immediately, with lemon wedges to squeeze on top.

FRIED ARTICHOKES

I include this recipe for anyone who has access to really good artichokes that don't require a second mortgage on your house to purchase. For so long California has been the only home for artichokes on this continent, but more and more farmers are beginning to realize that it doesn't require a Monterey Bay climate to succeed with these prickly thistles. I can even sometimes find them in farmer's markets in Maine in the early summer. When I do, I like to fry them in olive oil to serve with simple fried rabbit—an old Tuscan tradition that is very pleasing.

If you find small artichokes, they will not have an internal choke that has to be removed. If you must use larger artichokes, prepare them according to the instructions on page 201 and slice them into quarters, then again into eighths.

MAKES 4 SERVINGS AS AN ACCOMPANIMENT TO FRIED RABBIT OR CHICKEN

1 cup olive oil

1 cup unbleached all-purpose flour

Sea salt and freshly ground black pepper

12 small tender artichokes, prepared as described on page 201

Lemon wedges, for serving

HAVE ready a wire rack covered with paper towels for draining the artichokes.

PUT the oil in a deep skillet or wok over medium heat to warm up to 360°F. (Please use a frying or candy thermometer, if you have one; it's important to be accurate with deep-fat frying.)

TOSS the flour in a bowl with plenty of salt and pepper.

DRAIN the artichokes and cut them into smaller sections if necessary. Add them to the bowl of flour and toss to coat each section of artichoke well.

AS soon as the oil has reached 360°F (a small cube of bread will brown in just under a minute), add the artichoke pieces to the oil. Depending on the size of your pan, you may wish to do this in batches. Fry until the artichokes are golden, then remove with a slotted spoon and transfer to the rack to drain.

WHEN the artichokes are done, serve them immediately, with the lemon wedges. If you're serving them with fried rabbit or chicken, keep the artichokes warm in the oven while you prepare the meat, then serve both, piled up on a platter, with the lemon wedges to garnish.

BROCCOLI *or* CAULIFLOWER *with* LEMON, CAPERS, *and* BLACK OLIVES

The finishing sauce of lemon, capers, and black olives can be used to delicious effect with any number of greens, including all of those on page 199. Simply steam them as described and finish in the sauce of lemon, capers and black olives.

MAKES 4 TO 6 SERVINGS

About 1 pound broccoli or cauliflower

½ cup pitted black olives, coarsely chopped

1 heaping tablespoon salt-packed capers, rinsed and drained

2 tablespoons finely chopped flat-leaf parsley

Grated zest and juice of 1 lemon

Sea salt

Pinch of crushed red chile pepper

2 garlic cloves, crushed and chopped

⅓ cup olive oil, preferably a deep-flavored oil from Italy or Greece

TRIM the broccoli, if using, and cut the spears into 1-inch lengths. If using cauliflower, break the head apart into florets.

ON a chopping board, combine the olives, capers, parsley, and lemon zest and chop together to mix well.

BRING a pot of water large enough to hold the broccoli or cauliflower to a rolling boil. Add a big pinch of salt and, when it returns to a boil, add the broccoli or cauliflower. Cook until just barely tender, about 6 minutes (less if using very small cauliflower florets).

MEANWHILE, in a skillet large enough to hold all the ingredients, warm the chile pepper and garlic in the oil over medium-low heat until hot, 3 or 4 minutes. The chile and garlic should be starting to melt in the oil, rather than sizzling and browning. Stir in the lemon juice and cook for another 2 minutes, then add the olive-caper mix, give it a stir, take it off the heat, and set aside.

DRAIN the broccoli or cauliflower well, shaking the colander. Combine the broccoli or cauliflower with the olive-caper dressing in the skillet and set the skillet back over medium heat. Warm it up to serving temperature, taste to make sure the seasoning is right, and then serve.

Notes: You could also add 4 or 5 anchovy fillets, chopped, to the skillet with the crushed chile pepper and garlic. As the oil warms, crush the anchovies into the oil.

Pitted green olives could be used instead of black ones—just be sure they are olives with plenty of flavor.

BROCCOLI RABE *(Rapini)*, CAULIFLOWER, *or* BROCCOLI *with* TOMATOES *and* BLACK OLIVES

In this dish from Puglia, the heel of Italy's boot, broccoli rabe is braised in a small amount of liquid along with onions, tomatoes, little hot chile peppers, and black olives. It is also very successful with cauliflower or broccoli, the head broken into florets—in fact, a combination of cauliflower and broccoli works well and looks pretty. Traditionally this is served with a topping of grated cheese to make a great vegetarian main course, but if you plan to serve this as a *contorno*, or accompaniment, to fish or meat, the cheese topping seems to me excessive.

This is also an excellent "sauce" for pasta—short, curly shapes are best.

MAKES 4 TO 6 SERVINGS

1½ pounds broccoli rabe, cauliflower or broccoli

1 medium red onion, thinly sliced

⅓ cup olive oil, plus a little more if using cheese, preferably from southern Italy

1 dried red chile pepper, crumbled

Sea salt

15 to 20 small cherry or grape tomatoes, halved

15 to 20 pitted black olives, coarsely chopped

¼ cup boiling water, or more as needed

⅓ cup freshly grated pecorino or parmigiano reggiano cheese (optional)

TRIM the broccoli rabe and discard any yellow or wilted leaves. Cut into 2-inch lengths. If using broccoli or cauliflower, cut into florets.

COMBINE the onion with the oil in a pan that can be put under the broiler. Set over medium-low heat. As the onion starts to sizzle, add the chile and salt to taste. Now stir in the vegetable pieces and add the halved tomatoes and black olives. Add about ¼ cup boiling water, then cover the pan, reduce the heat, and cook for about 10 minutes. Check the vegetables for doneness, piercing the thick parts with the point of a knife. If they need to cook a little longer, you may wish to add a little more boiling water to keep the vegetables from scorching.

IF you wish to serve this as a pasta sauce, simply cook any kind of short, curly pasta until it is almost but not quite done, then drain and toss into the pan with the vegetables, letting the pasta finish cooking with the vegetables. (A ladleful of pasta water taken from the pot before draining and added to the vegetables with the pasta will help make a creamy sauce.)

IF you decide instead to use the cheese topping, turn the broiler on to high. When the vegetables are done, sprinkle the cheese over the top, dribble on a little more olive oil, and run under the broiler just long enough to melt the cheese. Serve immediately.

208

ROASTED CAULIFLOWER *with* TAHINI SAUCE

This is a recipe developed by my daughter Sara and often served during cauliflower season at her restaurant, Porsena, in New York's East Village. It comes from her cookbook, *Olives and Oranges*.

MAKES 4 TO 6 SERVINGS

1 large head cauliflower, cored and broken into florets

6 tablespoons olive oil

Sea salt and freshly ground black pepper

¼ cup plus 1 tablespoon tahini paste

Juice of 1 lemon (about 3 tablespoons)

1 garlic clove, minced to a paste

¼ cup finely chopped flat-leaf parsley

PREHEAT the oven to 400°F.

IN a large bowl, toss together the cauliflower with the oil, generously sprinkling it with salt and pepper. Spread the oily cauliflower out on a rimmed baking sheet and transfer to the hot oven. Roast, stirring and turning a couple of times, until the cauliflower is browned and tender, about 35 minutes.

MEANWHILE, in a blender puree the tahini paste, 6 tablespoons water, lemon juice, and garlic, adding a pinch of salt. Transfer to a serving bowl large enough to hold all the cauliflower.

AS soon as the cauliflower is done roasting, remove it from the oven and toss it in the bowl with the tahini sauce, adding the parsley. Serve immediately, while hot, or set aside to cool to room temperature.

CARROTS *and* CHICKPEAS *in a* CHERMOULA SAUCE

Chermoula is a great example of the many simple, highly flavored Mediterranean sauces that can be used in a variety of ways. Chermoula, which comes from Morocco, is often used as a splendid way to dress fish. But here I use it with plain carrots—not overcooked, just braised to the tender point. Try it with other vegetables too, especially root vegetables (turnips take on a new flavor dimension); or marinate fish fillets in chermoula before roasting in the oven for an impressively flavorful dish.

If you use red wine to braise the carrots, they will take on a nice, deep ruby color—a pretty contrast to the pale chickpeas.

You will have more punch from the spices if you toast the cumin and coriander seeds in a dry skillet over medium heat until the fragrance rises and the seeds begin to smoke, then grind them to a fine powder in a spice grinder.

MAKES 6 OR MORE SERVINGS

For the carrots:

2 to 3 pounds carrots, peeled and cut into irregular 2-inch chunks

¼ cup olive oil

Water or red wine, to cover the carrots

For the chermoula:

3 garlic cloves, crushed with the flat blade of a knife

1 bunch cilantro, finely minced

About ⅓ cup finely minced flat-leaf parsley

1 teaspoon harissa, or to taste

1 teaspoon sea salt

1 teaspoon mild paprika, preferably Spanish pimentón dulce

TO MAKE THE CARROTS: If the carrots are very thick, halve or quarter each chunk lengthwise. Put the carrots in a saucepan with the oil and cook over medium-high heat, stirring, until the carrots start to brown along the edges. Add water or red wine just to cover them and cook, partially covered, until they are barely tender, 10 to 15 minutes.

TO MAKE THE CHERMOULA: Chop the garlic, cilantro, and parsley together to make a very fine mince. Transfer to a bowl and stir in the harissa, salt, paprika, cumin, and coriander. Crumble the saffron into the mixture, then beat in the oil and lemon juice. Taste and adjust the seasoning. If it's not spicy enough (but you don't want to overpower the sweetness of the carrots), add a little chile pepper or more harissa.

continued

1 teaspoon ground toasted cumin seeds (see headnote)

½ teaspoon ground toasted coriander seeds (see headnote)

Pinch of saffron

½ cup olive oil

2 tablespoons freshly squeezed lemon juice or red wine vinegar, or more to taste

Ground hot red chile pepper (optional)

1 cup cooked chickpeas

1 cup cooked chopped spicy or bitter greens (optional)

AS soon as the carrots are done, drain them and, while they are still hot, pour the chermoula sauce over. Stir gently to cover the carrot pieces with the sauce. Set aside to marinate for at least 30 minutes before serving.

ADD cooked chickpeas and/or optional cooked spicy greens, if you wish. Serve at room temperature or a little warmer but neither piping-hot nor chilled from the refrigerator.

Carrots

Sweet, flavorful carrots are a neglected vegetable. Restaurant cooks mostly treat them as an opportunity for color on the plate rather than for their honeyed, earthy flavors. We should be more adventurous with a vegetable that is almost dazzlingly good for you.

Oven-roasted carrots (see page 198) are a terrific combination with beets, potatoes, and turnips to make a first-rate vegetarian offering. They also work well in an *à la grecque* treatment (see page 200), and stir-frying (see page 199) brings out a lot of their native sweetness.

LEEKS VINAIGRETTE

Leeks are very good prepared *à la grecque* (see page 200), and they are almost required in a good stir-fry. Leeks vinaigrette (*poireaux à la vinaigrette*) are a French classic, as good as a first course as they are for a side dish with, for example, a robust roast of pork.

MAKES 6 SERVINGS

6 fat leeks, or 12 slender ones

Sea salt

2 teaspoons French-style mustard

¼ cup aged red wine vinegar

Freshly ground black pepper

½ cup olive oil

Finely chopped flat-leaf parsley or fresh tarragon, for garnish

TRIM the root end and the tough green upper parts of the leeks, then slit them lengthwise from top to bottom but leave about an inch at the root end. Rinse very carefully under running water, opening the leaves up to let the water run through. Because leeks are blanched before harvesting, they often have a little mud in between the leaves. Remove all the mud and sand.

BRING liberally salted water to a boil in a skillet large enough to hold the full length of the leeks. When the water boils, add the leeks and cook until tender, 5 to 6 minutes. Remove from the heat and immediately add cold water to the pan to stop the leeks from cooking, then drain the leeks carefully but thoroughly.

IN a bowl, whisk together the mustard and vinegar, adding a pinch of salt and some ground pepper. Gradually whisk in the olive oil to make a smooth, creamy sauce for the leeks.

ARRANGE the leeks on a serving platter and spoon the vinaigrette over them. Garnish with chopped herbs. These are best served at room temperature. Chilling is not advised.

BATTER-FRIED EGGPLANT SLICES

Andalusian cooks serve their traditional salmorejo (see page 144) from Cordoba with plain, unbattered eggplant sticks—a little like fat french fries—fried in the region's best extra-virgin olive oil (see page 132). But in other regions, eggplant sticks (or slices or cubes) are dipped in a light batter before frying. Vary the seasonings in the batter, if you wish—use basil or mint, finely chopped, instead of the parsley; add a pinch of ground red chile pepper (my favorite is *piment d'Espelette*); or increase the quantity of grated cheese to make a decidedly cheesy coating. You could also use a very mild-flavored beer in place of the carbonated water. Lemon wedges served with the eggplant are a nice touch.

MAKES 4 TO 6 SERVINGS

1 medium eggplant (about 1 pound)

1 large egg

½ cup carbonated water (or beer)

4 to 6 tablespoons unbleached all-purpose flour

2 to 3 tablespoons finely grated pecorino or parmigiano reggiano cheese

1 teaspoon sea salt

1 garlic clove, crushed with the flat blade of a knife

⅓ cup chopped flat-leaf parsley or other fresh green herb

Freshly ground black pepper

1 to 2 cups olive oil

SLICE the eggplant horizontally or on the diagonal into ¼-inch-thick slices.

BEAT the egg in a bowl with the carbonated water until fully combined, then beat in 4 tablespoons of the flour, 1 tablespoon at a time. The batter should be as thick as heavy cream. If it is too thin, beat in another tablespoon or two until the batter is just thick enough to cling to the eggplant slices. Add the grated cheese and salt.

CHOP the garlic and parsley together to make a fine mince and stir it into the batter, then add the pepper. Set the batter aside to rest for at least 30 minutes.

HAVE ready a wire rack covered with paper towels. When you're ready to fry the eggplant slices, set the oil to heat in a deep-sided frying pan. The amount of oil depends on the size of the pan but should be at least 1 inch deep. Heat the oil until a deep-fry thermometer reads 350°F. (At that temperature, a small cube of bread should sizzle and turn golden in about a minute.)

WHEN the oil is hot, dip an eggplant slice in the batter, coating it on both sides. Hold it up to let the excess drip off and then slide it quickly into the hot oil. Don't do more than 4 or 5 slices at a time in order to maintain the temperature of the oil. Watch the temperature carefully and control it by raising or lowering the heat under the pan. Brown the eggplant slices on both sides, then transfer to the rack to drain.

WHEN all the eggplant slices are done, sprinkle with a little more salt, if you wish, and serve immediately, while the batter is still crisp and crunchy.

Eggplant

Eggplant, or aubergine, as the British call it, is an excellent vegetable for frying in extra-virgin olive oil. One caveat, though: if not handled properly, it will absorb frying oil like a sponge. *Handled properly* means:

1) The oil is at the correct temperature—350° to 360°F.
2) The eggplant pieces are thoroughly dry, and dried again just before dropping in the hot oil so that the pieces brown and crisp quickly and form a sort of shell to keep the inside from absorbing the oil.

Another important point: When frying eggplant, don't add oil to a pan that already has eggplant in it. The fresh oil will cool the oil in the pan so much that the eggplant pieces will start to absorb it. If you don't have enough oil in the pan, you must wait until you finish frying the current batch and remove it before adding more oil, then heating it to the correct temperature.

Alternatively, for many preparations you can toss sliced or chunked eggplant with olive oil and seasonings and roast them in a hot (400°F) oven before continuing with the recipe.

I used to follow religiously instructions to salt eggplant slices and drain them in a colander before using to get rid of any bitter juices. For most recipes, I no longer do that, as modern eggplant doesn't seem to require it. But if you wish to do so, by all means, be my guest!

ELIZABETH MINCHILLI'S "VAGUELY MIDDLE EASTERN" EGGPLANT SALAD

Elizabeth Minchilli is an enthusiastic gastronaut who divides her time between Rome and an olive farmlet in Umbria. She is apt to whip together something quite spectacular for lunch without really thinking about it. This eggplant "salad" is a good example. It works brilliantly as a first course on a hot summer day.

MAKES 4 TO 6 SERVINGS

Small pinch of crushed red chile pepper

1 or 2 garlic cloves, crushed with the flat blade of a knife

½ cup plain whole-milk yogurt or Greek yogurt

About ⅔ cup olive oil

2 large eggplants, cut into ½-inch-thick logs or batons

Sea salt and freshly ground black pepper

½ medium red onion, very thinly sliced

½ cup coarsely chopped pitted black olives

¼ cup coarsely chopped mint leaves

1 teaspoon crushed coriander seeds

¼ cup coarsely chopped roasted almonds

SEVERAL hours in advance, mix together the crushed chile and garlic with the yogurt. Stir in 2 tablespoons of the oil and set aside, refrigerated or in a cool place, to thicken slightly.

PREHEAT the oven to 400°F.

PUT the eggplant logs in a bowl and add the remaining ½ cup oil or enough to coat the logs thoroughly, turning and mixing with your hands. Spread the logs out on a baking sheet. Sprinkle with salt and pepper and transfer to the hot oven. Roast until the eggplant is tender and browned, 40 to 45 minutes, then remove from the oven and let cool.

ARRANGE the cooled (but not chilled) eggplant on a platter. Top with the sliced onion, the olives, and the mint, then spoon the yogurt mixture over the top and scatter the crushed coriander seeds and chopped almonds over the yogurt.

FAVA BEANS *or* GREEN PEAS BRAISED *with* PROSCIUTTO

I confess that I add this old-fashioned Roman recipe for fava beans or peas to almost every cookbook I write just because it is so easy and so good. But you must have very tender, young, just-picked beans or peas because the success of the recipe depends on these sweethearts, and if they come from your own garden, it's all the better. You can do this with just favas, just peas, or a mixture of both. Do keep in mind that in Rome there is no question of peeling the individual fava beans—they are so small and tender that there's no need to do that. Make sure the beans you select are the same.

In Rome they often use slices from a piece of lean guanciale (cured pork cheek), but prosciutto is easier for most North Americans to come by. If prosciutto is not available, use a good quality of slab bacon; if you wish, blanch the bacon in boiling water beforehand to rid it of any overly smoky flavor, which will detract from the sweetness of the vegetables.

MAKES 6 SERVINGS

1 medium white onion, halved and thinly sliced

½ garlic clove, crushed with a knife and chopped

2 or 3 slices prosciutto, diced

⅓ cup olive oil

3 to 4 pounds tender young fava (broad) beans or peas, shelled

1 cup light chicken broth or water, or more as needed

Sea salt and freshly ground black pepper

1 tablespoon minced flat-leaf parsley

COMBINE the onion, garlic, and prosciutto in a saucepan with the olive oil. Cook over medium-low heat, stirring occasionally, until the onion is soft but not beginning to brown and the prosciutto is releasing some of its fat. This will take 10 to 15 minutes.

STIR in the shelled beans and add the broth and a very little salt—the prosciutto may add plenty of salt to the dish. Add a couple of turns of ground pepper and raise the heat to a fast boil. Cook the vegetables quickly, uncovered, to retain their bright color and flavor. By the time the beans are tender, there should be just a few tablespoons of syrupy sauce in the bottom of the pan. If necessary, add a little more boiling broth or water while cooking.

WHEN done, serve immediately, sprinkled with the parsley and with chunks of crusty country-style bread to sop up the juices.

GREEN BEANS *with* TOMATO *and* OLIVE OIL

Called *loubiya bi zeit*, this is a standard offering in Lebanese kitchens. Something similar happens all over the Mediterranean, only the basic seasoning changes. At the western end of the Med, the red pepper and cumin would be dropped in favor of fresh herbs, chopped basil, parsley, or even a little very finely chopped rosemary.

MAKES 4 TO 6 SERVINGS

¼ cup olive oil

2 teaspoons cumin seeds

2 garlic cloves, finely chopped

½ medium yellow onion, thinly sliced

Sea salt and freshly ground black pepper

1 tablespoon tomato paste or concentrate

1 tablespoon Aleppo pepper or similar Middle Eastern crushed red chile pepper

1½ pounds green beans

1 (28-ounce) can whole peeled tomatoes, drained and crushed or chopped

HEAT the oil in a saucepan over medium-high heat; add the cumin seeds and cook, stirring often, until fragrant, about 1 minute.

ADD the garlic and onion, season with salt and pepper, and cook, stirring often, until soft and lightly browned, about 12 minutes.

ADD the tomato paste and Aleppo pepper, and cook, stirring occasionally, until the tomato paste is lightly caramelized, about 2 minutes. Add the green beans, tomatoes, and 1 cup water and bring to a boil. Reduce the heat to medium-low and cook, partially covered, stirring occasionally, until very tender. Let sit off the heat for at least 15 minutes before serving to allow the flavors to meld.

BRAISED WILD MUSHROOMS

In *Summer Cooking*, the great British food writer Elizabeth David introduced her recipe for mushrooms baked in grape leaves with the following observation:

"Many people who have a vine growing in their gardens will be glad to know of this excellent dish."

Indeed, it is an excellent dish, the grape leaves adding a slightly green and pleasantly acidic flavor to the mushrooms. Mrs. David suggests, unusually for her, that it can be made with canned grape leaves and ordinary store-bought cultivated mushrooms[1]. But the dish reaches an epiphany if the mushrooms are wild ones, gathered in some warm and sunny woodlot, and the leaves come from a vine growing over your garden shed. And if you don't have a grapevine in your backyard, or perhaps you don't even have a backyard, look for a neighbor with a vine and then just go over some dark night and remove a dozen or so leaves—no one will even notice they're gone.

MAKES 4 TO 6 SERVINGS

12 fresh grape leaves

Sea salt

⅓ to ½ cup olive oil

About 4 pounds fresh mushrooms, preferably wild porcini or cèpes, cleaned and trimmed, caps left whole but stems thickly sliced

Freshly ground black pepper

4 garlic cloves, peeled and split in half

PREHEAT the oven to 325°F.

BLANCH the grape leaves in boiling salted water, immersing them for about 2 minutes, then draining thoroughly.

SPREAD a thin film of the oil over the bottom of a shallow baking dish, one with a tight-fitting cover. Arrange 8 of the grape leaves over the bottom and sides of the dish and pour another thin film of the oil over the top. Scatter the sliced stems of the mushrooms over the grape leaves, then arrange the flat caps, spore side down, on top. Scatter more salt over the mushrooms along with plenty of pepper. Distribute the garlic cloves in and around the mushroom caps. Cover the caps with the remaining 4 grape leaves, put the lid on the dish (or secure aluminum foil tightly around it), and transfer to the oven. Bake for 35 minutes to 1 hour—smaller mushrooms will take less time. Remove the lid when the mushrooms are tender and cooked through, raise the oven heat to 375°F, and return the dish to the oven for an additional 10 minutes. When ready to serve, remove the top layer of grape leaves.

Note: You could treat small sweet onions in a similar fashion, first peeling them but otherwise leaving them whole.

1. I'm sure, if Mrs. D. were alive today, she would have a different opinion.

EASTERN MEDITERRANEAN STUFFED PEPPERS

Fresh red, yellow, or green sweet peppers, when hollowed out, make fine little receptacles for a savory filling. And the peppers themselves act as flavorful foils for whatever you put in them. This rice or bulgur filling is perfect for vegetarians.

MAKES 6 TO 8 SERVINGS

For the filling:

1 medium yellow onion, minced

3 or 4 scallions, white and green parts, minced

⅓ cup olive oil

¼ cup pine nuts

½ cup long-grain rice or medium-cut bulgur

2 medium ripe tomatoes, peeled, seeded, and chopped; or 2 canned tomatoes, drained and chopped

Sea salt and freshly ground black pepper

¼ teaspoon ground allspice, or to taste

¼ teaspoon ground cinnamon, or to taste

½ teaspoon crushed red chile pepper (optional)

2 tablespoons chopped fresh mint leaves

3 tablespoons black currants, soaked in hot water and drained

For the peppers:

4 large firm sweet peppers, preferably red and yellow

¼ cup olive oil

⅓ cup unseasoned dry bread crumbs

TO MAKE THE FILLING: Gently sauté the onion and scallions in the oil over medium heat until they are thoroughly softened but not brown. Add the pine nuts and continue cooking for a few minutes longer, until the pine nuts are golden. Add the rice and stir to coat thoroughly. Stir in the tomatoes, add salt and pepper, and then add ¼ cup very hot water. Mix well, cover the pan, and cook over low heat until all the liquid has been absorbed and the grain has started to soften, about 10 minutes. Remove from the heat, stir in the allspice, cinnamon, crushed chile pepper if using, the mint, and the drained currants. Set aside, covered, for 10 minutes, before using the mixture to stuff the peppers (see Note).

TO MAKE THE PEPPERS: Preheat the oven to 350°F.

CUT the peppers in half lengthwise and remove the seeds and internal white membranes.

SPREAD a thin film of the oil over the bottom of a roasting pan large enough to hold all the pepper halves side by side. Fill each half with the filling, allowing room for the grain to expand. When all the peppers are filled, sprinkle their tops with the bread crumbs and a thin thread of olive oil, adding the remainder of the oil to the pan. Bring water to a boil and add it to a depth of about ½ inch in the pan.

SLIDE the pan into the oven and bake for 1 hour. If the peppers aren't brown on top, increase the heat to about 425°F and dribble a little more oil over the tops. Return to the oven for 10 minutes or so, until the tops are brown.

THE peppers may be served hot from the oven, but they are almost better left to cool to room temperature before serving.

Note: It's a good idea to sauté a tablespoon of the filling in a little oil in order to test the seasoning before filling the peppers.

CRISPY OVEN-ROASTED KALE

This must be the healthiest snack imaginable—good-for-you kale with good-for-you olive oil, and a little salt to perk things up. What could be better?

MAKES 6 TO 8 SERVINGS

1 bunch green kale (about 1 pound), rinsed, thoroughly dried

¼ cup olive oil

Sea salt

PREHEAT the oven to 350°F. While the oven is heating, strip the kale leaves from the stems or central ribs and discard the ribs. Stack the leaves and slice them about ¼ inch thick, then add the sliced kale to a bowl. Toss with the oil until the leaves are thoroughly coated.

SPREAD the oil-coated leaves on a baking sheet, making a fairly even layer. Transfer to the oven and bake for about 10 minutes, removing the sheet and tossing the kale a couple of times. The kale should be crispy but not burned—watch it carefully and remove from the oven as soon as it reaches that stage. Sprinkle with sea salt and serve immediately.

Spinach

Spinach is great raw in a salad, but I think it really comes into its own when it's steamed and then braised, like the greens on page 199, in olive oil with a bit of garlic and maybe a little pinch of chile pepper. As with other greens, the steamed spinach must be drained thoroughly. Mediterranean cooks chop the steamed spinach in a colander, then, as soon as they can handle the hot greens, they pick up balls of the stuff and squeeze them between their hands to drain them even more thoroughly. (Save that tasty juice and add it to a vegetable stock.)

A pound of spinach will make roughly 1 cup of steamed, thoroughly drained cooked spinach, or enough for two people as a side. I like to reheat this quantity of spinach in 2 tablespoons olive oil in which I have very gently sautéed a chopped clove of garlic. While the spinach is reheating, I might add a pinch of *piment d'Espelette* or other not too fiercely hot chile. Then I take the pan off the stove and stir in ¼ cup plain whole-milk ricotta (or yogurt) and another tablespoon of oil.

Instead of the ricotta, Mediterranean cooks also may stir into the finished spinach a small handful of plumped golden raisins and another handful of toasted pine nuts.

PEPERONATA

Peperonata is found in one form or another all over rural Italy. This one has hot red chile peppers, indicating it's from Lucania, aka Basilicata—a part of Italy that's famous for the presence of hot peppers in its cuisine.

MAKES 4 SERVINGS AS A MAIN COURSE, 6 TO 8 AS A *CONTORNO*

2 medium yellow onions, halved and thinly sliced

⅓ cup olive oil

2 medium potatoes, peeled and sliced or cut into chunks

Sea salt and freshly ground black pepper

6 sweet peppers, preferably red and yellow

1 pound ripe red tomatoes, diced, to make 1 cup (or use canned, drained plum tomatoes, chopped to make 1 cup)

1 fresh or dried red chile pepper, or more to taste

COMBINE the onions and oil in a skillet large enough to hold all the ingredients and set over medium-low heat. Cook, stirring occasionally, until the onions begin to soften, then stir in the potatoes along with salt and pepper and continue cooking and stirring for about 10 minutes, until the potatoes are tender enough to pierce with the point of a knife.

WHILE the onions and potatoes are cooking, peel the sweet peppers, using a vegetable peeler to remove the thin skin on the outside. Cut the peppers into long, 1-inch-wide strips, discarding the seeds and white membranes.

AS soon as the potatoes are tender, add the pepper strips to the pan, stirring carefully to mix well without breaking up the potatoes. Let cook for about 15 minutes, or until the peppers are beginning to soften, then stir in the tomatoes. If you're using a fresh chile, cut it in half, discard most of the seeds and white membrane (which is where a lot of the heat is located), cut it into very thin slices, and add to the pan; if using a dried chile, break it, shake out and discard most of the seeds, and crumble into the pan. Stir once more and let cook for another 15 minutes. At this point, the tomato sauce will have thickened and all the vegetables will be very soft. If there is still a lot of liquid in the pan, raise the heat and boil rapidly until the liquid is reduced to a syrupy sauce.

REMOVE from the heat and serve immediately. Peperonata is also often served at room temperature.

VARIATION: To make a heartier dish, to serve as a main course at supper for instance, break 5 or 6 eggs into a bowl and beat them lightly with a fork. When the vegetables are tender, pour the beaten eggs over them and cook briefly, stirring and lifting the vegetables to let the egg slide underneath. If you wish, run the skillet under a preheated broiler to brown the top of the frittata lightly before serving.

VEGETABLES AND SALADS

Potatoes

Baked, fried, boiled, steamed, or roasted, potatoes seem created just to go with extra-virgin olive oil. I can't think of anything that shows off a high-quality oil more than a baked potato, cracked open at the table and doused with a glug of finest oil, a sprinkling of sea salt, and a couple of turns of black pepper. As for mashed potatoes, with olive oil mashed right in instead of butter—it's an exaltation of olive oil and of the glories of the humble spud. Spanish chef María José San Román, whose restaurants in the seaside town of Alicante, in southeastern Spain, should be a must on any gastronomic tour of that country, says that a full, fruity Cornicabra oil, a variety that is grown mostly in the provinces of Toledo and Ciudad Real, is a perfect foil for potatoes of any kind.

Fried Potatoes

Do we really need a recipe for fried potatoes? Doesn't everyone have his or her own way of doing them? Since she was a wee child, my daughter's favorite kitchen chore was frying thickly sliced potatoes in a big frying pan with plenty of chopped rosemary and garlic and a little ocean of olive oil. New Orleans chef Emeril Lagasse has an elaborate procedure for soaking cut french fries in the refrigerator, then rinsing and drying and frying at a low 325°F, removing from the fat, refrigerating again (even overnight!), then returning them to 350°F oil for a final fry up. My friend Fran Gage, an expert on California oils, soaks the potatoes before peeling and slicing them, and again once they've been prepped. Then she heats the oil to precisely 380°F and away she fries.

But the most extraordinary fried potatoes I ever had were in the little town of Baeza, in Andalusia, where Paco Vañó, who makes the excellent Castillo de Canena olive oil, had taken me to a favorite local restaurant. The chef showed us how he fries the sliced potatoes in oil heated to just 130° to 140°C (260° to 280°F), no more. He fries the potatoes gently in this fat until they are done, transfers the potatoes, dripping with oil, to a hot, deep dish, then raises the heat and fries eggs in that same, now very hot, oil for just 10 seconds and drops them on top of the potatoes, where they turn into a kind of egg sauce—delicious!

POTATO LATKES *for* HANUKKAH
(or all year round)

Hanukkah, of course, is the feast par excellence for olive oil, and it's no surprise that it comes in the middle of the olive harvest—or what would have been the olive harvest back in the time of the Jerusalem temple where the miracle supply of olive oil was found to keep the candelabra burning for eight days. Those ancient Israelites knew what they were doing—no other oil will suffice, and the very idea of low-fat latkes, promoted in diet magazines, is ridiculous. They're supposed to be as fat as possible!

MAKES 4 TO 6 SERVINGS

2 large russet potatoes, peeled

1 tablespoon freshly squeezed lemon juice

1 large yellow onion

2 tablespoons unbleached all-purpose flour

2 large eggs, beaten with a fork

Sea salt and freshly ground black pepper

Olive oil, for frying

⅛ teaspoon baking powder

ARRANGE a clean, lightly dampened kitchen towel over a colander and set the colander in the sink. Using the large holes of a grater, grate the potatoes into the towel. When the potatoes are grated, squeeze the towel firmly, extracting as much of the starchy juice as you can. Transfer the grated potatoes to a bowl and add the lemon juice, stirring to mix well.

USING the same grater, grate the onion directly into the bowl with the potatoes. Sprinkle the mixture with the flour and toss to distribute the flour evenly. Mix in the eggs, along with salt and pepper. This may be done ahead, even a day ahead, but refrigerate the bowl (covered) and don't add the baking powder until just before frying.

WHEN you're ready to fry the pancakes, add the oil to a heavy-duty skillet (black cast iron is perfect for this) to a depth of about 1 inch. Heat the oil over medium-high heat until it is just below the smoking stage—about 360°F. (Use a thermometer for accuracy.) Stir the baking powder into the potatoes, mixing well. Use a soup ladle or large soup-spoon to drop the potatoes into the hot oil, about ¼ cup at a time. Flatten the cakes gently with the back of the spoon. Fry on one side until brown and crisp, then turn and fry on the other side. Remove from the pan and drain on paper towels.

POTATO latkes are traditionally served with applesauce and a small dollop of sour cream.

OVEN-ROASTED WINTER SQUASH
with PANCETTA *and* ROSEMARY

Winter squash varieties that work well in this recipe include butternut, acorn, kabocha, and big blue Hubbards, but don't forget pumpkins, especially cheese pumpkin and *rouge vif d'Étampes*.

If you use bacon instead of pancetta, the dish will have a pleasantly smoky flavor. If you don't want that flavor, however, blanch the bacon before dicing by setting a chunk of slab bacon in a pot of simmering water for 5 or 6 minutes. This will cut down a lot on the smoky flavor. If you like the smoky flavor and want to emphasize it, use Spanish *pimentón de la Vera*, a smoky paprika, for the chile pepper in the dish.

MAKES 8 SERVINGS AS A SIDE DISH

5 tablespoons olive oil, plus more for the dish

¾ cup chicken or vegetable broth

⅓ cup diced pancetta or bacon

About 3 pounds winter squash, peeled and cut into 1-inch dice

1 medium red onion, very thinly sliced

1 tablespoon chopped fresh rosemary leaves

Pinch of ground red chile pepper, mild or hot to taste

Sea salt and freshly ground black pepper

1 cup fresh bread crumbs

½ cup finely grated parmigiano reggiano cheese

PREHEAT the oven to 375°F and use a little oil to grease a 9 by 13-inch baking dish. Bring the broth to a simmer in a saucepan.

SET a skillet over medium-high heat and combine the pancetta with 1 tablespoon of the oil. Cook, stirring, until the pancetta pieces have started to crisp and brown and give off some of their fat.

COMBINE the squash in a bowl with the sliced onion and rosemary. Add the ground chile pepper, salt and black pepper, and then 2 tablespoons of the oil. Toss with your hands to combine thoroughly and make sure all the squash dice are coated. Finally, stir in the browned pancetta with its oil and toss again. Transfer to the prepared baking dish, add the hot broth, cover the dish (with aluminum foil if necessary), and set it in the oven.

BAKE the squash for about 40 minutes, or until it is tender and a knife pierces it easily. Remove the dish from the oven and raise the oven temperature to 425°F. Scatter the bread crumbs and grated cheese over the squash and dribble the remaining 2 tablespoons oil on top.

RETURN the dish to the oven and bake for an additional 10 or 15 minutes, until the crust is golden.

THE dish can be served immediately, but it's better if allowed to cool a bit to something hotter than room temperature but not steaming hot.

GRATIN *of* TOMATOES *and* ZUCCHINI

Late in the summer, when tomatoes are at their peak of ripeness, the best thing to do with them is slice them onto a plate, pour over a generous glug of olive oil, add a few strategic drops of very good aged wine vinegar and a sprinkle of crunchy sea salt, and take the plate outside for a feast under the nearest shade tree, preferably with a water view to enjoy. Second best is to layer them with equally thick slices of real honest-to-god buffalo milk mozzarella plus an abundance of dark green basil leaves and oil-vinegar-salt for an *insalata caprese*, one of the most ingenious flavor combinations in the Italian kitchen. Third best is to bake them, as in this recipe: sliced tomatoes, sliced zucchini, sliced red onion, a scattering of chopped garlic and basil, and a few blobs of ricotta on top. The olive oil will pull this all together into a feast for the eyes and the palate.

Use smaller tomatoes for this, so that the slices almost match the zucchini slices in size.

MAKES 4 TO 6 SERVINGS

½ cup olive oil, plus more for the dish

2 pounds small ripe tomatoes, sliced about ¼ inch thick

3 dark green zucchini, sliced about ¼ inch thick

½ medium red onion, sliced about ¼ inch thick

Sea salt and freshly ground black pepper

3 garlic cloves, chopped

½ bunch of basil, leaves only, coarsely chopped

½ to ¾ cup ricotta cheese (see page 186)

¼ cup dry bread crumbs

¼ cup freshly grated parmigiano reggiano cheese

PREHEAT the oven to 375°F.

SPREAD a thin film of oil over the bottom of an oval gratin dish.

ARRANGE alternating slices of tomato, zucchini, and red onion in the dish, stacking them on a diagonal. If there is excess onion at the end, scatter the remainder over the top, along with a sprinkling of salt and pepper and the garlic bits. Arrange the basil on top.

SET aside 1 tablespoon of oil and dribble the remainder over the contents of the gratin dish. Add dabs of the ricotta all over, then sprinkle with the bread crumbs and grated cheese. Spoon the remaining 1 tablespoon oil over the top. Slide the gratin dish into the oven and bake for 45 minutes to 1 hour, until the top is brown and bubbly.

SERVE as soon as you remove the dish from the oven, or set aside to eat later—it's as good at room temperature as it is piping-hot.

SLOW-ROASTED TOMATOES *with* CAPERS *and* OLIVES

This is a long, slow recipe, but fortunately the cook is not required to do anything at all except occasionally peek in the oven to see how things are going. Just be prepared: It will take a good 3 hours before the tomatoes are ready.

You will need small tomatoes for this, not tiny grape tomatoes but the smallest size of plum tomatoes. These are delicious as a side with any kind of roast meats or fleshy fish—they're terrific with swordfish. But they also can be used almost as is, with pasta, especially short, stubby pasta shapes. Just break the tomatoes up a bit and mix them more thoroughly with the capers and olives to make more of a sauce.

A Tuscan olive oil or a Coratina oil from Puglia will marry well with the intense flavor of these tomatoes.

MAKES 4 TO 6 SERVINGS

2 pounds small ripe plum tomatoes

½ cup olive oil

Pinch of sugar

Pinch of sea salt

2 or 3 garlic cloves, coarsely chopped

¼ cup salt-packed capers, thoroughly rinsed and drained

½ cup pitted black olives, preferably salt-cured olives

2 tablespoons freshly squeezed orange juice

1 teaspoon crushed red chile pepper

Freshly ground black pepper

PREHEAT the oven to 250°F.

CUT the tomatoes in half lengthwise. Use a little of the oil to spread a thin film over the bottom of a roasting dish and set the tomatoes, cut side up, in the dish. Sprinkle each half with a little sugar and a little salt, then pour the rest of the olive oil over the tomatoes. Transfer to the oven and bake for about 1 hour.

REMOVE from the oven and sprinkle just a bit more salt and sugar, along with the chopped garlic, over the tomatoes, which should have settled in the pan and collapsed a bit as their juices evaporate. Give them a stir, just moving them around a bit with a wooden spoon, then return to the oven for another hour.

AFTER the second hour, give them another stir. By now they may be thoroughly collapsed and you can stir in the capers, olives, orange juice, chile pepper, and black pepper. Continue roasting for another hour, then remove from the oven and transfer to a serving bowl with all the juices. Or chop the tomatoes further and use them as a sauce. They're as great atop pasta as they are over steamed farro or a bulgur or rice pilaf.

SHAKSHOUKA
Spicy Tomatoes and Peppers

There's a famous restaurant in the old city of Jaffa called Dr. Shakshouka, an intriguingly old-fashioned kind of place where shakshouka, not surprisingly, is a featured attraction, most often served with eggs cooked right in the extremely tasty sauce. Israelis claim the dish for their own, but when I started investigating, I found it was almost ubiquitous all along the southern shore of the Mediterranean—even on the remote island of Pantelleria, part of Italy but almost in Tunisia, where there's a local favorite called *sciakisciuka*, which turns out to be very similar. Pantescans like to say the Arabs brought it from North Africa, and why not? Except . . . the two key ingredients are peppers and tomatoes, which were utterly unknown to the Arabs and everyone else in the Mediterranean until sometime well after 1492. So much for culinary history!

This is my adaptation of a number of Libyan, Egyptian, and Israeli ways of creating a robust dish that is served in Israel with eggs poached right in the sauce. It is equally good with fish fillets or fish cakes cooked in it. I could easily imagine this as the centerpiece for a breakfast buffet.

MAKES 4 TO 6 SERVINGS

3 sweet red peppers, cored and coarsely chopped

4 to 6 garlic cloves, chopped

⅓ cup olive oil

1 large or 2 medium tomatoes, peeled and coarsely chopped, plus 2 tablespoons tomato paste or concentrate; or 1 (28-ounce) can tomatoes with their juices

1 tablespoon mild paprika

1 teaspoon ground cumin, or more to taste

1 or 2 teaspoons medium-hot ground or crushed chile pepper (Aleppo pepper is best)

1 teaspoon ground coriander

GENTLY sauté the chopped peppers and garlic in the oil over medium heat until the vegetables are very soft, about 15 minutes.

IF you're using fresh tomatoes, stir them in. They will give off quite a lot of liquid. Cook until most of the liquid has evaporated, then stir in the tomato concentrate, along with the paprika, cumin, ground chile, coriander, caraway, and turmeric. Add 1 cup water along with the sugar and salt and pepper, and cook down for another 15 minutes or so to bring all the flavors together and thicken the sauce slightly.

IF you're using canned tomatoes, add them to the peppers and garlic along with the paprika, cumin, ground chile, coriander, caraway, turmeric, sugar, salt, and pepper, but do not add additional water.

TASTE and adjust the seasoning. If you add more chile or paprika, cook down again to get rid of the raw pepper flavor. When the sauce is ready, stir in the slivered salt-preserved lemon, if you have it (and if not, a good spritz of lemon juice will be fine).

continued

1 teaspoon ground caraway

½ teaspoon ground turmeric

Pinch of sugar

Sea salt and freshly ground black pepper

½ salt-preserved lemon, slivered, or a spritz of lemon juice

6 eggs; or 1½ pounds peeled fresh shrimp; or 1½ pounds salmon or other fish fillets

¼ cup chopped fresh cilantro (optional)

1 tablespoon za'atar (optional)

IF you want to cook eggs in the sauce (as they do in Jaffa), crack the eggs, one at a time, into a teacup, and slide the egg into the simmering sauce, first making a little indentation in the surface with a big serving spoon. Add each of the eggs—you should be able to get 6 in—and cook until the eggs are done to your taste. They are best, in my opinion, when the yolks are still a little runny, to contribute to the sauce.

BEFORE serving, sprinkle a little minced cilantro and/or za'atar on the eggs, if desired.

INSTEAD of eggs, you could add shrimp, being careful not to overcook them—they really only need about 1 minute in the simmering sauce. Or add fish fillets. Or arrange the fish fillets in an oiled baking dish and spoon the sauce over. Then transfer to a preheated 325°F oven and bake for 15 or 20 minutes, no more.

Salads

GIACOMO CASTELVETRO

Giacomo Castelvetro, an Italian exile in England, wrote his *Brieve racconto di tutte le radici, di tutte l'erbe e di tutti I frutti che crudi o cotti in Italia si mangiano* (*Brief Account of All the Roots, All the Greens and All the Fruits That, Raw or Cooked, Are Eaten in Italy*) back in 1614, hoping to introduce his British hosts to the whole concept of vegetable cookery, in which they were woefully remiss. Here's what he said about salad, freely translated and edited by me:

"Put a little salt in the bottom of the plate, then the greens, sprinkling on more salt, and then olive oil with a generous hand; turn the salad well with your hands, until every leaf is coated with oil."

This is still excellent advice for salad makers. Castelvetro went on to berate the Germans, who added too little salt, not enough oil, but way too much vinegar. "And some people do even worse," he added, "putting on nothing but salt and vinegar and sending them to the table like that for oil to be added when the greens are drunk with vinegar." The Italian salad law, *la legge salatesca*, goes like this:

Insalata ben salata, poco aceto, e ben oliata.

Salad well salted, a little vinegar, and very well oiled.

PALESTINIAN SALAD

Over the course of a three-week visit to Palestine a few years ago, in every home, it seemed, I was given a salad of stunningly crisp, fresh vegetables. The selection was more or less the same, sometimes with more cucumbers, sometimes with more radishes, but always with lots and lots of luscious Palestinian olive oil and freshly squeezed lemon juice to dress an abundance of slightly underripe tomatoes (treasured, as they are elsewhere in the Mediterranean, for their acid firmness in a salad), green peppers, small thin-skinned cucumbers sliced as half-moons, crisp radishes, green and white scallions, salt naturally, and lots and lots and *lots* of freshly chopped mint and parsley.

Years ago, I learned from a Palestinian friend to make salad dressing like this: Coarsely chop about half a clove of garlic and toss the pieces in the bottom of a salad bowl. Add a little more than ½ teaspoon fine sea salt and, using the back of a spoon, crush the garlic with the salt to make a paste. Then stir in 3 tablespoons fruity extra-virgin olive oil and 1 tablespoon freshly squeezed lemon juice. You can increase the quantity of the dressing, but always maintain the ratio of 3:1 olive oil to lemon juice.

MARINATED FETA *and* TOMATO SALAD

Feta is best for this treatment because its rough texture readily absorbs flavors from the marinade. It's often quite salty, so don't add any salt at all until you've tasted the final product. Other cheeses to consider are ricotta salata from southern Italy, a firm-textured chèvre from Provence, or Montenebro from Catalonia, in Spain. Crack the peppercorns in a mortar if you have one; otherwise, put them in a paper bag, set the bag on a bread board or wooden counter, and pound them gently with a rolling pin. The idea is to have roughly cracked but not crushed or ground peppercorns.

MAKES 4 SERVINGS

¼ pound Greek barrel-aged feta cheese (½ to ⅔ cup when broken up, as in the recipe)

⅓ cup olive oil, preferably very fruity Greek oil from Kalamata olives

1 to 2 tablespoons red wine vinegar

1 small dried red chile pepper, seeded and crumbled

Handful of coarsely chopped fresh basil, cilantro, or dill

1 tablespoon coarsely cracked black peppercorns

Sea salt (optional)

1 pound small ripe tomatoes (cherry, grape, or currant)

1 small red onion, halved and very thinly sliced

BREAK the cheese into small, irregular clumps if you can; otherwise, dice it not more than 1 inch to a side. Add the cheese pieces to a mason jar large enough to hold the cheese with the marinade. Combine in a small bowl the oil, vinegar, crumbled chile, green herbs, and peppercorns. Pour this mixture over the cheese in the jar, cover, and set aside in a cool place (not the refrigerator) for several hours or overnight.

WHEN ready to serve, taste the cheese mix and adjust the seasoning, adding salt if it seems necessary.

HALVE the little tomatoes and toss them in a salad bowl with the onion slivers. Pour the cheese and its marinade over the top. Bring the bowl to the table and toss just before serving.

POTATO *and* CAPER SALAD FROM *the* ISLAND *of* PANTELLERIA

You will probably never find an olive oil from Pantelleria, the little island in the middle of the ocean between Sicily and Tunisia, unless you take a ferry from Trapani and go there to get it yourself. The closest to the soft, delicate oils from the Biancolilla olive produced on the island are the Valle Trapanesi DOP oils from the western coast of Sicily, the area between Trapani and Marsala.

Capers from Pantelleria are world-renowned for their quality, but any salted capers will do if you can't find those from the island. Just be sure they are well rinsed before using. Vinegar- or brine-packed capers won't work well in this salad.

Pickled samphire, aka saltwort or salicornia, is made from a wild green that grows along the edge of the sea, on both the Atlantic and Pacific coasts. In Britain, pickled samphire is a treasure, and it is occasionally available in gourmet shops in North America. If you find it, by all means snatch it up for use in this and other salads. And if you can't find it, use pickled dilly beans instead. The flavor will be different but still quite acceptable.

MAKES 2 TO 4 SERVINGS

1 pound small, yellow-fleshed potatoes

⅓ cup salted capers, well rinsed and tossed dry

8 small ripe tomatoes (cherry tomatoes are fine), halved or quartered

8 to 10 salt-cured black olives, pitted and coarsely chopped

1 small red onion, halved and thinly sliced

Pickled samphire if available; otherwise use pickled dilly beans, slivered

¼ to ⅓ cup olive oil

Sea salt and freshly ground black pepper

Pinch of dried oregano

BRING a pan of lightly salted water to a rolling boil. Add the potatoes and cook, uncovered, until just tender, 20 to 25 minutes. Drain and let cool until they are still very warm but you can handle them.

PEEL the potatoes and slice them or cut them in chunks. Add to a bowl along with the capers, tomatoes, olives, onion slices, pickles, and oil. Toss gently to mix the ingredients, then taste and add salt and pepper. Spoon the potato salad onto a serving platter and sprinkle with the oregano. Serve immediately, while still a little warm or at least at room temperature. Do not refrigerate.

Note: Some Pantescan cooks use green olives rather than black, and some add a garnish of fresh basil or a very small amount of red wine vinegar. It's traditional to serve this salad with a type of small dried fish made on the island. The fish is shredded and the bones discarded, then the fish shreds are dressed with a little olive oil and served as an accompaniment to the salad. To mimic this flavor, try adding chopped anchovies or shredded dried cod to the salad.

SICILIAN ORANGE *and* RED ONION SALAD *(Insalata di Arance)*

A famous salad from Sicily, this combination of sweet blood oranges, pungent onions, and salty olives and anchovies, surprising as it may seem to North American palates, actually works very well. A similar salad from southern Spain uses shredded dried cod instead of the anchovies.

4 small oranges, preferably Sicilian Tarocco blood oranges

12 to 16 black olives, preferably salt-cured, pitted and halved

4 very thin slices red onion

6 anchovy fillets

3 tablespoons olive oil, preferably Sicilian

Freshly ground black pepper

PEEL the oranges thoroughly, cutting away the white pith as well as the outside membrane that covers the orange. Slice the oranges as thinly as you can manage on a plate to catch the juices.

ARRANGE the orange slices in a circle on a serving dish or on two salad plates. Distribute the olive halves over the oranges, then the red onion slices, and finally arrange the anchovy fillets on top.

POUR the orange juice over the salad, holding back any seeds. Spoon the oil over the salad and then sprinkle with pepper.

COVER lightly with plastic wrap and set aside at room temperature to let the flavors develop for at least 30 minutes before serving.

Note: Tarocco blood oranges are prized in Sicily for their deep orange flesh, liberally flecked with crimson, and their distinctive acid-sweet flavor balance. They are now grown in Florida and California but are not always widely available. If you cannot find these or other blood oranges (Moro and Sanguinello are two other varieties), use ordinary Florida juice oranges, but taste them before using. Tangy acidic oranges are to be preferred over sweet navel oranges, but if navels are all you can get, add lemon juice to taste to the orange juice on the plate.

WINTER SALAD *of* BRUSSELS SPROUT LEAVES

Who would believe that Brussels sprouts, the vegetable that generations of North American children have grown to hate, would become newly chic? Yet, along with kale and a few other farmer's market winter vegetables, Brussels sprouts are the new darlings of young chefs. Here the crisp leaves are teased apart and served as a fine salad.

MAKES 4 SERVINGS

1 pound Brussels sprouts

1 bunch flat-leaf parsley, finely chopped

2 or 3 scallions, thinly sliced, white and green parts

¼ cup roasted sunflower seeds

3 tablespoons olive oil

½ teaspoon Dijon-style mustard

1 tablespoon red wine vinegar

Sea salt and freshly ground black pepper

TRIM the Brussels sprouts of their stubby stems, then pull away as many whole leaves as you can. Coarsely chop the hearts of the sprouts. Combine the sprouts with the parsley, scallions, and sunflower seeds in a salad bowl and toss with the oil.

IN a small bowl, stir the mustard into the vinegar and add to the salad, along with salt and pepper to taste. Toss and serve.

TABBOULEH

Like most dishes that have been around for a couple of centuries or so, tabbouleh exists in many variations, but for me the classic will always be the way we had it in Lebanon in the early 1970s. It was very different from the New York deli version of soggy bulgur with green herbs scattered throughout. Instead it was a fresh and vibrant salad, with fragrant chopped parsley and mint as a base and bulgur added for substance. Good fruity Lebanese olive oil and the juice of freshly squeezed lemons added brightness, and cinnamon and allspice contributed their distinctive, slightly musky aromas. The result was a pyramid of complex and contrasting textures and flavors that was thoroughly satisfying.

MAKES ABOUT 4 CUPS (6 TO 8 SERVINGS)

½ cup medium-cut bulgur

1 pound ripe tomatoes, diced

1 bunch scallions, white and green parts, thinly sliced

3 large bunches flat-leaf parsley, finely chopped (3 cups)

1 or 2 bunches mint, leaves only, finely chopped (1 cup)

½ cup olive oil, preferably Lebanese (or Greek or Palestinian)

Juice of 1 lemon (about ¼ cup)

¼ teaspoon ground allspice (optional)

¼ teaspoon ground cinnamon (optional)

Sea salt and freshly ground black pepper

Pinch of crushed red chile pepper (optional)

Large crisp romaine lettuce leaves, for serving

COVER the bulgur in a bowl with cold water to a depth of about 1 inch. Let soak for 20 to 30 minutes. When the grains are plump, drain them, squeezing out as much water as you can; then turn the bulgur grains into a clean kitchen towel and squeeze out the remaining water. Each grain should be plump and moist but with no trace of liquid left.

ADD the bulgur to a salad bowl with the diced tomatoes and scallions and mix with your hands, squeezing slightly to release the flavors. When the salad is well mixed, stir in the parsley, mint, and oil. Squeeze the lemon juice into a small bowl and add the allspice and cinnamon, if using, stirring to mix well before adding to the salad. (Otherwise, just squeeze the lemon juice right onto the salad.) Add plenty of salt and pepper, and a small pinch of chile pepper as well, if you wish.

TASTE the salad—it should have lively flavors of lemon and mint, undercut by the musky tones of the bulgur and spices. Adjust the seasoning, then arrange the salad heaped on a platter and surrounded by overlapping romaine leaves. Use the leaves as edible scoops for the salad.

Notes: Purslane is often used in tabbouleh. If you can find it (it may be growing as a weed in your garden), add a handful of plump purslane leaves along with the scallions.

In Palestine and Israel, tabbouleh is sometimes served garnished with bright red pomegranate seeds—a handsome presentation.

FATTOUSH, DAKOS, PANZANELLA, *and* OTHER BREAD SALADS

Mediterranean kitchens are a treasure trove of bread salads, from Tuscan panzanella to Lebanese fattoush to Cretan dakos made with crunchy barley rusks—and half a dozen others scattered around the shores. It's a thrifty way of using up stale or leftover bread, and the bread soaks up the delicious salad juices and becomes soft and savory. This Lebanese fattoush saved me many times from fainting with hunger after getting lost in the library stacks at the American University of Beirut when I was a student. After hours of wandering in the library, I would stagger out into the daylight and head for home, where a bowl of fattoush, made by our Lebanese housekeeper, often awaited me.

MAKES 6 SERVINGS

2 small rounds Arab pita bread, preferably a couple of days old

¾ cup olive oil, preferably Greek, Lebanese, or Palestinian

1 or 2 garlic cloves, crushed and chopped

Sea salt

Juice of 1 lemon (about ¼ cup)

8 radishes, halved or sliced

8 scallions, white and green parts, sliced

3 medium tomatoes, cut into thick chunks

2 medium cucumbers, preferably thin-skinned Middle Eastern or Armenian cukes, sliced

2 plain brine-pickled cucumbers (not sweetened, not heavily flavored with garlic or dill), sliced

1 small head romaine lettuce, coarsely chopped

½ cup coarsely chopped fresh mint leaves

PREHEAT the oven to 400° to 450°F. Split the rounds of Arab bread and set the 4 separated rounds on a baking sheet. Sprinkle the rounds with 2 tablespoons of the oil and transfer to the oven. Bake until the breads are crisp and toasted, then remove from the oven and set aside.

ADD the garlic and about ½ teaspoon salt to a small bowl and crush together, using the back of a spoon, to a paste. Stir in the lemon juice and remaining 10 tablespoons olive oil.

BREAK up the toasted bread into small pieces and put most of the pieces in the bottom of the salad bowl, reserving a few for the top of the salad. Pile on the radishes, scallions, tomatoes, cucumbers, pickles, lettuce, mint, and parsley. Beat the garlic-lemon dressing with a fork to mix well, then pour over the salad. Grind the black pepper over the top and sprinkle on the sumac. Garnish with the reserved bits of toasted bread.

½ cup coarsely chopped flat-leaf parsley

Freshly ground black pepper

2 tablespoons ground sumac

TAKE the salad bowl to the table and toss the ingredients together just before serving to keep the bread from getting soggy.

BEAN, LENTIL, CHICKPEA, FARRO, *and* OTHER HEARTY SALADS

Salads made from legumes and/or grains can make delightful main courses, especially for vegetarians or anyone trying to cut back on overconsumption of meat. But for the rest of us, a little meat or fish added will also contribute to the appeal of the dish. Think of something as simple as chopped bits of salami or a grilled fresh sausage, very thinly sliced and stirred in. Or leftovers—chunks of roast chicken or ham or shredded roast pork sound delicious, and the remains of an oven-roasted halibut or swordfish could add a lot. But, as with most salads, be judicious. The focus should be on the grains or the beans, alone or in combination, and the rest is a savory garnish.

Almost any kind of legume can be turned into a salad—tiny green French lentils or equally small gray ones from Umbria, fat white cannellini beans, sulphur or soldier beans from Maine, anasazi or pinto beans from New Mexico, little pale green flageolets; the list is almost limitless. One good source for dried beans in an enormous variety is www.ranchogordo.com in California. Although their selection is focused on beans of the Southwest, they are constantly expanding their offerings, which do include some Italian and New England beans.

Farro is a popular grain for salads—and I have to insist that, many translations to the contrary notwithstanding, farro is *not* usually spelt (*Triticum aestivum spelta*), but a much more interesting, antique variety of hard durum wheat called emmer (*T. turgidum dicoccum*). (Spelt is in a different branch of the vast wheat family, and in many regions outside of France and Germany it's considered a grain for animals.) Other types of wheat that can be cooked as whole berries (kamut, for instance) are also appropriate, as are transformed wheat products like couscous (especially large-grain Middle Eastern couscous) and bulgur.

Whatever you select, cook it in the simplest way possible, soaking overnight if necessary and then boiling in salted water and a spoonful of olive oil until tender but not mushy. Drain thoroughly before mixing in the salad.

A salad is best made when the grains or legumes are still quite warm and will absorb other flavorings rapidly, but that's not to say that you can't refrigerate or even freeze part of your harvest and keep it for later use. Let's say you've soaked 2 cups of beans overnight and cooked them until tender. You should have enough for 8 servings. If that's too much, freeze half the beans with some of their cooking liquid and use them another day—or in another recipe.

To 2 to 3 cups cooked, drained beans, you might add:

1 garlic clove, minced

¼ cup finely chopped flat-leaf parsley

1 medium red sweet pepper, seeded and chopped

1 small fresh green chile pepper, seeded and finely chopped

1 medium yellow or red onion, chopped; or 4 scallions, thinly sliced; or 3 or 4 shallots, chopped

2 medium ripe tomatoes, finely chopped; or a handful of little grape tomatoes, halved

1 bunch very firm radishes, halved or sliced

For aromatics, think about adding:

¼ cup slivered fresh basil, chervil, tarragon, cilantro, or other fresh green herbs—chives and lovage are two I especially like

¼ cup chopped fresh mint leaves

1 teaspoon ground cumin

¼ teaspoon ground allspice

½ to 1 teaspoon crushed or ground red chile pepper—piment d'Espelette, Aleppo pepper, or smoky pimentón de la Vera

DON'T feel you must include all of the suggested ingredients. Sometimes, indeed often, it's better to err on the side of discretion. Less is more, as Mies van der Rohe so tellingly noted.

AGAIN, be cautious and judicious with your seasoning. Of course you will add a good sprinkling of sea salt and freshly ground black pepper, and then several healthy glugs of olive oil. Most of these salads can take well to a robust oil such as a Koroneiki from Greece, a Moraiolo from Umbria, or a Picual from Spain. And finally, a good spritz of lemon juice.

TOSS this all together to mix well and set aside for at least 30 minutes (but do not refrigerate) for the flavors to develop and meld together.

Note: Keep in mind that a blend of different beans, or of legumes and grains (chickpeas and bulgur wheat, for instance), can also make an eminently satisfying dish.

SEAFOOD

O N THE EAST COAST OF SICILY, the daily Catania seafood market is so clamorous, so vigorous, so replete with fishy delights, that it should go to the top of every gastronome's bucket list. Sicilians really know seafood and how to experience it, from the simplicity of raw sea urchins, cracked open and eaten with a shot of lemon juice, to the complexity of multi-layered seafood stews garnishing *cuscussu*, the Sicilian version of North African couscous. It's no wonder I turn to Sicily for the most appropriate way to mix fish with olive oil, especially the green, fruity oils of the hills overlooking the coast. There I find the simplest, most delicious garnish in a sauce called salmoriglio. All it calls for is the finest kind of olive oil, the freshest lemon juice, the most pungent wild oregano, and Sicilian sea salt. Here's a recipe for 1 cup of sauce, 6 to 8 servings:

¾ cup olive oil, preferably Sicilian

¼ cup freshly squeezed lemon juice

Sea salt

1 tablespoon crumbled dried oregano

Freshly ground black pepper

1 or 2 garlic cloves, finely minced (optional)

Crushed red chile pepper to taste (optional)

COMBINE all the ingredients, including the optional ones if desired, and beat vigorously with a wire whisk or a fork to amalgamate. Serve immediately, spooning over prepared fish steaks, fish fillets, or whole fish cooked on the grill or roasted in the oven. Pass extra sauce to be added at the table.

Salmoriglio complements almost any kind of grilled, broiled, or poached fish—a whole sea bass is ideal, big tiger shrimps are quite wonderful, but one of the finest uses for salmoriglio, curiously enough, is as a dipping sauce to accompany a whole steamed Maine lobster. It's a long way from the Mediterranean, but the two are almost perfect together.

In general with seafood, I prefer to use a light, fruity, sweet, not overly pungent or bitter oil to go with white-fleshed fish, shrimps, and lobster and clams. A Tunisian oil, like that from Maisons Mahjoub in the Mejerda Valley of northern Tunisia, is perfect, and so is an Arbequina from Catalonia or some of the better-made Provençal oils, such as Castelas from the Vallée des Baux appellation. For what Italians call *pesce azzurro*, or blue fish—meaning the range of oily fish, from sardines to mackerel to true bluefish to salmon and swordfish—you want an oil with more character, more pungency, and for that I would go with a Koroneiki oil from the island of Crete—Biolea is an optimal selection—or a Coratina from Italy's Puglia region. Squid and octopus are strong enough in flavor to balance against that kind of oil, but, much as I love Tuscan oils, I don't think their robust character goes well with any fish except possibly yellowfin or albacore tuna. (Bluefin tuna is on my don't-buy list and it should be on yours because it is one of the most endangered creatures in the ocean, at serious risk for extinction.)

As with vegetables, there are a number of techniques that can be applied to different types of fish and seafood, most but not all from the Mediterranean.

FRIED SHRIMP, CALAMARI, *and* CHUNKS *of* FISH

For frying fish, Italian cooks favor a basic coating of plain flour, seasoned simply with salt and pepper, or with fresh or dried herbs. In Andalusia, the champion region for frying in Spain, cooks use a special *harina para freir*, flour for frying, a mix of all-purpose flour and semolina, sometimes with a little cornstarch added for crispness.

But the Brits—and we don't usually think of British cooks when we think of frying—are world leaders in the simple but seductive delights of fish and chips, batter-fried fish with fried potatoes (french fries), and for that you must have a proper batter. This easy batter originated in an Elizabeth David cookbook.

MAKES ENOUGH BATTER TO COAT 2 TO 3 POUNDS OF SEAFOOD (8 SERVINGS)

2 cups unbleached all-purpose flour

3 tablespoons olive oil

Pinch of sea salt

10 ounces (1¼ cups) tepid fizzy water or beer

1 egg white

2 to 3 pounds seafood (see recipe)

Olive oil, for frying

Lemon wedges, for garnish

IN a bowl, mix together the flour, oil, salt, and fizzy water, cover with plastic wrap, and let stand for about 2 hours. After that time, beat the egg white in a separate bowl until it is quite stiff, then fold it into the batter. Use this to batter a variety of seafood—small, fresh shrimps; calamari rings or whole baby calamari, cleaned; scallops, cut in half if they're very large; clams or mussels; chunks or cubes of firm-textured fish (such as swordfish, halibut, shark)—all are ideal.

WHEN ready to cook, heat olive oil in a pan deep enough for frying until a deep-fry thermometer reaches 360° to 365°F. It's important that the oil be hot enough in the first place, and that it doesn't overheat during the course of frying. Have ready a wire rack covered with paper towels to drain the fish. Set the oven on 200°F to keep early batches warm while you finish frying.

WHEN the oil is hot enough, drop whatever you're frying into the batter, let excess batter drip back into the bowl, then drop into the hot oil. Let the pieces bubble in the oil, turning them evenly on all sides so they turn beautifully golden and crisp. Keep testing the oil with your thermometer, and if it drops too low (say, below 350°F), stop frying and wait for the oil to heat up again. Be careful, too, not to let the oil get so hot that it burns the fish before cooking it through. Remove the pieces when done with a slotted spoon and set to drain on the rack, then transfer to the warm oven until you've finished.

SPRINKLE with salt and serve immediately, with lemon wedges.

AN OLIVE OIL VERSION *of* JASPER WHITE'S CLAM FRITTERS

Jasper White is the king of New England seafood—or of New England seafood cooks. This batter comes from *Jasper White's Cooking from New England*. It makes enough for 5 pounds of clams, steamed open in a pot with ½ cup dry white wine. Shuck and coarsely chop the clams and reserve a cup of their broth to use in the batter. These are clam fritters, not fried clams—an important distinction. Note that the batter must be refrigerated before cooking.

Instead of clams, try fritters with oysters, chopped-up scallops, or other seafood.

MAKES 4 TO 6 SERVINGS

2 cups unbleached all-purpose flour

1 cup cornmeal, preferably stone-ground

2 teaspoons baking powder

4 large eggs

1 cup milk

1 cup broth from the steamed clams

¼ cup olive oil, plus 1 to 2 cups for frying

Chopped meat from 5 pounds steamed littleneck clams

½ cup chopped scallions, white and green parts

Sea salt and freshly ground black pepper

COMBINE the flour, cornmeal, and baking powder, tossing with a fork to mix well. Lightly beat the eggs in a large bowl with a fork, and stir in the dry ingredients. Then stir in the milk, clam broth, and the ¼ cup oil. Fold in the chopped clams and scallions and add salt and pepper. Refrigerate the mix for 1 hour before cooking.

WHEN ready to cook, prepare a wire rack lined with paper towels for draining the fritters. Set the oven on 200°F to keep early batches warm while you finish the frying. Heat the 1 to 2 cups oil in a pan deep enough for frying until a deep-fry thermometer reaches 360° to 365°F. It's important that the oil be hot enough in the first place, and that it doesn't overheat during the course of frying.

DROP spoonfuls of clam fritter batter into the hot oil and let them bubble in the oil, turning them to brown evenly on all sides. Remove one fritter and cut it open to be sure they are cooked all the way through—sometimes you can have a beautifully browned exterior and a still gummy interior. That's an indication either that your oil is too hot or that your fritters are too large. One to 2 tablespoons batter should produce the right size fritter.

TRANSFER the fritters to the rack as they finish cooking. Keep warm in the oven until you are done, then serve immediately. May be served with a dipping sauce—a spicy aioli (see page 301) is good, but so is a tart-sweet tomato sauce. Or just serve the fritters plain—they will disappear very quickly, in any case.

OVEN BAKING WHOLE FISH, FILLETS, *or* STEAKS

Whole fish are ideal for roasting in the oven, but in my experience it is not easy to find a whole fish, even in seaside communities. Fish purveyors have become convinced that North American consumers like their fish cut up, just like their meat. To our loss on both counts.

So, even though whole fish are preferable for oven roasting, I give directions for fillets or steaks. If you do come across a whole fish, you can follow the same principles, adjusting cooking times to reflect the thickness of the fish.

Most thick fillets or fish steaks (think halibut, salmon, swordfish, or sea bass) benefit from oven baking, which is so quick and easy that you should be able to have dinner on the table in 30 minutes. A further plus: The vegetables and potatoes get cooked right along with the fish so there's much less cleanup. You start by arranging the fish in an oven dish that has been liberally spread with a film of olive oil. Next, sauté very gently a few sliced onions and/or leeks and/or garlic in olive oil, then, when soft, pile them on the fish, sprinkle with some fresh herbs (flat-leaf parsley, basil, fennel tops, chives) and some grated lemon zest, squeeze a few drops of lemon juice over the top, sprinkle with salt, pepper, and a pinch of chile pepper if you wish, add a little more olive oil and some bread crumbs, and transfer the whole thing to a preheated 400°F oven. Bake for 15 minutes, then lower the heat to 350°F and bake for an additional 10 to 25 minutes, or until the fish is cooked through.

Add other vegetables to the roasting pan if you wish, depending on the season—thickly sliced potatoes or carrots, button mushrooms, chunks of zucchini or summer squash, florets of broccoli or cauliflower, little plum tomatoes—or add a handful of pitted black olives and a scattering of capers, rinsed first to remove the salt.

Sometimes a fish for roasting will benefit from marinating in savory, spicy, or herbal mixtures. A marinade that I like to use for swordfish steaks (although it works just as well with other dense-fleshed white fish such as hake, haddock, or sea bass) calls for wild fennel pollen, which you can find at some fancy food shops. Zingerman's in Ann Arbor stocks it. Or use ½ cup or so fresh greens from the tops of bulb fennel in the supermarket produce section. Finely chop the greens and sprinkle them liberally, along with salt and pepper, over the swordfish steaks. Then whisk together ¾ cup olive oil with 3 tablespoons freshly squeezed lemon juice and 2 minced garlic cloves, and pour that over the fish. Cover it and let it marinate for 3 to 4 hours before roasting as above.

BECCHINA'S OVEN-ROASTED FISH
Pesce Arrosto

This is a Sicilian recipe from Gianfranco Becchina, producer of fine Olio Verde oil, who is also a superb home cook. In his Castelvetrano kitchen, he roasts a whole *cernia*, or grouper, including the head and tail, but I've adapted his recipe to halibut or similar steaks.

For 6 to 8 servings, 2 pounds of boneless fish should be adequate; with the bone in, count on another half pound—2½ pounds in all.

MAKES 6 TO 8 SERVINGS

2 pounds potatoes, preferably yellow Finns or Yukon gold, peeled

¼ cup plus 2 tablespoons olive oil, preferably Sicilian

1 medium yellow onion, chopped

1 plump garlic clove, chopped

1 cup dry white wine

2 or 3 plum tomatoes, peeled and chopped, or use whole canned plum tomatoes, to make about ⅔ cup chopped

Crushed red chile pepper (optional)

¼ cup salted capers, well rinsed

4 halibut or other similar fish steaks, cut ¾ to 1 inch thick

2 pounds small, slender zucchini, cut in half lengthwise

½ cup pitted black olives, preferably salt-cured

Sea salt and freshly ground black pepper

¼ cup freshly squeezed lemon juice

¼ cup minced flat-leaf parsley

CUT the potatoes into chunks, about 1½ inches to a side, and drop into a pan of rapidly boiling water. Return to a boil and cook for 5 minutes; drain and set aside.

ADD the ¼ cup oil to a sauté pan along with the onion and garlic and set over medium-low heat. Cook gently just until the vegetables soften, stirring occasionally. Raise the heat slightly, and add the wine and chopped tomatoes, along with a good pinch of crushed chile pepper, if you wish. Cook rapidly, stirring, until the wine has reduced by about one-third and the tomatoes are melting in the liquid. Remove from the heat and stir in the capers.

PREHEAT the oven to 325°F.

USE some of the remaining olive oil to coat the bottom and sides of a roasting pan large enough to hold all the fish in one layer. Set the fish in the pan and arrange the blanched potatoes and zucchini pieces around the sides. Scatter the olives among the potatoes and zucchini. Spoon the prepared onion-wine sauce over the fish and vegetables, sprinkle with salt and pepper, and add the remaining oil in a thin thread over the top.

TRANSFER the pan to the oven and bake for 10 minutes; using tongs, turn the potatoes and zucchini and return to the oven for another 10 to 15 minutes, or until the potatoes are tender, by which time the fish should be cooked through. Test with a fork to make sure it flakes tenderly.

TRANSFER the fish to a heated serving platter, arranging the vegetables and olives around it. Stir the lemon juice and minced parsley into the pan juices and spoon over the fish. Serve immediately.

SEAFOOD

253

POACHING FISH *in* OLIVE OIL

The technique is a little tricky, but once you gain confidence in your ability to maintain the oil at a constant low temperature, you will turn to it for delicious results. I learned about poaching with olive oil back in the long-ago 1990s, from a wonderful Maine chef named Tom Gutow, who had a restaurant in Castine on Penobscot Bay. He poached a center cut of native-raised salmon, and what arrived at the table was so fresh-tasting, so silken in texture, so utterly delicious, that it seemed quite miraculous. Chef Tom poached his fish on top of the stove and so did I at first, despite the fact that stovetop poaching requires constant vigilance to be sure the temperature never goes over about 150°F. Then I learned about oven poaching and changed my approach.

A center cut of salmon is ideal for this (the cut the French call *darne de saumon*), but a thick halibut steak will also do well. In Sicily I've had an oil-poached round of swordfish, cut from the tail end in one thick 3-inch piece. I imagine a center cut of yellowfin or albacore tuna, if you could find it, would be similarly fulfilling. But failing a center cut, thick fillets of fish will also work, though they will take less time to cook all the way through—which could be a plus.

A frying or candy thermometer, one that can go right down into the oil, is useful.

Having selected your fish, preheat the oven to 200°F—very low but that's the whole point. Take a pan that can go in the oven or a baking dish that can sit on top of a stove burner (because you'll need to use both cooking areas), and add your fish to the pan. It's best if the fish just fits in the pan, without too much empty space—you'll use less oil that way. In Sicily, cooks sprinkle the fish with dried oregano, grated lemon zest, salt, and pepper. Elsewhere, a cook might add a couple of garlic cloves, peeled but left whole, a couple of branches of fresh thyme, and perhaps a few small chile peppers. Next, add olive oil to come just to the top of the fish and cover it with a thin film of oil.

Set the pan on a stovetop burner over minimal heat—the smallest flame on a gas burner, the lowest setting on electric. Use a thermometer to be exact and, when the oil in the pan has reached 200°F, carefully transfer the pan to the oven.

(Some cooks like to craft a sort of bain-marie by setting the pan with the fish and oil into a larger roasting pan, then adding boiling water to the roasting pan to come about 2 inches up the sides. I don't see the necessity of this, but it seems worth noting.)

Let the fish cook for 1 hour, then test for doneness. It is difficult to give times since so much depends on the thickness of the fish, but in any case it is almost impossible to overcook unless you forget the fish and leave it in all day. If you're planning for a dinner party, put the fish in the oven at least 2 hours before you're expecting to serve it. Keep in mind that some fish (salmon and tuna among them) are preferred on the rare side, while others (swordfish, halibut, and the like) are better cooked through.

If the fish is not quite done to your taste, return it to the oven, turn the heat off but leave the oven door closed, and the fish will continue to cook in the residual heat of the oven and the oil. If the fish is much more underdone than you prefer, simply continue cooking it for another 30 minutes or so.

When the fish is done to your taste, remove the pan from the oven. Use a slotted spatula or fish turner to transfer the fish to a warm serving platter, leaving behind the oil and the white "patina"—actually the juice of the fish that has solidified during cooking. Use the savory oil from the pan to make a sauce for the fish—perhaps the salmoriglio on page 248.

Note: Another beauty of this preparation is that because the oil is treated in such a gentle manner, it can be used two or three more times, first filtering it through a fine-mesh sieve. It will, however, be redolent of fish, so use it advisedly.

CEVICHE
Marinated Raw Fish Fillets

All fish, obviously, should be as fresh as you can find it, but it's even more important with ceviche, which is a way of "cooking" fish simply by marinating it in citrus juice. This is an old Mediterranean way of preserving fish for a short period of time; the technique arrived in Latin America with the Spanish incursions and was transformed, deliciously, by the addition of chopped fresh cilantro, tomatoes, and green chile peppers.

Note that this is also a splendid way to treat very fresh wild shrimp or scallops. Just be absolutely certain that the scallops have not been treated with phosphates to plump them and, not incidentally, increase their weight. It will leak into any preparation to which they are added. Always ask for "dry," meaning untreated, scallops.

Serve this as a first course with a small green salad or with avocado slices dressed with oil and lemon. Made the day before, it also makes a great Saturday lunch, perhaps after a morning at the beach or on a hiking trail.

MAKES 8 SERVINGS AS A FIRST COURSE

1½ pounds fresh fish fillets

1 cup combined citrus juices—lemon and lime; lemon, lime, and grapefruit; lime and orange; or lime and bitter (sour) orange

¾ cup fruity, not bitter, olive oil

⅓ cup finely chopped cilantro

1 small red onion, minced

1 ripe red tomato, peeled, seeded, and chopped

2 small fresh jalapeño or serrano chile peppers, seeded and minced

Lemon wedges, for serving

COVER the fish fillets with the citrus juice in a bowl. Cover the bowl with plastic wrap and refrigerate for at least 6 hours, or overnight.

DRAIN the fish and arrange on a serving platter. Mix together the oil, cilantro, onion, tomato, and chiles and spoon over the fish. Cover once more and set aside until ready to serve. (If it's very warm weather, refrigerate the fish; otherwise, cool room temperature is fine for an hour or so.) Before serving, taste a small piece of fish. You probably will not need to add more acid since the citrus flavors will have penetrated the fish, but serve it with lemon wedges (or limes) in case someone wants to add more.

Note: No salt is added to prevent too much liquid from leaching out of the fish.

NORTH AFRICAN SEAFOOD TAGINE

A proper Moroccan tagine, with its high-peaked lid, is not required to make this dish. While I highly recommend that remarkable method of stovetop cooking, any covered casserole, especially if made of terra-cotta, will work instead.

When I had this in Morocco, down on the Atlantic coast below Essaouira, it was made with the big succulent red shrimps that are harvested just offshore. That kind of shrimp is hard to find, and the quality of most frozen imported shrimp is questionable. So at various times I've substituted big chunks of swordfish or halibut—big enough so that three pieces make a serving. It's also an excellent treatment for plump sea scallops. Just be sure you buy "dry scallops," meaning they haven't been treated with phosphates, which, while apparently harmless, leak out during cooking to make an unsightly mess. Quick clue: Phosphate-treated scallops are pure snow-white, without the pale cream color of non-treated fish.

If you use a ceramic (earthenware) tagine or casserole, follow the manufacturer's directions for stovetop cooking. Some are perfectly safe to use with a direct flame, while others require a heat diffuser.

The recipe calls for sweet Spanish paprika (*pimentón dulce*): Note that this is not *pimentón de la Vera*, with its smoky flavor. There are a great many different Spanish *pimentones* (paprikas), including the prized ones from Murcia in the southeast of Spain, which are sun-dried and consequently have a fresher flavor. (Of course, if you want a smoky flavor in the dish, by all means, use *pimentón de la Vera*.)

Toast saffron to crisp the stamens and make them easier to crumble. To do that, fold them into a small sheet of regular white paper, set the folded paper in a skillet, and toast over medium heat until the paper starts to change color. Salt-preserved lemons are easy to purchase online, but they're so useful in the kitchen that I recommend making your own from organic lemons bought during the peak of the season (plenty of directions, also online).

If you wish, serve the tagine with couscous or rice to absorb the delicious sauce.

continued

3 tablespoons finely chopped cilantro

⅓ cup finely chopped flat-leaf parsley

½ cup olive oil, plus more for the tagine

1 teaspoon ground ginger

3 teaspoons sweet mild Spanish pimentón or other fragrant paprika

1 teaspoon saffron threads, toasted

Freshly squeezed juice of 1 lemon

24 large shrimps, shelled and deveined; or 2 pounds swordfish or halibut, cut into large chunks (2 or 3 to a serving); or 2 pounds dry sea scallops

8 medium ripe red tomatoes, peeled, seeded, and chopped (or the equivalent in whole canned tomatoes)

3 garlic cloves, minced

1½ teaspoons ground cumin

1 teaspoon ground coriander

Sea salt and freshly ground black pepper

1 large red onion, thinly sliced

4 medium red potatoes, peeled and thinly sliced

2 red sweet peppers, seeded and slivered

½ salt-preserved lemon, slivered (optional)

½ cup small green Mediterranean olives, pitted

MIX the chopped cilantro and parsley with ⅓ cup of the oil in a large bowl. Add the ginger, *pimentón*, saffron, and lemon juice and mix with a fork to blend well. Add the seafood and turn to coat thoroughly in the marinade. Cover the bowl and set in the refrigerator for several hours or overnight.

IN a medium saucepan, combine the tomatoes with the remaining 3 tablespoons oil, plus the garlic, cumin, and coriander. Set over medium heat and cook, stirring, until the sauce thickens and the excess juices boil away. Add salt and pepper to taste.

OIL the bottom of a large heavy casserole. Arrange the onion and potato slices over the bottom and season with salt and pepper. Layer the pepper slivers on top. Spoon the thick tomato mixture over the vegetables, cover the pan, and set over medium-low heat. Cook, covered, until the potatoes are tender, 30 to 40 minutes. If necessary, add a very little boiling water to the pan to keep the vegetables from burning. If there's too much liquid, uncover the pan, raise the heat slightly, and boil rapidly to evaporate.

WHEN the vegetables are tender, layer the seafood on top, adding the preserved lemon slices, if using, and the olives. Scrape the rest of the marinade over the top of the seafood, cover with a lid (or the top of the tagine) and cook on the stovetop over medium-low heat just until the shrimp are cooked through.

REMOVE and serve immediately.

Note: If the sauce seems too liquid at the end, remove the seafood and raise the heat, boiling the sauce, uncovered, to reduce. Then add the seafood back to the sauce to serve.

HAKE FILLETS *with* GARLIC *and* CAPER SAUCE

I make this with a lightly flavorful oil from Chile, which makes an elegant sauce without competing with the strong flavors of garlic and capers.

Don't feel limited to hake—the recipe works just as well with haddock, halibut, swordfish, monkfish, or indeed any firm-textured, white-meat fish.

To toast blanched almonds, preheat the oven to 350°F. Spread the almonds in one layer on a baking sheet and set in the preheated oven for 10 to 15 minutes, stirring occasionally, until the almonds are golden. Do not overcook: Keep in mind that they will continue to darken for a minute or so longer once removed from the oven.

MAKES 6 TO 8 SERVINGS

1 head garlic

4 boneless hake fillets (6 to 8 ounces each)

Sea salt and freshly ground black pepper

⅓ cup olive oil

¾ cup dry white wine

½ cup toasted almonds (see headnote), chopped

1 small onion, chopped

¼ cup salt-packed capers, well rinsed and dried

PREHEAT the oven to 350°F.

SEPARATE the individual cloves of garlic but do not peel them. Set the cloves on a baking sheet and roast for 15 to 20 minutes, until soft.

SPRINKLE the fish fillets on both sides with salt and pepper.

USE a little of the oil to grease an ovenproof baking dish just large enough to hold the fillets without much overlap. Arrange the fillets side by side in the dish. Combine the wine and the remaining oil in a small saucepan and heat just until it is very hot. Pour the wine and olive oil over the fish, cover the dish (use aluminum foil if the dish has no lid), and transfer to the oven to bake for 20 minutes.

MEANWHILE, peel the garlic and chop the cloves. Combine the garlic with the almonds and onion in the bowl of a food processor. Add 3 tablespoons of the capers and pulse briefly, just to crush the ingredients and mix well, but do not make a paste.

WHEN the fish is done, remove the fish from the baking dish and keep warm on a platter. Bring the broth left in the baking dish to a boil, then reduce the heat to low. Stir in the almond mixture and simmer until the sauce is thick. Top the fish with the sauce and garnish with the remaining 1 tablespoon capers.

SEAFOOD

261

HALIBUT *with a* SAFFRON-ALMOND SAUCE

In Spain, this is called *en pepitoria*. Think of it as a master recipe that can be used for many different kinds of seafood (scallops, swordfish, monkfish, and so forth). It's also a delicious treatment for chicken, cut into parts, with the timing adjusted accordingly.

MAKES 6 TO 8 SERVINGS

Pinch of saffron threads

½ cup slivered almonds

About ¾ cup olive oil

4 garlic cloves, thinly slivered

1 or 2 slices stale bread, crusts removed, cubed (1½ cups bread cubes)

1 cup finely chopped onion

1 cup finely chopped leeks

Unbleached all-purpose flour, for dredging

Sea salt and freshly ground black pepper

2½ pounds halibut, swordfish, or other seafood, cut into 8 serving pieces

1 cup white wine

⅓ cup chopped flat-leaf parsley

⅓ cup chopped cilantro

SEVERAL hours before you're ready to cook (or in the morning, before you go to work), set the saffron to steep in about 1 cup of very hot water.

SET a skillet over medium heat. When the pan is hot, add the almond slivers and half the oil. Sauté gently just until the almonds are golden, then remove and transfer to a blender or food processor. Add the slivered garlic to the oil and toast until golden but not dark brown. Remove the garlic and add to the almonds. Add a little more oil to the pan if necessary, and toast the bread cubes in the oil until golden. Remove and add the bread cubes to the almonds.

IF necessary, add a little more oil to the pan, along with the chopped onion and leeks. Lower the heat and cook gently until the vegetables are soft. Remove with a slotted spoon and set aside.

PREHEAT the oven to 375°F.

TOSS about ½ cup flour with salt and plenty of pepper, then spread the flour on a plate. Dredge the fish pieces lightly in the flour.

ADD all the remaining oil to the pan and raise the heat again. Brown the floured fish pieces on both sides in the hot oil, then transfer the fish to an ovenproof dish and spoon the onion-leek mixture over the top. Cover with aluminum foil and bake in the oven for about 10 minutes, or until the fish is almost done. Keep warm but don't finish cooking it just yet.

WHILE the fish is baking, add the wine to the skillet in which you sautéed everything and set the skillet over medium heat. Bring the wine to a boil and boil for 5 minutes to reduce.

GRIND or process the almonds, garlic, and bread, adding the saffron water with the saffron threads. With the motor running, add the parsley and cilantro and as much or as little of the boiled-down liquid in the frying pan as is necessary to make a creamy mixture. Remove the fish from the oven and spoon the sauce all over, mixing it with any juices in the oven dish. Return the dish to the oven, uncovered, for another 10 minutes. Then serve immediately.

ZUPPA DI ARAGOSTA DELLA CANTINA SICILIANA

This is a sumptuous soup made by Chef Pino Maggiore at his tiny restaurant, Cantina Siciliana, on a back street of the old port town of Trapani, in far western Sicily. It is served as a main course, which is why I've included it here instead of in the soups chapter.

To make the fish broth, Sicilians have access to a whole range of what we would call "trash fish": tiny, bony, tasty specimens of the salty Mediterranean that lend incredible flavor to any soup they're added to. If you want fish like that in North America, you almost have to go catch it yourself. Alas, that's impossible for most of us. Instead, ask your fish purveyor to set aside some heads and racks (meaning the skeletons) of fish that he or she is filleting. It's the kind of stuff that gets thrown out otherwise, a tremendous waste of the goodness of the sea. Add to the heads and racks a few pieces of the cheapest fish on offer, but do not use oily fish such as sardines, mackerel, or bluefish because they don't work for a broth.

Almond flour may sound exotic, but I find it easily in health food stores and many supermarkets, where it may be sold as ground almonds. Just be sure it has not had any sugar added to it.

The lobsters Chef Pino uses are very small Mediterranean lobsters, weighing not more than ½ to ¾ of a pound each. We can't legally buy lobsters that small in the United States, so I have adapted the recipe to 1-pound Maine lobsters, the smallest we can purchase.

MAKES 6 SERVINGS

6 pounds fish, for the broth (see headnote)

3 garlic cloves, crushed with the flat blade of a knife and chopped

1 small onion, coarsely chopped

½ cup olive oil, preferably Sicilian, plus more for garnish

2 tablespoons tomato paste or concentrate

RINSE the fish and, if necessary, gut them. Cut the larger ones into smaller pieces—no bigger than the palm of your hand. Set aside.

MIX the garlic, onion, and oil in the bottom of a stockpot over medium-low heat. Cook, stirring, until the onion is soft. Then add the tomato paste and a little water and stir to dissolve.

continued

SEAFOOD

1 tablespoon sea salt

Freshly ground black pepper

Big pinch of crushed red chile pepper

1 (2-inch) cinnamon stick

Small bunch flat-leaf parsley, coarsely chopped

Small bunch basil

3 lobsters, weighing 1 pound each, if available; otherwise use 2 larger lobsters, for a total weight of 3 to 4 pounds

⅓ cup almond flour (very finely ground blanched almonds)

Pinch of ground cinnamon

About ⅓ pound spaghetti, broken into approximate 3-inch lengths

WHEN the tomato is completely dissolved, add 3 quarts (12 cups) water to the stockpot. Add the prepared fish, the salt, plenty of black pepper, the chile pepper, cinnamon stick, and parsley. Separate the leaves from the stems of basil. Add the stems to the broth, setting the leaves aside to use for a garnish.

BRING the broth to a simmer over very low heat. Cover and simmer gently for 1 hour 15 minutes. When the broth is done, strain it through a fine-mesh sieve or through cheesecloth, pressing down on the fish to extract as much flavor as possible. Discard the fish and other solids.

THE broth can be prepared well ahead of time up to this point and refrigerated or even frozen until ready to use.

WHEN ready to cook the soup, bring the broth back to a simmer. Add the lobsters and cook until they are done, 6 to 7 minutes, or longer for larger lobsters. Remove the lobsters and set aside to cool, then crack the shells and remove all the meat inside. Set the whole claw meat aside to use as a garnish, if you wish. Otherwise, cut all the meat into bite-size portions.

BRING the broth back to a boil and add the almond flour and ground cinnamon. Stir to mix well and let simmer for 5 minutes or so to fix the flavors.

JUST before you're ready to serve, add the broken spaghetti to the broth and cook until the pasta is done—about 8 minutes, no more. Sliver the reserved basil leaves.

SERVE the soup while it's still very hot. Either add the lobster pieces to the broth and serve from a cauldron; or plate up individual servings, putting a quantity of lobster in the center of each plate, spooning the broth and pasta generously over the lobster, and garnishing each plate with a piece of the claw meat and a sprinkle of slivered basil. Finally, dribble a generous thread of olive oil on top.

WHOLE SMALL FISH *or* FISH FILLETS *in a* TUSCAN TOMATO SAUCE

Tuscany might not seem a go-to place for fish dishes, but the whole 150-mile-long coastline from Carrara south to Orbetello is a paradise for fish lovers. This traditional way of frying fish and finishing it in a rich tomato sauce comes from Livorno, aka Leghorn, midway on that long coastline. There it's made with whole small red mullet, a Mediterranean species that is almost impossible to find in North America. But the sauce is delicious with fried fish fillets as well.

MAKES 6 SERVINGS

6 plump fillets white-meat fish (haddock, hake, or other)

Sea salt and freshly ground black pepper

1 celery rib, white part only, finely chopped

½ medium fennel bulb, finely chopped

½ cup finely chopped flat-leaf parsley

1 garlic clove, finely chopped

About ¾ cup olive oil

1 cup canned whole tomatoes, with their juices, chopped

1 tablespoon sugar

2 tablespoons tomato paste or concentrate, dissolved in ¼ cup hot water

Unbleached all-purpose flour, for dredging

Minced fresh basil or flat-leaf parsley, for garnish

Lemon wedges, for garnish

RINSE the fish and pat dry. Sprinkle with salt and pepper on both sides and set aside.

IN a saucepan or skillet large enough to hold all the fish, gently sauté the celery, fennel, parsley, and garlic in ¼ cup of the oil over medium-low heat until the vegetables are soft. Stir in the chopped tomatoes with their juices and the sugar, and simmer for 15 to 20 minutes, until the tomatoes have condensed to a thick sauce. Add the dissolved tomato paste and continue cooking until the sauce is thick and almost jammy. Add salt and pepper to taste and set aside, keeping warm while you fry the fish.

SPREAD the flour on a plate and dredge each piece of fish to coat lightly. In another skillet or saucepan, heat the remaining ½ cup oil, and when it is hot—shimmering but not smoking—fry the fish until crisp and lightly golden on each side. Do this in batches if necessary. Remove the fillets when they're done and set on a rack to drain.

WHEN all the fish is done, heat the tomato sauce to simmering and add all the fish, nestling the fillets into the sauce. Cook for no more than 3 minutes, then serve immediately, sprinkled with the basil and with the lemon wedges on the side.

SHRIMP *and* SAUSAGE GUMBO

Just to prove that it doesn't have to come from the Mediterranean for a recipe to feature fish and olive oil, here's an olive oil treatment for that old and treasured southern Louisiana dish, gumbo. Try to find wild-caught shrimp for this, since most farmed shrimp, unless you can be certain of their origin, are raised in highly questionable circumstances. In any case, don't feel constrained to use only shrimp in this recipe. Oysters are often added to gumbo, as is crabmeat, although already cooked crabmeat should be added at the very end.

Gumbo is usually served over steamed white rice, but I like it almost better over a creamy bed of polenta (see page 195).

You will first have to beef up your regular chicken stock, adding the shells from the shrimp you will use in the gumbo, and to make a very peppery spice mix to be used in the gumbo.

MAKES 8 TO 10 SERVINGS

For the beefed-up (shrimped-up) chicken stock:

½ cup extra-virgin olive oil

1 cup coarsely chopped yellow onion

1 cup coarsely chopped celery

2 quarts chicken stock

¼ cup tomato paste or concentrate

2 bay leaves

Shells and heads from 2 pounds shrimp

For the spice mix:

1 tablespoon ground hot red chile pepper, such as cayenne

1 tablespoon crushed white peppercorns

1 tablespoon crushed black peppercorns

1 teaspoon crumbled dried thyme

TO MAKE THE CHICKEN STOCK: In the bottom of a stockpot, combine the oil with the onion and celery and cook over medium-low heat until the vegetables are soft. Bring about ½ cup of the stock to a boil in a small saucepan, then remove from the stove and stir in the tomato paste until it is thoroughly dissolved. Add to the vegetables in the stockpot, along with the bay leaves, the rest of the chicken stock, and the heads and shells from the shrimp. Bring to a simmer, cover, and simmer gently for at least 30 minutes, or let the stock keep simmering while you prepare the rest of the gumbo.

TO MAKE THE SPICE MIX: Combine all of the ingredients in a spice grinder or coffee mill and grind to a soft powder. You will only need 2 tablespoons for the gumbo; the rest can be kept sealed in a tin or jar for another time.

TO MAKE THE GUMBO: Heat the oil in a heavy Dutch oven or similar pot over medium heat until it is very hot but not smoking. Whisk in the flour and continue whisking constantly, to make a smooth, dark roux. Watch carefully and do not stop whisking. In 8 to 10 minutes, the roux will turn dark brown.

1 teaspoon crumbled dried oregano, preferably Greek

3 bay leaves, broken or crumbled into bits

½ teaspoon whole cumin seeds

¼ cup fine sea salt

For the gumbo:

1 cup extra-virgin olive oil

1 cup unbleached all-purpose flour

1 cup chopped yellow onion

1 tablespoon chopped garlic

¾ cup chopped sweet green peppers

¾ cup chopped celery

2 pounds andouille or other fresh spicy sausage, sliced

1 cup diced chorizo or other dry spicy sausage

¼ cup tomato paste

2 tablespoons Worcestershire sauce

1 (1-pound) package frozen okra (or 1 pound fresh okra, if available, trimmed and sliced)

Sea salt (optional)

1 pound oysters or scallops (optional)

2 pounds peeled fresh shrimp

½ pound cooked crabmeat

1 cup sliced scallions, green and white parts

STIR in the onion, garlic, peppers, and celery, and continue stirring, using a wooden spoon, until the vegetables start to soften. Add the 2 tablespoons spice mix and the fresh sausage and cook, stirring, until the sausage meat has changed color. Stir in the dried sausage and then ladle 6 cups of the stock into the pan using a strainer to hold back shrimp shells. When the stock begins to simmer, extract about ½ cup and use it to dissolve the tomato paste in a small bowl, then stir the paste mixture into the stock, along with the Worcestershire sauce.

CONTINUE to simmer the gumbo for about 10 minutes, stirring to remove any lumps, then add the okra. If using fresh okra, cook for 15 to 20 minutes, or until the okra is tender. If using frozen, follow package directions; the cooking time will be much shorter.

WHEN the gumbo is finished, it should be a velvety brown. Taste and add salt if necessary and/or more of the spice mixture, if you wish. Add the oysters, if using, and cook, simmering, for 3 to 5 minutes, then stir in the shrimp and turn off the heat. The shrimp will cook in the residual heat of the gumbo. Finally, stir in the crabmeat and serve immediately, garnished with the scallions.

MEAT *and* POULTRY

BILL BRIWA'S TITLE AT THE CULINARY INSTITUTE OF AMERICA AT GREYSTONE, in California's Napa Valley, is chef-instructor, but that modest appellation doesn't begin to describe what this masterful cook and master palate can do when he gets going with a group. Said group could be a class of young students from the school's culinary training programs, or it could be a bunch of curious consumers visiting the school's kitchens, or a select audience of top sensory scientists from around the globe, or an exclusive club of California olive oil producers, intent on learning more about their craft before they go out to tackle the U.S. market.

Whatever their interests, however, Chef Briwa's introduction is guaranteed to open their minds and their palates to the possibilities of olive oil. He usually sets out just three super-premium oils, of widely varying profiles, then a selection of simple items to taste, with and without the oils. One of the oils is almost always Tuscan, with its typical bitter-pungent profile. But a curious thing happens to that oil when it is tasted with one of Chef Briwa's favorite foods to include—a small slice of rare roast beef or steak. Tasting the oil on its own can produce a coughing fit among those not used to it. But pour a little spoonful of bitter oil over the meat and then taste the two together, and something very interesting takes place. The bitterness disappears completely, even though the oil is exactly the same—nothing has been done to it. And that's the reaction between a super-premium olive oil and a food that Briwa is looking for. What is it that different oils do to different foods, and how can we use this perception in the professional kitchen?

Which leads me to understand the foundation of that time-honored Tuscan tradition of a handsomely grilled beefsteak garnished with nothing but the finest olive oil that Tuscany produces—a tradition that harks back over the ages to when the Etruscan ancestors of modern Tuscans sliced slabs of meat off their white Chianina beef cattle, grilled them over the glowing embers of a wood fire, and served them up with a dollop of green olive oil and a sprinkle of salt.

I haven't included a recipe for *bistecca alla fiorentina* or *bistecca chianina* in this collection because it's not the kind of preparation that depends on a recipe. Rather, it's the quality of the meat and the quality of the olive oil that determine the quality of the dish. And beyond that, it's just a question of hot coals and a willing audience.

But there are many other recipes and preparations for meat dishes from the Mediterranean that feature olives and their oil, and I've been experimenting over the years with ideas for using olive oil in dishes that you might not think, at first glance, would benefit (Southern fried chicken? murgh masala?)—but they do! Above all, I encourage you to make olive oil a distinctive part of any meat cookery that you try, or any favorite recipes in your repertoire, from meat loaf to *boeuf bourguignon* to Hungarian goulash to chicken-taco salad to sweet-and-sour pork. You'll be very glad you did.

ROAST CHICKEN *with* OLIVE OIL

For years, I've roasted chickens the way I learned from cookbook author Elizabeth David, first in a very hot oven, then turning the oven down to finish the cooking. But Marcella Hazan, another of my kitchen goddesses, starts the bird off at a medium temperature and then raises it for the finish. Which is correct? Try it both ways and see which you prefer.

MAKES 4 TO 6 SERVINGS

1 (4-pound) roasting chicken

Fine sea salt and freshly ground black pepper

½ cup finely chopped fresh herbs (such as flat-leaf parsley, rosemary, thyme)

½ cup olive oil, plus a little more for the roasting pan

2 lemons, preferably organic, cut in half

2 bay leaves

IF you want to do this the David way, preheat the oven to 450°F. If you prefer the Hazan way, preheat it to 350°F.

RINSE the bird inside and out and pat dry with paper towels. Put a pinch of salt and plenty of pepper in a bowl and add the chopped herbs. Stir in the oil and the juice of a lemon half.

RUB the bird all over, inside and out, with the olive oil mix, being generous. Put a couple tablespoons of mix inside the cavity. Add the remaining lemon halves to the cavity, squeezing each one gently to release a bit of juice and soften the lemon (do not squeeze out all the juice). Add the bay leaves to the cavity. Truss the bird, tying the legs together and folding in the wings to keep its shape. Spoon a little olive oil (not the herb mix) over the bottom of a roasting pan just large enough to hold the bird.

IF following the David way, set the chicken, breast side up, in the pan and transfer to the preheated 450°F oven. Roast the chicken about 15 minutes, until the breast looks golden, then turn the heat down to 350°F and roast another 15 minutes. Turn the bird over and continue roasting another 30 to 45 minutes, until done—when a leg joint moves easily; when if you prick a leg with a skewer, the juice runs clear yellow and not at all rosy; or when a thermometer inserted into the breast registers 165° to 170°F or inserted into the thigh (but not touching the bone) registers 175° to 180°F.

IF following the Hazan way, put the chicken in the preheated 350°F oven breast side *down*. After 30 minutes, turn over to face the breast up, and let it cook another 30 to 35 minutes. Turn the oven heat up to 400°F and cook 20 minutes more, until the breast skin is crisp and brown.

REMOVE the bird when done and let it rest for 10 or 15 minutes so the juices retract, then serve immediately, carving at the table. The juices left in the pan are served as a sauce for the chicken.

BRAISED CHICKEN *with* VEGETABLES *from the* WINTER FARMER'S MARKET

Use a small roasting pan, just large enough for the bird and the vegetables. This also works well in one of those lidded terra-cotta roasters, such as a Römertopf.

1 (4-pound) chicken

½ lemon, preferably organic

Sea salt and freshly ground black pepper

2 tablespoons chopped fresh herbs (such as flat-leaf parsley, sage, rosemary, thyme)

2 bay leaves, crumbled

2 garlic cloves, crushed and chopped

¼ cup olive oil

1 pound small fingerling potatoes, halved lengthwise; or larger potatoes cut into chunks

½ pound small carrots, trimmed

½ pound small turnips, trimmed

½ pound small onions, peeled

¼ cup dry white wine, or more if needed

PREHEAT the oven to 475°F.

RUB the chicken all over with the cut side of the lemon, squeezing to release the juice. Then place the lemon half in the cavity and sprinkle the inside liberally with salt and pepper.

COMBINE the chopped fresh herbs, bay leaves, and garlic with 2 tablespoons of the oil and rub this mix liberally all over the chicken. Set the chicken on a rack in a roasting pan just large enough to hold the bird and all the vegetables.

MIX the remaining 2 tablespoons oil with the potatoes, carrots, turnips, and onions, making sure they are coated well with oil. Season with salt and pepper and toss, then pile the vegetables around the chicken in the roasting pan. Pour 2 tablespoons of the wine into the bottom of the pan. Cover the pan with its lid or with a sheet of aluminum foil.

TRANSFER to the oven and roast for 45 minutes to 1 hour. Halfway through the roasting time, check the pan and, if it is dry, add the remaining 2 tablespoons wine, or a bit more if necessary. Remove the lid and return to the oven, turning the roaster, if necessary, to make sure everything roasts evenly.

THE chicken is done when a thermometer, inserted near the thigh but not touching the bone, registers 170°F. Remove from the oven and let rest for 10 to 15 minutes before carving the bird and serving it with the vegetables.

Note: You can turn this into Braised Chicken with Vegetables from the Summer Farmer's Market simply by varying the vegetables. A good mix might include eggplant cut into chunks, zucchini (small ones halved lengthwise, larger ones cut into chunks), and small tomatoes to roast whole. Whole small leeks would make a nice addition too.

MURGH MASALA
Chicken Curry from Northern India

Indian cooks are wholeheartedly adopting the use of olive oil because of its healthful properties, which suggests that it's time for the rest of us to do likewise with our favorite Indian recipes. When used instead of the traditional peanut oil or ghee (melted, clarified butter), olive oil lends a subtle presence even to this spicy dish. But because of the dominant flavors of Indian spices, use an oil that does not have an aggressive flavor profile, perhaps Miller's Blend from California Olive Ranch or Olisur from Chile.

This makes a very mild but deliciously fragrant curry. If you prefer a spicier dish, increase the amount of fresh chiles in the marinade and the crushed chile pepper in the cream at the end. Or use a very spicy brand of garam masala.

Grating the onion makes the sauce quite creamy, but it also, I find, produces buckets of tears. If you prefer, chop the onion to a fine mince in a food processor.

MAKES 8 SERVINGS

3 to 4 pounds chicken parts (breasts, legs, thighs), skin removed

For the marinade:

4 garlic cloves, finely minced

1 (2-inch) piece fresh ginger, minced

2 fresh green jalapeño chile peppers, seeded and minced

Sea salt

1 teaspoon garam masala (Indian curry spice mixture), or more to taste

½ teaspoon ground turmeric

¼ cup plain whole-milk yogurt

RINSE and dry the chicken pieces and set in a bowl.

TO MAKE THE MARINADE: Combine the garlic, ginger, and jalapeños and process or chop further to a fine paste. In a bowl, combine the garlic mixture with salt to taste, the garam masala, turmeric, and yogurt. Pour the mixture over the chicken pieces, turning the chicken to coat each piece completely. Cover the bowl and set aside for a couple of hours at cool room temperature, or 5 to 6 hours in the refrigerator.

TO MAKE THE SAUCE: Combine 6 tablespoons of the oil and the onion in a large heavy saucepan and cook over medium-low heat, stirring frequently, until the onion is very soft and melting. Do not let the onion brown at this point.

ADD the cinnamon stick and cardamom and continue cooking and stirring until the onion starts to turn brown. Stir in the garlic and about ¼ cup water. Add the yogurt, raise the heat slightly, and continue cooking and stirring for about 5 minutes more or until all the elements are well combined.

VIRGIN TERRITORY

For the sauce:

½ cup olive oil

1 large red or yellow onion, coarsely grated or minced (1½ cups)

1 cinnamon stick (about 4 inches)

1 teaspoon ground cardamom

1 tablespoon very finely minced or crushed garlic (3 or 4 garlic cloves)

¾ cup plain whole-milk yogurt

1 tablespoon grated fresh ginger

2 teaspoons mild paprika

1 teaspoon ground turmeric

1 teaspoon ground cumin

1 teaspoon ground coriander seeds

Sea salt

For the cream:

Pinch of saffron

½ teaspoon crushed red chile pepper, or more to taste

½ cup heavy cream

NOW add the ginger, paprika, turmeric, cumin, and coriander, along with 1 cup water. Let the sauce come to a simmer, and cook gently for about 5 minutes.

IN a separate pan or skillet, brown the chicken pieces in the remaining 2 tablespoons oil. As the chicken pieces brown, add them to the spicy onion sauce. When all the chicken is done, scrape any remaining marinade from the bowl into the sauce and stir to coat the chicken well. Taste and add a little salt if necessary. Cook at a low simmer for about 30 minutes.

MEANWHILE, TO MAKE THE CREAM: Stir the saffron and crushed red chile into the cream and let it sit for 30 minutes to 1 hour. Add the cream to the sauce and bring to a simmer. Cook for another 4 or 5 minutes, until the cream has boiled down and thickened.

SERVE immediately, with steamed basmati rice if you wish.

M'SAKHAN
Chicken, Onion, and Sumac Pie

This sumptuous combination is a favorite with Palestinian and Jordanian cooks alike. In northern Palestine, it's traditionally served at the feast at the end of the olive harvest. Rich green Middle Eastern olive oil, from Palestine, Lebanon, or Israel, will add flavor, while tart, dark red sumac, available in Middle Eastern markets, balances the sweetness of the slightly caramelized onions. A small amount of butter also contributes to the opulence of what is essentially a dish for a country feast, baked in the wood-fired oven, or *taboun*, of the farmhouse.

MAKES 6 SERVINGS

About 1 cup olive oil

3½ to 4 pounds chicken parts (legs, thighs, breast halves)

Sea salt and freshly ground black pepper

4 large yellow onions, finely chopped (4 cups)

¾ cup chicken or veal stock

2 tablespoons unsalted butter

1 cup pine nuts

⅓ cup ground sumac

½ teaspoon mixed ground allspice and cinnamon

2 or 3 large rounds (or 4 or 5 smaller rounds) Arab pita bread

PREHEAT the oven to 350°F.

USE about 2 tablespoons of the oil to grease the bottom of a 10 by 12-inch ovenproof dish. Arrange the chicken pieces in a single layer in the dish and sprinkle liberally with salt and pepper. Dribble another ¼ cup oil over the chicken and rub to make sure the chicken parts are thoroughly coated with oil, salt, and pepper. Sprinkle about 1 cup of the onions over the chicken parts. Add the stock and transfer the dish to the oven. After about 20 minutes, turn the chicken pieces over. Continue cooking for another 20 to 30 minutes, until the chicken is just cooked through—it will be cooked again later. Remove from the oven and set aside.

MEANWHILE, gently cook the remaining onions in ⅓ cup of the oil over low heat until the onions are thoroughly softened but not starting to brown. (This will take 20 to 30 minutes.) When the onions are done, remove them from the pan, leaving the oil behind, and place in a bowl. Melt the butter in the oil remaining in the pan and toast the pine nuts over medium heat until they are golden. (Be careful not to burn the pine nuts. Remove them from the pan with a slotted spoon as soon as they have started to turn color. They will continue to cook in their residual heat for a bit after they are removed from the pan.) Add the nuts to the onions in the bowl, then add the sumac and mixed allspice and cinnamon.

RAISE the oven temperature to 425°F.

CAREFULLY separate each piece of Arab bread into two by cutting around the outside edge and gently pulling the top and bottom sections apart. You should have enough bread to cover the bottom surface of another, slightly larger baking dish that is deep enough to hold all the ingredients. Grease the bottom and sides of the dish with ¼ cup oil and arrange half the bread sections over the bottom, slightly overlapping the pieces and letting the bread come up the sides of the dish. Arrange the chicken pieces, tucking them together, on top of the bread. Pile the onion–pine nut mixture over the chicken. Dip the remaining pieces of Arab bread in the juices remaining in the chicken pan, soaking the bread thoroughly in the juices, and then arrange the pieces, overlapping in the center, over the top of the chicken. (Think of this as a chicken pie, with the bread being the "crust.") Pour all the remaining pan juices, together with the onions that cooked with the chicken, over the top of the bread. Transfer to the hot oven and cook for 20 to 30 minutes, or until the bread is golden on top and crisp around the edges. (If the bread on top starts to burn, cover it with a sheet of aluminum foil.)

WHEN the top is golden, remove from the oven and let sit for 20 minutes or so before serving. Be sure to include plenty of the onion mixture and a wedge or so of crisp, flavorful bread with each serving.

SOUTHERN-FRIED CHICKEN *in* OLIVE OIL

Surprisingly, Georgia (the state, not the country) is rapidly developing new olive plantations and making olive oil. What better time, then, to add a healthy touch of olive oil to that traditional Georgia treat, Southern-fried chicken, in place of time-honored pork lard or Crisco.

Old-fashioned recipes call for jointing a whole bird, but the breasts are often dry and disappointing, so I concentrate on thighs and drumsticks.

MAKES 4 TO 6 SERVINGS

4 pounds chicken parts (preferably 4 thighs and 4 drumsticks)

Sea salt and freshly ground black pepper

2 cups buttermilk

2 tablespoons olive oil, plus more for frying

⅔ cup unbleached all-purpose flour

⅓ cup finely ground cornmeal

Well-flavored paprika, sweet or hot, as desired (or smoky pimentón de la Vera)

THE day before (or the night before), season the chicken parts with salt and pepper and put them in a bowl. Beat together the buttermilk and oil and pour over the chicken—there should be enough to cover all the parts. Cover the bowl with plastic wrap and refrigerate to marinate. Be sure to allow time for the chicken to come back to room temperature before cooking.

WHEN you're ready to cook the chicken, combine the flour and cornmeal in a medium bowl and add the paprika, along with a little more salt and black pepper. Toss with a fork to combine well.

GET out your big black cast-iron skillet and add about 1½ inches of oil to it. Set over medium heat to warm while you flour the chicken. Shake the chicken pieces to let the excess marinade drip off (but don't wipe them dry; the marinade will help flavor the chicken and also make it easier for the flour coating to stick). Roll the pieces in the seasoned flour to coat thoroughly.

NEXT to the stove, have ready a wire rack lined with paper towels to drain the chicken when it's done.

THE oil should have reached frying temperature by the time you're done coating the chicken, but be sure to check before adding the chicken; a frying or candy thermometer should read 350°F. A small cube of bread dropped into the hot oil will sizzle and turn golden in about a minute.

ADD the chicken pieces to the hot oil in one layer (you may have to do this in batches), cover the pan, and turn the heat down so that the chicken simmers in the oil rather than fries. After 5 to 6 minutes, uncover, turn the pieces over, cover again, and let sizzle-simmer for another 6 minutes.

REMOVE the cover, turn the heat up, and fry the chicken pieces until they are a deep golden brown all over. Transfer to the rack and let them drain while you continue with the rest of the chicken. Total cooking time for each batch should be 20 to 25 minutes.

Note: If you want a more Italian/Tuscan flavor to this, add to the buttermilk-oil combination 1 clove garlic, smashed and chopped, and 1 tablespoon finely minced fresh rosemary leaves.

CHILE-STUFFED STEAK

Another in the great American repertoire of standard, favorite, traditional dishes that benefit greatly when you substitute olive oil for the more common butter. For the fresh chile peppers, use whatever is available and suits your taste. Some people like very hot chiles, while others prefer the milder, warm flavor of Anaheims or poblanos.

MAKES 4 SERVINGS

6 tablespoons olive oil

3 garlic cloves, crushed and finely minced

½ teaspoon freshly ground black pepper

¼ teaspoon ground hot red chile pepper

2 (10-ounce) top sirloin or New York strip steaks, 1½ to 2 inches thick, excess fat cut away

6 fresh green chile peppers— Anaheim, Sandia, or other medium-hot peppers

1 tablespoon unbleached all-purpose flour

Pinch of Greek, Sicilian, or Mexican oregano

½ cup chicken stock

IF you're using a charcoal grill, start the fire in advance so that the coals will be ready when it's time to cook.

AT least 30 minutes before you're ready to start cooking, mix together 4 tablespoons of the olive oil with half the minced garlic, the black pepper, and the ground chile pepper. Cut a deep pocket in each steak, being careful not to pierce through along the sides. Rub the steaks all over, inside and out, with the spiced oil and let marinate. (This can be done several hours in advance.)

WHEN the charcoal is ready, roast the chile peppers, turning them constantly, until the skins are black and blistered. (You can also do this in advance, roasting over a gas flame or in the oven, but the charcoal is preferable and will give the peppers a nice smoky flavor.) Place the peppers in a paper bag to steam slightly. Then rub the skins off and trim the peppers of their stems, internal white membranes, and seeds. Slice one of the peppers lengthwise in quarters and set aside for a garnish. Chop the remaining peppers rather coarsely and set aside.

IN a small saucepan, heat the remaining 2 tablespoons oil over medium heat. Add the remaining garlic and cook briefly, stirring with a wooden spoon, until the garlic starts to turn golden. Add the flour and continue cooking, stirring, until it thickens to a roux. Stir in the oregano and add the stock. Cook, stirring, until the stock has formed a creamy sauce. Then stir in the chopped chiles and mix well. Remove about ½ cup and reserve for a garnish; use the rest to stuff the pockets in the steaks.

TRANSFER the steaks to the grill—or, if you prefer, use a preheated oven broiler—and cook until done, approximately 8 minutes per side for medium-rare. Cut each steak into two serving portions and serve immediately on a heated platter, garnished with a little of the reserved chile sauce. Drape a chile strip over the top of each steak.

PROVENÇAL DAUBE *of* BEEF *or* LAMB *with* GREEN OLIVES

A daube is nothing more or less than a rich stew of meats, a few vegetables, and lots of wine for the sauce. It was originally always cooked in a special terra-cotta vessel, called appropriately enough a daube, and either sent to the village oven or popped into the farmhouse oven on baking day, after the bread came out and the intense heat of the oven was starting to fall. As such, it captures or encapsulates all those flavors we romantics associate with the rustic country cuisine of southern France—garlic, wild and fragrant herbs, wine and citrus, olives and their oil and, inevitably, the pungent fragrance of burning Gauloise cigarettes. I've left the Gauloises out of this recipe, but it is still very similar to what you always used to find in small-town bistros on market day.

Traditionally, a *daube avignonaise*, from the great old town of Avignon, was made with lamb, but this treatment is just as good with beef. Also note that it is traditionally served with noodles but can be served with rice or even with polenta (see page 195), which is especially good.

MAKES 8 SERVINGS

For the marinade:

½ cup olive oil, preferably a Provençal oil from the Vallée des Baux

1 medium yellow onion, sliced

1 celery rib (including the green leaves), sliced

1 medium carrot, sliced

2 garlic cloves, crushed and chopped

3 or 4 bay leaves

2 sprigs fresh rosemary

2 sprigs fresh thyme

1 tablespoon black peppercorns, cracked in a mortar

1 teaspoon juniper berries

TO MAKE THE MARINADE: Add the oil to a heavy sauté pan along with the onion, celery, and carrot. Cook gently until the onions are translucent, then add all the remaining marinade ingredients. Simmer for 10 minutes. Remove from the heat and let cool completely. Put the meat in a deep bowl and pour the marinade over it. If it should happen that there's not enough marinade to cover the meat, add more red wine. Cover the bowl with plastic wrap and leave in a cool place to marinate for 24 hours, refrigerating if you think it necessary.

TO MAKE THE STEW: Remove the meat from the marinade, reserving the marinade, and dry it completely with paper towels. Sprinkle it all over with instant flour. Heat the oil over medium-high heat in a skillet with high sides. Brown the meat in the hot oil, turning to give it a good toasted crust on all sides. Transfer the browned meat to a roasting dish with a cover (if you're using a terra-cotta casserole, be sure it is safe to use on the stovetop) that is large enough to hold all the ingredients. Add the carrots and onions to the roasting dish, tucking them in and around the pieces of meat.

Zest of ½ orange, cut into 3 or 4 narrow strips

¾ cup robust red wine, preferably from the Rhône Valley, plus more as needed

2 tablespoons red wine vinegar

2 tablespoons cognac or Armagnac

2½ pounds boneless beef or lamb, preferably from the shoulder

For the stew:

A little instant flour, for sprinkling on the meat

3 tablespoons olive oil

8 medium carrots, trimmed and cut into chunks

18 small onions, trimmed

24 pitted green olives

Sea salt and freshly ground black pepper

PREHEAT the oven to 325°F.

STRAIN the remaining marinade, discarding the solids, into the skillet in which you browned the meat. Bring to a simmer, scraping up any browned bits left in the bottom of the skillet, and simmer until the marinade is reduced by about half. Add the reduced marinade to the roasting dish and bring to a simmer. Cover the roasting dish and transfer to the oven. Bake for 3 to 4 hours, or until the meat is falling apart. Remove from the oven and lift the meat from the sauce. Set the sauce in the refrigerator to cool, then lift off the fat layer.

REHEAT the sauce, adding the olives, then the meat. Season with salt and pepper. Simmer for 15 to 20 minutes, or until the sauce is slightly thickened and the beef is warmed through. Serve immediately, if you wish, with boiled noodles, rice, or polenta to accompany it.

PORK LOIN *or* CHOPS *with a* SPICY ADOBO RUB *or* MARINADE

In North America, we often think of adobo as a Filipino (or Puerto Rican) dish, but the original came from Spain, where olive oil is used instead of the soy sauce of the Philippines. It is simply a Spanish way of making a rub to add extra flavor and tenderness to very simple meat dishes. Pork is ideal for this, but the rub could also be used with a firm-textured fish like swordfish or shark. This is from Extremadura, the western region of Spain.

2 bay leaves, crumbled or minced

Sea salt

2 garlic cloves, crushed and minced

1 tablespoon pimentón de la Vera (smoked Spanish paprika)

1 tablespoon dried oregano

⅓ cup olive oil

2 tablespoons red wine vinegar or freshly squeezed lemon juice

1 small red sweet pepper (or ½ medium pepper), very finely minced

About 1½ pounds pork loin, or 4 meaty pork chops

CRUSH the bay leaves with the salt in a mortar. Add the garlic and continue working to make a smooth paste, then stir in the *pimentón* and oregano, crushing to make as fine a mixture as possible. Stir in the oil and vinegar, to make a thick paste. Stir in the minced red pepper. Smear the paste all over the outside of the pork loin or on both sides of each pork chop, and set the meat aside, covered lightly with plastic wrap, to marinate for at least 2 hours but better overnight in the refrigerator.

WHEN ready to cook, prepare a medium-hot charcoal fire. Or, if you don't have a grill, preheat the oven to 350°F.

GRILL the meat, using the marinade to baste the meat as you turn it on the grill.

OR, to cook in the oven, brown the meat all over in a little more oil in a frying pan, then transfer to the oven and bake for 45 minutes to 1 hour, basting every 15 minutes with the marinade, or until the meat is thoroughly cooked—145°F on a meat thermometer. The time will depend on the thickness of the cut you are using. Remove from the grill or oven and let sit for 15 minutes or longer to retract the juices, then serve, hot or at room temperature, with any delicious juices that have accumulated as a garnish.

Note: This is also an excellent marinade or rub for a whole roast chicken, or for lamb or chicken parts to grill, using the marinade to baste the meats.

LAMB WITH BLACK OLIVES

The olives used in this preparation are fresh, uncured, ripe black olives right off the tree. If you happen to have an olive tree in your backyard, drop a handful of ripe olives in rapidly boiling water for about 20 minutes to get rid of some of the bitterness, then drain and use in the recipe. Otherwise, wrinkled, salt-cured black olives will do just as well.

This is very good served with the creamy polenta on page 195.

MAKES 6 SERVINGS

2 pounds lamb shoulder or leg, cut into small stewing pieces

Sea salt and freshly ground black pepper

2 or 3 garlic cloves, finely chopped

Leaves from 2 sprigs fresh rosemary, finely chopped

½ cup olive oil

½ cup dry white wine, plus more as needed

1 cup black olives, pitted if you prefer

2 tablespoons tomato paste dissolved in ¼ cup warm water

PAT the pieces of lamb dry with paper towels and sprinkle generously with salt and pepper.

IN a heavy saucepan or casserole, gently cook the garlic and rosemary in the oil over medium-low heat until the garlic is soft but not brown, about 10 minutes. Add the seasoned lamb, raise the heat to medium, and brown the lamb pieces, turning frequently, until they are brown on all sides. Add the wine, let it come to a simmer, and cook until the wine is reduced by half.

STIR in the olives and the dissolved tomato paste, mixing everything together, then cover the pan and continue cooking on very low heat for about 1 hour, or until the sauce is very thick and the lamb is cooked through. Check the sauce periodically and add more wine or water if it seems necessary.

WHEN the lamb is done, serve it immediately, accompanied by polenta, if you wish, or by plain small potatoes, simmered until tender and then rolled in olive oil.

Note: Delicious as this stew is, this is also a fabulous recipe for lamb shanks: Brown the shanks first and set them aside. Proceed with the recipe, then add the lamb back to the sauce with the olives and tomato paste. Instead of cooking them on the stovetop, transfer them to a 325°F oven and cook, tightly covered, for about 2 hours or until they are thoroughly cooked and falling off the bone. You could also add some small peeled potatoes and carrots to the pot to enjoy with the lamb.

LEBANESE LAMB *and* BULGUR MEATBALLS

This is a great example of how small quantities of meat can be stretched to serve large numbers of people. In Lebanese kitchens, bulgur—wheat that has been steamed, dried, and cracked—is the grain of choice for this Middle Eastern "hamburger helper." Bulgur comes in three grades: fine, medium, and coarse. Medium, I find, is best for this treatment.

MAKES 6 SERVINGS

For the meatballs:

1 cup medium-cut bulgur

1½ pounds lean ground lamb

⅓ to ½ cup grated red onion, drained

¼ cup olive oil, plus more for frying

¼ cup ground or crushed Aleppo or Turkish red pepper

2 teaspoons ground cumin

1 teaspoon ground coriander

½ teaspoon ground allspice

½ teaspoon ground cinnamon

½ cup minced mint leaves

½ cup minced flat-leaf parsley

Sea salt and freshly ground black pepper

1 large egg, lightly beaten, if necessary

For the yogurt sauce:

8 ounces feta cheese, grated

¼ cup plain whole-milk yogurt

2 tablespoons extra-virgin olive oil

1 garlic clove, minced

1 tablespoon minced mint leaves, or more to taste

TO MAKE THE MEATBALLS: Set the bulgur in a bowl and add warm water to cover by a depth of 1 inch. Set aside to soak while you prepare the lamb. Combine the ground lamb and drained grated onion in a bowl and knead lightly with your hands to mix thoroughly.

IN a small saucepan over medium-low heat, warm the ¼ cup olive oil with the Aleppo pepper, cumin, coriander, allspice, and cinnamon. Cook about 3 minutes, then pour over the meat, scraping the pan. Mix thoroughly, kneading the meat.

DRAIN the bulgur thoroughly, squeezing handfuls of the grain to get rid of as much liquid as possible. It should be quite dry and fluffy. Knead the bulgur into the mix. As you knead, mix in the mint and parsley. When everything is thoroughly combined, knead in some salt and pepper.

DAMPEN your hands and shape the meat mixture into 12 slightly flattened meatballs, a little fatter than a traditional burger and a little flatter than a traditional meatball. The mix should hold together without crumbling or falling apart, but if it does not, mix in the lightly beaten egg. Once all the meat has been shaped, set the meatballs on a plate in the refrigerator for 30 minutes to firm up.

WHEN ready to cook, heat about ½ inch or less of oil in a deep skillet over medium heat. When the oil is hot, add 6 of the meatballs and cook on both sides until they are nicely browned. Transfer to a platter and set aside. Repeat with the remaining meatballs.

TO MAKE THE YOGURT SAUCE: In a bowl, mix together the feta, yogurt, oil, garlic, and mint.

SERVE the meatballs with the yogurt sauce.

VEAL SHOULDER *with* CAPER-ANCHOVY SAUCE

This is my adaptation of a recipe developed by Eleonora Console, who had a cooking school in her home under the shadow of Mount Etna, on Sicily's east coast. It makes a savory sauce that even anchovy haters will adore. In fact, the sauce would be good with other roast meats too, especially pork or chicken.

MAKES 6 TO 8 SERVINGS

For the meat:

A little unbleached all-purpose flour, for sprinkling on the meat

Sea salt and freshly ground black pepper

1 boned veal shoulder (about 3 pounds), tied

¼ cup olive oil

1 small onion, coarsely chopped

1 or 2 sprigs rosemary

1 or 2 sprigs sage

1 star anise pod

¾ cup chicken stock, veal stock, or water, plus more as needed

For the sauce:

1 garlic clove, chopped

¼ cup olive oil

8 anchovy fillets

2 tablespoons capers, well rinsed

2 to 3 tablespoons aged red wine vinegar

2 tablespoons slivered fresh mint leaves

Sea salt

TO PREPARE THE MEAT: Combine the flour with salt and plenty of black pepper and sprinkle it all over the veal, patting to make it adhere. Add the oil to a heavy saucepan in which the veal will fit comfortably, and set it over medium heat. Stir in the onion, rosemary, and sage, then add the veal and brown it in the hot oil, turning it often until it is thoroughly browned all over. Add the star anise and the stock. Lower the heat, bring the liquid to a simmer, cover the pan, and cook gently for 1½ to 2 hours. Turn the veal over occasionally and, if necessary, add more boiling stock to the pan.

WHEN the veal is done, remove it from the pan and set aside to rest for at least 10 minutes. Strain the pan liquid, discarding the solids. You should have 1 cup liquid. If you have more than you need, put the liquid in a small saucepan and reduce to 1 cup.

TO MAKE THE SAUCE: Sauté the garlic in the oil in a small frying pan over medium-low heat until just barely golden. Stir in the anchovies, crushing them into the garlicky oil. Add the capers and 2 tablespoons vinegar, along with the mint. Stir the pan juices into the sauce. Taste and adjust the seasoning, adding more vinegar or salt if necessary.

SLICE the veal, discarding the string; arrange the slices on a warm serving platter and spoon the sauce over them. Serve immediately, passing any extra sauce to be added at the table.

SAUCES

THE *SAUCIER*, OR SAUCE CHEF, IN A FRENCH PROFESSIONAL KITCHEN is the number three in command, after the chef and the sous-chef, which indicates in just how high regard sauces are held in those gastronomic temples. Indeed, traditional *cuisine française* is dramatic with its list of necessary sauces. Today we tend, even in professional kitchens, even in France, to simplify. Yet there is an important role that sauces play in bringing to life many dishes. A basic tomato sauce that can be used to dress pasta, to mix with a green vegetable, or to top a simple grilled chicken breast is something every cook needs in his or her freezer; while slightly more complicated pounded nut sauces like pesto, or egg-and-oil emulsions like mayonnaise and aioli, will quickly dress up a plain poached fish or even something as simple as a dish of hard-boiled eggs, peeled and halved and arranged on a bed of fresh greens. Olive oil is essential in all of these sauces, and for uncooked sauces like pesto or mayonnaise it should be the very best you can afford, because the flavor of good oil has an important role to play in the virtue of the sauce as a whole.

SIMPLE BASIC TOMATO SAUCE

This is the most elemental sauce imaginable—in fact, it almost doesn't deserve the name "sauce" since it's just pureed tomatoes with olive oil. Make it in quantities when fresh, red, ripe tomatoes are available in local markets, then freeze or can it in jars. All winter long, it will be a pleasure to find in the pantry, a quick sauce for pasta (add some garlic, some rosemary, some basil) or the foundation for a more complicated meat ragù, as an addition to a soup or stew, or a topping, with mozzarella and grated parmigiano reggiano, for pizza. The best tomatoes to use for this are so-called paste tomatoes or plum tomatoes, which have a better ratio of sweet flesh to juice and seeds; beefsteak tomatoes and their ilk are great in salads but they give off far too much juice to use in this recipe. And if the right kind of fresh tomatoes isn't available, you can also make this sauce with best-quality canned tomatoes. Use two 28-ounce cans of whole tomatoes and cook them down with the olive oil, just as directed.

MAKES 4 CUPS

4 pounds tomatoes, preferably paste or plum tomatoes

⅓ cup olive oil

Sea salt

Pinch of sugar (optional)

BRING a large pot of water to a rolling boil and add the tomatoes in two or three batches. Let simmer for 10 seconds, then remove with a slotted spoon and transfer to a colander in the sink. Run cold water over them.

WHEN all the tomatoes are done, peel them by simply lifting the skin off with a paring knife. It should come away easily. If it doesn't, you have not left them long enough in the boiling water.

CUT the peeled tomatoes directly into a heavy saucepan and set them over medium heat. Add the oil and a pinch of salt, stir to mix, and let the tomatoes slowly come to a simmer. Lower the heat and simmer slowly for an hour or so, or until the sauce is thick and most of the juice has evaporated. If you wish, turn them into a food processor or use an immersion blender to make a puree, or leave them as is, a little rough and all the more pleasurable for that. In any case, taste the sauce and adjust the seasoning, adding a little sugar if necessary to boost the flavor. But if you do add more seasoning, give the sauce another 5 minutes of simmering to blend the salt and/or sugar well with the other ingredients.

continued

SAUCES

293

THE sauce is ready to use as is. Or, freeze the sauce in 1-cup freezer containers. Or can it in half-pint or 1-pint jars. If you pour the simmering sauce into scrupulously clean canning jars and top the jars immediately with their equally clean lids, the lids will seal without further processing and the sauce will keep well in a cool, dark place for several months.

YOU can also gussy this sauce up in any number of ways—just add chopped black olives, capers, and anchovies to make something approaching a puttanesca sauce for pasta; add it to a hearty winter soup to lend a welcome touch of summer; use a couple of spoonfuls in a braise for roasted meats or fish, perhaps adding a little balsamic or aged sherry vinegar to give it sparkle; or sauté fresh sausages, sliced onions, and plenty of garlic, then add the tomato sauce and serve over grilled polenta squares for a wonderful quick lunch. Truth is, with this sauce in your pantry or freezer and a good bottle of olive oil in your larder, you have some very special ingredients to work with.

TABLETOP DIPS *from the* EASTERN MEDITERRANEAN

ZA'ATAR DIP

Za'atar, a favorite spice blend in the Levant, is served in Lebanon and Palestine on *man'oushe*, a sort of flatbread that is griddle-baked in a neighborhood bakery or by a vendor who sets up his *saç* griddle (it looks like an upside-down wok) right on the street. The flat rounds of bread, sprinkled liberally with this blend of tart sumac, wild oregano or thyme,[1] toasted sesame seeds, and sometimes roasted melon seeds, mixed with olive oil, are rolled up and served hot for breakfast. You can buy ready-made za'atar at many Middle Eastern shops, or make your own by mixing 5 table-spoons dried fragrant thyme or Greek oregano with half that quantity of sumac and a tablespoon or more of sesame seeds, plus a pinch of salt. Adjust the seasoning to your taste, and grind it to a coarse powder in a coffee mill just before using.

Combine za'atar with olive oil to make a spread or, with more oil, a dip. Or use za'atar and oil to make this tasty dip.

MAKES ABOUT 1 CUP

3 tablespoons coarsely ground za'atar

6 garlic cloves, very finely minced

1 bunch cilantro, coarsely chopped

½ cup olive oil

Sea salt

Ground or crushed Middle Eastern red chile pepper, preferably Aleppo or Turkish pepper

COMBINE the za'atar, garlic, cilantro, and olive oil in a bowl and mix vigorously. Season with salt and ground chile pepper to taste. If you want more of a puree, combine in a blender or food processor and pulse, adding more or less oil to make the mixture more or less like a spread or a dip, depending on which you prefer.

Note: This makes a magnificent rub or marinade for chicken—a whole chicken for roasting, or chicken parts for grilling or baking. Rub the za'atar mix into the chicken several hours before cooking; if you're dealing with a whole bird, loosen the skin on the breast and slide some of the mix underneath.

---

1. The wild thyme used is *Origanum siriacum*, which grows all over the Lebanese mountains—confusingly it's also called za'atar in Arabic, so you have to know whether you're talking about the wild herb or about the spice mixture in which the wild herb is featured.

MUHAMMARA

A sumptuous spread from that region of the Middle East where the finest culinary traditions of Lebanon, Turkey, and Syria all blend together with a little Armenian influence as well. The best chile pepper to use in this muhammara (*moo-HAMM-a-rah*) is coarsely ground or crushed dried Aleppo pepper, although other kinds of Turkish and Syrian chile peppers are good too. They are all available from World Spice Merchants in Seattle (www.worldspice.com) or from Kalustyan's in Manhattan (www.kalustyans.com).

Sweet peppers are best when roasted over live fire—either a gas flame on your stovetop or charcoal embers in the fireplace or on the outside grill. Roast, turning frequently, until the skins are black and blistered. Failing gas or charcoal, you can also roast peppers under the oven broiler until they are collapsed and the skins are blistered—but they will not have the intense flavor of flame-roasted peppers. Whatever the method, put the roasted peppers in a paper bag and set aside for 15 to 20 minutes to steam in their own heat and soften. At that point, it's easy to remove the blackened skin, using a paring knife to pull it away. Then cut the peppers open, draining any liquid into a small bowl. Discard the stems, seeds, and white inside membranes.

Roast the walnuts, the pine nuts, and the bread crumbs in a 350°F oven for 10 to 15 minutes. The walnuts are ready when their thin skins start to flake off; the pine nuts and the bread crumbs are done when they are golden.

Toast cumin seeds in a small skillet on top of the stove, stirring and tossing until the fragrance starts to rise. Remove immediately and grind to a powder in a spice grinder, or pound in a mortar.

MAKES 2½ TO 3 CUPS

4 roasted red sweet peppers, peeled and seeded, juices reserved

2 or 3 plump garlic cloves, crushed with the flat blade of a knife

1 teaspoon sea salt, plus more as needed

1½ cups walnuts, roasted

1¼ cups bread crumbs, toasted

CHOP the peppers coarsely and transfer to a food processor. Process in pulses until you have a textured puree.

IN a mortar, pound the garlic cloves to a paste with the salt. Add the roasted walnuts and continue pounding, adding a tablespoon or two of the reserved pepper juices. Once the walnuts are quite pasty, pound in the bread crumbs. (If you don't have enough pepper juice, use a tablespoon or two of lemon juice instead.) Transfer the ingredients in the mortar to the food processor and process very briefly, just enough to mix everything together.

continued

1 to 3 tablespoons freshly squeezed lemon juice, plus more as needed

1 tablespoon ground or crushed Middle Eastern red chile pepper, preferably Aleppo or Turkish pepper

2 tablespoons pomegranate syrup, plus more as needed

1½ teaspoons cumin seeds, toasted and ground

4 to 6 tablespoons olive oil

Pine nuts, roasted, for garnish

WHY, you may ask, do I not just put everything into the food processor to start with? Muhammara is supposed to have a rather coarse texture from the walnuts and bread crumbs; in order to control that texture, I think it's better to pound the walnuts, bread crumbs, and garlic in the mortar and mix them very quickly into the pepper puree.

SCRAPE the contents of the food processor into a bowl and stir in the chile pepper, pomegranate syrup, ground cumin, and 4 to 5 tablespoons of the oil. Stir in 1 tablespoon lemon juice and taste. If necessary, adjust the seasoning with more salt, lemon juice, or pomegranate syrup.

WHEN you're ready to serve, pile the muhammara in an attractive bowl and dribble the remaining olive oil over the top. Garnish with roasted pine nuts and serve with crostini (toasted bread crusts) or crackers or, to be most authentic, toasted triangles of Arab pita bread.

Note: Muhammara is also a beautiful relish to serve with any sort of roast or grilled lamb.

TZATZIKI

Tzatziki (*cacik* in Turkish) is simply yogurt with something else chopped and mixed in, just like the raitas of India. That something, however, varies enormously. It could be chopped cucumber and a little garlic, or chopped garlic and a little red sweet pepper, or hot chile pepper and fresh dill, or a combination of garlic, mint, and cumin, or fresh basil and parsley. The list goes on and on. In Israel, where avocados are practically the national vegetable (or fruit), they even make avocado tzatziki, whizzing the green avocado right in with the yogurt.

Here's the simplest, most classic kind of tzatziki, but let your imagination roam. It's a good idea to use Greek-style yogurt, which is simply yogurt that has been strained through a very fine sieve until thick (there are special plastic cones to do the job, but a couple of layers of cheesecloth in a colander will work in a pinch if you want to make your own). But if you want to make a last-minute tzatziki, perhaps to go with a roast leg of lamb (an ideal pairing), don't worry—regular yogurt will do the trick even if the sauce might be a little runny.

MAKES ABOUT 2 CUPS

1½ cups plain whole-milk yogurt, preferably Greek-style

1 long English cucumber, peeled and seeded

2 garlic cloves, chopped

Sea salt

1 tablespoon white wine vinegar

2 to 3 tablespoons olive oil, preferably Greek or Lebanese

Pinch of crushed Aleppo or Turkish red chile pepper (optional)

2 tablespoons chopped fresh mint or dill leaves, plus some whole leaves for garnish

IF using regular yogurt instead of Greek-style, set the yogurt to drain in a very fine-mesh sieve or a cheesecloth-lined colander over a bowl for at least 3 hours, or leave it to strain overnight in the refrigerator.

CHOP the cucumber very fine, or grate it on the large holes of a cheese grater.

USING the back of a spoon, crush the garlic to a paste with about ½ teaspoon salt in the bottom of a bowl. Stir in the cucumber, vinegar, and oil. If you wish, add a pinch of crushed chile pepper. Add the fresh mint and the yogurt and stir to blend well.

Notes: If you want to make avocado tzatziki, simply substitute 1 avocado, pitted, peeled, and chunked, for the cucumber. Crush it with a fork in the bowl with the garlic paste, making it as smooth or as rough as you wish.

For a slightly different flavor and a more interesting texture, substitute 8 ounces Greek feta for the yogurt. Whiz it in the food processor or the blender with ¼ cup plain yogurt and 2 tablespoons olive oil. Then use it like the yogurt in the recipe.

SAUCES

MAYONNAISE, AIOLI, ALLIOLI, AND THE LIKE

Making mayonnaise, and its offshoots aioli, rémoulade, and the like, should not be considered rocket science. These are easy sauces, especially as you grow accustomed to the fact that any sauce that fails to emulsify can be rectified by starting over again. I do have to admit that I once had a spectacular failure in the midst of a class in the teaching kitchen at Boston University. Remembering those old French housewives' tales, I turned to the student with whom I was working. "Are you menstruating, by any chance?" I asked. "Well, yeah," she said, somewhat puzzled. And there it was—confirmation that menstruating women can't make mayonnaise.

But I still don't believe it.

I've also seen mutterings on the Internet, at sites like Chowhound for instance, that olive oil is made bitter by vigorous beating, such as with a food processor, blender, or immersion blender. I must confess, honestly, that I've not had that experience, nor have any of several other cooks and chefs I've queried. If you find that mayonnaise made in a machine, instead of by hand, is too bitter for your taste, try simply using a less bitter oil—Arbequina, Biancolilla, and Taggiasca are among several olive cultivars that tend to produce sweet oils with a great deal of delicacy. Another tip, from one of the Chowhound correspondents: Refrigerate bitter mayonnaise for a day or two and the unpleasant flavor disappears.

I suspect it may also be because our palates have grown so used to the taste and texture of commercial mayonnaise that we simply can't adjust to the real stuff. But the real stuff has an enormous amount of virtue, not least the fact that it's made by real people (you) in a real kitchen, rather than by machines in a factory somewhere.

I do like to make these mayonnaise-type sauces in a blender or food processor, however, because you can use a whole egg, making a sauce that's lighter in texture as well as flavor. Mayo made by hand must be made with the yolk only—otherwise it will never emulsify. The following are directions for a blender, but a food processor operates in exactly the same fashion. An immersion blender is a little more difficult, simply because you must carefully control the amount of oil you're adding at first and it's difficult to do that if you're also focusing on moving the blender around the bowl.

BASIC MAYONNAISE

MAKES 1 TO 1¼ CUPS

1 large egg

1 egg white

Sea salt

Juice of ½ lemon, or more as needed

1 to 1½ cups fruity olive oil, as needed

WHIZ the egg and egg white in a blender with a pinch of salt to mix completely. Add just a few drops of lemon juice and whiz again. Now, with the center knob from the blender lid open and the blender going full tilt, start to pour in the oil, a very thin thread at first, until the mixture starts to thicken. Keep pouring and, as the mayonnaise thickens, you can add oil in a thin but constant stream. When you've added ¾ cup of the oil, stop the blender and add the remaining juice of the lemon half, being careful to hold back seeds. Turn the blender back on and continue to add the oil, and the mayonnaise will thicken even more. When the sauce has reached the right consistency (and that depends on your personal taste), turn off the motor and taste. Add more salt or more lemon juice if necessary. Otherwise, simply scrape the mayonnaise into a bowl.

IF the mayonnaise breaks down or fails to emulsify while you're blending it, remove it all from the blender and start over again with a fresh egg. Whiz it until it's light and foamy, then start adding the broken-down mayo and more oil and lemon juice. It should reconstitute easily.

Note: French cooks often add a spoonful of Dijon mustard to the mayonnaise right at the beginning; others might whiz in a pinch of cayenne or milder ground red chile pepper (like *piment d'Espelette*, my old standby) or a spoonful of fragrant curry powder.

Aioli

The famous garlic mayonnaise from Provence is also made in neighboring Catalan country, where it's called allioli. Catalan mayonnaise traditionally has no egg in it—an omission that gives it a paler color and a pleasant, almost waxen texture. But modern cooks tend to add an egg, just to make it easier.

When aioli is made by hand, the garlic and salt are pounded in a mortar as a first step, then the egg and salt are added and the oil, slowly, slowly, until it all emulsifies. I'm convinced that garlic is indeed made bitter by the vigorous beating of a blender, yet I want that lighter texture I get from using a whole egg. So, with a bow to the orthodox, I make the mayo, then pound the garlic (4 to 8 cloves, coarsely chopped) in a mortar with a little salt until I have a homogeneous paste. That gets stirred into the mayonnaise after it's removed from the blender.

Note: Fausto Luchetti, former head of the International Olive Oil Council and no mean cook himself, thoroughly crushes a small boiled potato with the garlic and salt in order to make a more stable sauce.

RÉMOULADE

If aioli is simply mayonnaise with garlic added, rémoulade is simply mayonnaise with a lot of mustard, vinegar, pickles, and green herbs. Maybe not quite that simple, but it's close. Note that other herbs can be used if you don't have chives—tarragon is good, and chervil is often used in France, though it's difficult to find in North America unless you grow it yourself.

This is the sauce that is traditionally used in France to make *céleri rémoulade*, the salad of celery root that is often served as part of an hors d'oeuvre of crudités, or raw vegetables.

1 large egg

1 hard-boiled egg yolk

2 tablespoons white wine vinegar, or more to taste

2 tablespoons Dijon mustard, or more to taste

¾ to 1 cup olive oil

Sea salt and freshly ground black pepper

½ cup minced flat-leaf parsley

½ cup minced chives

¼ cup chopped cornichons

¼ cup coarsely chopped capers, soaked first to remove salt

COMBINE the egg, hard-boiled egg yolk, vinegar, and mustard in a blender and blend briefly. Then, with the motor running, slowly pour a very thin thread of oil through the feed tube, emulsifying the mixture exactly like a mayonnaise. When you have added ¾ cup of the oil, stop the blender. Taste the sauce and add salt, pepper, and if necessary a little more vinegar or mustard. If the sauce is not quite as stiff as you'd like, add more of the oil with the motor running, but always in a thin stream.

MIX the parsley, chives, cornichons, and capers, chopping further if needed to make a fine mince. Scrape the sauce out of the blender and mix in a bowl with the minced herb mixture.

ANCHOVY SALAD DRESSING

This very simple dressing is traditionally made for puntarelle, or chicory shoots, a delight of the early spring table in Rome. But the pungent sauce could be used for other greens as well, especially bitter greens like endive and chicory. It's even good with plain romaine lettuce and sensational with a Caesar salad.

MAKES ENOUGH FOR 4 TO 6 SERVINGS

2 garlic cloves, crushed with the flat blade of a knife

4 to 6 oil-packed anchovy fillets; or 2 whole salt-packed anchovies, rinsed, deboned, and coarsely chopped

1 tablespoon red wine vinegar or sherry vinegar, or more to taste

¼ cup olive oil (use a pungent oil, such as a Tuscan, a Coratina from Puglia, or a fine Picual from Andalusia)

Freshly ground black pepper (optional)

USING a mortar and pestle, pound the garlic cloves to a paste with the anchovy fillets. When the paste is very smooth, stir in the vinegar. Slowly beat in the oil, using a fork to mix well. Taste and adjust the seasoning, adding pepper if desired. (There should be sufficient salt from the anchovies.)

ROMESCO SAUCE

With its intriguing flavors of dried chiles, almonds, garlic, and sweet peppers, this sauce is a natural complement to all kinds of seafood. And that's precisely what it's used for on its home turf of Catalonia. But it's also a splendid garnish for roasted or grilled vegetables. Witness the early springtime treat called *calçots*, which are long, skinny members of the onion family that are treasured in Catalonia and unknown elsewhere. *Calçots* are grilled in huge batches at outdoor festivals, often on a grill that is a set of discarded bedsprings set up over burning embers—a memorable sight. The *calçots* are served to hungry crowds in a festive event called a *calçotada*—always with romesco to accompany them.

When you're grilling a piece of fish, throw some onions or leeks on the grill and roast until they're blistered and burned on the outside. Serve them up like that and let guests peel the burned part off and dip the sweet, tender insides into the romesco. It's not quite a *calçotada*, but it's close.

MAKES ABOUT 2 CUPS

2 dried New Mexico or Anaheim chile peppers (or use Spanish dried ñora peppers, if available)

1 small dried hot red chile pepper, or more to taste

¾ cup olive oil, preferably from Catalonia or southern France

½ cup blanched whole almonds

4 garlic cloves, peeled but left whole

1 (2-inch-thick) slice crusty country-style bread, crusts removed

1 red sweet pepper, roasted (see page 198) and peeled

1 medium very ripe tomato, cut in half and seeded

BREAK up the dried chiles, discarding some or all of the seeds (which is where much of the heat is concentrated). In a dry skillet over medium-low heat, toast the chiles until they are aromatic and the color starts to change. Transfer the chiles to a small bowl and add hot water to cover. Let them steep for 20 minutes or so.

WHILE the chiles are steeping, heat 2 tablespoons of the oil in a small skillet over medium-low heat and fry the almonds carefully until they are golden brown. Using a slotted spoon, transfer them to a blender or food processor. Add another 1 tablespoon oil to the pan and fry the garlic cloves gently until they are brown. Remove the garlic and add to the almonds. Finally, add 2 more tablespoons of the oil to the pan and fry the bread on both sides until toasted crisp and golden brown. Add to the almonds and garlic, along with any oil remaining in the skillet. Add the chiles, leaving behind their soaking water. Process the contents in brief spurts, stirring down occasionally, to get a coarse texture, like bread crumbs.

2 tablespoons aged sherry vinegar, or more to taste

Sea salt and freshly ground black pepper

CHOP the sweet pepper and the tomato and add to the blender, along with the vinegar. Process to a coarse paste. Add salt and pepper and then, with the motor running, add the remaining oil in a thin, steady stream to emulsify with the rest of the ingredients. The sauce should be thick and still a little rough in texture. Taste and adjust the seasoning, adding more salt or pepper or vinegar.

PILE in a bowl and serve. (The sauce may also be refrigerated for a week or more without damage.)

SWEETS *and* DESSERTS

SWITCHING FROM VEGETABLE OIL TO OLIVE OIL IN MOST COOKING APPLICATIONS IS EASY—if a recipe calls for ¼ cup vegetable oil, you simply substitute ¼ cup olive oil. Switching from *butter* to olive oil, in most of the recipes in this book, is an equally easy one-to-one proposition. But when it comes to baking, especially cakes and cookies, things get a little trickier. That's because butter is much denser, with less liquid, than olive oil. Even though all butter contains some liquid, it's much less than fluid olive oil. That extra liquid must be accounted for in any baking recipe because it changes the way other ingredients will react. As a general rule, olive oil should be substituted at three-quarters the amount of butter called for. For example, if the recipe calls for 1 teaspoon butter, use ¾ teaspoon olive oil; similarly for 1 cup butter, use ¾ cup olive oil, and for 1 stick butter (8 tablespoons), use 6 tablespoons olive oil.

However, as that wonderfully helpful website www.oliveoilsource.com points out, it isn't always a good idea to use liquid fat, that is, olive oil, instead of solid fat, that is, butter, margarine, or lard. For instance, the good people at that site remind us, "since cake frosting must stay solid at room temperature, butter and powdered sugar work nicely, but olive oil and powdered sugar don't."

Similarly, even though I'm a dedicated olive oil baker, I use butter for the cake pan or cookie sheet when it's called for. It sticks to the sides of the pan, for one thing, and is much easier to manipulate over a tricky surface, such as a Bundt pan.

One thing I've noticed over the years, but which I've been playing around with: Most cake and cookie recipes conventionally call for creaming butter and sugar together right at the start. That doesn't work so well with olive oil, as the mixture never reaches the fluffy stage the recipes call for. I often change a recipe like that to begin by creaming together eggs and sugar, then adding the olive oil later, along with any other liquid ingredients (milk, cream, wine, water, whatever).

If you're interested in developing your repertoire of baked goods with olive oil, I suggest you try out these recipes to get a sense of what is involved, then go on to experiment with your own favorites.

YOGURT *and* OLIVE OIL CAKE

This is a lovely plain tea cake, the kind Europeans might serve on a breakfast buffet. It's not overly sweet so it can be gussied up, if you wish, with a dollop of homemade jam or whipped cream or even a little ice cream. Arbequina, either from Spain or from a New World grower, is a good choice for this cake, especially if you can find a fresh oil from a recent harvest. But any lightly fragrant oil will do.

MAKES 8 DESSERT SERVINGS OR 16 SMALLER SERVINGS

Unsalted butter, for greasing the pan

½ cup plain whole-milk yogurt

⅔ cup granulated sugar

3 large eggs

1½ cups unbleached all-purpose flour

2 teaspoons baking powder

Pinch of sea salt

1 tablespoon grated lemon zest

½ cup lightly fragrant olive oil

¼ cup powdered sugar (optional)

PREHEAT the oven to 350°F.

USE a scant tablespoon of butter to grease the bottom and sides of a 9-inch round cake pan, preferably a springform pan. Line the bottom with parchment paper and grease the paper.

IN a large bowl, beat together the yogurt, granulated sugar, and eggs. Sift together the flour, baking powder, and salt, and fold into the yogurt mixture. Stir in the lemon zest, then add the oil and fold in until well blended. Pour the batter into the prepared cake pan.

BAKE for 25 to 35 minutes, until a toothpick inserted in the middle comes out clean and the cake pulls away from the sides of the pan.

COOL on a wire rack for 15 minutes. Loosen the edges from the pan with a knife and then release the cake from the pan.

SERVE the cake as is, or sift the powdered sugar over the top.

APPLE–OLIVE OIL POUND CAKE

This variation on an old-fashioned pound cake, so called because the ingredient quantities are determined by relative weight, uses olive oil instead of butter for a light, fresh flavor. The weight of the eggs should be matched by the weight of each remaining ingredient. Originally, everything was supposed to weigh a pound, but that makes a huge amount of cake, so I've cut it back. Three eggs should weigh about 6 ounces; for any variation in weight, adjust the quantities of sugar, flour, and olive oil accordingly. If you are using a kitchen scale, simply weigh the ingredients as described in the recipe. But for those who lack a kitchen scale (a terrific addition to any kitchen, by the way), I've included volume measurements in the list below.

Use a mild, sweetly fruity oil here—an Arbequina, or a Taggiasca from Liguria would be just fine, as would any of the lightly flavored California oils.

MAKES 8 DESSERT SERVINGS OR 16 SMALLER SERVINGS

A little unsalted butter, for greasing the pan

About 1¼ cups unbleached all-purpose flour, plus more for dusting the pan

3 large eggs (about 6 ounces)

¾ cup plus 2 tablespoons sugar

About ¾ cup olive oil

1 teaspoon vanilla extract

Sea salt

2 to 3 cups peeled and chopped apples

PREHEAT the oven to 350°F. Grease and flour a 9-inch round cake pan, preferably a springform pan. Line the bottom of the pan with parchment paper.

FIRST, weigh your eggs in their shells. This is your baseline and allows you to expand or reduce the recipe as much as you wish. The eggs should weigh around 2 ounces each, 6 ounces in all. Once weighed, separate the whites from the yolks and set the whites aside. Weigh an amount of sugar equal to the weight of the eggs (6 ounces). Take out a couple of tablespoons and set aside to add to the whites when you beat them. Set the remaining sugar in a large bowl. Measure out the same amount, again 6 ounces by weight, of flour and set aside. Finally, measure the oil, again by weight, and set aside. (If you are not weighing your ingredients, use the measurements given in the ingredients list.)

ADD the egg yolks to the sugar in the bowl and, using an electric mixer, beat together until the mixture is very thick and light-colored. Beat in the olive oil, a few ounces at a time, until all the oil has been absorbed into a thick emulsion. Add the vanilla and beat on high speed for a couple of minutes, then remove the beater and add the flour. Using a rubber spatula, fold the flour into the batter.

NOW clean the beaters scrupulously (the least trace of fat will stop the egg whites from mounting). Add a pinch of salt to the egg whites and beat to soft peaks. Sprinkle the reserved sugar over the whites and continue beating to very stiff peaks. Using a spatula, gently fold the egg whites into the batter until thoroughly combined.

TURN half of the batter into the prepared cake pan. Distribute about three-quarters of the chopped fruit over the batter in the pan, then top with the remaining batter. Finally, distribute the remaining fruit over the top and transfer to the preheated oven. Bake for about 45 minutes, or until the top of the cake is golden brown, the sides pull away from the pan, and a slender toothpick inserted in the middle comes out clean. Transfer to a cake rack and let cool before removing from the pan.

QUINCE *and* GINGER OLIVE OIL CAKE

This recipe was inspired by one developed by my friend Patricia Shea, an artist and passionate baker who lives in Belfast, Maine. Quinces give an astonishingly lush pink color to the glaze. The quinces should be prepared first and can be done several days in advance.

MAKES 8 TO 10 SERVINGS

For the quinces:

1 lemon

1 pound quinces (about 3 medium quinces)

½ cup sugar

½ cup honey

1 (1- to 2-inch) piece fresh ginger, peeled and very thinly sliced

1 teaspoon ground cardamom, preferably freshly ground

For the cake:

Unsalted butter, for greasing the pan

2 cups cake flour, unbleached if available

2 teaspoons ground ginger

1 teaspoon ground cardamom

1 teaspoon baking powder

Pinch of salt

3 large eggs plus 1 egg yolk

¾ cup sugar

½ cup olive oil

1 teaspoon vanilla extract

½ cup Greek-style yogurt

TO MAKE THE QUINCES: Grate the zest of the lemon and set aside. Cut the lemon in half and add the juice of half the lemon to a bowl of cool water to make acidulated water for the quinces—it will keep them from turning brown.

PEEL and core the quinces and slice all but one of them into wedges. As you finish, add the quince wedges to the acidulated water. Chop the final quince into small pieces and add to the acidulated water. This will be mixed into the cake batter.

ONCE all the quinces are sliced or chopped, combine the sugar, honey, ginger, and cardamom in a saucepan with the lemon zest and the juice of the second lemon half. Add 2½ cups water, bring to a simmer, and add all the quince, both sliced and chopped. Cover and simmer the quince for about 20 minutes, or until they are tender all the way through. Remove the quince from the syrup and set aside, separating the chopped pieces from the slices. Boil down the syrup until it is thick and syrupy. This can be done well ahead of time. Refrigerate both the quince and the syrup if you're going to keep them longer than a couple of hours.

TO MAKE THE CAKE: Preheat the oven to 325°F.

BUTTER the bottom and sides of a 9-inch springform pan. Line the bottom with parchment paper and butter the paper. Arrange the slices of quince in a pattern over the bottom of the cake pan.

SIFT together in a bowl the flour, ginger, cardamom, baking powder, and salt.

continued

BEAT the eggs and egg yolk briefly in another bowl. Beat in the sugar, a little at a time, until the mixture is fluffy, then beat in the oil and vanilla. Using a spatula, fold in a few tablespoons of the flour mixture and the yogurt. Then fold in the chopped quince and the rest of the flour mixture.

SPOON the cake mixture over the quince slices, transfer the cake pan to the oven, and bake for 40 to 50 minutes, until the cake is golden on top and pulling away from the sides of the pan.

REMOVE the cake from the oven and set on a wire rack to cool slightly, then invert it onto a serving platter. Remove the paper from the bottom (now the top), leaving the quince slices in place. If the reserved quince syrup has gelled, set it over very low heat until it loosens, then spoon it over the top of the cake, letting it dribble down the sides, to make a glaze.

OLIVE OIL CAKE *with* ROASTED PEARS

Firm-textured Bosc pears, with lovely russeted skin, are what you need for this cake. Green cardamom is available in many gourmet stores, or online from www.worldspice.com. Open the cardamom pods and crush the dark seeds in a mortar. Use any late-harvest wine, or a Moscato or Moscatel; fruit wines may also be used, as long as they are sweet. And if you don't want to use anything alcoholic, substitute a sweet apple cider.

MAKES ONE 9-INCH ROUND CAKE (8 TO 10 SERVINGS)

For the roasted pears:

4 very firm pears, peeled, quartered lengthwise, and cored

⅓ cup sweet dessert wine

2 tablespoons olive oil

2 tablespoons sugar

For the cake:

Small amount of unsalted butter, for greasing the pan

1 cup unbleached all-purpose flour

½ cup semolina

2½ teaspoons baking powder

Pinch of sea salt

⅔ cup sugar

2 large eggs

1 cup olive oil

½ cup sweet dessert wine

⅓ cup whole milk

Finely grated zest of 2 lemons

1 tablespoon crushed green cardamom seeds

TO MAKE THE ROASTED PEARS: Preheat the oven to 350°F. Set the pear quarters in a roasting dish and sprinkle with the wine, oil, and sugar. Roast for 45 minutes, turning occasionally, until the pears are tender and starting to caramelize. Set aside to cool to room temperature.

TO MAKE THE CAKE: Lightly butter a 9-inch round cake pan, preferably a springform pan. Line the bottom with parchment paper. Sift together both flours, the baking powder, and salt. Arrange the cooled pears in a circle on the bottom of the cake pan. Scrape all the remaining syrup in the roasting dish into a small saucepan and set aside.

BEAT the sugar and eggs together in a large bowl until pale and creamy.

BEAT in the oil, then the wine, then the milk with the lemon zest and cardamom, thoroughly beating in each ingredient before adding the next. Using a rubber spatula, fold in the flour mixture until just combined. Turn the batter into the prepared pan, covering the pears completely, and transfer to the oven.

BAKE the cake for 40 minutes, or until a toothpick inserted into the middle comes out clean and the cake pulls away from the sides of the pan. Remove the cake from the oven and set on a wire rack to cool slightly, then invert the cake and release it from the pan.

REHEAT the reserved syrup in the small saucepan and dribble it over the cake. Serve immediately.

THIS cake keeps well for a day or two, but it will get a little soggy if you try to keep it longer than that.

SWEET CHEESE RAVIOLI *with* BITTER HONEY

These lightly sweetened cheese tarts are made on the island of Sardinia, where they're called *sebadas* (say-BAH-dahs) or *seadas*. They are always served with the island's famous *miele amaro*, bitter honey. If you can't find *miele amaro*, use a richly flavored honey—chestnut honey, for instance, is excellent. (Adding a bit of orange juice and rosemary perks it up for this recipe.)

Fresh sheep's milk ricotta cheese with a pleasantly acid tang is not easy to find except in the finest cheese shops. Be careful that you are actually buying ricotta and not just curdled milk. Ricotta is made from the whey left after cheese making; it is *not* made by adding lemon juice or vinegar to whole milk. The folks at Old Chatham Sheepherding Company in New York's Hudson Valley (www .blacksheepcheese.com) will happily ship their ricotta for overnight or second-day delivery. If you can't find it, you could substitute a creamy fresh goat's milk chèvre instead.

MAKES 16 TO 20 *SEBADAS* (5 OR 6 SERVINGS)

For the dough:

1½ cups semolina

½ cup unbleached all-purpose flour

1 large egg

3½ tablespoons olive oil

Big pinch of salt dissolved in ½ cup very warm water

For the filling:

2 abundant cups fresh sheep's milk ricotta cheese

½ cup hot water

2 to 3 tablespoons semolina

1 teaspoon sugar, or more or less to taste

continued

TO MAKE THE DOUGH: Toss the two flours together in a bowl and make a well in the middle. Add the egg and oil to the center and mix with your hands, rubbing the oil into the flour until the dough is quite sandy in texture and the oil is evenly distributed throughout. Then start adding the salty water by the tablespoon—5 to 6 tablespoons should be the right amount, but you may need more or less depending on relative humidity. The dough should be quite soft and malleable but not sticky. Knead the dough a few strokes on a very lightly floured board, just to incorporate everything very well. Shape it into a ball, cover with a damp towel or a piece of plastic wrap, and set aside to rest while you make the filling.

TO MAKE THE FILLING: In a small saucepan over medium-low heat, combine the cheese with the hot water. As soon as the mixture starts to bubble around the edges, stir in 2 tablespoons of the semolina and continue to cook very gently, stirring with a wooden spoon, until the cheese thickens. Add all or part of the remaining semolina if needed. The cheese mixture should be thick but not solid—about the

continued

Grated zest of 1 medium lemon, preferably organic

Grated zest of 1 small orange, preferably organic

2 cups olive oil

¾ cup Sardinian bitter honey (miele amaro) or chestnut honey

Up to ¼ cup freshly squeezed orange juice

Leaves from 1 sprig fresh rosemary, coarsely chopped

consistency of commercial sour cream. Remove from the heat and stir in the sugar and citrus zests. Taste and add a little more sugar if the cheese is still very acidic, but keep in mind that the cheese should not be noticeably sweet.

DIVIDE the pasta dough into quarters. Roll one portion out on the very lightly floured board until it is very thin—less than ¹⁄₁₆ of an inch. (Italian cooks say you should be able to read a newspaper through the pasta—but whatever you do, do *not* roll the pasta out on a newspaper, as it will pick up a nasty taste and possibly other nasty things as well from the newsprint.)

USE a circular biscuit cutter 3¼ to 3½ inches in diameter to cut circles from the pasta dough. Drop about 1 teaspoon of the filling into the center of half the circles. Dip your finger in warm water and run it around the edge of the circle, then cover with the remaining circles and press the two together with the tines of a fork. Set the completed *sebadas* on a rack while you continue with the remaining pasta dough and filling.

WHEN all the *sebadas* have been shaped, heat the oil in a heavy pot until a thermometer reads 350° to 360°F. Have ready a wire rack with paper towels underneath to drain the fried *sebadas*. Drop 3 or 4 *sebadas* into the hot oil and let them fry, turning them once after they have risen to the surface of the oil. They should be lightly golden rather than brown in color. As soon as they are ready, remove with a slotted spoon and set on the draining rack. Then continue with the remaining *sebadas*.

MEANWHILE, warm the honey in a small saucepan, adding the orange juice and the chopped rosemary, until it is liquid and quite warm. Serve the *sebadas*, 2 or 3 to a serving, with the liquid bitter honey drizzled over the top.

OLIVE OIL BROWNIES

Well, why not? Brownies are never going to be considered health food, but we can make them minimally better for us by using olive oil. And don't forget the walnuts, which add a powerful quotient of omega-3 fatty acids. Truly, though, forget about health food for the moment and just enjoy these luscious treats for what they are, made even more delectable with olive oil.

MAKES 16 BROWNIES

Unsalted butter, for greasing the pan

4 ounces dark chocolate (at least 70% cacao)

⅓ cup fruity olive oil

2 large eggs

¾ cup sugar

½ cup unbleached all-purpose flour

2 teaspoons vanilla extract

1 cup chopped walnuts

PREHEAT the oven to 350°F. Butter an 8-inch square baking pan.

BREAK up the chocolate in small pieces into an ovenproof bowl or pan and set it in the oven to melt thoroughly. When it is completely soft, combine it with the olive oil, beating with a fork to mix thoroughly. Let cool.

BEAT the eggs until they are thick and foamy, then beat in the sugar, about ¼ cup at a time. When the sugar is thoroughly incorporated and the chocolate mixture has cooled down, combine the two, stirring them together with a spatula or wooden spoon (do not beat).

USING a rubber spatula, stir in the flour, vanilla, and walnuts. Spread the mixture in the prepared brownie pan and transfer to the preheated oven. Bake for about 25 minutes, or until the edges start to pull away from the pan. Remove from the oven and set on a wire rack to cool completely before cutting into squares.

MOUSSE AU CHOCOLAT *with* OLIVE OIL

An amazingly easy but very elegant dessert, this has been a favorite of mine for years. It is a perfect ending for any sort of festive meal.

MAKES 6 TO 8 SERVINGS

6 ounces high-quality bittersweet chocolate

2 tablespoons Armagnac or cognac

2 tablespoons very strong brewed coffee

4 large eggs

½ cup olive oil

1 tablespoon finely grated orange zest (optional)

Pinch of sea salt

2 tablespoons sugar

CHOP or grate the chocolate to make it easier to melt and combine it in the top of a double boiler with the Armagnac and coffee. Set it over simmering, but not rapidly boiling, water and let melt thoroughly, stirring occasionally. Once all the chocolate has melted, remove from the heat and let cool slightly.

SEPARATE the eggs, setting the whites aside. Using a handheld mixer, beat the chocolate while adding the egg yolks, one after the other, beating continuously. Still beating, pour in the oil. When all of this is fully amalgamated into a dark, shiny, unctuous mass, beat in the orange zest, if using.

CLEAN and dry the beaters thoroughly, then beat the egg whites, first adding the salt and later, as the whites mount and firm up, the sugar. Beat until the eggs are very stiff.

FOLD about one-quarter of the beaten whites into the chocolate mixture and then, once it is thoroughly incorporated, continue with the rest of the egg whites, about one-quarter at a time, until all the whites have been folded in and no trace of white can be seen.

SPOON the mousse into a serving bowl or into 6 to 8 individual ramekins and set in the refrigerator for a couple of hours to become totally firm.

THE mousse may be kept in the fridge for several days, but it should be thoroughly wrapped in plastic wrap to prevent it from picking up other refrigerator odors.

MRS. FANCELLI'S OLIVE OIL COOKIES

Feliciano Fancelli runs the oil mill, or *frantoio*, that has been in his family for umpteen generations. An old-fashioned crush-and-press operation, it is one of the last still functioning in the hills near Assisi, in Umbria. This simple cookie recipe, typical of Italian country sweets, comes from Mrs. Fancelli, who has been making them, she says, for years. For sweet wine, she uses a local Sagrantino passito from nearby Montefalco, but a sweet Moscato will do very well instead.

Toast the nuts in a 350°F oven until they are golden; when they are cool enough to handle, chop or process briefly in the food processor to make a coarse mix, not at all pasty.

MAKES 34 TO 40 COOKIES

2¼ cups unbleached all-purpose flour

1 cup sugar

1½ teaspoons baking powder

Pinch of sea salt

1½ cups chopped toasted almonds or hazelnuts, or a mixture

1½ cups raisins, chopped

2 large eggs

⅔ cup olive oil

⅔ cup sweet wine

PREHEAT the oven to 350°F. Spread sheets of parchment paper on two or three cookie sheets.

TOSS together in a bowl the flour, sugar, baking powder, and salt, then stir in the nuts and raisins.

IN another bowl, whisk together the eggs and combine, whisking, with the oil and wine. Pour over the flour mixture. Stir and knead slightly with your hands to mix the liquids thoroughly into the flour.

DROP the cookie mixture by tablespoons onto the prepared cookie sheets and transfer to the preheated oven.

BAKE for about 20 minutes, or until the cookies are lightly golden. Remove and transfer the cookies immediately to a wire rack to cool.

VARIATIONS: Use dried cranberries in place of the raisins. Make olive oil Toll House cookies by substituting walnuts and chocolate chips for the almonds and raisins and adding ½ teaspoon vanilla extract. Or make lemon drops by omitting the almonds and raisins entirely and adding ¼ teaspoon vanilla extract, the grated zest of 1 lemon (organic, preferably), and 2 tablespoons freshly squeezed lemon juice, then top each cookie before baking with 4 or 5 pine nuts.

OLIVE OIL GELATO *with* VANILLA *or* ROSE WATER

This is adapted from a remarkable recipe for ice cream that America's premiere *gelataia*, Jeni Britton Bauer, developed for the website Food52. After trying innumerable eggy ice cream recipes, I came across this. It makes an astonishingly smooth, creamy ice cream that really has the texture of frozen cream and not, like so many others, frozen custard. It is, in my not inconsiderable experience, much more akin to Italian gelato than it is to American ice cream.

Try the recipe at different times with a variety of different oils to see which you prefer. I like to make it with a sturdy Tuscan-style oil with its assertive flavors, but you might prefer a subtler Catalan Arbequina or a softer oil from California or Chile. Rose water is a lovely flavor to add, but vanilla is almost as good, and almond extract brings out the almond flavors in that Catalan oil.

If you use a modern canister-style ice cream maker, such as the Cuisinart ICE-21 that I prefer, be sure to set the canister in the coldest part of your freezer for a full 24 hours before using it, and do not remove it from the freezer until you're ready to add the chilled cream to it.

Read through the recipe and you will see that this is not something you can do in a couple of hours. Best to start preparations at least a day before you intend to serve the gelato—and even better to start two days ahead. But, believe me, it is worth the wait.

MAKES 2 PINTS

2 cups whole milk

4 teaspoons cornstarch

1½ ounces cream cheese, at room temperature

⅛ teaspoon fine sea salt

¾ cup heavy cream

½ cup olive oil

1 teaspoon rose water or vanilla extract, or other flavoring

⅔ cup sugar

2 tablespoons light corn syrup

NOTE that the gelato mixture must be thoroughly chilled before it's added to the equally thoroughly chilled canister of the ice cream maker. You may simply put the gelato mixture in the refrigerator, well covered so it doesn't pick up off-odors, overnight; or you can prepare an ice bath, using a large bowl into which the bowl of gelato mixture will fit, and filling the larger bowl with ice and a little water. If you decide to do this, have the bowl of ice ready before you start to make the gelato.

ADD 2 tablespoons of the milk to a small bowl and stir in the cornstarch to make a smooth, lump-free slurry.

IN a medium bowl, combine the cream cheese and the salt, mixing with a fork to get rid of any lumps.

COMBINE the cream, olive oil, rose water, sugar, and corn syrup with the remaining milk in a 4-quart saucepan. Bring the cream mixture to a rolling boil over medium heat and set a timer. The mixture should boil for precisely 4 minutes. Remove from the heat and use a wire whisk to stir in the cornstarch mixture. Return to the stovetop over medium heat and continue cooking until the mixture thickens slightly, about 1 minute. Remove from the heat.

GRADUALLY add the hot milk mixture to the cream cheese in the medium bowl, whisking steadily until it is smooth. Do this a little at a time to avoid lumps. Now, either set the bowl into the ice water bath, stirring it occasionally and adding more ice, until it is very cold, or set the bowl in the refrigerator overnight. After about 20 minutes, when the mixture has lost most of its heat, cover the bowl with plastic wrap to avoid picking up refrigerator odors. (If you cover it before it is chilled, you risk creating condensation, which will drip back into the gelato mixture.)

ONCE the gelato mixture is as cold as you can get it without freezing it, add it to the frozen canister of the ice cream maker and proceed according to the manufacturer's directions. Once the machine has stopped freezing (with the Cuisinart I mentioned above, that takes 25 to 30 minutes) and the mixture is pulling away from the sides, indicating that it's well on its way to becoming gelato, transfer it to a container with an airtight lid and set in the freezer for at least 4 hours before serving.

GRIDDLE-BAKED SEMOLINA PANCAKES *with* SWEET DATE-ORANGE FILLING

This griddle cake, which comes from Tunisia, derives its sweetness solely from the dates in the filling. It is delicious with afternoon tea or midmorning coffee, but it could also be a special treat for Sunday breakfast. If you don't have a griddle, you can use a heavy cast-iron frying pan, preheated until it's very hot.

MAKES 10 TO 12 SERVINGS

¾ pound dates, pitted

1¼ cups olive oil

2 tablespoons freshly grated orange zest

1 tablespoon crumbled dried orange peel

4¼ cups semolina

Sea salt

PROCESS the dates in the bowl of a food processor until they are quite smooth, then, with the motor running, slowly pour in ¼ cup of the oil. Add the fresh and dried orange and continue processing until you have a smooth paste. Set aside.

PLACE 4 cups of the semolina in a large bowl. Add the remaining 1 cup olive oil, working the semolina until the oil is absorbed. Dissolve about 1 teaspoon salt in ¾ cup warm water and slowly add that to the semolina dough, working the dough in the bowl until you have a kneadable consistency. Knead in the bowl briefly, then transfer to a board and knead until the dough is quite smooth. Use the remaining ¼ cup semolina if necessary to keep the dough from sticking to the board.

WHEN the dough is well kneaded, it should feel soft but not at all sticky. Set aside, covered with plastic wrap or a kitchen towel, to rest for about 30 minutes.

WHEN ready to proceed, start to heat a stovetop griddle or cast-iron skillet over medium heat. (You should not need additional fat on the pan.) Divide the semolina dough into quarters. Shape a quarter into a ball, then pat it out into a circle on the board. Use a rolling pin to roll an even circle 8 to 9 inches in diameter and ⅛ to ¼ inch thick. Spread half the date mixture over the circle, then top with another circle made from a similarly shaped quarter of the dough. Use the remaining dough and date mixture to make a second cake—or, if you wish, make long skinny rectangles. The cakes may be cooked as they are, or they may be cut into smaller lozenges, squares, rectangles, or other shapes.

AS soon as the cakes are made, transfer them to the very hot surface of the griddle and cook for about 4 minutes per side, or until the surfaces are brown and crisp and the inside is cooked through. Adjust the heat as necessary so the cakes don't burn. If you need to cook in batches, keep the cooked cake or smaller pieces warm until ready to serve.

SERVE immediately, although they are also very good set aside and served later at room temperature.

APPENDIX

HOW TO BUY OLIVE OIL:
Some extra-virgins to seek out

Like most people who pretend to the least bit of knowledge of olive oil, I am constantly asked what my favorite is, what one should buy, what's the best, and what's a good deal. It was in part to answer these kinds of questions that I set out to write this book. And I have to confess, at the end, there are no easy answers.

American consumers are used to having what they want when they want it, where they want it, and at a price they can afford. Many of the reasons why this is difficult with fine extra-virgin olive oil are detailed elsewhere in the book, but one stands out: Most of these oils are made by very small producers with limited distribution, and exported and distributed in small quantities as compared to big industrial oil companies. Thus, a first-rate oil in a Boston specialty foods shop just might not be available in San Francisco, say, or Seattle or Toronto. And for people in more remote areas, it may be even more difficult. Fortunately, the Internet presents a constantly growing solution to the problem of access. Even Amazon.com offers a huge gamut of olive oils from all over the world. I don't actually approve of the site, however, because of a distressingly cavalier attitude toward important questions like harvest date.

RECOMMENDED SOURCES FOR HONESTY, GOOD SERVICE, AND A GOOD REPRESENTATION OF EXCELLENT OILS:

DI PALO FINE FOODS
200 Grand Street
New York, NY
212-226-1033
www.dipaloselects.com
(100 percent Italian)

GUSTIAMO
718-860-2949
www.gustiamo.com
(website only; 100 percent Italian)

MARKET HALL FOODS
5655 College Avenue
Oakland, CA
510-250-6000; 888-952-4005
www.markethallfoods.com
(especially good for California oils)

OLIO2GO
8400 Hilltop Rd, Suite H
Fairfax, VA
866-654-6246 (866-OLIO2GO)
www.olio2go.com
(another 100 percent Italian source)

ZINGERMAN'S DELI
422 Detroit Street
Ann Arbor, MI
888-636-8162
www.zingermans.com

NOTE: www.manicaretti.com and www.therogerscollection.com are two importers of fine olive oils who supply retail outlets; information is available on their websites about where to find specific oils.

RECOMMENDED OLIVE OILS

For all-purpose cooking oils, there are a number of good ones, sold in 3- or 5-liter tins at acceptable prices, ones that won't evaporate the household budget if you use them with a fairly lavish hand. Among ones I would recommend are:

Academia Barilla from Italy
Iliada from Greece
Trader Joe's Kalamata from Greece
California Olive Ranch
Costco's Kirkland Signature

The following is a list of finer olive oil brands, including estates and producers, many of whom make more than one brand.[1] Keep in mind that not every oil listed below will be widely available in North America, and that there is no guarantee the oils will have been correctly maintained in an undamaged state once the producer has shipped them.

SPAIN

Castillo de Canena (www .castillodecanena.com): Francisco and Rosa Vañó, Jaen, Andalusia

Masia El Altet (www.masia-el-altet.com): Alicante, southeast Spain

Dauro (www.roda.es; www .aceitesdauro.es): Bodegas Roda (Mauro Rottlant and Carmen Daurella), Girona, northern Catalonia

Aubocassa (www.roda.es; www .aceitesaubocassa.es): DO Oli de Mallorca, Bodegas Roda (see above), Mallorca

Portico de la Villa, DO Priego de Cordoba: Manuel Montes Marin, Sierras Subbeticas, south of Cordoba, Andalusia

Señorio de Vizcantar, DO Priego de Cordoba, Sierras Subbeticas, south of Cordoba, Andalusia

Marques de Valdueza (www .marquesdevaldueza.com): Fadrique Alvarez de Toledo, Merida, Extremadura

Melgarejo (www.aceitesmelgarejo .com): Aceites Campoliva and the Melgarejo family, Pegalajar, Jaén, Andalusia

Oleum Viride (www.oleumviride .com): Luis Lucero, Zahara de la Sierra, Andalusia

FRANCE

Castelas (www.castelas.com), AOC Vallée des Baux: Jean-Benoît and Cathérine Hugues, Les Baux de Provence

ITALY

Pianogrillo (www.pianogrillo.it): Lorenzo Piccione, Chiaramonte Gulfi, southeast Sicily

Olio Verde (www.olioverde.it): Gianfranco Becchina, Tenuta Pignatelli, Castelvetrano, southwest Sicily

Titone (www.titone.it), certified organic, DOP Valli Trapanesi: Nicola Titone and daughter Antonella, Trapani, western Sicily

Cantholio (agricolabiovona@ yahoo.it): Giuseppe and Filippo Bivona, Menfi (Agrigento), southern Sicily

Cutrera (www.frantoicutrera.it): Giovanni Cutrera and children, Piano dell'Acqua, Chiaramonte Gulfi, southeastern Sicily

Librandi (www.oliolibrandi .it), certified organic: Pasquale Librandi, Vacarizza Albanese, Calabria

Crudo (www.crudo.it): Schiralli family, Bitetto, Puglia

Pascarosa (www.pascarosa.com): Brian and Catherine Faris, Martina Franca, Puglia

---

1. I don't mean to suggest that oils not on this list are in any way defective, simply that I have not personally experienced them.

Il Tratturello (www.parcodeibuoi
.com): Francesco Travaglini, Parco
dei Buoi, Molise

Colonna (www.marinacolonna.it):
Marina Colonna, Masseria Bosco
Pontoni, S. Martino in Pensilis
(Campobasso), Molise

Tiburtini (www.tibvrtini.com):
Bulgarini and Lolli di Lusignano
families, Tivoli (Rome), Lazio

Cru di Cures, (www.laurafagiolo
.it), DOP Sabina: Passo Coresi, Fara
Sabina (Rieti), Lazio

Olivastro (www
.olioquattrociocchi.it), certified
organic: Amerigo Quattrociocchi,
Alatri (Frosinone), Lazio

La Quagliera (www.laquagliera.it):
Prisca Montani, Spoltore (Pescara),
Abruzzi

Decimi (www.decimi.it): Graziano
Decimi, Bettona (Perugia), Umbria

Marfuga (www.marfuga.it):
Gradassi family, Campello sul
Clitunno, Umbria

Badia a Coltibuono (www
.coltibuono.com): Stucchi-Prineti
family, Gaiole (Chianti), Tuscany

Cafaggio (www.castellodicafaggio
.com): Enrico and Valentina Benci,
Impruneta (Florence), Tuscany

Primo Olio (www.montecastelli
.com), certified organic: Jens and
Ruth Schmidt, Montecastelli,
Monteriggioni (Siena), Tuscany

**Laudemio di Marchesi Frescobal-
di:** Pontassieve (Florence), Tuscany
(Laudemio is a trademark of 21
separate Tuscan estates, of which
Frescobaldi is one)

Castello di Ama (www
.castellodiama.com), DOP Chianti
Classico: Lorenza Sebasti and
Marco Pallanti, Gaiole, Tuscany

Capezzana (www.capezzana
.it): Contini-Bonacossi family,
Carmignano (Prato), Tuscany

Poggio Etrusco (www
.poggio-etrusco.com), certified
organic: Pamela Sheldon Johns;
Montepulciano, Tuscany

Vicopisano (www
.vicopisanolio.it): Nicola Bovoli,
Palazzetto, Vicopisano (Pisa),
Tuscany

San Cassiano (www
.aziendagricolasancassiano.it):
Mirko Sella, Mezzane di Sotto
(Verona), Veneto

Antichi Uliveti (www.oliopinna.it):
Pinna family, Sassari, Sardinia

CROATIA

Ol Istria (www.agrokor.hr):
Agrolaguna, Poreč, Istria

GREECE

Biolea (www.biolea.gr), certified
organic: Christine and Giorgios
Dimitriadis, Astrikas (Kolymbari),
Crete

Mani Bläuel (www.mani-blauel
.shop.com), certified organic: Fritz
Blauel, Pyrgos-Lefktrou, Messinia,
southern Peloponnese

Kritsa (www.kritsacoop.gr):
Agricultural Cooperative of Kritsa,
Lasithi, Crete

Gaea (www.gaea.gr; www.catcora
.com): Gaea Products, Agrinion,
quality DOP and organic olive oils,
mostly sold in the United States
under the Cat Cora label

PALESTINE

Canaan Fair Trade (www
.canaanfairtrade.com): Canaan
Fair Trade cooperative, Burqin
(Jenin), West Bank

TUNISIA

Moulins Mahjoub (www
.moulinsmahjoub.com), certified
organic: Mahjoub family,
Tebourba, northern Tunisia

CALIFORNIA

Pasolivo (www.pasolivo.com):
Dirk family, Paso Robles, San Luis
Obispo County

McEvoy Ranch (www
.mcevoyranch.com): Nan McEvoy
and son Nion, Petaluma, Marin
County

Séka Hills (www.sekahills.com):
Yocha Dehe Wintun Nation,
Brooks (Cache Creek, Capay
Valley), Yolo County

Corto (www.corto-olive.com):
Cortopassi family, Lodi, San
Joaquin County

California Olive Ranch (aka COR)
(www.californiaoliveranch.com):
Oroville, Butte County

CHILE

O-Live (www.o-liveandco.com):
Olisur (Alfonso Swett), La Estrella
(Colchagua Valley)

SOUTH AFRICA

Morgenster (www.morgenster
.co.za): Giulio Bertrand, Somerset
West, Western Cape

BIBLIOGRAPHY

Two websites of special interest, with frequently updated information about extra-virgin olive oil:

www.oliveoilsource.com
www.oliveoiltimes.com

Anderson, Burton. *Treasures of the Italian Table.* New York: William Morrow, 1994.

Capano, Giuseppe, & Luigi Caricato. *Olio: crudo e cotto.* Milano: Tecniche Nuove, 2012.

Chatterton, Brian. *Growing Olives for Quality Oil.* Kindle edition: Pulcini Press, 2011.

————. *Inside the Olive Jar.* Kindle edition: Pulcini Press, 2012.

Columella, Lucius Iunius Moderato. *De Re Rustica,* Book V. Cambridge: Loeb Classical Library, Harvard University Press, 1954.

Counihan, Carole M. *Around the Tuscan Table: Food, Family, and Gender in Twentieth-Century Florence.* Oxford and New York: Routledge, 2004.

Dalby, Andrew. *Siren Feasts: A History of Food and Gastronomy in Greece.* London & New York: Routledge, 1997.

Dalby, Andrew, and Sally Grainger. *The Classical Cookbook.* Los Angeles: J. Paul Getty Museum, 1996.

Delgado, Claudia, and Jean-Xavier Guinart. "How do consumer hedonic ratings for extra virgin olive oil relate to quality ratings by experts and descriptive analysis ratings?" *Food Quality and Preference,* vol. 22:2, pp. 213–225, March 2011.

Eitam, David, "Olive Culture in Ancient Israel," www.gemsinisrael.com/e_article000008705.htm.

Frankel, Rafael, Shmuel Avitsur, and Etan Ayalon. *History and Technology of Olive Oil in the Holy Land.* Tel Aviv and Arlington, VA: Olearius Editions, 1994.

Friedrich, W. L. Report for the Second International Scientific Congress on Santorini, Thera and the Aegean World, published 1980 (www.therafoundation.org/articles/environmentflorafauna/fossilplantsfromweichselianinterstadialssantrinigreeceii).

Gage, Fran. *The New American Olive Oil.* New York: Stewart, Tabori and Chang, 2009.

Garnsey, Peter. *Food and Society in Classical Antiquity.* Cambridge: Cambridge University Press, 1999.

Helstosky, Carol. *Garlic and Oil: Food and Politics in Italy.* New York: Bloomsbury, 2004.

Higgins, Charles. "Less Olive Oil Improves Quality." www.oliveoiltimes.com, April 3, 2012.

Kalua, C. M., M. S. Allen, D. R. Bedgood Jr., A. G. Bishop, P. D. Prenzler, K. Robards. "Olive oil volatile compounds, flavour development and quality: A critical review." *Food Chemistry* 100 (2007) 273–286, www.elsevier.com/locate/foodchem.

Keyder, Virginia. *Law and Olive Oil: The New Green Gold.* JURIST - Forum, August 1, 2012, http://jurist.org/forum/2012/08/virginia-keyder-olive-oil.php.

Kiritsakis, Dr. A. *Olive Oil from the Tree to the Table, 2nd ed.* New York: Wiley-Blackwell, 1998.

Mueller, Tom. *Extra-Virginity.* New York: W.W. Norton, 2011.

Oreggia, Marco. *FlosOlei: Guida al mondo dell'extravergine/A guide to the world of extra-virgin olive oil* (in Italian and English). Published annually, Rome.

Pollan, Michael. *Botany of Desire.* New York: Random House, 2001.

Quiles, José L., M. Carmen Ramírez-Tortosa, Parveen Yaqoob. *Olive Oil and Health.* Wallingford (England): CABI, 2006.

Rosenblum, Mort. *Olives: The Life and Lore of a Noble Fruit*. New York: Macmillan, 1996.

Speranza, Rossella. *Olive Oil: Sense and Sensibility*. Galatina (Italy): Congedo Editore 2008.

Van Andel, Tjeerd H., and Curtis Runnels. *Beyond the Acropolis: A Rural Greek Past*. Redwood City, California: Stanford University Press, 1987.

Varela, Gregorio. *Frying Food in Olive Oil*. International Olive Oil Council, Madrid: nd.

Wilkins, John, and Shaun Hill. *Archestratus: Fragments from the Life of Luxury, revised edition*. Totnes, Devon: Prospect Books, 2011.

Some publications of interest on the nutritional science behind possible health effects of extra-virgin olive oil:

Beauchamp, Gary K. et al. "Phytochemistry: Ibuprofen-like activity in extra-virgin olive oil." *Nature*: 437, September 1, 2005.

Fistonić, I., M. Situm, V. Bulat, M. Harapin, N. Fistonić, D. Verbanac. "Olive oil biophenols and women's health." Gynecology, Obstetrics and Menopause Clinic, Preradovićeva 10, 10000 Zagreb, Croatia, www.ncbi.nlm.nih.gov/pubmed.

Hardy, S., W. El-Assaad, E. Przybytkowski, E. Joly, M. Prentki, Y. Langelier. "Saturated fatty acid–induced apoptosis in MDA-MB-231 breast cancer cells. A role for cardiolipin." Molecular Nutrition Unit, Centre de Recherche du Centre Hospitalier de l'Université de Montréal, and the Institut du Cancer de Montréal, Université de Montréal, Québec, Canada, www.ncbi.nlm.nih.gov/pubmed.

Harvey, Kevin A., Candace L. Walker, Zhidong Xu, Phillip Whitley, Thomas M. Pavlina, Mary Hise, Gary P. Zaloga, and Rafat A. Siddiqui. "Oleic acid inhibits stearic acid-induced inhibition of cell growth and pro-inflammatory responses in human aortic endothelial cells." www.ncbi.nlm.nih.gov/pubmed.

Kalua, C. M., M. S. Allen, D. R. Bedgood Jr., A. G. Bishop, P. D. Prenzler, K. Robards. "Olive oil volatile compounds, flavour development and quality: A critical review," *Food Chemistry* 100 (2007) 273–286, www.elsevier.com/locate/foodchem.

Konstantinidou, Valentini, Maria-Isabel Covas, Daniel Muñoz-Aguayo, Olha Khymenets, Rafael de la Torre, Gullermo Saez, Maria del Carmen Tormos, Estefania Toledo, Amelia Marti, Valentina Ruiz-Gutiérrez, Maria Victoria Ruiz Mendez, and Montserrat Fito. "*In vivo* nutrigenomic effects of virgin olive oil polyphenols within the frame of the Mediterranean diet: a randomized controlled trial." *Journal of the Federation of American Societies for Experimental Biology* (FASEB), www.fasebj.org/content/24/7/2546.abstract.

Mizushina, Y., T. Takeuchi, F. Sugawara, H. Yoshida. "Anti-Cancer Targeting Telomerase Inhibitors: β-Rubromycin and Oleic Acid." Laboratory of Food & Nutritional Sciences, Department of Nutritional Science, Kobe-Gakuin University, Nishi-ku, Kobe, Hyogo, Japan, mizushin@nutr.kobegakuin.ac.jp; www.ncbi.nlm.nih.gov/pubmed.

Monti, Maria Chiara, Luigi Margarucci, Alessandra Tosco, Raffaele Riccio, Agostino Casapullo. "New insights on the interaction mechanism between tau protein and oleocanthal, an extra-virgin olive-oil bioactive component." *Journal of the Royal Society of Chemistry*; cited as DOI: 10.1039/c1fo10064e (www.rsc.org/foodfunction); June 2011.

Terés, S., G. Barceló-Coblijn, M. Benet, R. Álvarez, R. Bressani, J. E. Halver, and P. V. Escribá. "Oleic acid content is responsible for the reduction in blood pressure induced by olive oil." www.ncbi.nlm.nih.gov/pubmed.

INDEX

Note: Page references in *italics* indicate recipe photographs.

S

Saffron-Almond Sauce, Halibut with, 262–63
Saganaki (Grilled Halloumi or Kasseri Cheese), 136
Salad Dressing
  Anchovy, 303
  preparing, tips for, 235
  simple, made with olive oil, 101
Salads
  Bean, Lentil, Chickpea, Farro, and Other Hearty, 244–45
  Eggplant, Elizabeth Minchilli's "Vaguely Middle Eastern," 216, 217
  Fattoush, Dakos, Panzanella, and Other Bread, 242–43
  Marinated Feta and Tomato, 236, 237
  Orange and Red Onion, Sicilian (*Insalata di Arance*), 239
  Palestinian, about, 235
  Potato and Caper, from the Island of Pantelleria, 238
  Tabbouleh, 241
  Winter, of Brussels Sprout Leaves, 240
Salmorejo, 144
Salmoriglio, 248
San Román, María José, 105, 226
Sauces. *See also* Dips; Mayonnaise
  Caper-Anchovy, 289
  Chermoula, 211–12
  Romesco, 304–5
  Salmoriglio, 248
  Tahini, 128
  tomato, made with olive oil, 101–2
  Tomato, Simple Basic, 293–94
  Yogurt, 288
Sausage and Shrimp Gumbo, 268–69
Seafood. *See* Fish; Shellfish
Sella, Mirko, 50
Semolina
  note about, 158
  Pancakes, Griddle-Baked, with Sweet Date-Orange Filling, 324–25
Sfiha (Middle Eastern Pizza), 168, 169–70
Shakshouka (Spicy Tomatoes and Peppers), 232, 233–34

Shellfish
  An Olive Oil Version of Jasper White's Clam Fritters, 250
  Arroz Caldoso con Almejas (Soupy Spanish Rice with Clams), 184, 185
  Fried Shrimp, Calamari, and Chunks of Fish, 249
  North African Seafood Tagine, 258, 259–60
  Shakshouka (Spicy Tomatoes and Peppers), 232, 233–34
  Shrimp and Sausage Gumbo, 268–69
  Shrimp Fritters from the South of Spain, 130, 131–32
  Zuppa di Aragosta Della Cantina Siciliana, 264, 265–66
Shrimp
  Calamari, and Chunks of Fish, Fried, 249
  Fritters from the South of Spain, 130, 131–32
  North African Seafood Tagine, 258, 259–60
  and Sausage Gumbo, 268–69
  Shakshouka (Spicy Tomatoes and Peppers), 232, 233–34
Singletary, Bob, 53
Sinolea, 56
Small dishes
  Bruschetta, 113
  Classic Provençal Black Olive Tapenade, 121, 122
  Eggplant Fries, 132
  Epityrum, 29
  Falafel (Bean or Chickpea Fritters)—The Real Thing, with Tahini, 128–29
  Fett'unta (Bruschetta), 113
  geographic specialties, 112
  Greek Zucchini Fritters (*Kolokythokeftedes*), 127
  Green Olive Tapenade, 121, 123
  Marinating Cured Olives, 119
  New England Codfish Balls, 132
  Olive Oil with Popcorn, 120
  Pa amb Tomaquet (Bread with Tomato), 113
  Pane Cunzata (Garnished Bread) from a Sicilian Frantoio, 114
  Pinzimonio, 122

Roasted Red Peppers with Anchovies and Tomatoes, 124, 125
Saganaki (Grilled Halloumi or Kasseri Cheese), 136
serving as main dishes or sides, 113
Shrimp Fritters from the South of Spain, 130, 131–32
Sicilian Fried Almonds, 115–16
tapenades, about, 120
Tarte au Chèvre (Fresh Cheese and Tomato Tart), 133–34, 135
Tortilla Española, 8
Soups. *See also* Stews
  Bean, Savory, with Spicy Greens, 149
  Chickpea, 154–55
  Chickpeas and Greens, 193
  cold, from Andalusia, 140
  Gazpacho, 141
  Lentil and Bulgur, with Chile-Mint Garnish, 153
  Pistou, 150, 151–52
  Ribollita, 12–13
  Roasted Squash, with Cumin, 148
  Salmorejo, 144
  Tomato, Classic, 145
  Tomato-Cucumber, with Avocado Cream, 142, 143
  Tuscan Bean and Farro, for the Olive Harvest, 61
  Vegetable, Pureed (Chunky, Creamy, or Silken, Your Choice), 146–47
  Zuppa di Aragosta Della Cantina Siciliana, 264, 265–66
Spaghetti Aglio-Olio-Peperoncino (Spaghetti with Garlic, Oil, and Hot Red Peppers), 177
Spaghetti Ajo-Ojo-Peperoncino, xii
Spices, for recipes, 109
Spinach
  Risotto alle Erbe (Green Herb Risotto), 186–87
  serving ideas, 223
  steaming, 223

INDEX

"*Olive oil* may be the most important food in Western cooking, and Nancy Jenkins is a rare expert. No one brings more love and knowledge to the subject with all its fascination and complexity. She is one of our finest writers, and she happens to be a talented cook."

— ED BEHR, editor and publisher of *The Art of Eating*

"*Nancy Harmon Jenkins* takes a deep look at the complexities of a key component in Mediterranean cooking—extra-virgin olive oil—and draws on her years of experience to tell us what it's all about; why some is good, some is bad, and how to know the difference; and, most importantly, with lots of appealing recipes, how to use this healthy ingredient in our kitchens and on our tables."

— PAULA WOLFERT, author of *The Food of Morocco* and many other books